Entrepreneur
MAGAZINE'S

LEGAL GUIDE

Intellectual Property

- Patents
- Trademarks
- Copyrights
- Trade Secrets

Additional titles in Entrepreneur's Legal Guides

Helen Cicino, Esq.
Managing Editor

Bankruptcy for Businesses: The Benefits, Pitfalls and Alternatives

Business Contracts: Turn Any Business Contract to Your Advantage

Business Structures: How To Form a Corporation, LLC, Partnership, Sole Proprietorship (Available November 2007)

Estate Planning, Wills and Trusts

Forming an LLC: In Any State

Forming a Partnership: And Making It Work

Harassment and Discrimination: And Other Workplace Landmines (Available November 2007)

Hiring and Firing

Incorporate Your Business: In Any State (Available October 2007)

The Operations Manual for Corporations (Available November 2007)

Principles of Negotiation: Strategies, Tactics, Techniques to Reach Agreements (Available November 2007)

The Small Business Legal Tool Kit

Small Claims Court Guidebook (Available January 2007)

Tax Planning for Business: Maximize Profit, Minimize Taxes (Available December 2007)

Entrepreneur MAGAZINE'S

LEGAL GUIDE

Catherine J. Holland, Vito A. Canuso III,
Diane M. Reed, Sabing H. Lee,
Andrew I. Kimmel, and Wendy K. Peterson
Attorneys at Law

Intellectual Property

- **Patents**
- **Trademarks**
- **Copyrights**
- **Trade Secrets**

EP
Entrepreneur
Press

Editorial director: Jere L. Calmes
Cover design: Desktop Miracles, Inc.
Composition and production: Alicen Armstrong Brown

This publication is designed to provide accurate and authoritative information in regard to the subject matter covered. It is sold with the understanding that the publisher is not engaged in rendering legal, accounting, or other professional services. If legal advice or other expert assistance is required, the services of a competent professional person should be sought.

Scales ©Rzymu

Library of Congress Cataloging-in-Publication Data
    Intellectual property: patents, trademarks, copyrights and trade secrets/by Catherine J.
        Holland. . . [et al.].
        p.   cm.
    ISBN-13: 978-1-59918-147-9 (alk. paper)
    ISBN-10: 1-59918-147-9 (alk. paper)
        1. Intellectual property—United States—Popular works. I. Holland, Catherine J.
    KF2980.I539 2007
    346.7304'8--dc22   2007008528

Printed in Canada

12 11 10 09 08 07   10 9 8 7 6 5 4 3 2 1

Contents

Preface xvii

PART ONE
Identifying Your Intellectual Property

CHAPTER 1
Intellectual Property 3

How Different Types of IP Protect
Different Aspects of Your Business 4

    Driven by Innovation: Patent Protection 5

    Brand Recognition or Goodwill:
       Trademark Protection 9

    Know-How and Valuable Secrets:
    Trade Secrets 10

Creativity and Fixed Expressions: Copyrights 11
Brief Summary of Intellectual Property Types 11

CHAPTER 2
Find Your IP 13
Your Company: Rain Alert Inc. 17

PART TWO
Protecting the Keys to Your Business
Subpart A—Protect Your Company's Name, Brands, Product Names, and Logos

CHAPTER 3
Protecting Your Company Name— Incorporating Is Not Enough 21

CHAPTER 4
Finding a Good Trademark 23
What Is a Trademark? 24
Selecting a Strong Mark 24
    The Strongest Trademarks: Coined and Arbitrary Marks 24
    The Gray Zone: Descriptive Marks 25
    The Gold Standard: Suggestive Marks 26
    The Words That Will Never Be Trademarks: Generic Words 27
    Evaluating Trademarks for Your Umbrella 27
What Other Trademarks Do You Own? 29
    Product Configuration Marks 29
        Registering Product Configuration Marks 30
    Sound Marks 31

CHAPTER 5
Searching and Registering Your Trademarks 33
Making Sure Your Mark Does Not Infringe the Rights of Others 33
    Searching the Internet 34
    Searching the Database of the USPTO 34
    Professional Search Companies 34
    Obtaining a Legal Opinion 35

Buttoning up your Trademark Rights 36

    Federal Registration 37

    The Application 37

        Filing a Trademark Application Before Using a Mark 37

        Describing the Goods 38

        Classifying the Goods 38

    The Office Action 39

    Publication for Opposition 39

    Statement of Use 40

    Fraud 41

    Cost to Obtain a Federal Registration 41

    Length of a Federal Registration 42

  State Registration 43

CHAPTER 6

Care and Maintenance of Your Trademarks **45**

  Marking Your Products and Marketing Materials
    with a Trademark Notice 45

  Using a Mark 46

    Trademark Genericide 47

  Policing Your Trademark 47

    Watching Services 48

  Trademark Goodwill and Assignments 48

  Trademark Licensing 49

  Trademarks and Domain Names 49

CHAPTER 7

Trademark Oppositions and Cancellation Actions **51**

  Filing an Opposition or Cancellation Action 52

  Answer 52

  Discovery 53

  Testimony Period 53

  Trial 54

  Fear Not, Oppositions and Cancellation Actions
    Are Rather Common and Usually Mild 54

CHAPTER 8

Trademark Protection in Foreign Countries. **55**

Foreign Filing Strategies for Trademarks 57

Foreign National Applications. 57

The Madrid Protocol: Another Way to Obtain

Foreign Trademark Protection. 59

The Cost to Obtain Foreign Trademark Registrations. 61

PART TWO

Subpart B—Protecting Your Innovative New Product

CHAPTER 9

What Is a Patent? **65**

The Three Types of United States Patents 66

Patents Provide Only a Right to Exclude 68

What Can You Patent? 72

Design Patents 73

CHAPTER 10

Filing Your Patent Application **77**

When to File Your Patent Application. 80

File Within One Year to Preserve United States Rights 80

File Before Any Public Disclosure

to Preserve Foreign Rights 82

Requirements to File a Patent Application 83

The Specification 85

Written Description, Enablement, and Best Mode 88

Written Description 89

Enablement 91

Best Mode 92

Claims. 93

Items to File with a Patent Application. 98

Filing Fees. 99

Inventorship. 99

Other Documents 102

CHAPTER 11

Requirements for Patentability. **103**

Utility, Novelty, and Nonobviousness 104

    Anticipation 104

    Obviousness 105

The Different Types of Prior Art. 106

What Is an Interference? 112

The Examiner and Prior Art 115

Patent Searching 117

CHAPTER 12

Examining a Patent Application **119**

The Office Action 120

    Anticipation Rejection 121

    Obviousness Rejection 123

A Final Rejection. 125

    Filing an Amendment after Final. 126

    Filing a Request for Continued Examination (RCE) 126

    Filing a Continuation Application 126

    Filing an Appeal 127

How Does My Patent Get Allowed? 127

CHAPTER 13

Continuing Applications, Provisional Applications, and Patent Publication **129**

Continuation Applications 130

Continuations 130

Divisionals 131

    Restriction Requirements. 132

Continuations-in-Part. 133

Example 134

Establishing Priority 136

    Inventorship 136

    Pendency. 136

    Disclosure 136

Priority Claim. 137
Continuing Application Limits. 138
Continuing Applications and Patent Term 139
A Provisional Patent Application 139
After a Patent Application Publication. 142
18–Month Publication 142
Non-Publication Requests. 143
Provisional Rights. 146

CHAPTER 14
Getting Worldwide Patent Protection. 149

CHAPTER 15
Once Your Patent Issues 155
Marking a Product with the Patent Number. 156
Errors in an Issued Patent 156
A Reexamination. 160
Patent Term. 164
Measuring Terms 166
Ways to Extend the Patent Term. 166
Ways a Patent Term Can Be Cut Short 170

CHAPTER 16
IP Audits and Developing a Patent Strategy 175
IP Audits 176
The Offensive Plan: Developing a Patent Portfolio 177
Whether to Patent 177
Maintaining Inventions as Trade Secrets 178
Searching to Assess Patentability. 178
Considering the Useful, Marketable Life of Your Technology 179
Requesting Nonpublication of Your Patent Application 180
What to Patent. 180
When to File Your Patent Applications 181
Filing Provisional Patent Applications to Defer Costs. 182
Filing Under the Patent Cooperation Treaty to Defer Costs 183

Where to Apply for Patent Protection 185
Cost Considerations 186
Defensive Analysis: How to Avoid Infringing
    Someone Else's Patents 188
Establishing Ownership 190
Purchasing Patent Protection 192
Generating Licensing Revenue from Your Patent Protection 193

PART TWO

Subpart C—Protecting Company Secrets

CHAPTER 17

Trade Secrets **197**

The Legal Requirements for Trade Secrets 199

CHAPTER 18

Protecting and Enforcing Your Trade Secrets **201**

What Information Should Be Secret 202
Inform Employees About Your Confidential Information 202
Employee Entrance Interviews 203
Reminders 203
Confidentiality Agreements 204
Exit Interviews 204
Using Technology to Safeguard Your Trade Secrets 205
Losing Trade Secret Protection 205
Enforcing Your Trade Secrets 206
Non-disclosure Agreements with Third Parties 207

PART TWO

Subpart D—Protecting Catalogs and Marketing Materials

CHAPTER 19

Copyrights and How They Can Protect
Your Marketing Materials, Web Sites,
and Other Artistic Expressions **213**

Overview of Copyrights 214

CHAPTER 20

What Can Be Protected by Copyright 217
Expression That Is Not Copyrightable 218
The Minimal Amount of Originality Requirement. 218
Copyright in Your RAINGOD Umbrella 219
Copyright Only Protects the Expression of an Idea 219
Copyright Protection Limited to Artistic Expression 220
Copyrighting a Web Site 221

CHAPTER 21

Who Can Claim Copyright? 223
Author's Rights 223
Contract Workers 224
Work Made for Hire. 225
Other Works Made for Hire 226
Co-Authors of Copyright 227
Copyright Ownership in Your RAINGOD Umbrella 227
Copyright in the Overall Umbrella Design 228
Copyright in the Handle Design. 228
Copyright in the Fabric Design. 229
Copyright in the Software 229
Copyright in Your Marketing Materials 230
Getting Ownership of Copyrights You Do Not Own. 230

CHAPTER 22

Copyright Protection and How Long It Lasts 233
Derivative Works 234
The Test for Copyright Infringement 234
Remedies for Copyright Infringement 234
Length of a Copyright 236
Works Created on or After January 1, 1978 236
Works Created and Published or
Registered Before January 1, 1978 237
Works Created Before January 1, 1978,
But Not Published or Registered Before January 1, 1978 237

Other Factors Affecting the Term of Copyright. 237
Publication 238
The Public Domain 238

CHAPTER 23
Using Copyrighted Work Owned by Others in Your Business 239
Using Derivative Work. 239
Using Copies of Works. 240
Using Only a Small Portion of a Copyrighted Work 240
Obtaining Permission 241
Fair Use. 241

CHAPTER 24
Registering Your Copyright 245
Advantages to Registering a Copyright 246
When to Register a Copyright 246
The Importance of Registration 247
The Process and Cost of Registering. 248
The Mechanics 248
Application Forms. 249
The Fees 249
The Deposit Copy Requirement for Registration 249
The Mandatory Deposit Requirement 250

CHAPTER 25
**Marking Catalogs and Marketing Materials with
Copyright Notice: Foreign Copyright Protection 251**
Protecting Copyrights in Foreign Countries. 253

PART TWO
Subpart E—Registration of Patents, Trademarks, and Copyrights

CHAPTER 26
The Benefits of IP Protection 257
The Myth About Patents: Getting a Patent on Your Product
Guarantees that You Can Sell It Freely. 258

The Rights Provided by a Trademark Registration. 258

The Rights Provided by a Copyright Registration 259

PART THREE

Protecting Yourself from Infringing the IP Rights of Others
How to Make Sure You Can Sell and/or Continue to Sell a New Product
Subpart A—Pre-design and Pre-launch Product Evaluations

CHAPTER 27

Protecting Yourself from a Patent Infringement Claim 265

The First Step: Focus on the New Features 265

Conducting a Technology/Patent Search: Figuring Out
What Is Unprotected and What Is Protected 266

Hire a Professional Patent Searcher. 267

Reliability of Patent Searches. 269

Analyze the Results of Your Patent Search 270

Look at the File History. 271

After the Patent Search 272

Design-Arounds 273

The Need for an Opinion of Counsel 274

Patents Are Complicated 274

Your Investors Insist on It 275

Protect Yourself from an Accusation of Willful Infringement 275

The Cost of an Opinion of Counsel 277

Being Sued—And the Chances of Winning 278

Patent Trolls. 280

Risk-Aversion and Problematic Patents 281

Obtaining Rights to the Problematic Patent 282

Buying the Patent vs. Obtaining a License Under the Patent 282

Patent Licenses vs. Product Licenses 283

Obtaining a License Under Someone Else's Patent 285

The Terms of a Patent License 285

What You Pay for a Patent License. 286

Invalidating the Problematic Patent. 286

Telling If a Patent Is Invalid. 286

Show That the Invention Is Not Novel or Is Obvious 286

Show Insufficient Written Description, No Enablement,
No Best Mode, and/or the Claims Are Indefinite 287
Legal Opinions on Patent Invalidity 288

CHAPTER 28
Cease-and-Desist Letters and Infringement Suits 289
Assess the Seriousness of the Threat 290
Options in Responding 291
Stopping Competitors from Sending Cease-and-Desist Letters 292
What To Do If You Are Sued for Infringing Patents,
Trademarks, or Copyrights 293
Move Quickly—Time's-a-Tickin' 293
Options 294
Hire a Lawyer 294
Assess the Allegations in the Complaint 296
Do a Cost-Benefit Analysis of
Fighting vs. Settling the Case 296
Think About the Intrusion of Litigation into Your Business . . . 297

PART FOUR

Stopping Others from Infringing Your IP Rights

CHAPTER 29
Enforcing Your IP 301
The Copier: Individual, Group of Individuals, and/or
Company or Companies 302
Do You Need the Infringer to Stop? 302
Available Resources 305
The Costs of Discovery 305

CHAPTER 30
The Nature and Cost of IP Litigation: Going to Trial 309
The Complaint 311
Location of the Lawsuit 311
Whom Should You Sue? 311
Allegations in the Complaint 313

The Answer of the Defendant Infringer 313
   Affirmative Defenses 313
   Counterclaims. 314
The Plaintiff's Reply to Counterclaims 314
The Pleadings 314
The Case Management Conference. 315
The Discovery Process 316
Claim Construction and Markman Hearings
   (aka Markman Proceedings). 319
Expert Witnesses. 320
The Trial 321
   Pre-trial Proceedings 322
      Witness Lists, Summaries of Testimony, and Exhibit Lists 322
      Trial Briefs. 322
   Pre-trial Costs. 322
   Jury Focus Groups and Jury Experts. 323
   Jury Instructions. 323
   Trial Costs. 323
Post-trial Proceedings. 324
   The Costs of Post-trial Proceedings 324
   Appealing Your Case 325
The Overall Costs of Litigation. 325

Appendix A **325**

Appendix B **339**

Appendix C **351**

Glossary **375**

About the Authors **395**

Index **399**

Preface

It's the American dream. You invent an innovative new product, you launch the product, the product takes the market by storm, you make billions selling your new product, and you ride off into the sunset, rich and happy. Does that sound too good to be true? Certainly it has happened to some entrepreneurs, but all too often the American dream is dashed.

How does the dream fail? There are the usual reasons such as lack of money to finance the product, poor market acceptance, or a general lack of business savvy by the entrepreneur. But let's assume that you invent the world's most innovative new product, you have great financial backing, you have keen business

> What are IP rights? Intellectual property, or IP, refers to creations of the mind, whether they are inventions, literary pieces, art, music, designs, photographs, slogans, or names. IP rights can take the form of patents, trademarks, copyrights, trade secrets, and other rights granted to you by governments or case law.

acumen, and your product does take the market by storm. Could anything go wrong that could completely knock you off your horse? You bet. Unfortunately for the entrepreneur and business owner, an increasingly common reason for business failure is lack of understanding regarding intellectual property rights, also known as IP rights.

What are IP rights? Intellectual property, or IP, refers to creations of the mind, whether they are inventions, literary pieces, art, music, designs, photographs, slogans, or names. IP rights can take the form of patents, trademarks, copyrights, trade secrets, and other rights granted to you by governments or case law. Once you get IP rights, they can help protect you and your business. If you don't get them, or if you get them but don't protect them, you may lose your business, your ideas may be stolen, and/or your products may be copied. In addition, if you accidentally or intentionally violate the IP rights of others, your business could be shut down.

This all sounds hopeless, right? Wrong. That's where this guide comes in. The keys to avoiding the IP missteps and mishaps of other entrepreneurs and business owners is to become educated about IP rights and to make good, informed decisions about IP rights so that your business can thrive. This guide is designed to help you, the entrepreneur and small to medium business owner, protect some of your most vital assets—your inventions, trade names, and logos. It will help you to avoid infringing the IP rights of others. It also will assist you in spotting critical patent, trademark, and IP issues early in order to prevent problems down the road. Our goal is to take a somewhat mystifying and often intimidating area of the law and to break it down into easy-to-understand principles that you can begin applying immediately.

Here's an overview of some common questions that entrepreneurs and small businesses have about IP rights:

1. What do I have that needs to be protected? What are patents, trademarks, trade secrets, and copyrights? Why do they need to be protected?
2. How do I protect:
   • My business name, brands, product names, and logos?
   • My innovative new product?
   • My business secrets?
   • My catalogs and marketing materials?
3. If I get a patent and register my trademarks and copyrights, does that guarantee that I can sell my products?
4. How do I make sure that I don't infringe the IP rights of others so that I can sell or continue to sell my new product without worry? What do I do if I receive a cease-and-desist letter from a competitor or get sued for infringement?
5. What can I do to stop competitors who are copying my product? What can I do if competitors are using my name, brands, product names, or logos?

Each of these questions will be addressed in this guide. Now, let's start down the path toward your American dream.

P.S. No legal guide would be complete without the normal disclaimer, so here goes. We would be remiss if we didn't remind you that this guide is *not* intended to be comprehensive legal advice that can be applied to every situation. Rather, it is intended to give you the tools to help you understand basic principles of IP law and the IP issues that will most likely arise in your business. The information here is current only as of the date of publication, and any updates in IP law will not be reflected. Therefore, this guide is not intended to be a substitute for legal advice, which you should seek from your own IP attorney.

In addition, this guide refers to a number of registered trademarks owned by various companies. The references are for illustration purposes only. The authors fully acknowledge the ownership of the trademarks by their owners and the authors make no claim to such trademarks.

❑ ❑ ❑

The authors wish to thank all of the people who assisted them with this guide. First, we thank Jere Calmes and Helen Cicino for giving us the opportunity to share our knowledge of intellectual property law with entrepreneurs and small business owners. We thank all of the dedicated people at our firm, Knobbe, Martens, Olson & Bear, who assisted with this project—including Roberta Bustillos, Ruth Carpenter, Ashanti Falcon, Debbie Munson, Judy Perkins, Nikki Ramos, Amar Sehmi, Sherry Spitzer, Moira Timney, and Lynette Williams. We also thank those Knobbe, Martens partners who assisted us by providing valuable feedback on our manuscript—Gerard von Hoffmann, Paul Stewart, and Karoline Delaney. Finally, we express our appreciation to our spouses, Mark, Renee, Terry, Peggy, Ioana, and Dale, and our children, Claire, John, Elissa, Vito IV, Jack, Annie, Jacob, Sophia, Kelly, and Sara, for giving up their time with us so that we could write this guide.

Identifying Your Intellectual Property

PART ONE

Intellectual Property— An Overview

Intellectual property (IP) can exist in almost all areas of a company. From the research and development laboratory to the sales and marketing department, employees create IP. However, as an entrepreneur and business leader, it is up to you to identify the IP in your organization and determine which types of IP should be protected. Entrepreneurs and business people who are aware of the differences between the four major types of IP (patents, trademarks, copyrights, and trade secrets) and who are able to identify IP-related issues add valuable leadership and guidance to a business venture. For example, venture capitalists often investigate a target investment's

"IP position" prior to investing. Also, investors and boards of directors often expect the leadership of the company to understand IP issues and to protect and enforce a company's intellectual capital. This section will explain, in general, the four major types of IP and how you can identify these invisible assets to add value to your business.

How Different Types of IP Protect Different Aspects of Your Business

When you think about intellectual property, it helps to step back and take a broad view of the driving forces behind your business. What does your business do to create value? What drives sales and profitability? Is your company a first-to-market innovator, or a later-to-market, extra-efficient manufacturer? Does or will brand recognition command a price premium in the market, or will your company merely supply goods for others to brand and market? These are some questions to ponder when you consider how intellectual property might serve your needs.

Even if your particular business plan does not include product manufacturing or marketing, intellectual property can help implement your business goals, such as attracting capital or successfully executing an exit strategy. An exit strategy is the ultimate goal an entrepreneur establishes when embarking on a new business venture. For example, your exit strategy may involve merging with or being acquired by another company. Whether your exit strategy involves going public or being acquired, and whether you're an innovator, manufacturer, and/or marketer, understanding IP issues helps maximize business value so that you reap maximum returns when you implement your exit strategy. If your business goal is to remain a privately held company, understanding your IP will help to maximize your returns on your business investments.

An IP strategy provides a plan to protect your business's driving forces. The following sections provide a brief review of the four types of IP that should be evaluated and understood when you develop your business's IP strategy: patents, trademarks, copyrights, and trade secrets. Table 1.1 on page 12 summarizes some of the differences between these types of intellectual property.

Driven by Innovation: Patent Protection

Will your company research and develop solutions, such as new products, processes, and methods, or improvements to existing technologies? If so, patents may provide valuable protection. Patents provide the right to prevent others from "practicing" your invention. For example, a patent will allow you to stop others from manufacturing, using, selling, offering to sell, or importing into the United States, products that are covered by your patent. In addition, if you've patented a process, or a method of doing something, the patent laws allow you to prevent others from "practicing" your patented methods. Patents are discussed further in Chapters 9 to 16.

The "right to stop others," sometimes referred to as the "right to exclude," is often confused with the "right to practice," sometimes referred to as "freedom to operate." The right to exclude allows a patent holder to sue another to stop patent infringement (i.e., the unauthorized making, using, selling, offering to sell, or importing into the United States, the patented invention, which are collectively referred to as the unauthorized "practicing" of an invention). However, a patent does not provide you with a "right to practice." This means that even though you may receive a patent on your innovation (which means that you will have the right to prevent

> **You Should Know** Patents are issued by the U.S. Patent and Trademark Office (often referred to as the Patent Office, the USPTO, or just the PTO). The Patent and Trademark Office is an agency of the federal government, like the Food and Drug Administration (FDA), the Federal Communications Commission (FCC), and the Securities and Exchange Commission (SEC). The Patent and Trademark Office is responsible for evaluating and examining all patent applications and deciding whether or not to grant patents. The Patent Office is supposed to grant patents only for new, nonobvious, and useful inventions.

Myth vs. Reality	**Myth:** A patent gives you a right to practice the invention covered by the patent.

Reality: A patent only gives you the right to stop others from practicing (making, using, selling, offering to sell, or importing into the United States) your invention. This concept is very important, and frequently misunderstood. For example, it would not be correct to say, "We can't be sued for making our products because we have patents that cover our products." Instead, it would make more sense to say, "We have the right to prevent others from making the products covered by our patents."

---

others from practicing your innovation), you may not be able to make, use, sell, offer to sell, or import, your innovation yourself.

If this doesn't make sense, think about a patent that describes an improvement to existing technology. An improvement to existing technology may sometimes be patented. For example, let's say you obtain a patent on the existing technology plus the improvement (e.g., a car that automatically adjusts its windshield wiper's wiping speed based upon the rate of rainfall hitting the windshield). You would be precluded from practicing your invention if someone else holds a patent on the underlying existing technology (e.g., windshield wipers). Similarly, the person holding the underlying technology patent would be precluded from practicing your improvement because you now hold a patent on the improvement. You and the other patent holder have "locked horns," and neither one of you can practice the new improvement. However, a license or cross-license of the patents could resolve this impasse. License and cross-license strategies are discussed in greater detail in Chapter 27.

Although an issued, granted patent is presumed to be valid and enforceable, an accused infringer has the right to challenge the validity and enforceability of a patent in federal court. In fact, accused infringers are often successful in proving that patents are actually invalid, and should not have been issued, or that the patent is not enforceable. For example, a patent can be found to be invalid if a defendant is able to identify "prior art" that illustrates that the patented invention is not new. In addition, a patent can be found to be unenforceable if a defendant can show that the patent applicant or his representative committed a fraud upon the Patent and Trademark Office. Therefore, you should understand that the discussions in this guide related to licensing and litigation (see Part 2, Chapters 16, 29, and 30) assume that you plan to license and assert valid and enforceable patents. You may not know whether your patent is invalid or unenforceable until it is asserted and its validity and enforceability is challenged in court. This is one of the risks to consider and review with your patent attorney when developing licensing and litigation strategies.

The purpose of the patent system is to stimulate innovation. In exchange for providing an inventor with the right to exclude others from practicing for a period of time, the public receives a complete disclosure of an inventor's invention and instructions how to practice that invention. When the patent's term expires, the disclosed invention falls into the public domain, which means that anyone and everyone can practice the invention freely. In the meantime, during the term of the patent, the public receives information about the invention so that it may develop improvements and refinements, which may be patentable in and of themselves.

Patents can be used to protect the innovations you and your employees conceive, whether or not those innovations are ultimately embodied within

---

Did You Know? Did you know that in the United States, holding an intellectual property right usually does not guarantee you an unfettered right to practice an invention? Although you can reduce risks by studying the patents held by others, securing licenses, entering contracts, seeking indemnification, and/or obtaining opinions from counsel, there is no way to be 100 percent certain that you will not be sued by another for patent infringement. Patent attorneys can help identify risks to entrepreneurs and provide risk assessment and management strategies.

your company's (or your competitor's) products, methods, systems, user manuals, etc. In addition, innovations need not be breakthrough technological findings, flashes of genius, or results of divine stimulation. In fact, incremental improvements to long-standing, existing technologies can sometimes be perfectly patentable subject matter as well (as long as the improvements are not mere obvious variants or changes, as will be discussed in greater detail in Chapter 11).

Inventing does not necessarily occur in the engineering laboratory. In fact, the mere act of conceiving of a solution to a problem can sometimes suffice as an inventive act. Therefore, identifying product- or company-related problems, such as user problems, technical problems, manufacturing problems, testing problems, reliability problems, etc., and finding solutions to those problems often leads to a finding of patentable subject matter that you could consider pursuing with patents.

Invention can, therefore, occur in the marketing, sales, service, quality control, or any other department that solves problems relevant to your company. In addition, the patent system allows not only things, such as machines and devices, to be patented but also allows processes, such as methods of using machines and devices, to be patented as well. Finally, patents can be granted on improvements to existing devices, such as new features in a second-generation product.

To help identify the inventions generated within your company, you might consider holding periodic patent review meetings. For example, during a patent review meeting a patent review committee could invite members from different departments to discuss department-specific innovations. You might also consider implementing a system to encourage innovation and invention disclosure by providing financial incentive to employees to submit written invention disclosure documents. Some incentive programs provide employees with a small bonus for filing an invention disclosure, and a larger bonus if the patent review committee decides that the invention is worth patenting and a patent is filed. Some programs provide an additional bonus after a patent is issued.

While most patents protect the useful aspects of your technologies (such patents are called *utility patents*), there are also some patents, called *design patents*, that are used to protect more aesthetic features, such as the ornamental features of your product's design. So if your product has a unique shape or look, you might think about pursuing design patents as well. See Chapter 9 for more on design patents.

Brand Recognition or Goodwill: Trademark Protection

Will you invest in developing brand recognition and company goodwill? Will you launch marketing campaigns and/or develop logos, slogans, and/or distinctive packaging or product configurations? If so, trademarks may provide valuable protection. Trademarks allow a consumer to identify the source of a good or service. In other words, when consumers see your logo or product name, they will think of your company and will come to expect a certain level of product (or service) quality.

Trademark law allows consumers to rely on trademarks when making purchasing decisions. Trademark law gives consumers confidence that they are selecting the products and services that they want (which have the quality they expect). Trademark law also helps businesses protect their reputation and goodwill. However, not all marks (e.g., names, symbols, logos, etc.) provide the same level of protection. Before you invest marketing dollars and other resources to develop brand recognition and goodwill, be sure to investigate the strength of the trademarks that you want to use. Investigating the ability to register a trademark and assessing strength of a potential trademark is discussed in Chapters 4 and 5.

In addition, a product's overall configuration as well as certain features, such as colors, background design, the product wrapping or packaging, its label, or other physical features, such as the product itself or the shape of its container, may be protectable as a form of trademark called *trade dress*. However, trade dress protection, like all other forms of trademark protection, is available only if such features are distinctive and nonfunctional, as discussed in the trademark chapters.

Know-How and Valuable Secrets: Trade Secrets

Have you developed a process that provides a commercial advantage and cannot be reverse engineered (or figured out by analyzing the products you sell)? Does your company have information that you would not want a competitor to have, such as customer or supplier lists, manufacturing methods, proprietary processes, etc.? Are you concerned that an employee might leave your company to join or start a competing venture that uses your secret information? If so, trade secrets may provide valuable protection.

A trade secret is any formula, pattern, device, or compilation of information that is used in your business and that provides an opportunity to obtain an advantage over competitors who do not know or use it. For information to be considered a trade secret, the secret holder must take reasonable steps to keep it confidential. If the secret holder needs to share the secret with outside parties (such as vendors that will be manufacturing parts), then there must be an agreement of confidentiality (often called a non-disclosure agreement, or NDA) between the secret holder and the recipient, or the secret holder must put the recipient on notice of the secret status of the information.

Courts will look at several factors in determining whether information is a trade secret, including the secret holder's efforts to protect secrecy of the information, how widely the information is known within and outside of the holder's organization, and whether information provides a commercial, competitive advantage over others.

In general, if one of your employees (or former employees), without your permission, discloses or sells your trade secrets to someone outside of your company and by doing so breaches a duty of confidentiality to your company, you can then bring an action in court for "misappropriation" or stealing of the trade secret. It is, therefore, important that you establish either an express or implied duty of confidentiality (e.g., a confidentiality agreement, non-disclosure agreement, consulting agreement, employment agreement, etc.) prior to disclosing valuable, secret information to third parties (including your own employees). Chapters 17 and 18 provide more detailed information regarding trade secret protection.

Creativity and Fixed Expressions: Copyrights

Will you develop written or musical pieces in connection with your business, including web pages, animations, commercials, infomercials, or videos? Perhaps you plan to hire employees or consultants to write software, create technical drawings, models, or designs. If so, copyrights may provide valuable protection. Copyrights protect "original works of authorship" that are "fixed in any tangible medium of expression." This includes literary works, musical works, dramatic works, pictorial, graphic, and sculptural works, motion pictures and other audiovisual works, sound recordings, architectural works, as well as others. Copyright law protects computer programs (including embedded software and other code), user interfaces, and in some situations, design features of manufactured products (sometimes referred to as articles of manufacture) as well.

A copyright owner has the exclusive right to do or authorize the reproduction, distribution, public performance, and display of his copyrighted work. In addition, unlike patents, copyrights are not granted or issued by a federal agency—instead, rights in a copyrightable work are created as soon as the work is created. It is, therefore, important for you to understand where copyrights can arise during daily operations, and to take steps to assure that those rights belong to you. Chapters 19 to 25 provide more detailed information regarding copyright protection.

Brief Summary of Intellectual Property Types

Table 1.1 summarizes some of the differences among the various types of intellectual property. The four major types of IP protect different things in different ways. Not only does each type of IP have different requirements, but the manner of obtaining and time required to obtain the IP protection, the duration of the IP protection, and costs differ significantly as well. Some of these differences will be discussed in greater detail below.

TABLE 1.1. **Comparison of Different Types of Intellectual Property**

	Utility Patents	Design Patents	Trademarks	Trade Secrets	Copyrights
What does it protect?	Processes, machines, manufactures, or compositions of matter, or any new and useful improvement thereof	Designs for articles of manufacture	Identity of source of goods or services	Anything that can be kept secret	Expression
Rights conferred?	Exclude others from making, using, selling, offering for sale, or importing	Exclude others from making, using, selling, offering for sale, or importing	Prevents use of confusingly similar marks	Prevents misappropriation of ideas by third parties	Prevent others from copying without permission
Requirements for protection?	Useful, new, and nonobvious	New, original, and ornamental	Use in commerce and "distinctiveness"	Subject to reasonable measures to preserve secrecy	Original and creative, and fixed in a tangible medium
How to obtain protection?	Apply in Patent Office	Apply in Patent Office	Automatic with use; registration optional	Keep it secret	Automatic with use; registration to enforce
Time to obtain?	3 years +	1 year +	1 year +	Immediate	3 months
How long does protection last?	20 years from filing	14 years from issuance	Can be perpetual	Until disclosed	Life + 70 years; 95 or 120 years for work for hire
Filing cost?	$5,000 to $20,000 +	$750+	$1,500+	N/A	$500+

Find Your IP

The following fictional company products and service descriptions are provided for you to test your current IP knowledge. While reading each of the following descriptions, think of the various types of IP discussed above, and see if you can identify examples of each type of IP embodied in each description. Also, think about how much value each form of protection might add to a company offering such products and/or services.

1. A new soft drink called "Buzz Cola," which has a unique bottle shape
2. A children's book called "Larry Potter"

3. A new business idea called "Ship-Ex," used to deliver packages over the internet

4. A statuette used as a hood ornament for a car

5. A new formulation for motor oil

6. A method for performing a catheter-based surgical procedure on a patient's heart

7. A new machine for forming metallic components

Here are some sample answers to the different types of intellectual property that might be protected in each of the examples provided above. These are just a few examples, and these lists are not comprehensive.

1. A new soft drink called "Buzz Cola," which has a unique bottle shape.
   - *Patent.* You might be able to patent the method of making the new drink, including the process of mixing the ingredients together and controlling the mixing parameters (e.g., temperature, pressure, rate of delivery, mixing speeds, etc.). If you have designed special equipment to manufacture the drink and to bottle it, the equipment might be patentable as well. If the bottle has certain ornamental features, design patent protection might be available.
   - *Trademark.* The product name, "Buzz Cola," might be a trademark, and the unique bottle shape might be protected as trade dress.
   - *Copyright.* Artwork used on the bottle, as well as any music, lyrics, video, animation, etc., used to market the product could possibly be protected with copyrights.
   - *Trade secrets.* Instead of filing a patent on the formulation used to make the product, you could treat the recipe as a trade secret. Also, the names of suppliers and customers could be protected as trade secrets as well.

2. A children's book called "Larry Potter."
   - *Patent.* Any new machines used to manufacture the book could be patented. Ornamental features of the book itself, such as the shape or overall look of the book, might be protectable with design patents.
   - *Trademark.* You might want to protect the mark, "Larry Potter," not only for books, but other related products, such as videos, toys, dolls, etc. Distinct packaging of the book could be protected as trade dress.

However, the owner of the HARRY POTTER® mark may object to your use and/or registration of your mark.

- *Copyright*. The book itself can be copyrighted, as well as any original artwork appearing within it. You could copyright other "expressions" of the book, such as a version of the book that is read and recorded on cassette or compact disc, or a movie based upon the book.
- *Trade secret*. Prior to publication you might be able to treat the manuscript of the book as a trade secret.

3. A new business idea called "Ship-Ex" used to deliver packages over the internet.
   - *Patent*. Any new methods or process of taking orders, routing delivery, and delivering packages could possibly be patented.
   - *Trademark*. Your service mark, Ship-Ex, might be protected. Any logo that you design might be protected as well. Again, the owner of the FEDEX® mark may object to your use and/or registration of your service mark.
   - *Copyright*. Software or other code used to implement your system could be copyright-protected.
   - *Trade secret*. Instead of filing patents, you might be able to protect the methods you use to accept and process orders as trade secrets.

4. A statuette used as a hood ornament for a car.
   - *Patent*. Any new methods or process of manufacturing the statuette, including manufacturing equipment, and packages, could possibly be patented. The ornamental features of the statuette could be protected with design patents.
   - *Trademark*. If the hood ornament is used to identify the source, such as the manufacturer of the car, the ornament could be protected as a trademark for the car.
   - *Copyright*. Copyright protection might be available for the statuette as a sculptural work.
   - *Trade secret*. If a secret process is used to create the statuette, the process could be protected as a trade secret. Customer lists could be protected as trade secrets, too.

5. A new formulation for motor oil.
   - *Patent.* The method of manufacturing the motor oil could be patented as well as the oil itself if it contains a new combination of materials.
   - *Trademark.* Marks used to market the oil could be trademarked. If the oil has a distinct color or smell that is used to market the oil, the color or smell might be trademarked as well.
   - *Copyright.* Written text, graphics, and artwork on the packaging of the motor oil might be copyright protected.
   - *Trade secret.* Instead of filing patents, you might be able to protect the methods you use to produce the oil as trade secrets.

6. A method for performing a catheter-based surgical procedure on a patient's heart.
   - *Patent.* The method itself as well as any new devices used to perform the method could be patented.
   - *Trademark.* Any name, logos, or other marks used to market the method or the devices to perform the method could be trademarked. If you establish a teaching program to educate others how to perform the method, any name or logo that you use in connection with the marketing of such training services could be protected as a service mark.
   - *Copyright.* Written instructions for use, as well as training videos or audio recordings could be protected with copyrights.
   - *Trade secret.* The method itself could be kept as a trade secret.

7. A new machine for forming metallic components.
   - *Patent.* The machine itself, as well as the method employed by the machine, could be patented.
   - *Trademark.* Marks used to sell the components as well as marks used to market the service of forming components could be protected with trademarks.
   - *Copyright.* Software or other code used by the machine to operate could be copyright-protected.
   - *Trade secret.* The machine and the processes performed by the machine could be maintained as trade secrets.

Your Company: Rain Alert Inc.

To help illustrate how each type of intellectual property can arise, the following sections refer to Rain Alert Inc., a hypothetical corporation that you have formed to develop, manufacture, market, and sell your brainchild: An umbrella that receives a wireless radio signal and tells its owner if the weather forecast predicts rain. We apply the principles and rules of intellectual property law to this hypothetical corporation to illustrate how patents, trademarks, copyrights, and trade secrets can be developed and enforced.

Your inspiration for starting Rain Alert Inc. comes from having been caught in the rain without an umbrella once too often. You don't have time every morning to check the weather report, so you think, "Wouldn't it be great if I could look at my umbrella as I walk out the door and immediately know whether I need to bring it or not?" After thinking about the problem for awhile, you realize that if an umbrella incorporated a wireless receiver, such as a weather signal receiver, it could directly receive weather forecasts from a weather bureau. The umbrella could then communicate the weather forecast to its owner by flashing a light, beeping, or providing some other audible or visual signal.

After you raise some seed capital, form a corporation, and hire an engineer and a marketing guru, Rain Alert Inc. is born. You and your team decide that your umbrella will have a fabric with a thatched-roof pattern and the handle will be in the shape of a tiki. The tiki's eyes will flash red as it emits the sounds of thunder and lightning to indicate predicted rain. Only one thing remains to decide—the product's name. You conduct market research and ultimately decide upon the name Rain Alert.

When you try to raise capital, you encounter the same question over and over again: How are you protecting this novel invention? What have you done to lockup your innovation and to keep competition at bay? In addition, you anticipate that as the company becomes successful, knock-offs and copycat products will appear. You realize the importance of integrating an intellectual property strategy into your business plan, and you begin to think about the different forms of intellectual property, and how each form might add value to your company:

- Patents seem ideal to protect the overall invention of a wireless communication-enabled umbrella as well as the methods of receiving wireless information and informing a user of a weather condition.
- Trademarks seem ideal to protect your product's name, and perhaps its overall configuration, including the tiki handle.
- Trade secrets might help protect a new process that you've developed to fabricate the umbrella canopy, and your customer lists.
- Copyrights seem useful to protect the software that controls system operations, and also protect any artwork you might provide on the umbrella's canopy.

The following chapters describe your intellectual property strategy.

PART TWO

Protecting the Keys to Your Business

Subpart A

Protect Your Company's Name, Brands, Product Names, and Logos

You have a great idea for a product. Now you need to figure out what to call the product, what to call the company, and what the product is going to look like. All of these decisions will affect the attractiveness of the product to potential customers. After all, if no one wants to buy your product, everything else is academic. So, the first order of business is to pick a trademark (also called a mark) that will enhance your ability to sell the product. Equally important, however, are picking a mark that does not infringe any one else's rights and being able to stop others from using a confusingly similar mark on competing products. The day after your product launch, you do not want to receive a letter from a company demanding that you immediately stop using your mark because it infringes its rights. Similarly, three months after your wildly successful product launch, you do not want to find out that you cannot stop a flood of cheaper competitive products from using your exact mark. Therefore, you will need to put some thought into what you will call your business and your product.

CHAPTER 3

Protecting Your Company Name— Incorporating Is Not Enough

Most businesses form a corporation or LLC, or file a fictitious business name statement. It may come as a shock to you to learn that neither the certificate of incorporation nor the fictitious business name statement gives you the right to use the business name, or "trade name," if it is likely to cause confusion with a trademark or service mark that someone else used first.

The state or county agencies that issue the certificates of incorporation and fictitious business name statements do not perform searches to determine if your business name infringes someone else's prior rights. The only way to make sure

Did You Know? Neither a fictitious business name statement nor a certificate of incorporation gives you the right to use your business name in the advertising, promotion, or sale of goods or services.

your company name does not infringe the rights of others is to do a trademark search.

If a court decides there is confusion between your name and someone else's trademark, it can make you stop using your business name, even if you have a fictitious business name statement or a certificate of incorporation. The legal test used by the court does not even require that the names or marks be identical; it requires only that the names or marks be similar enough to cause a likelihood of confusion.

Another thing to consider is whether your company name makes a good trademark. In your rush to set up your corporation, you picked Rain Alert Inc. as your company name. It sums up the essence of your product—an umbrella that alerts you when it is going to rain. You like the name. It helps your employees, your partners, your investors, and everyone else involved with your company by focusing them on the distinguishing feature of your product. It is short, easy to spell, easy to understand, and to the point. It is a fine company name.

It is also a terrible trademark. How, you ask, could a name with these wonderful attributes be a bad trademark? What is a trademark anyway?

CHAPTER 4

Finding a Good Trademark

The prudent business owner can save a tremendous amount of time and expense in the long run if he chooses his trademarks carefully at the beginning. Potential marks should be evaluated not only for their marketability, but also for their inherent strength and the likelihood they may infringe the rights of others. The first step, of course, is to figure out what a mark is and how it differs from a company name or a description of the products.

What Is a Trademark?

A trademark is usually a brand name for a product. It can be a word, phrase, logo, design, color, sound, smell, product configuration, or virtually anything that is used to identify the source of the product and distinguish it from competitors' products. More than one trademark may be used in connection with a product.

BIG MAC® is a word mark for hamburgers and the "Golden Arches"® is a logo mark. "Don't Leave Home Without It"® is an example of a phrase registered as a servicemark for charge card services.

A trademark represents the goodwill and reputation of a product and its source. Its owner has the right to prevent others from trading on that goodwill by using the same or a similar trademark on the same or similar products in a way that is likely to cause confusion as to the source, origin, or sponsorship of the products.

A service mark is like a trademark, except it is used to identify and distinguish services rather than products. The terms "trademark" or "mark" are often used interchangeably to refer to either a trademark or service mark.

Selecting a Strong Mark

A strong trademark can do a lot of heavy-lifting for your company. It will be a mark that clearly distinguishes your products from those of your competitors. It will be instantly recognizable by your customers. It will, in short, stand out in the crowd.

A weak trademark, on the other hand, has a lot more competition. It will be easier for your competitors to use similar marks, and yours could just get lost in the shuffle. It is important to understand the difference between inherently strong marks and inherently weak marks, and to choose yours accordingly.

Example of a Service Mark: McDONALD'S® is a service mark for restaurant services.

The Strongest Trademarks: Coined and Arbitrary Marks

All trademarks are not created equal. Some are inherently very strong, and their owners can stop pretty much everyone else in the world from using them in connection with any goods or services, whether or not the goods and services are related to those of the trademark owner. These marks are usually coined words that do not exist but for their creation as a trademark. Examples of such marks include EXXON® or KODAK®. There is no reason for any person or company to use those words, except to refer to the trademark owners. For example, if you saw a company named Exxon Knitting Supplies, you might automatically associate the store with the energy company, even though it seems highly unlikely that the energy company would be in the knitting supply business. The mere fact that you thought of the energy company when seeing the mark, even in the most incongruous context, could be sufficient for the energy company to stop use of the mark by the knitting supply company.

Although coined or fanciful marks are the strongest and most protectable marks from a legal point of view, marketing people generally don't like to use them. They do not give the public any clue as to what product is being sold in connection with the mark, and the company must commit to a substantial investment in marketing and advertising to develop consumer recognition of the brand. Once established, however, these brands have enormous power. Eventually, even the marketing people learn to love them.

Another kind of mark which is very strong is an "arbitrary" mark. This is a word that already exists, but does not have any connection with the goods or services being sold. Examples include APPLE® for computers and AMAZON® for electronic retail services. There is no reason for competitors to use these words to describe any aspect of their goods. Of course, the public is still free to use "apple" in connection with fruit, and "Amazon" in connection with strong women. Marketing people typically do not like arbitrary marks much more than they do coined words, and for the same reason—it costs more to educate the public as to what the company is actually selling.

The Gray Zone: Descriptive Marks

Inevitably, the marketing people will think along the same lines that you did when you selected your company name. They want a mark that says it all, and says it quickly. It is much easier to let the customer know what you are selling if you just say it right up front. The problem with this approach is that if your

Examples of descriptive marks that have acquired secondary meaning include AMERICAN AIRLINES® and SPORTS ILLUSTRATED®.

mark describes your product, or a quality or characteristic of your product, you cannot stop others from using the same words to describe their products. In general, a descriptive term cannot be a proprietary trademark owned by one company to the exclusion of others. So, the more descriptive your mark is, the less likely you will be able to stop anyone else from using it.

There is an exception to this rule. If you can show that you have extensively advertised the mark and have a significant volume of sales, and can demonstrate that a substantial portion of your potential market recognizes that the descriptive name is a trademark that refers to your goods, then you can stop others from using confusingly similar marks on related products. This concept is called "acquired distinctiveness" or proving "secondary meaning" in your mark.

As you can appreciate, proving secondary meaning can be expensive. Therefore, if you think it will bother you if other people use your mark to describe their competing products, one simple way to bypass a potentially significant expenditure of money and energy is to avoid choosing descriptive terms as trademarks.

The Gold Standard: Suggestive Marks

Examples of suggestive marks include CHICKEN OF THE SEA® tuna fish and MINUTE MAID® orange juice.

The true art in trademark selection arises when companies develop brands that suggest a quality of the product yet stop short of describing it. Suggestive marks are inherently distinctive. Suggestive marks are the middle ground, where the marketing department and the lawyers can be equally enthusiastic. The marketing people like them because they suggest a positive attribute of the product, the lawyers like them because the company will not have to establish secondary meaning before it can protect and enforce its trademark rights.

The Words That Will Never Be Trademarks: Generic Words

Finally, there is a category of terms that can never function as trademarks. These are generic words. Let's say you own a dealership that sells red sedans, and you call yourself THE RED SEDAN DEALERSHIP. There is nothing to prevent you from using this name. Unfortunately, there is also nothing to prevent every other company that sells red sedans from also using THE RED SEDAN DEALERSHIP, even if they set up shop across the street from you.

Figure 4.1 shows the spectrum of strength of a trademark, from the strongest types to the weakest.

FIGURE 4-1. **Trademark Spectrum of Strength**

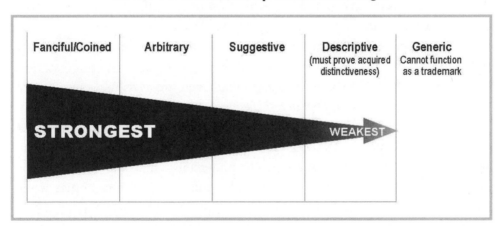

Evaluating Trademarks for Your Umbrella

You have asked the marketing department to come up with a trademark to be used on your umbrella. They have presented you with a list of the following potential marks: RAIN ALERT, RAINMAN, SMARTBRELLA, TIKI-BRELLA, and RAINGOD.

> **You Should Know** | ## What is a trade name?
>
> A trade name is the name of a business. Unlike trade-marks, a trade name can be used as a noun. It need not be followed by generic terms. It is permissible to use all or a portion of a trade name as a trademark or service mark. "Ocean Pacific Apparel Corporation" is a trade name. OCEAN PACIFIC® is a trademark when used on clothing, and may be a service mark when properly used with surfing competitions.

Knowing what you now know, you reject RAIN ALERT as a trademark because you believe it may be descriptive. You do not want to have to go through the hassle and expense of having to prove significant sales and advertising in order to prove you have a protectable trademark. You can still use Rain Alert Inc. as a company name, however, and may develop trade name rights in it.

You reject RAINMAN (even though you loved the movie) because you are worried that the movie studio may object to your use of the mark. You have heard that they can be fairly aggressive in protecting their properties. SMARTBRELLA and TIKIBRELLA are interesting possibilities. A customer seeing both marks would immediately understand that the product is an umbrella. Without much more additional mental work, the customer would also understand that the SMARTBRELLA probably incorporates some electronics. TIKIBRELLA clearly refers to one of the distinguishing aspects of the umbrella's appearance—the handle shaped like a tiki. Unfortunately, both marks do such a good job of conveying this knowledge to the customer, that they move into the uncomfortable "gray zone" between descriptive marks and suggestive marks. There is a very good chance that you will have to go to the expense of arguing that these marks are not descriptive in order to prove that you have protectable rights. If you are not successful in the argument, you will have to go to the expense of proving secondary meaning.

You are determined not to spend money unnecessarily. Because it is easy and inexpensive to brainstorm product names, you decide to keep looking.

The last mark on the list is RAINGOD. What, you wonder, were the marketing people thinking? You turn it over in your mind. Then, like a bolt from the blue, it hits you. RAINGOD suggests many attributes of your umbrella, without describing anything at all. In a sense, your umbrella acts like a rain god—it tells you when it is going to rain. The tiki handle with the flashing eyes could be a representation of a rain god. It is a clever name which customers will remember. In addition, there is no reason that your competitors would need to use the word to describe any aspect of their umbrella. You decide that this is the mark that is going to sell a million umbrellas, and you are ready to take the next step.

What Other Trademarks Do You Own?

In addition to the word mark you use on your umbrella, you should keep in mind that there may be several other distinctive things that function as trademarks for your company and your products. Colors, sounds, and even smells have been registered as trademarks. The owner must prove that these features are not important to the function of the product, and that consumers recognize that they identify the source of the products. You should consider carefully all aspects of your umbrella, and decide if you wish to claim other trademarks. If so, you can develop your marketing materials with this goal in mind.

Product Configuration Marks

One interesting feature of your umbrella is the handle shaped like a tiki. If you would like to stop others from selling umbrellas with tiki handles, you should market your umbrella so that consumers recognize that tiki handles are your trademark. If you are successful, you may be able to stop others from selling umbrellas with any kind of tiki handle, not just a tiki that looks like your tiki.

One easy way to establish trademark rights in the tiki handle configuration is to do "look for" advertising. Your hang tags, advertisements, and product information should all promote the tiki handle as a trademark of Rain Alert Inc. They can include statements like "When you see the tiki,

---

Did You Know? | ## Is My Product's Shape or Packaging Protectable?

The nonfunctional features of a product's shape or packaging (its "trade dress") may be protectable if they are sufficiently distinctive to identify the owner of the trade dress. Product shapes are being protected with ever-increasing frequency. For example, the appearance of a C clamp, a Ruger 22-caliber pistol, a fingernail polish bottle, and the red border and format of TIME® magazine have all been protected against look-alike competitive products.

     To obtain this type of protection, you should select nonfunctional and distinctive product features or packaging. These features should then be promoted through image advertising or "look for" advertising so that customers recognize the product shape or packaging and associate it with a single source.

---

you know you've got RAINGOD" or "Get a tiki handle, get a handle on the weather." Another idea would be to make your hang tag in the shape of a tiki.

Registering Product Configuration Marks

At the same time that you position your marketing to promote the tiki handle, you can also file an application to register the tiki handle as a trademark in the USPTO. The USPTO treats product configuration marks the same way it treats descriptive marks. The examiner will require that you provide evidence that your tiki handle has acquired secondary meaning before she will allow you to register it as a trademark. You will need to show that you have advertised and sold umbrellas with the handle, and that consumers recognize the handle as a trademark of your products. You can provide the examiner with copies of your marketing materials, which will be very helpful in establishing that the tiki handle is a trademark, not just an ornamental design.

> **You Should Know** | **Can I Register My Trade Dress?**
> If your trade dress is nonfunctional and is either inherently distinctive or has acquired customer recognition from sufficient promotion of the protectable features, it may be registered as a trademark. For example, the shape of the WEBER® barbecue grill and the clear tip of a SHAKESPEARE® fishing rod have been registered with the U.S. Patent and Trademark Office.

It would be more expensive to prosecute this product configuration application than it would be to prosecute a simple word mark application. If the tiki handle is important to you, however, and if you want to prevent others from doing the same thing, you may decide that it is worthwhile. If you have set up your marketing materials correctly, the cost to prove secondary meaning should not be exorbitant.

Sound Marks

Another possible trademark could be the sound of thunder and lightning that come from the umbrella handle. Like the shape of the handle, if you can demonstrate that consumers recognize the sound as a trademark identifying your umbrella, you may be able to claim it as trademark. This will allow you to stop others from selling umbrellas issuing confusingly similar sounds. Once again, your marketing materials can be instrumental in helping you establish your sound trademark. The USPTO will allow you to register sound marks. Like product configuration marks, however, it is more expensive to prosecute these applications.

CHAPTER 5

Searching and Registering Your Trademarks

You have selected the perfect mark. It is catchy. It is clever. It is strong. It would be a shame if someone else thought of it first. If they did, they could demand that you stop using your mark. They might even be able to make you pay them money for the damage you have caused. They could really rain on your parade.

Making Sure Your Mark Does Not Infringe the Rights of Others

The first step to ensure that you are not stepping on the toes of others is to conduct some searches. There are several kinds of searches you can do. The more thorough your searching, the higher your confidence that you will not infringe the rights of others.

Searching the Internet

Being the fiscally conservative person that you are, you decide that you do not want this to happen to you. You will conduct a search to see if there is anyone out there who might think that RAINGOD umbrellas would infringe their rights. You turn first to the marvelous repository of all knowledge—the internet. A half hour of browsing turns up many hits for "rain gods," none of which refers to umbrellas or any other kind of electronic device that relates to weather forecasting.

Searching the Database of the USPTO

Another valuable resource for searching the availability of trademarks is the web site of the United States Patent and Trademark Office, www.uspto.gov. On that site, you can search the database of the Trademark Office at no cost and see all active, abandoned, or cancelled trademark applications and registrations. You can also access the official examination record or "prosecution history" of all of the pending applications and registrations, and learn quite a bit about the problems other companies have had trying to register similar marks. See Appendix B.

Professional Search Companies

Up until now, you have really only invested time and creative muscle in selecting and searching your mark. If your goal is to have the highest level of assurance possible that you can safely use your mark without infringing the rights of others, you will take the next step and invest money in a more thorough search performed by a professional searching company. For approximately $500, a searching company will provide you with a search report. The report will show pertinent applications and registrations in the U.S. Patent and Trademark Office and pertinent state registrations. In addition, it will include a large section of companies and marks that are not registered in the USPTO

> **You Should Know** | ## What Is a Trademark Search?
> There are a number of professional searching companies that may be used to help ensure that your mark or trade name does not conflict with the rights of another business. The goal of these searches is to avoid spending time, effort, and money promoting a product name or business name, only to find out that it conflicts with someone else's rights.
>
> These searches are typically performed through trademark lawyers who evaluate the search report to determine if there is an actual or potential conflict with another name or mark. This evaluation depends upon the consideration of numerous legal factors and case law decisions.

or state trademark offices. These unregistered marks are obtained by searching telephone and trade directories, and the internet. It is important to know about these companies because they can have protectable rights in unregistered marks. In other words, even if a company hasn't registered its mark anywhere, it could still stop you from using your mark.

Most search reports are around 150 pages long. There probably will be a few marks that are exactly the same as your mark, and hundreds of marks that are only similar to your mark in some way. In a search for RAINGOD, for example, you will probably find lots of marks that include the word RAIN and lots of marks that include the word GOD. Some of these marks may be used on umbrellas or rainwear; most of the marks will be used on other things, like clothing or entertainment services. How do you decide if any of these prior marks are a problem? You may need to enlist the help of a professional, namely, a trademark lawyer.

Obtaining a Legal Opinion

The last step to take in your effort to minimize the risk that you will encounter an infringement claim is to obtain the written opinion of a lawyer. Your lawyer will analyze the search results and provide you with an opinion as to the likelihood that your proposed use of the mark RAINGOD might infringe any of the marks revealed in the search report. You should discuss with your lawyer your business plans, including any plans you have to expand your use of the RAINGOD mark beyond umbrellas. This will enable her to provide you with a comprehensive opinion. Hopefully, of course, the lawyer's opinion is that there is a very low risk of infringement. Once you have this opinion, you and your lawyer will keep it in a safe place. In the unlikely event that someone ever claims that you are infringing their rights, you should be protected from any claim that your infringement was willful or intentional. After all, you took the time to get a lawyer's opinion, and you relied on her opinion that it should be OK to use the mark.

Buttoning up Your Trademark Rights

You have your mark. You have your search. You have your legal opinion from your trademark lawyer. You now want to make sure that no one else can use your mark. The best way to immediately establish your rights in the mark is to file an application to register it in the USPTO.

There is no requirement to register your mark, but there are many advantages to doing so:

1. If you have a federally registered mark, it is presumed to be a valid mark, and you are presumed to have the exclusive right to use it throughout the United States on the goods or services listed in the registration.

2. A registered mark will be revealed in searches conducted by other businesses in their effort to avoid selecting marks that may conflict with those of others.

3. Only federally registered trademarks or service marks may use the ® symbol.

4. After five years, the registration may become incontestable, which significantly limits the grounds on which competitors can attack it.

Federal Registration

One of the chief benefits of filing a federal application is that you establish instant nationwide priority in your mark. This means that you will have grounds for objecting to any other company that begins using a confusingly similar mark after the filing date of your application. There is an obvious advantage to filing your application as soon as possible. The early filing date can be critical when combating competitors, infringers, and other third parties down the road. More often than you would think possible, completely unrelated companies or individuals file applications for similar marks within months, weeks, or even days of each other. Unless one of the companies was using the mark before the filing date of the other applications, the first to file almost always wins.

> You can record your registered mark with U.S. Customs, and it will stop infringing and counterfeit imports from entering the country. Imagine, your tax dollars actually working for your direct benefit!

The Application

Filing an application to federally register a trademark is a fairly straightforward procedure that can be done via the www.uspto.gov web site. Appendix C has a print out from the web site showing a basic application. You can prepare and file the application yourself, or you can have a trademark lawyer do it for you. Unless you are very familiar with trademarks, the electronic form can be tricky.

Filing a Trademark Application Before Using a Mark

You can file your application based on your intent to use the mark. This means that you don't actually need to be using the mark when you file the application, although you will need to use the mark before the registration will issue. If you are already using the mark, you can file your application based on actual use. This involves a few extra steps upfront, but you avoid having to file a Statement of Use later on. Because most

> It will take at least a year for you to obtain a federal registration for your mark, but your rights in your mark will go back to your filing date.

people are interested in obtaining the earliest filing date possible, they file their application based on their intent to use the mark. They decide that they do not want to take the extra time to prepare a use-based application, even though they may have already begun to use the mark.

Describing the Goods

You will need to describe the goods or services upon which you plan to use the mark. The wording of this description may depend on whether or not you plan to file applications in foreign countries. In general, you should try to keep your description as broad as possible. After the application is filed, you will not be able to add any other goods or services, although you will be allowed to more specifically define your original description. The www.uspto.gov web site provides a manual of acceptable ways to describe your goods. See Appendix C.

You know that you are going to use the RAINGOD mark on umbrellas. In the back of your mind, however, you can imagine expanding the use of the mark to a variety of other accessories and products—raincoats, boots, hats, tote bags, tiki key chains, and flashlights. You should consider including all of these goods in your application to register the mark. You will have to pay additional filing fees to the USPTO; however, the benefit of obtaining the early filing date for the mark on all of the goods almost always outweighs the cost of the filing fees. When the money starts pouring in from the sale of your RAINGOD umbrella, you will not be pleased to learn that you cannot expand your use of the mark to tiki key chains because someone else beat you to the punch.

> An application for a federal registration may be filed before a mark is used in commerce, assuming you have a good-faith intent to use the mark. Actual use must begin before the registration will issue.

Classifying the Goods

You will also need to classify your goods. The USPTO has broken down all goods and services into different classifications, which can be completely arbitrary. For example, potato chips fall in Class 29 and corn chips fall into Class 30. The www.uspto.gov web site provides a classification manual for you to consult when deciding how to classify your goods. See Appendix C. An attorney experienced in this area of the law can save you quite a lot of time in the application process and minimize the chance that there will be any serious errors in the application.

The Office Action

Your application will be examined by a lawyer at the USPTO, and in about four to six months, she will send you an office action with her objections. These objections can be major or merely procedural. The two most common "major" objections are that your mark is descriptive, and that your mark is confusingly similar to a mark registered by someone else. If you have done your homework ahead of time, you can minimize the chances that the examiner will raise these objections to your application. A common procedural objection is that the examiner wants you to reclassify or amend your description of goods.

You will have six months in which to respond to the examiner. After receiving your response, the examiner may issue a second office action. You will have an additional six months to respond. This process of office actions and responses is called the prosecution of the application. It is unusual for an examiner to approve an application without raising any issues for prosecution, so you can count on getting at least one office action.

If you fail to respond to an office action, your application will be abandoned. It may be possible to revive your application if your failure to respond was an accident, but the timeline for reviving an application is fairly short. If the application is important to you, it is critical that you keep track of the response deadlines.

Publication for Opposition

Once the examiner approves the application, it will be published for opposition. Any company or individual that objects to your application will have 30 days in which to oppose it. Typically, a company will oppose an application if it believes that it has superior rights in a mark that is confusingly similar to the mark in the application. The opposer can obtain an extension of time up to 180 days past the publication date. Once the 180 days has expired, the opposer must file a Notice of Opposition or the application will proceed to allowance. For more information, see Chapter 7, Trademark Oppositions and Cancellation Actions.

Statement of Use

Once the opposition period has passed, the USPTO will issue a Notice of Allowance. You then will have six months to submit evidence that you have used the mark on the goods listed in the application. This evidence is called a specimen. For trademarks, acceptable specimens include labels, tags, and product packaging showing the mark on the goods. Advertising materials are usually not sufficient. For service marks, acceptable specimens include promotional materials advertising the services. You will need to provide one specimen for each class of goods in the application.

You also will need to tell the examiner the date you first used the mark anywhere, and the date you first used it in interstate commerce or in commerce with another country. A mere token shipment of goods is not sufficient. The mark must be used on goods or services in the normal course of your business. It is perfectly fine to submit a date of first use that precedes the filing date of your application.

It is possible to wait up to three years after the Notice of Allowance has issued before filing your Statement of Use. The down side to waiting this long, however, is that you will need to purchase extensions every six months, at a cost of $150 per class of goods. Also, your registration will not issue until you have submitted the Statement of Use.

When you file your Statement of Use, you can decide whether or not you want to drop any goods from the application. When you filed your application, you may have covered classes of goods that you thought you might need, but you still aren't using the mark with those goods. If necessary, there is a procedure that permits you to split the application in two, and obtain a registration for the goods upon which you have used your mark and keep an application pending for the goods which you have not begun to sell.

> **Warning!** If you sign a Statement of Use that declares that you have used your mark on all of the goods and services listed in the application, and that is not true, your entire registration may be vulnerable to cancellation on the grounds that you committed fraud.

Fraud

It is important that you carefully review your list of goods and services, and sign your Statement of Use only after you have used the mark on all of the goods and services. If you sign the declaration stating that you have used the mark on all of the goods and services when you actually have not, your entire registration may be vulnerable to a cancellation action brought by another company on the grounds that you committed fraud. The bottom line is that you can obtain a registration for your mark only for the goods that you have actually sold.

Cost to Obtain a Federal Registration

The filing fees for a federal application depend on whether you file it electronically or by paper. The cost is lower if you file electronically. Say no more—you decide to file your application electronically. Appendix C has the USPTO fee chart. For the typical application, the USPTO charges $325 per class of goods or services included in the application. If you use a law firm to file the application, it will probably charge you an additional $400 to $500 to prepare the description and correct classification of goods, and to strategize the best way to file the application in view of prior registrations owned by other companies, your business plans, and your desire for foreign protection. Most law firms charge a flat fee to prepare and file trademark applications.

The cost to prosecute the trademark application will depend on a number of different things. If you use a lawyer to respond to the office actions, the cost will depend upon the number and type of office actions that are issued. Your lawyer should provide you with an estimate. It can cost anywhere from $200 to $500 to respond to a run of the mill office action that raises no big substantive issues. It can cost between $2,000 and $4,000 to respond to a very difficult office action that raises several prior registrations as obstacles to your application or that objects to your mark on the ground that it is descriptive. Of course, if you decide to respond to these office actions yourself, there will not be any out-of-pocket costs to prosecute the application.

Either during prosecution of the application or after the Notice of Allowance has issued, you will need to file a Statement of Use. The USPTO fee for that is $100 per class of goods. If an attorney assists you in preparing and filing the Statement of Use, you will probably pay between $200 and $300 per class of goods to select appropriate specimens and identify the correct dates of use.

After the Notice of Allowance issues, you will have six months in which to file your Statement of Use. If you have not used the mark by that deadline, you can purchase a six-month extension. A total of five such extensions are available. The USPTO filing fee is $150 for each class of goods.

From start to finish, if you file and prosecute the application yourself, it should cost you approximately $500. If you hire a lawyer to file and prosecute your application and there are no major issues raised during prosecution, you will probably spend around $1,500. Both of these estimates assume that the application is for one class of goods, and that you begin using your mark relatively soon after you file your application, so that you do not have to obtain extensions to file your Statement of Use.

Filing and prosecuting trademark applications can quickly become very complicated. If the mark you are seeking to register is critical to your business, you should seriously consider hiring an attorney who specializes in the field.

Length of a Federal Registration

Once your Statement of Use has been accepted, the USPTO will issue a registration certificate. See Appendix C for an example. You should carefully read the registration certificate, and note the deadlines to maintain and renew your registration.

Between the fifth and sixth anniversaries of the registration date, you will need to file a declaration to maintain the registration. You may also file a declaration making your registration incontestable. This means that no one can challenge the validity of your registration based on their use of a similar mark, even if their use began before your use and application date. The USPTO fees to file these two declarations is $300 per class.

Every ten years from the registration date, you will need to file a renewal declaration, and pay the USPTO a renewal fee. The renewal fee is $500 per class. You may maintain and renew your registration as long as you continue to use your mark on all of the goods and services included in the registration. With each declaration, you will need to submit proof that you are still using the mark. Like the specimens you submitted with your application, the proof of use must show the mark used on labels, tags, or packaging for the goods, or on promotional materials advertising the services.

If you are no longer using the mark on all of the goods or services included in the registration, you must specifically delete them from the registration. If you do not do so, and sign the renewal declaration anyway, another company could attack your registration on the ground that you have committed fraud. Do companies really do this? Yes, they do.

State Registration

You may also decide to register your mark in one or more states. The examination process for state registrations is fairly minimal and varies by state. Many states seem to rubber stamp applications although they should reject

---

| You Should Know | **Where May I Get More Information on State and Federal Registrations?** |

Information on state registrations may be obtained from the Trademark Unit of your Secretary of State's Office. See Appendix C. Information on federal registrations may be obtained from the U.S. Patent and Trademark Office at www.uspto.gov.

> **Did You Know?** Marks may be registered in each of the 50 states. The advantages of a state registration vary according to the laws of each state. Most states require that you use a mark on goods or services before applying the registration. A California trademark registration, for example, is usually faster, cheaper, and less difficult to obtain than a federal registration. It also allows its owner to sue infringers under several California statutes that offer advantages not available under federal law. A California trademark registration, however, has no force outside of the state.

your application if your mark is similar to a prior registered mark or if your mark is descriptive. The prosecution procedure is not as sophisticated as it is on the federal level, and your ability to overcome these rejections varies by state.

One difference between state and federal procedure is that you must use your mark on the goods *before* you can file your state application. There is no "intent to use" provision like there is on the federal level. In addition, the protection given by a state registration is only statewide.

Even though a state registration usually costs less than $500 to obtain, most companies decide that it is much more important to get a federal registration with its nationwide priority and protection. In some situations, however, it may be beneficial to get state protection. Perhaps your business is very small, or perhaps trademark laws in your state give you a legal advantage not found in the federal statutes.

In most cases, a state registration is valid for ten years, and can be renewed for additional ten-year periods, assuming you are still using the mark.

CHAPTER 6

Care and Maintenance of Your Trademarks

There are many things you must do to properly maintain your trademarks. These things include marking your products and marketing materials with a trademark notice, using, assiging, and licensing your marks correctly, and policing your marks.

Marking Your Products and Marketing Materials with a Trademark Notice

Once you have decided what your identifying features, or trademarks, are, you should use trademark notice. TM or SM may be used right away to identify your trademarks and service marks, even before you file your trademark application. You may not use the ® notice until the mark is registered in the USPTO. As you know, it could be a year or two before you obtain your registration. In the meantime, though, use TM or SM. They enhance your trademarks in the minds of your customers, and serve as "Keep off the Grass" signs to your competitors.

Ideally, you should use trademark notice every time you use your trademark, RAINGOD™. The marketing people usually object to this, claiming that trademark notice is too busy, and ruins the look of the text and advertising. Once again, your first priority is to create and market a product that is appealing to consumers. If it is too ungainly to always use RAINGOD™, use the TM notice every time the RAINGOD mark is prominently featured on the marketing materials, advertising, and hang tags, and use the trademark notice at least once on every page, if there is a multipage user manual.

You also should use trademark notice in connection with your tiki handle and the sound marks. This notice can be placed in the marketing materials, hang tags, and other written materials. Perhaps your umbrella will have a cloth label sewn into a seam. On this label, and in your other materials, you can include language such as "RAINGOD™, Tiki Handle™, and the Sound of Thunder and Lightning™ are trademarks of Rain Alert Inc."

Using a Mark

Trademarks must be used properly to maintain their value. Marks should be used as adjectives, not as nouns or verbs. To prevent loss of trademark or service mark rights, the generic name for the product should appear after the mark. For example, Yamaha Motor Corporation refers to its product as the WAVERUNNER® personal watercraft—it uses its registered trademark first, followed by the generic name for the product.

In addition, the mark should appear visually different from the surrounding text. Use different font size, and style, color, or quotation marks for the trademark or service mark, as in OAKLEY® sunglasses, APPLE® computers, or CARL'S JR.® restaurant services. You may also use an asterisk (*) after a mark where the asterisk refers to a footnote explaining the ownership of a mark.

Trademark Genericide

If you do not use your mark correctly, you may lose the exclusive right to use it. In a worst case scenario, your mark could become the generic name for the product. If that happens, the whole world can use your trademark. Because competitors need to be able to describe their products, no one can own the exclusive right to use generic terms.

> Kerosene, escalator, trampoline, and nylon were once trademarks, but are now generic names.

Policing Your Trademark

After you spend all of the time, energy, and money to select and protect your nice, strong trademark, it is very important you police it as well. Policing does not mean that you ask for its papers and send it home before curfew. It means that you monitor the market, and make sure that no one else starts using a mark that is too similar to yours.

It is important to police your mark. If you don't and other companies begin using marks that are similar to yours, the zone of protection around your mark will gradually be eroded. Your competitors will be able to use marks that are increasingly similar to your mark. Eventually, you may find that you have lost your ability to stop your biggest competitor from using a mark that is virtually identical to your mark. Why? Because the customers have become so good at sifting through a lot of similar trademarks owned by different companies, they aren't likely to think that any of them come from the same source.

How similar is too similar? It varies, but you tend to know it when you see it. If you are selling the RAINGOD® umbrella, which of the following competing umbrella marks would you

> BAND-AID® brand adhesive strips, JELL-O® brand gelatin, and KLEENEX® brand tissues are examples of trademarks that are fighting the battle not to become generic words. Their owners spend millions of dollars advertising the fact that those trademarks refer to their specific products, and not adhesive strips, gelatin and tissues generally.

object to? RAIN UMBRELLA, RAIN-BE-GONE, DON'T RAIN ON ME, RAIN SPIRIT, WEATHERGOD, or TIKIGOD? What if you saw someone using the mark RAINGOD on waterproof handbags?

Every company draws the line at a different point, but it is important that you decide how far you want to keep your competition away from your mark, and that you take steps to make sure they do. These steps can vary from making a telephone call, sending a letter, hiring a lawyer to send a stronger letter, or filing a lawsuit. In any event, you should document your policing efforts, so that you can prove that you have diligently protected your trademark from infringers.

Watching Services

In addition to keeping your eyes and ears open in the market, you can also enroll your mark in both United States and foreign watching services. These services will notify you if another company files an application to register a similar mark. You can then decide if you want to send any of these companies a letter or oppose their application. Watching services are a very effective way to police your trademark and monitor the competition. Both United States and worldwide watching services cost only $200 to $400 per year.

Trademark Goodwill and Assignments

You want customers to know that RAINGOD® refers to your products only. Even better, you want your products and your RAINGOD® mark to have such a good reputation that customers who see the RAINGOD® mark on non-umbrella items are compelled to buy them because they have a warm and fuzzy feeling about the RAINGOD® mark. This is called the goodwill associated with the trademark, and it can become an extremely valuable asset.

Under United States law, a trademark and its goodwill cannot be separated. If you ever assign your trademark to another company, it is very important that you also assign the goodwill associated with the trademark. If you do not, the trademark will become void. You can guess what that means—it no longer exists. And if it no longer exists, that means that you have just invalidated your registration and all of the rights you have built up in the mark.

Trademark Licensing

You may want to consider licensing other companies to man-ufacture goods bearing your RAINGOD mark. This can be an easy way to generate revenue, because it involves no capi-tal investment by you, other than the cost to have a good license agreement prepared. You may also have to invest in a letter opener so that you can open up all of the envelopes containing royalty checks.

One important thing to remember in any licensing agreement is that it must contain a provision that gives you control over the quality of the products being sold with your trademark. Not only must the license give you the right to control the quality of the products, but you must also take steps to ensure that the quality standards are being met, and you must have the right to terminate the license if they are not.

If the license does not contain a quality control provision, it is called a *naked license*. If you do enter into a naked license, you may lose your exclu-sive right to use your mark. Yes, this means that not only your licensee but also anyone else who wants to will be able to use your RAINGOD mark with abandon, and they will not have to pay you one red royalty cent. Brrrrr.

> It has been estimated that if all of the hard assets of the Coca-Cola Company burnt to the ground, the company would still be worth bil-lions based on the value of the COCA-COLA® trademark alone.

Trademarks and Domain Names

Trademarks and domain names are not the same thing, and registering a domain name does not give the owner any trademark rights. At their core, domain names are merely addresses on the internet. They are no more a trademark than is 2040 Main Street.

A domain name can become a trademark only if it leads to a web site that offers goods or services. AMAZON.COM® is an example of domain name that is also a service mark for computerized online ordering services. GOOGLE.COM® is an example of a domain name that is also a service mark for the retrieval of information from the internet.

> A trademark assign-ment must include an assignment of the goodwill associated with the trademark. If it does not, the mark will become void.

> Having a federal trademark registration for your mark is essential if you want to stop others from using confusingly similar domain names.

An owner of a domain name should not be able to stop you from using your trademark, unless he is selling goods or services from his web site that are related to the ones you are selling. Likewise, you probably will not be able to stop others from using domain names that are similar to your trademark, unless they are selling goods and services on their web site that are related to the ones you are selling.

If you expect that you may be doing any business on the internet, you should consider registering a domain name as soon as possible. It is relatively inexpensive. The web site www.icann.org has information about the procedure for obtaining domain name registrations and objecting to the domain name registrations of others.

CHAPTER 7

Trademark Oppositions and Cancellation Actions

An opposition is a proceeding brought by a company or an individual who wants to oppose a pending trademark application. A cancellation action is a proceeding brought by a company or individual who wants to cancel a trademark registration. Although one proceeding concerns applications and one concerns registrations, the procedure and cost of oppositions and cancellation actions are essentially the same.

Trademark oppositions and cancellations in the United States take place before the Trademark Trial and Appeal Board, or TTAB. The TTAB is like a court, but it handles only appeals from the trademark branch of the USPTO, and opposition and cancellation proceedings. The only issue decided by the TTAB is whether a mark is entitled to registration. It cannot award money damages or issue injunctions to stop a company from using a trademark.

Filing an Opposition or Cancellation Action

After your trademark application has been examined by an examiner at the USPTO and all of the issues have been resolved, the examiner will approve the application for opposition. A 30-day window opens, and any company or individual who believes he would be damaged by your registration may file an opposition or obtain an extension of up to 180 days in which to file an opposition. The usual reason that someone files an opposition is because he thinks your mark is too similar to a mark he is using.

There are a number of reasons a person may file a cancellation action against a registration. One of the most common reasons is if he believes that the trademark owner has abandoned his mark. A cancellation action with this basis may be brought at any time. Another common reason for filing a cancellation action occurs when a person believes your mark is confusingly similar to his mark, and he used his mark before your use or application date. This kind of cancellation action cannot be brought against an incontestable registration.

The cost to prepare and file a notice of opposition or a petition to cancel is approximately $1,000, which includes the $300 filing fee. If the application or registration contains more than one class, however, the filing fee increases $300 for each class.

Answer

The TTAB will notify the applicant or the registrant that an opposition or cancellation has been filed. The applicant must file an answer within 40 days after receiving official notice of the opposition or cancellation.

The opposition or cancellation may be withdrawn without prejudice any time before the answer is filed. This means that the opposer can re-file the opposition later if he wants to. After an answer is filed, the opposition or cancellation may not be withdrawn without prejudice except with the written consent of the applicant.

The cost to prepare and file an answer depends on the facts of each case, but is usually between $1,000 and $3,000.

Discovery

Effective November 1, 2007, the parties must participate in a pre-discovery conference to discuss discovery issues and possible settlement. Once an answer has been filed with the TTAB, the TTAB will set dates for taking discovery. After the opening of the discovery period, the parties must make initial disclosures. Only then may they proceed with traditional discovery. Each party may serve written interrogatories, requests for production of documents, and requests for admissions on the other party. Upon receipt of the discovery requests, the recipient will have 30 days to respond, but it is very common for the parties to agree to extend these deadlines.

The cost to prepare discovery and to respond to the other party's discovery depends on the issues in the case, but can run between $10,000 and $25,000 depending upon how much discovery the other party requests.

Depositions may also be noticed during this phase of the proceedings, allowing each party to question the other party's witnesses under oath. Depending on where the deposition is located, the cost for each deposition is likely to be anywhere from $5,000 to $15,000.

Testimony Period

The TTAB will also assign to each party the time for taking testimony. It is very unusual for the TTAB to have live testimony at hearings. The way a party can present its own witnesses is by having its lawyer schedule a deposition of her own client or other witnesses. The client will answer the lawyer's questions, and the whole thing will be recorded by a court reporter. This written record is then submitted to the TTAB. Obviously, testimony evidence is usually favorable to whichever side is giving the testimony. Assuming that each party takes the testimony of two witnesses, and attends the testimony-depositions of the other party's two witnesses, the testimony phase generally costs between $20,000 and $60,000.

Trial

In the final phase of an opposition or cancellation proceeding, each party submits a brief setting forth its arguments and files a reply brief to the other party's arguments. Oral arguments may also be requested. The TTAB has recently started to allow attorneys to attend hearings and present oral arguments via videoconference. This can substantially reduce the cost to attend such hearings.

After a number of months, the TTAB issues a written opinion based upon the evidence, the parties' briefs, and the oral arguments. The cost for this phase runs generally between $25,000 and $50,000.

Fear Not, Oppositions and Cancellation Actions Are Rather Common and Usually Mild

After reading the above, you have quickly concluded that oppositions and cancellation actions are extremely expensive and that they are to be avoided at all cost. You will be relieved to hear that the vast majority of oppositions and cancellation actions settle before any discovery takes place. Many settle before an answer is filed. Some settle before the notice of opposition is even filed. In fact, a very small percentage of oppositions or cancellation actions ever go all the way to a final decision by the TTAB.

Like you, most people quickly realize that it is in their best interest to settle their differences as quickly as possible, and avoid the cost of going through discovery. Attorneys who practice in this area are well aware that the opposition and cancellation procedure usually serves as a lever to negotiate a mutually beneficial solution that will address not only the registration of the mark, but also the use of each party's mark in the marketplace. Such an agreement is usually far more practical than pushing for a decision by the TTAB. After all, the TTAB will only determine if a mark should be registered. It will not decide who has the right to use the trademark in the marketplace or if a party is entitled to damages or recover its attorneys' fees. Those kinds of decisions can be made only by a federal or state court.

In fiscal year 2006, there were 22,500 extensions to oppose filed in the TTAB. Only 6,581 oppositions were actually filed, and only 80 decisions were issued by the TTAB.

Trademark Protection in Foreign Countries

Your umbrella is a thundering success. Orders are pouring in and business is booming. You have increased your investment in advertising, and you are buying booths at national trade shows. The increased volume of sales is making you consider moving your manufacturing to Asia. Also, you want to invest some of your hard-earned profits into expanding your market to foreign countries.

Others have been watching your success as well. Enterprising individuals from around the world attend the same trade shows you do. They walk up and down the aisles, and in addition to collecting lip balm, squeeze balls, and other giveaways, they take

> **You Should Know** Trademark owners who have not registered their marks in foreign countries may find that the mark has been appropriated by a third party who was the first to register in that country. Many foreign countries regard the first to register in that country as the owner of the mark, even if it is a pirate who saw the mark in the United States and stole it. This pirate may even be a trusted foreign distributor of the United States trademark owner.
>
> Foreign pirates may be able to prevent the original United States trademark owner from using or registering the mark in one or more foreign countries. In some cases, it may be possible to recover the mark, but the United States owner may face expensive litigation or exorbitant demands from the pirate.

photographs and notes. They hop a plane back to Spain or Korea, and they immediately file applications there to register the trademark RAINGOD for umbrellas, coats, and tote bags. The Spanish individual, fully embracing the concept of a unified Europe, filed a Community Trademark application, which covers all 28 countries in the European Union.

You have talked to potential manufacturers in China. At some point in the discussions, you learn that one of them has filed an application to register RAINGOD in China. They tell you that this is to protect your rights, but you notice that the application was filed listing the manufacturer as the owner of the mark, not Rain Alert Inc.

In almost all foreign countries, the first to file a trademark application is the owner of the mark. Guess what? You have just been aced out of the European Union, China, and Korea. The application owners in these countries can stop you from using the RAINGOD mark there. They are free to sell RAINGOD umbrellas in their countries, and there is not much you can do about it. Some of these individuals may not want to compete with you, but will use their application to negotiate a favorable license, distribution, or manufacturing agreement with you.

Can companies really do this? Yes, they can. Do companies really do this? Yes, they do—all the time. It keeps lawyers very busy.

What can you do to avoid the horrible problem of not being able to use your own trademark in foreign countries? It's simple. Be the first to file trademark applications there.

Foreign Filing Strategies for Trademarks

You may have plans to market your product globally. If that is the case, then you should consider registering your marks in other countries.

Foreign National Applications

In a perfect world, you could file one application which would instantly protect your trademark everywhere around the globe. Unfortunately, we do not live in a perfect world. To protect your trademark, you must file separate applications in every country where you want protection. One exception is the Community Trademark application, or CTM, which covers all of the countries in the European Union.

It is usually unnecessary, and extremely impractical, for most companies to file applications in every country in the world. Each company should analyze its business and determine where its primary markets will be, where its manufacturing will take place, and where counterfeits and knock-offs are most likely to come from. You can then prioritize these countries, and file foreign trademark applications accordingly.

| You Should Know | The European Community Trademark Application, or CTM |

As of January 1, 2007, the following countries are members of the European Union: Austria, Belgium, Bulgaria, Cyprus, the Czech Republic, Denmark, Estonia, Finland, France, Germany, Greece, Hellenic Republic, Hungary, Ireland, Italy, Latvia, Lithuania, Luxembourg, Malta, the Netherlands, Poland, Portugal, Romania, Slovakia, Slovenia, Spain, Sweden, and the United Kingdom.

Even the largest companies—the ones that can afford it and whose products are knocked off regularly—do not want the expense of extensive foreign filing until they know if a product will be successful. How do they avoid having trademark "pirates" filing applications all over the world within a few hours after their product launch?

The United States and other countries have signed treaties that help combat the problem of the foreign trademark pirate. If a company files an application for a mark in the United States, it may file an application for the same mark on the same goods or services virtually anywhere else in the world and get the benefit of its United States filing date, as long as it files the foreign application within six months of the United States filing date. This means that the company's foreign application will have priority over any intervening applications. Figure 8.1 illustrates this concept.

By taking advantage of these treaties, you can spread your trademark filing costs out over six months. You can file first in the United States. If you will be manufacturing products in China, you can file an application there in two months. If you attend a trade show and some individuals from Mexico are taking great interest in your product, you can file there in four months. If you are receiving lots of orders for your product and know that it is a "keeper," in six months you can file in countries where you expect to

FIGURE 8-1. **Trademark Foreign Filing Priority**

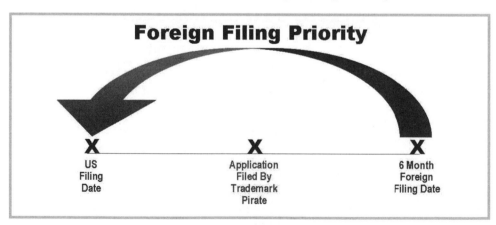

expand your business, perhaps in the European Community, Canada, Japan, and Australia.

All of these foreign applications will have the early United States filing date, even if they are filed two, four, or six months after the United States application. These foreign applications will have priority over any applications filed by other companies after your United States filing date. In the "first to file owns the mark" system followed in most countries, this six-month priority filing system can be a very effective tool for keeping would-be trademark pirates at bay.

A company can file foreign trademark applications at any time, but cannot claim the benefit of its United States filing date for any applications filed after six months from the United States filing date. Also, the company cannot claim the United States filing date for a foreign application for a mark that is different from the mark in the United States application or which includes different goods or services from those in the United States application. In other words, the foreign application must be virtually identical to the United States application in order to obtain the priority filing date. If you anticipate that you will be doing foreign filing, you should prepare your United States application with this in mind. There are ways to describe your goods and services that will give you better protection abroad.

Foreign trademark protection is a highly specialized field. Unless you have connections to filing firms in different countries, you will almost certainly need to hire a United States lawyer with those connections to coordinate your foreign filings.

The Madrid Protocol: Another Way to Obtain Foreign Trademark Protection

Another way to obtain protection abroad is by filing an international application under the Madrid Protocol. The Madrid Protocol is an international trademark treaty which provides a single International Registration covering multiple countries. Under this system, the United States applicant files an application to register her mark in the USPTO. She then pays an additional fee to the USPTO to have the application extended to other countries. The application is sent to the World Intellectual Property Organization, or WIPO,

> **Did You Know?** Foreign protection through the Madrid Protocol has been available to United States trademark owners since November 2, 2003, but the vast majority of United States companies continue to file national applications in each country where they want protection, rather than rely on an International Registration.

in Geneva, Switzerland. WIPO forwards the application to the countries selected by the applicant, and each foreign trademark office examines the application using its regular examination standards. If the foreign trademark office issues an office action, the applicant must hire foreign lawyers to respond. Assuming the applicant can satisfy the examiner's requirements, each country will grant protection under the International Registration issued by WIPO.

One disadvantage of an International Registration is that it will cover only the exact goods included in the underlying United States registration. In many countries, the applicant would probably be able to obtain broader protection with a national application, because most foreign trademark offices allow a broader description of goods than is allowed by the USPTO.

Another disadvantage is that the foreign protection hangs upon the fate of the underlying United States application. If the applicant doesn't obtain the United States registration for any reason, for example, the applicant is not able to overcome the objections of the examiner or the application is successfully opposed by another company, the International Registration will be cancelled. Also, if the United States registration is later cancelled because the owner fails to maintain it, or it is cancelled by another company, the International Registration will also be cancelled.

Using the Madrid Protocol may reduce filing and maintenance costs and may simplify management of an international trademark portfolio. In many cases, however, it is less expensive to simply file national applications in each foreign country where protection is desired. The cost of filing a Madrid Protocol trademark application varies widely, depending upon the number of countries in the application, the countries chosen, and the number of classes designated in the application. Appendix B has a copy of the fee calculator from the WIPO web page.

The Cost to Obtain Foreign Trademark Registrations

The cost to file a trademark application varies from country to country, but averages approximately $1,500 per country, including filing fees and the fees of United States and foreign lawyers. The cost to file a Community Trademark Application is approximately $2,500. These estimates are based on filing an application for goods in one class. If the goods fall into more than one class, the filing fees may be higher.

The foreign application will be examined by the foreign trademark office, which in almost all cases will issue office actions similar to those issued by the USPTO. The applicant will then have a chance to respond. The prosecution of the application is similar to the prosecution of an application in the United States, although each country may have different examination criteria. The cost to prosecute each foreign application depends on the number and type of objections raised by the examiner. Assuming that there are no serious obstacles to registration, such as prior registrations for similar marks, the cost to prosecute a foreign application may range from $1,500 to $2,500. In addition,

---

Strategy Tip | Trademark Notice in Foreign Countries

If a United States product is sold overseas, care must be taken to ensure the United States federal registration symbol ® is not used unless the mark is registered in the foreign country where the product is being sold. Some countries have both civil and criminal penalties for using the ® symbol with a mark not registered in that country. Improper use of the ® symbol may also make the mark unenforceable in some countries. It may be necessary to use different labels on products being sold outside of the United States. Another option is to use ® and an * or other symbol (RAINGOD®*), leading to clarifying language like "*RAINGOD® is a registered trademark in the United States and selected countries."

some trademark offices, such as the Japan Trademark Office and the Community Trademark Office, charge registration fees that may range from $1,500 to $2,500.

From start to finish, a foreign trademark registration usually costs between $4,000 and $5,000. A European Community Registration may cost between $5,000 and $6,000.

Protecting the Keys to Your Business

Subpart B

Protecting Your
Innovative New Product

You have a great idea for a new product, and as you've learned in Part A, you now know what to call it. But how do you protect yourself from someone else stealing your great idea? Generally, that's what patents are for. But before seeking patent protection, it's important to know what you can get out of your patent, and what you can't. For example, would you want to get a patent on your RAINGOD umbrella even if it means that you can't sell the umbrella yourself? Sometimes the answer is yes, and sometimes the answer is no. This part of the book explores when it's right to get a patent, when it's not, and what to expect out of the patent process. This will help you to make good decisions so that your time and money are spent wisely.

CHAPTER 9

What Is
a Patent?

A patent is a property right granted by the United
States government and authorized by the United
States Constitution for the purpose of protecting
inventions. Article I, Section 8 of the United States
Constitution specifically gives Congress the authority
"To promote the Progress of Science and useful Arts,
by securing for limited Times to Authors and Inventors the exclusive Right to their respective Writings
and Discoveries." Under this authority, Congress created the laws governing patents (to protect "Discoveries") and copyrights (to protect "Writings"). The
patent laws are found in Title 35 of the United States
Code, so sometimes you'll hear lawyers refer to the

> **Strategy Tip** Get patents to protect your inventions. A United States patent applies nationwide, allowing you to stop someone who steals your invention (also called an infringer) anywhere in the United States. But be warned that a United States patent by itself does not give you foreign rights, so if someone sells your invention in Europe, your United States patent may be powerless to stop the sale.

patent laws as "Title 35" or "35 U.S.C." Patents are issued by the U.S. Patent and Trademark Office, which is also referred to as the USPTO, PTO, or U.S. Patent Office.

Because the patent laws are part of federal law, the rights granted by patents are nationwide in scope. This means that even if you're only selling your patented product in California, you can still assert your patent against someone selling an infringing product in Massachusetts. However, this also means that obtaining a United States patent does not give you rights outside the United States. If you want to protect your invention outside the United States, you will also want to seek foreign patent protection. For more information on foreign patent protection, see Chapter 14.

The Three Types of United States Patents

There are three different types of patents provided, or granted, by the United States government:

1. Utility patents are used to protect any new and useful process, machine, manufacture, or composition of matter, or any new and useful improvement thereof.
2. Design patents are used to protect any new, original, and ornamental design for an article of manufacture.
3. Plant patents are used to protect any asexually reproduced distinct and new variety of plant.

Utility patents are by far the most popular type of patent, and they will be the primary focus of this section. You would use a utility patent to protect what's useful about your invention, such as the way your RAINGOD umbrella is made, operates, or receives and transmits information about the weather. You might use design patents, discussed below, to protect what's unique about the appearance of your invention, such as the tiki handle of your RAINGOD umbrella. Plant patents give the owner the right to exclude others from asexually reproducing a patented plant, or from selling or using an asexually reproduced patented plant. Because plant patents provide a very specific type of protection not commonly encountered by most entrepreneurs, they would not be applicable to your RAINGOD umbrella and will not be discussed further in this book.

Because patents are *intellectual* property, a patent holder's property right is by its very nature intangible. This is in contrast to *real* property, such as real estate or an automobile, which is a physical thing that the property holder owns. By obtaining a patent, you will obtain something that is defined simply by words, as would typically be printed on sheets of paper. Figures 9.1, 9.2, and 9.3 illustrate examples of the cover pages of utility, design, and plant patents, respectively. You can tell the difference between the three types of patents by the way the patent numbers are written. Design patent numbers are preceded by "D" or "Des.," plant patent numbers are preceded by "Plant" or "PP," and utility patents are indicated simply by the patent number itself.

Did You Know? The United States government has issued over seven million utility patents, far outnumbering design patents and plant patents. The term "patent" is often used synonymously with "utility patent." Other terms used to describe utility patents are "regular patents" or "non-provisional patents," to distinguish them from provisional patent applications, discussed in Chapter 13.

> **Myth vs. Reality** | **Myth:** If I obtain a patent on my invention, that means I have the right to make, use, and sell my invention.
>
> **Reality:** Obtaining a patent on your invention does not give you the right to make, use, and sell your invention. Patents only provide a right to exclude or prevent others from making, using, or selling your invention. So, while you might be able use your patent to stop your competitor from making and selling your patented product, you could be stopped from selling your product if another competitor also has a patent that you might infringe.

Patents Provide Only a Right to Exclude

Don't assume that once you obtain your patent, you will then be able to make and sell your invention free and clear. One of the most common misconceptions about obtaining a patent is that it will give you the right to practice your invention. The term "right to practice" refers generally to the right to make, use, and sell your invention without impinging on the rights of others. In fact, the only right granted by a patent is the right to exclude. More particularly, a patent provides the right to exclude or prevent others from making, using, selling, or offering for sale your invention in the United States, or importing your invention into the United States. In the case of utility patents, this right to exclude is provided generally for a term of 20 years from the filing of your patent application. For design patents, this right lasts for 14 years from the issuance of your patent. Additional information on patent terms is provided in Chapter 15.

To give an example, let's assume that you successfully obtained a patent covering your RAINGOD umbrella described above. Let's also assume that the original patent for the standard umbrella is still alive (meaning that its 20-year term has not yet expired). Therefore, you don't have the right to make and sell your umbrella without impinging on the rights of the owner of the other patent. For you to make and sell your new umbrella, you would need to obtain a license from the owner of the original umbrella patent, or else you could be sued for patent infringement by the holder of that patent.

FIGURE 9.1 **Cover Page of a Utility Patent**

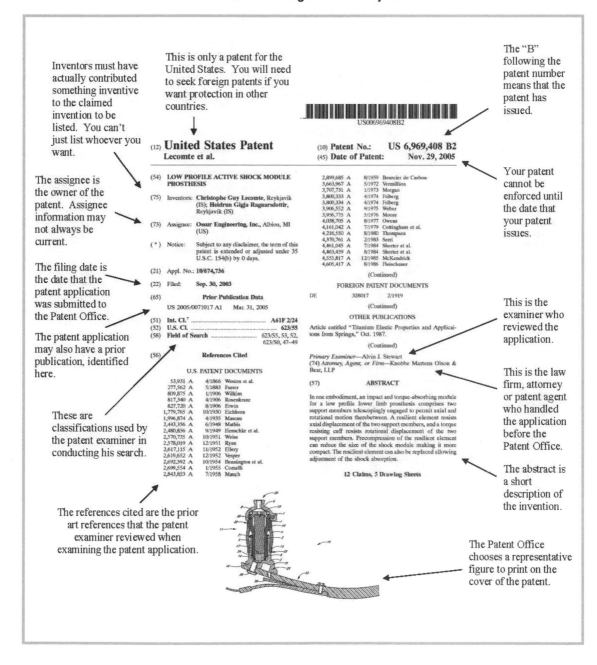

Inventors must have actually contributed something inventive to the claimed invention to be listed. You can't just list whoever you want.

This is only a patent for the United States. You will need to seek foreign patents if you want protection in other countries.

The "B" following the patent number means that the patent has issued.

The assignee is the owner of the patent. Assignee information may not always be current.

The filing date is the date that the patent application was submitted to the Patent Office.

The patent application may also have a prior publication, identified here.

These are classifications used by the patent examiner in conducting his search.

The references cited are the prior art references that the patent examiner reviewed when examining the patent application.

Your patent cannot be enforced until the date that your patent issues.

This is the examiner who reviewed the application.

This is the law firm, attorney or patent agent who handled the application before the Patent Office.

The abstract is a short description of the invention.

The Patent Office chooses a representative figure to print on the cover of the patent.

FIGURE 9.2 **Cover Page of a Design Patent**

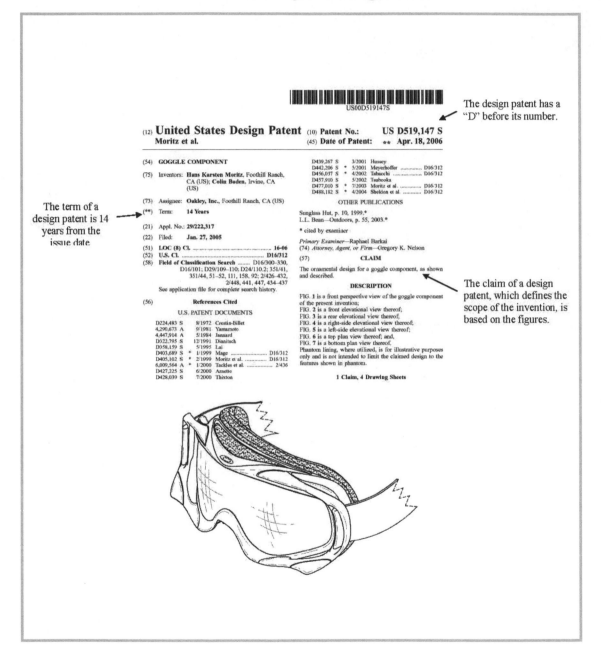

The design patent has a "D" before its number.

The term of a design patent is 14 years from the issue date.

The claim of a design patent, which defines the scope of the invention, is based on the figures.

FIGURE 9.3 **Cover Page of a Plant Patent**

US00PP10165P

United States Patent [19]

Fear et al.

[11]	**Patent Number:** **Plant 10,165**
[45]	**Date of Patent:** **Dec. 30, 1997**

[54] APRICOT TREE 'SUAPRISEVEN'

[75] Inventors: **Carlos D. Fear**, Aptos; **Bruce D. Mowrey**, La Selya Beach; **David W. Cain**, Bakersfield, all of Calif.

[73] Assignee: **Sun World, Inc.**, Bakersfield, Calif.

[21] Appl. No.: **694,186**

[22] Filed: **Aug. 8, 1996**

[51] Int. Cl.^{6} A01H 5/00

[52] U.S. Cl. Plt./39
[58] Field of Search Plt./39

Primary Examiner—James R. Feyrer
Attorney, Agent, or Firm—Knobbe, Martens, Olson & Bear, LLP

[57] **ABSTRACT**

A new and distinct apricot tree variety characterized by its large, round fruit which exhibits a high external red blush.

1 Drawing Sheet

1

BACKGROUND AND SUMMARY OF THE INVENTION

This invention relates to the discovery and asexual propagation of a new variety of hybrid apricot tree, *Prunus armeniaca* cv. 'Suapriseven'. The variety produces a relatively large, round apricot, having attractive external red blush, and cultivated for the fresh fruit market. It was discovered on May 17, 1990 in Wasco, Kern County, Calif., the new variety being hybridized by Carlos D. Fear, and evaluated and selected by Bruce D. Mowrey and David W. Cain.

The variety has as its seed parent, Apricot tree cv. 'Suapritwo' (U.S. Plant Pat. No. 7,550), and its pollen parent is an unnamed, unpatented apricot tree seedling of unknown parentage and identified in the breeders' plant collection as seedling F18. The parent varieties were first crossed in February 1987, and the resulting seed was harvested and sowed in September 1987, with the date of first flowering being February 1990. The new 'Suapriseven' variety was first propagated by Bruce D. Mowrey in June 1990, in Wasco, Kern County, Calif. by budding onto Nemared rootstock.

The new variety cv. 'Suapriseven' may be distinguished from other presently available commercial apricot tree cultivars by the following combination of characteristics: the fruit of the new 'Suapriseven' apricot variety ripens early mid-season about with the Katy variety (an unpatented variety) and, thus, is usually eating ripe in Wasco, Calif. about May 18; but the 'Suapriseven' fruit can be distinguished from the Katy variety by having a larger size, more external red blush and superior eating quality.

The new variety may be distinguished from its pollen parent, seedling F18, by the following combination of characteristics: the fruit of the 'Suapriseven' has a higher external blush, improved apricot flavor and a more rounded, more desirable shape than seedling F18. The new variety may be distinguished from its seed parent, 'Suapritwo' by the following combination of characteristics: the 'Suapriseven' fruit generally ripens with the 'Suapritwo' variety and has nearly the identical appearance and eating quality as that of 'Suapritwo'; however, the new 'Suapriseven' variety is pollen fertile, whereas 'Suapritwo' is pollen sterile and requires a pollenizer. Furthermore, the 'Suapriseven' variety exhibits a more consistent bearing habit and is more productive than the 'Suapritwo' in years having a low accumulation of winter chilling hours (hours of temperatures between 32° F. and 45° F.). The new 'Suapriseven' variety has been shown to maintain its distinguishing characteristics

2

through successive asexual propagations by, for example, budding.

BRIEF DESCRIPTION OF THE FIGURE

The accompanying drawing in FIG. 1 illustrates, in full color, a typical stem and mature leaves of the new apricot tree variety, and the outer surface of ripe fruit as viewed perpendicular to the suture line plane and looking at the suture line. The drawing also illustrates the fruit of the new variety sectioned in half from end to end, with the stone removed from the flesh.

DETAILED BOTANICAL DESCRIPTION OF THE INVENTION

Throughout this specification, color names beginning with a small letter signify that the name of that color, as used in common speech, is aptly descriptive. Color names beginning with a capital letter designate values based upon R.H.S. Colour Chart, published by The Royal Horticultural Society, London, England.

The descriptive matter which follows pertains to 'Suapriseven' plants grown in the vicinity of Wasco, Kern County, Calif. during 1994, and is believed to apply to plants of the variety grown under similar conditions of soil and climate elsewhere:

TREE

General:
  Size.—Large.
  Vigor.—Vigorous.
  Habit.—Semi-upright.
  Density of foliage.—Medium.
  Shape.—Topped.
  Hardiness.—Hardy in Wasco, Calif.
  Productivity.—Very productive.
  Fruit bearing.—Regular bearer.
  Root stock.—Nemared.
Trunk:
  Shape.—Medium to stocky.
  Surface texture.—Medium.
Branches:
  Shape.—Stocky.
  Surface texture.—Medium.
  Surface appearance.—Semi-glossy.
Lenticels:
  Number.—Medium.
  Size.—Large.

Why would you want to seek a patent for something that you can't necessarily make? Your patent still has value in that it prevents anyone else from making, using, or selling your invention. Your business goal may not be to sell a product, but simply to sell your patent or license it to someone else who wants to make the product. Or if you are interested in making and selling your product, your patent may give you the leverage to negotiate a cross-license with another party, especially if that other party is the holder of the original patent. With a cross-license, you might license your patent to the other party in exchange for that other party giving you a license for its patent. This would then allow you to sell your product without infringing the original patent.

What Can You Patent?

You realize that your invention has many neat features. For example, your RAINGOD umbrella has the ability to communicate with the National Weather Service to tell you when it's going to rain. It also has a special type of sensor that detects the humidity in the air, and is made of a new type of material that makes it more weather-resistant. The design of the umbrella is unique having the tiki handle with glowing red eyes.

With an unlimited budget, you could probably seek separate patents for all of the above features and more. There's no rule that says you can't seek several patents even if they all cover different aspects of the same product. You may think that your umbrella is just one invention, but the U.S. Patent Office might see six or seven.

With utility patents in particular, something qualifies as an invention that can be patented if it is a "new and useful process, machine, manufacture, or composition of matter, or any new and useful improvement thereof" (quoting the language from Section 101 of Title 35). These requirements have been interpreted broadly, and often quoted is the standard that "anything under the sun that is made by man" may be patented. Patents in the United States have therefore been issued on medical methods, computer software, microorganisms, and business methods, although business methods are often not patentable in foreign countries. There are, of course, limits to what may be patentable (e.g., laws of nature, physical phenomena, and

> **Strategy Tip** Patents in the United States can be sought for almost any kind of invention, and multiple patents can be sought for different features of your invention. However, just because something can be patented doesn't mean that it will be patented. As is discussed in Chapter 11, all inventions must still be "new" and "nonobvious," and the USPTO will often use these requirements to try to limit the types of patents that it will issue.

abstract ideas are not patentable), but in general, virtually any invention is a candidate for patent protection.

So think about your product and consider how many different inventions you might have, and what in particular should your patent or patents protect? With the RAINGOD umbrella, likely you'd want to protect the umbrella itself, perhaps incorporating a wireless transmitter and receiver. But if you considered closely the different categories of invention specified by Title 35, Section 101, you'd probably realize that you also invented a new method of conveying weather information, a new sensor that can detect weather conditions, and a new weather-resistant material. Because you can seek patents on all sorts of inventions, you may decide that you want to file for multiple patents to cover each of your many inventions. Of course, your finance people will tell you that your company doesn't have the money to file for so many patents all at once. For tips on how to save money while still getting the most out of your patent protection, see Chapter 16.

Design Patents

Most of the discussion on patents so far has been on utility patents. But you may also have heard or read about design patents. Depending on your product, they might be a good alternative to a utility patent application, or something you might want to get in addition to a utility patent.

Design patents are used to protect any new, original, and ornamental design for an article of manufacture. Articles of manufacture can encompass almost any tangible products made, such as lamps, sunglasses, bottles, tables, etc. Usually design patents are used to protect unique shapes, configurations, or styles of products or their packaging, but they cannot be used to protect functional (or useful) features of the products. For example, if filing a design patent for a bottle, the design patent might protect the unique shape of the bottle, but it would not protect the functionality of the opening at the end of the bottle through which liquid is poured. However, if the opening itself has a unique design, such as a triangular shaped opening, that feature, being ornamental, could also be protected by design patent.

Preparing a design patent application involves creating drawings of the article of manufacture being protected. Drawings are usually made from multiple angles in order to capture every relevant part of the design. Aspects of the design that are considered limiting of the invention are shown in the drawings in solid lines, whereas optional features are shown in dashed or phantom lining.

The application process for design patents is similar to the application process for utility patents described further in Chapter 10. Design patent applications are examined by a patent examiner who may reject your application in one or more office actions before giving you a Notice of Allowance. As with utility applications, patent examiners review design applications for novelty and nonobviousness. However, with a design application, the examiner also is looking for ornamentality, which means that the features shown in a design application cannot be entirely functional—they need to be ornamental.

The examiner can search for prior art for a design patent from all sorts of locations, and is not limited to only looking for other design patents as prior art. The examiner looks for anything (for example, products in advertisements, catalogs, or web sites) that would show that your design is not unique, is obvious, or is functional. Design patent applications are often examined much more quickly than utility patent applications, which means a quicker route to obtaining a patent if your invention has both functional and ornamental features that you wish to protect by both design and utility patents. Design patents also have a different term from utility patents—14 years from issuance as opposed to 20 years from filing, as is discussed in Chapter 15.

You Should Know The protection offered by design patents can overlap a bit with trade dress protection. For example, the unique configuration of the umbrella handle shown above might be protected not only with a design patent but also using trade dress, as described in Chapter 4.

Infringement of a design patent is evaluated a little bit differently than that for a utility patent because a design patent does not have the same kind of claims as a utility patent. As shown in the sample cover page of a design patent in Figure 9.2, the claim of a design simply reads "The ornamental design for a goggle component, as shown and described." Thus, the drawings are critical to determining what your design patent protects. Infringement is assessed using what's known as the "ordinary observer" test, where a competitor's product infringes if an ordinary observer would think that the other design and the patented design are so similar that the consumer would be deceived into buying one product instead of the other. The competitor's product must also incorporate what makes the design patent novel, i.e., the feature or features of the patented design that make it unique over the prior art. For example, if the design for the umbrella handle is different from prior designs because of the tiki handle, that feature must be found in the competitor's product in order to be infringing.

CHAPTER 10

Filing Your Patent Application

Once you've determined what invention or inventions you want to protect, you're ready to go get your patent. All patents, whether utility, design, or plant patents, are obtained by the filing of a patent application in the USPTO. Filing of a patent application by itself doesn't give you any rights that you can enforce against others. With the exception of so-called provisional rights provided for patent publications, discussed later in the chapter, a patent cannot be enforced until the patent issues. All the patent application filing gives you is a date ("the filing date") that is used to determine who your patent may be used against and what can

> Filing a patent application does not give you the right to enforce your patent. A patent cannot be enforced until the patent issues.

be used against your patent, and it puts you in line to have your patent examined.

The USPTO, located in Alexandria, Virginia, is an agency of the Department of Commerce and employs thousands of patent examiners. You don't need to go to the USPTO in person to apply for a patent application. Patent applications are typically mailed to the USPTO, and most correspondence with the USPTO is done in writing by mail, or fax, or electronically. After you file a patent application, it is assigned to a particular technology center where it will be handled by an examiner specializing in that technology. A patent examiner examines your patent application by applying the patent laws found in Title 35, rules found in Title 37 of the Code of Federal Regulations (known as 37 C.F.R.), and procedures set forth in the Manual for Patent Examining Procedure (known as the MPEP). The patent examiner will mail to your designated correspondence address the results of the examination of your patent application. However, you will likely have to wait a long time (often well more than a year) for an examiner to provide you with the results of the examination.

Once you receive these results (likely in the form of a document referred to as an "office action"), you may need to respond to the examiner to try to convince him of why you deserve to get the patent. This negotiation process with the examiner is known as the "prosecution" of the patent application. If you are successful convincing the examiner, he will send to you a Notice of Allowance. Within a few months of paying an issue fee, you will get your patent. Chapter 12 provides further information regarding the examination of a patent application.

As soon as a patent application is filed, the patent applicant (also known as the "patentee") may mark any product covered by the patent application as "Patent Pending." Although this marking is optional, it provides potential infringers with notice that you are attempting to obtain a patent, and may deter them from copying your product. The "Patent Pending" marking can be used no matter whether the patent application filed is a utility, design, or plant patent application.

Patent applications are filed in the name of the inventor or inventors. If the invention is owned by someone other than the inventor(s), that party may also have the authority to file the patent application, although the inventors' names will always still be identified, and inventor signatures should be obtained. Most likely, your company will own the rights to your employees' inventions because most employees will have signed agreements assigning the rights to all inventions made during the course of employment to your company. While an inventor or owner can file a patent application himself, most patent applicants use a registered patent attorney or agent to file their patent applications. Patent attorneys and agents must have a technical degree and pass an exam to qualify to practice before the USPTO. Patent attorneys also have a law degree, so they are able to handle litigation, licensing, and other legal matters.

Hiring a patent attorney or agent costs money, of course (maybe lots of it). And having an attorney or agent prepare a patent application for filing isn't cheap. Costs can run anywhere from $5,000 for a simple mechanical invention to $15,000 or $20,000 for a complicated software invention. These are just the filing costs, and there will no doubt be examination costs, issue fees, and maintenance fees (all discussed below). Filing a patent application is a huge investment, which is a major reason why you may want to consider hiring a professional to get it done right.

You Should Know As between utility patents and design patents, utility patents usually offer the best form of protection. But there is no requirement for the patent marking to indicate whether the application filed is a utility or design patent. Therefore, when you see a product marked with "Patent Pending," don't just assume that the owner of the patent will be able to obtain strong utility patent protection. Sometimes the patent owner's only protection will be for a very specific design. Or sometimes the patent owner gets a utility patent, but the patent only protects a few obscure features of the product.

When to File Your Patent Application

Imagine this: You came up with the great new idea for your RAINGOD umbrella back in 2005, but you don't have the money to file a patent application on it, and instead you take the idea to a trade show, print up flyers showing your new umbrella, and try to find investors in your product. One potential investor you meet sounds interested, but you don't end up negotiating a deal until 2007. At that time the investor says he's only interested if you have a patent application for the idea. You talk to a patent attorney, and the attorney tells you that it's now impossible to get a patent. Without the patent, your deal falls through, and the investor creates his own company ripping off your idea, and makes a ton of money selling the same umbrella you invented.

Could this nightmare scenario really happen? Unfortunately, it could, because there are very specific rules on when you must file a patent application in order to preserve rights.

File Within One Year to Preserve United States Rights

The question of when to file often depends on whether you are interested in protecting rights just in the United States, or if you're also interested in protecting rights in foreign countries as well. To maintain United States protection, your patent application must be filed within one year after any public disclosure, sale, or offer for sale of your invention. This is what's known as the one-year grace period in the United States, the Section 102(b) bar (referring to Section 102(b) of Title 35) or the on-sale bar. The reason behind the rule is to prevent an inventor from commercially exploiting an invention for too long without filing a patent application. Figure 10.1 illustrates application of the one-year United States grace period.

> **Strategy Tip**   To protect your patent rights in the United States, file your patent application within one year of any public disclosure, sale, or offer for sale of your invention.

FIGURE 10.1 **Timeline to Preserve United States Patent Rights**

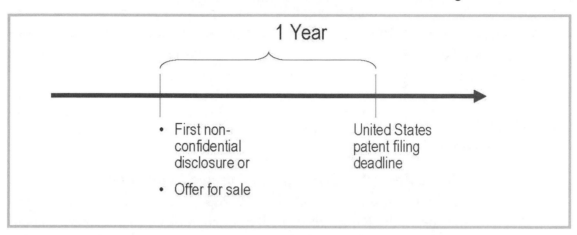

In the above example, your showing of the umbrella at the trade show was the kind of disclosure that triggers the start of the one-year grace period. Other examples of public disclosures or on-sale events that may start the clock running are:

- Putting pictures of your invention on a web site
- Selling your product over the internet
- Publishing a scientific article that describes your invention
- Presenting your invention at a scientific conference

It's not always easy to determine whether a particular activity starts the clock for the one-year grace period. For example, whereas an outright sale or publication of an article will certainly start the clock, if the activity is experimental or if the invention has not yet been completed, whether the clock starts to run may be questionable. It's always best to ask your patent attorney to determine whether a particular activity will trigger the start of the grace period.

One way you can prevent the triggering of the one-year grace period is to get a non-disclosure agreement from the people who will be seeing or hearing about your invention. Confidentiality or non-disclosure agreements are often used to maintain the secrecy of an invention so as not to create a public disclosure. Let's say that you want to demonstrate your invention to

Use non-disclosure agreements to avoid creating a public disclosure and extend the time you have to file a patent application.

a potential new customer, but you're not sure whether that would be a public disclosure and you sure don't want that one-year clock to start ticking. You should try to get a non-disclosure agreement from the potential customer, which your patent attorney can help you prepare. Though not always easy to get someone to agree to sign, you'll want to be extra careful about disclosing your invention if you don't have a patent application yet on file.

File Before Any Public Disclosure to Preserve Foreign Rights

The United States grace period, however, does not apply for most other countries in the world. Rather, the rule in most countries is that the patent application must be filed *before* your invention is made available to the public. This does not mean, though, that you have to file your patent application in every country that you want before your public disclosure. Most countries in the world and the United States have signed a treaty to recognize the filing of a United States application to avoid a bar, so long as a corresponding foreign application is filed within one year of the United States application. Thus, most inventors will want to ensure that at least their United States patent application is on file before any disclosure of the invention to outsiders. In other words, as long as you have filed your United States application before you make a public disclosure, sell, or offer to sell your invention and you file your foreign application within a year after you file your United States application, you have preserved your right to file for patents in most foreign countries. Figure 10.2 illustrates this timeline.

Strategy Tip To protect your patent rights outside of the United States, file your United States patent application *before* making your invention available to the public. You will then have one year to file additional patent applications for foreign patent protection.

FIGURE 10-2 **Timeline to Preserve Foreign Patent Rights**

Because most companies have at least some interest in pursuing patents both in the United States and abroad, you'll most likely want to make sure your patent application is filed before any public disclosure or sale. If this becomes difficult, you'll want to try to use non-disclosure agreements to keep your invention under wraps.

Requirements to File a Patent Application

Now that you know what a patent is and you have decided to file a patent application, you need to know what is involved in preparing and filing your patent application. This is where it might start to get expensive, because the filing of the patent application is usually where you'll want the help of a patent attorney.

A typical utility patent application includes a specification, claims, and one or more drawings, as discussed further below. Once these items are submitted, the USPTO will give you what's known as a filing date, and other required items (such as the inventors' declaration, filing fee, and other formalities) can be submitted later. The date that you file your application is important because the USPTO will recognize that date as the date of your invention. While you may have actually made and prototyped your invention months or

> **Myth vs. Reality** **Myth:** I must have completed a working prototype in order to file a patent application.
>
> **Reality:** You do not need to have made a prototype of your invention in order to file a patent application.

even years before your patent application was filed (often called "actual reduction to practice"), the filing of your patent application provides what is known as a "constructive reduction to practice." This date could become important, especially if you are trying to prove that your invention predates someone else's invention.

You do not need to have made a prototype of your invention in order to file a patent application. Because of the detail required to go into a patent application, the patent application itself is considered to be a "constructive reduction to practice" of an invention, eliminating the need for a working prototype. If you have created a prototype, there is also no requirement to deposit it with the USPTO. You may choose, however, to try to demonstrate your prototype by meeting with the examiner in person at an examiner interview, as discussed in Chapter 12.

> **Did You Know?** Patent applications must be submitted by Express Mail in order to receive the date of mailing as the filing date. If you send your application by regular first class mail, the USPTO will only give you the date the Patent Office receives it. This could be important if someone else files for a similar invention around the same date as you. Although the USPTO does not allow for submission of patent applications by fax, they have recently established an electronic filing system (EFS) that allows you to file patent applications electronically.

The Specification

The patent specification (also referred to as the "disclosure") usually forms the bulk of the text of a utility patent application. An example of a simple patent specification describing the RAINGOD umbrella is found in the patent application set forth in Appendix A. The text of the specification most commonly includes the following sections in the following order:

- *Title of the Invention.* A brief title referring to the subject matter of the invention. The title of our umbrella invention is "Smart Umbrella."

- *Field of the Invention.* A single sentence or two at the beginning of the patent application, describing the general field of technology. This information is helpful to the examiner in performing her search for relevant patents, publications, or other information predating your invention. In our umbrella patent application, the Field of the Invention reads: "The field relates to wireless communication, and in one case, wireless communication with an umbrella."

- *Background of the Invention.* The Background contains a description of the technology related to the invention. Sometimes the Background will identify and describe prior patents or publications addressing the same or similar problem that the patent application itself is intending to address. For example, the Background of the umbrella invention might identify and describe prior patents for umbrellas with various displays or electronics. It can also be more general, simply describing in brief some of the prior ways others have attempted to solve similar problems. The patent application found in Appendix A includes a brief example of a Background section.

- *Summary of the Invention.* The Summary provides a brief overview of the invention, usually in just a few paragraphs. Some patent attorneys use the Summary to summarize or paraphrase the language found in the claims, discussed below.

- *Brief Description of the Drawings.* The specification will usually include a series of drawings, or figures, and the specification should list and briefly describe each of them. Usually a sentence per drawing will suffice.

- *Detailed Description of the Preferred Embodiments.* The Detailed Description forms the majority of the text of the specification, generally providing a full and thorough description of the invention. This description is usually written with extensive reference to the drawings or figures, with each component of each figure labeled with a reference number that is described in detail in the specification. Figure 10.3 below provides an example of a drawing of the umbrella invention, with reference numbers 102 through 108 pointing to different components of the umbrella.

You'll see in the sample patent application in Appendix A that the umbrella invention is described with a large amount of detail,

FIGURE 10-3 **Drawing Found in Patent Application for Umbrella Invention**

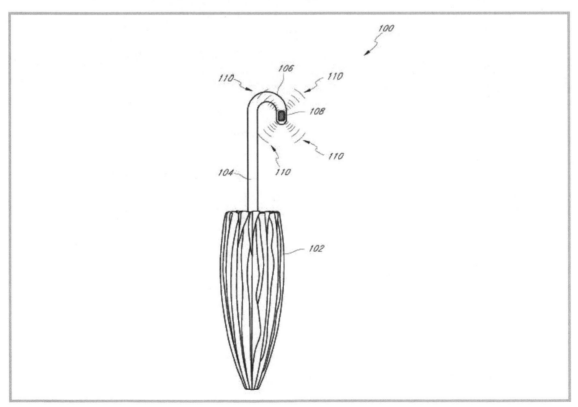

describing, for example, the material that the umbrella is made of, the number of spokes it has, and the different types of alarms or indicators it might use to alert the user that it is going to rain. You might think that with all of this detail, the scope of the patent application will be narrow. However, these features provided in the detailed description are simply the preferred embodiments, or examples, of how the invention is made and operates. Including this detail does not necessarily mean that the patent itself will be narrow and easy to get around. As discussed below, it is the claims, not the Detailed Description, that define the legal scope of the patent.

- *Claims.* Claims are the numbered paragraphs at the end of the specification that provide the legal definition of the patent. When you want to determine how broad a patent is, the first section you should read is the claims. A claim recites limitations, or features, that must be found in another party's product in order for that product to be infringing. The longer the claim is, the more limitations it has and the narrower it is; a shorter claim has fewer limitations and is thus broader. Claims will be addressed in greater detail in the next section.
- *Abstract of the Disclosure.* This section provides a brief narrative of the disclosure in 150 words or less.
- *Drawings.* The specification also includes the drawings themselves which, as discussed above, are referred to frequently in the Detailed

Did You Know? A patent application might also "incorporate by reference" another patent or patent application. If another patent is incorporated by reference, this means that the text of the other patent application is considered to be part of the patent application that includes the incorporation by reference. An example of how the incorporation by reference might be written is as follows: "Further details regarding the umbrella and its operation may be found in U.S. Patent No. 8,321,987, the entirety of which is hereby incorporated by reference."

Description. They are sometimes grouped separately from the rest of the specification, but they do form part of the specification as well. There are several different types of drawings that may appear in a patent application. For example, the patent application for the umbrella includes, as Figures 1–4 of the patent application, a structural illustration of the umbrella itself, a schematic showing the transmission of information from a weather station to the umbrella, a block diagram of umbrella components, and a flowchart illustrating a method of communicating with an umbrella. Drawings may also include circuit diagrams, photographs, or any other sort of illustration that will help convey the invention.

Written Description, Enablement, and Best Mode

In preparing your patent application with your patent attorney, you may wonder, "Why is this patent application so long?" Or, "Why do you have to put in so much information? My invention isn't really that complicated, and I don't want everyone to know exactly what I'm doing."

Your patent attorney isn't just trying to rack up your legal fees. Rather, she has good reason to ask for all this information: it's required by the USPTO. In exchange for the rights that the United States government is going to give

Strategy Tip Although photographs are permitted in patent applications, most patent applications include computer-drawn illustrations instead of photographs of a product. The computer-drawn illustrations allow for illustrations from different angles, through different cross-sections, and with parts shown assembled or separated. Because drawings can sometimes be time-consuming and expensive to produce, the USPTO allows for filing of "informal" drawings, which may include hand-drawn sketches. The USPTO will typically require you later to turn your informal drawings into formal drawings at some time before issuance of the patent.

you by granting you a patent, the USPTO wants something in return. They want to know details on how your invention is made and your best way of making it, so that they can publish it for the entire world to see. The level of detail that you are required to include in your patent application is the trade-off that you make for being granted the patent monopoly. Because you are receiving a patent, in exchange you are teaching the public how to make your invention so that it can benefit from your invention, such as by seeking a license to your invention or by making improvements to it. And once your patent expires, your invention will be in the public domain, meaning that anyone at that time is free to copy it and sell it.

The USPTO accomplishes these goals by imposing the requirements for written description, enablement, and best mode when preparing a patent application. These are three requirements found in Section 112 of Title 35 of the patent law, and you'll sometimes hear lawyers refer to them as the Section 112, first paragraph requirements. The actual language of Section 112, first paragraph reads as follows:

> The specification shall contain a *written description* of the invention, and of the manner and process of making and using it, in such full, clear, concise, and exact terms as to *enable* any person skilled in the art to which it pertains, or with which it is most nearly connected, to make and use the same, and shall set forth the *best mode* contemplated by the inventor of carrying out his invention.

These Section 112, first paragraph requirements are typically satisfied by the description of the invention in the Detailed Description portion of the specification, though they can also be satisfied in other sections of the specification, including the summary, the claims and the figures. Failure to satisfy these requirements can render a patent invalid. Each is discussed below.

Written Description

The purpose of the "written description" requirement is to prove that you invented what you say you've invented, and to ensure that the invention is sufficiently described to put the public in possession of the invention. Oftentimes, this simply means that the applicant must have described somewhere in the specification the feature that is being claimed. In other words, the patent specification must tell the public what the invention is that the applicant is claiming. In the umbrella example, if a claim is made for an umbrella having a curved handle, the specification somewhere must describe both an umbrella and a curved handle.

Let's say that you always meant for your umbrella to have a curved handle, but you forgot to include it in the description of your invention when you filed the patent application. Can you later revise your patent application to include the curved handle? The answer, unfortunately, is no. The USPTO measures whether you are in possession of your invention as of the date of filing of the patent application. After your patent application is filed, you are not allowed to add new subject matter, or "new matter," to the application. You can, however, consider filing a new application for the umbrella having a curved handle, though you will no longer receive the benefit of the date you filed your first patent application.

As another example, let's say that you forgot to include in your specification text describing the curved handle of the umbrella. But you did happen to include in your figures a drawing showing the umbrella with a curved handle. Will this now be enough to provide written description for a claim for an umbrella with a curved handle? This answer is probably yes. If it is readily apparent that the figures do indeed show a curved handle, most likely you will be allowed to make a claim for the curved umbrella handle. You may be required to amend your written specification to explicitly identify the curved handle, though this will not be considered to be adding new matter because the figures have always shown the feature.

The claims themselves can also be used to satisfy the written description requirement, if the language of the claim was found in the application when it was first filed. For example, if the only place the curved umbrella handle is described when the application is first filed is in the claims, but not in the summary, the figures, or the detailed description of the invention, this will still provide you with written description support for claiming the curved handle. This is because the claims themselves prove that you were in possession of the invention having a curved handle at the time the patent application was filed.

> **Did You Know?** Did you know that some patent attorneys use the Summary of the Invention section simply to paraphrase the language of the claims in the patent application? The reason for this is that even though the claims themselves can satisfy the requirement for written description, including this language in the Summary of the Invention may help further demonstrate to a patent examiner that the patent applicant was in possession of the subject matter being claimed.

As with the figures, you may be required to amend your specification to explicitly identify the curved handle, but this will not be considered to be adding new matter. But if your claims as filed did not include the curved handle, you cannot amend your claims after filing to recite a curved handle unless the feature is described elsewhere in the specification, such as in the Summary, Detailed Description, or the Figures.

Enablement

A second requirement of Section 112, first paragraph is the enablement requirement. Enablement requires that you describe your invention in a manner to allow one skilled in the art to make and use the invention. In other words, the patent must include enough details about the invention so that someone who is familiar with how to make an umbrella can read the patent and then make the umbrella. This does not mean, however, that every little detail of the invention needs to be described to enable the invention. With the umbrella, for example, one skilled in the art (i.e., an umbrella maker) may already know how a traditional umbrella is constructed, and thus, the patent application need not describe every screw and every stitch holding the umbrella together. But especially for those features that really make your invention unique, you will want to describe how those features are made and how to make them work.

Written description and enablement are separate requirements, although sometimes it's not always easy to draw the line between the two. Table 10.1 provides some examples.

In each of these examples, assume that the language being claimed did not appear in the application as first filed. In the first example, a claim for a car with six wheels would not have written description support in a specification describing a car with four wheels because the specification clearly does not describe six wheels. However, such a claim might be enabled because once the specification describes how to make a car with four wheels, one of skill in the art would likely also know how to make a car with six wheels.

In the second example, a claim for a perpetual motion machine would have written description support in a specification that describes a perpetual motion machine; however, such a claim would not be enabled because the specification could not describe how to make such a machine operate.

In the third example, a claim for a perpetual motion machine would not have written description support based on the description of a clock, nor would it be enabled. This is because the description of the clock would not demonstrate that the patent applicant had actually made a perpetual motion machine, and it would not show the public how to make a perpetual motion machine.

Best Mode

The third requirement of Section 112, first paragraph is the best-mode requirement. Best mode requires that the specification disclose the preferred manner of carrying out the invention. This is the reason the Detailed

TABLE 10.1 **The Differences Between Written Description and Enablement**

Specification	Claim	Written Description?	Enablement?
A car with four wheels	A car with six wheels	No	Yes
A perpetual motion machine	A perpetual motion machine	Yes	No
A clock	A perpetual motion machine	No	No

> **Warning!** If you try to keep your best ideas out of your patent application, you may not be able to enforce your patent. If a court finds that you withheld the best mode for practicing your invention, your patent may be found legally invalid.

Description is often referred to as a "Detailed Description of the Preferred Embodiments." For example, in the umbrella invention, if there is a particular radio frequency that you as the inventor know to be the best frequency for making the invention work, that detail must be described in the specification. You cannot keep your best ideas secret if you want to get a patent on them.

Although a patent examiner will likely never know whether or not you've disclosed your best mode, this kind of information can be discovered later in litigation. For example, let's say you knew the preferred frequency for transmitting the weather information when you filed your application but you didn't include it in the specification. Years later, after your patent issues, you sue a competitor who has copied your invention. If the competitor finds evidence (because you admit it or it's somewhere in your notes) that you knew about the preferred frequency when you filed your application, the court may find that you've violated the best mode requirement and you could lose your lawsuit.

The best mode requirement only applies at the time of filing the application. Thus, if you only learn of the preferred frequency after filing of the application, you do not then need to inform the USPTO of this. The best mode needs to be included when you file your application, so you cannot amend your specification after filing to include your best mode.

Claims

The claims are the numbered paragraphs found at the end of the patent, each written as a single sentence. Claims provide the legal definition of the invention—in order for someone to infringe a patent, he must infringe at least one claim of the patent. For a claim to be infringed, the accused product or process must include each and every limitation, or requirement, found in the claim.

> **Myth vs. Reality**
>
> **Myth:** If I describe the invention in too much detail in my patent application, the patent will be too narrow and easy to get around.
>
> **Reality:** While the written description, enablement, and best-mode requirements may cause you to include many details of your preferred invention in your patent application, the scope of your invention is defined by the claims, not by your specification. Thus, your claims can be broad while your specification description is detailed.

Claim 1 below is a simple example of a claim directed to a conventional umbrella.

1. An umbrella, comprising:
   an elongate shaft having a first end and a second end;
   a curved handle provided at the first end of the elongate shaft;
   a plurality of spokes connected to the second end of the shaft,
   the spokes being moveable from a collapsed configuration
   aligned with the shaft and an expanded configuration extending
   away from the shaft; and a covering supported by the spokes
   and forming a concave surface facing toward the handle.

Figure 10.4 illustrates how each component of this claim is found in a drawing of the umbrella.

For Claim 1 above to be infringed, an accused device must have every limitation, or requirement, of the claim. Thus, an umbrella that has an elongate shaft, spokes, and covering, but a straight, rather than a curved handle, would not infringe Claim 1.

Most claims can be considered as having three parts: (1) the preamble, (2) the transition, and (3) the body. The preamble serves to introduce the claim and provide an indication of the nature of the subject matter to follow. The preamble can usually be identified as the language preceding the transition, discussed below. In the above Claim 1, the preamble is the language "An umbrella."

FIGURE 10.4 **An umbrella as defined by Claim 1**

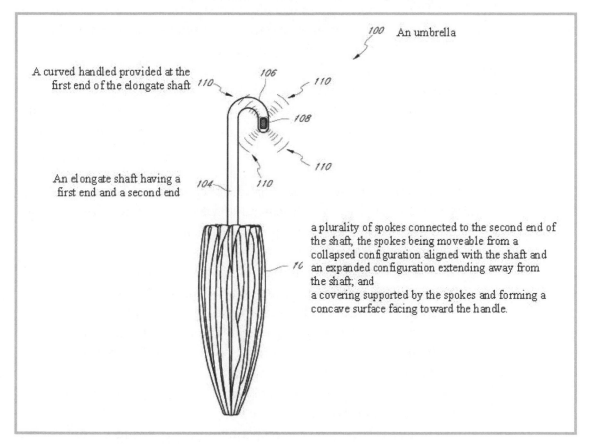

The transition phrase bridges the preamble with the body of the claim, and determines whether the claim is open-ended or close-ended. An open-ended claim is infringed even if the infringing product includes more than just what is recited by the claim. A close-ended claim is infringed only if the infringing includes the limitations recited by the claim, and nothing more. The most common transition phrases are "comprising," "consisting of," and "consisting essentially of."

comprising:

Claims using the transition phrase "comprising" are open-ended, indicating that the claim requires all of the limitations that follow, but can still be infringed if an infringing device includes more than just those limitations. For example, in the above Claim 1, the transition phrase, "comprising," is followed by four different limitations constituting the body of the claim. A competitive umbrella including the four limitations of the body of the claim would still infringe even if the umbrella included an additional feature, such as a radio transmitter or an LED. That the umbrella with the additional feature may be patentable itself is irrelevant to whether or not the new umbrella infringes.

consisting of:

The transition phrase "consisting of" is close-ended, meaning that to infringe the claim, the accused device must have only the limitations specified in the claim. Consider the following modified claim:

2. An umbrella, consisting of:

 an elongate shaft having a first end and a second end;

 a curved handle provided at the first end of the elongate shaft;

 six spokes connected to the second end of the shaft, the spokes being moveable from a collapsed configuration aligned with the shaft and an expanded configuration extending away from the shaft; and

 a covering supported by the spokes and forming a concave surface facing toward the handle.

In the above example, if the competing umbrella includes eight spokes, instead of six spokes, the claim would not be infringed because the "consisting of" language indicates that the umbrella can only have six spokes.

consisting essentially of:

The transition phrase "consisting essentially of" is similar to "consisting of," but allows for immaterial differences. Consider Claim 1 rewritten with the "consisting essentially of" transition phrase:

3. An umbrella, consisting essentially of:

 an elongate shaft having a first end and a second end;

 a curved handle provided at the first end of the elongate shaft;

 a plurality of spokes connected to the second end of the shaft,

the spokes being moveable from a collapsed configuration
aligned with the shaft and an expanded configuration extending
away from the shaft; and

a covering supported by the spokes and forming a concave surface facing toward the handle.

The "consisting essentially of" language provides that the claim can only
be infringed by an umbrella having each of the four limitations specified in the
body of the claim, and no other features that materially change the nature of
the invention. Thus, a competitor umbrella that adds an insignificant feature,
such as a decorative pattern on its covering, might still be infringing, while an
umbrella with a more significant feature, such as an LED display, might not
be infringing.

Claims can be of different types for different inventions, as suggested by
Section 101 of Title 35. Thus, the invention for the umbrella may have claims
not only for the umbrella itself, but also for a method, such as follows:

4. A method of transmitting information to an umbrella, comprising:
   transmitting weather information from a weather station to a
   receiver on an umbrella; and
   activating a signal on the umbrella when the receiver receives
   weather information indicating that it is going to rain.

Claims can also be in either independent or dependent form. An independent claim, such as Claim 1, 2, or 3 above, stands by itself, and does not
refer to any other claim. A dependent claim refers to a previous claim, and
then specifies further limitations. For example:

Strategy Tip Your patent claims should use the transition phrase "comprising," because it offers you the broadest protection. The transi-
tion phrases "consisting of" and "consisting essentially of" are found more often in
chemical patent applications, where specific formulations may be important to
patentability and how the invention works.

---

5. The umbrella of Claim 1, further comprising an indicator displaying a weather condition.

Claim 5 is an example of a dependent claim, which includes all of the limitations of Claim 1, and further specifies an indicator on the umbrella. Claim 5 is thus a narrower claim than Claim 1, in that to infringe this claim, the accused product must have every feature specified by Claim 1 *and* Claim 5. Why would you want a claim like this? The dependent claim may be valuable if the independent claim is too broad, and could be invalidated in court. The dependent claim serves as a fallback claim that could still be asserted and infringed, even if the independent claim is invalid.

Patent applications can often include a large number of independent and dependent claims to cover different aspects of an invention. Thus, a patent application for the new umbrella might include three or four or more different independent claims for umbrellas having different features, methods of transmitting information to an umbrella, etc. However, the number of claims included in a patent application is limited practically by cost, as well as by the requirement that a patent can only be granted for a single invention. Regarding cost, when more than 20 total claims are filed, or more than three independent claims are filed, the USPTO begins to charge excess claim fees, e.g., $50 for each claim over 20 and $200 for each independent claim over three. See Appendix B. Regarding the single invention requirement, if a patent examiner determines that your patent application claims multiple inventions, she might require you to only pursue claims to a single invention. Remaining claims can be pursued via continuation or divisional applications, discussed in Chapter 13, which will cost more money.

> Patent claims can be invalidated in court, but just because an independent claim is invalidated doesn't necessarily mean that the dependent claims will be invalidated as well. This is why you'll often see patents with many dependent claims.

Items to File with a Patent Application

Preparing the specification, drawings, and claims covers most of what you need to file your patent application, and if you send only these items to the USPTO, it will be enough to get you your filing date. If you only filed your specification, drawings, and claims with your patent application, the USPTO will mail a Notice to File Missing Parts, specifying a due date of two months from the date of mailing the notice (this due date may be extended five more months by paying a fee). It also will include the amount of money due for the patent application, and a requirement to file the inventor's oath or declaration.

Filing Fees

The current USPTO fee schedule, effective as of September 30, 2007, is provided in Appendix B and may be found at http://www.uspto.gov/go/fees/index.html. Filing of a utility patent application requires payment of a filing fee (currently $310), search fee (currently $510), and examination fee (currently $210). If these fees are not paid with the filing of the application, the USPTO will impose a surcharge (currently $130) for submitting these items late. You can save some money if you qualify for small entity status, which cuts most of your fees in half. Small entities are typically independent inventors, small businesses (less than 500 employees), or nonprofit organizations. If you don't qualify as a small entity, by default you will be a large entity, and pay the normal, large entity fees. Be sure to talk to your patent attorney before paying small entity fees, because paying the wrong fees can be considered fraud, causing your patent to be invalid.

> You don't even need to pay a fee to obtain a filing date for a patent application. Filing a specification with drawings and claims alone is enough to be able to say "Patent Pending." Of course, patents aren't free, and the USPTO will send you a bill for your filing fees due within a few months.

Inventorship

A patent application is filed in the name of the true inventors, even if the patent is owned by a company or other entity. Each inventor must sign an oath or declaration to complete the filing of the patent application. A typical inventor's declaration form is found in Appendix B.

In thinking about who should be listed as an inventor of your patent application, you'd like to recognize all of the employees who were involved in the project. Can you list as inventors the marketing person who came up with the name RAINGOD, the clerk who ordered all the parts for the

> **Warning!** The government fees associated with filing of a patent application are only a small part of the cost of a patent application. Attorney fees for preparing a patent application can run anywhere from a few thousand dollars to tens of thousands of dollars, and this is only for preparing the patent application. Additional attorney time and government fees will be required to prosecute your application (i.e., navigate your patent through the Patent Office) as well as for issuance and maintenance of your patent. Be sure to budget appropriately.

umbrella, and the president of the company just because he likes to see his name on patents?

If you list any of the people mentioned above, you could get into trouble for not listing true inventors, and you may lose the ability to enforce your patent. Inventorship in the patent context is a strict legal requirement, and not everyone should be listed as an inventor. Each named inventor must have contributed, either individually or jointly with another inventor, to the subject matter of at least one claim in the application. Conception of the invention is generally considered to be the touchstone of inventorship, and is usually obtained by arriving at a definite and fixed idea of the invention. If you merely reduced the invention to practice, such as by following someone else's instructions to make a prototype, this normally does not qualify you as an inventor unless you also contributed something inventive to the claimed invention.

Take, for example, a claim for an umbrella comprising an indicator for

> **Did You Know?** Only the first and original inventor(s) may obtain a valid patent. Thus, you cannot obtain a patent in the United States for an invention you saw overseas, because you are not the first or the original inventor. Similarly, someone who sees your invention cannot obtain a valid patent on it because that person is not the first or original inventor. Someone else could, however, improve your invention and then patent the improvement.

transmitting weather information. If Joe was the person who conceived of the original idea of having an umbrella with the indicator, Joe would be an inventor of that claim. If Joe then instructed Jill to make a prototype of the invention, merely following the instructions of Joe, Jill would not qualify as an inventor. However, if Jill, in making the prototype, realizes that the umbrella should have an audible alarm for telling the user that it's going to rain, Jill would then become an inventor if the patent application also included a claim for the umbrella having an audible alarm.

In identifying inventors to the USPTO, it is not necessary to identify which inventors invented which claims. Nor does it matter if not all the inventors contributed to the invention to the same degree. As long as each individual makes a not insignificant contribution to the claimed invention, he or she must be listed as an inventor.

Although inventorship is important and you should do everything you can to make sure it's correct, having an inventorship error is not necessarily fatal to your patent. If you find that during the prosecution of your patent application, or even after your patent issues, there has been an inadvertent error made in the listing of inventors, the error is usually easily correctable by filing a petition to correct inventorship. For example, if an inventor was accidentally omitted, or if a non-inventor was listed by mistake, the USPTO will generally allow the inventorship to be amended provided that the person left off or the person to be added signs a statement indicating that she did not try to deceive the USPTO in being included or being left off. Usually such petitions are fairly easy to get approved. However, you should not rely on the ability to correct inventorship later instead of ascertaining proper inventorship up front.

> **Strategy Tip** You should confirm inventorship from time to time while the application is pending. Because claims can change during prosecution, inventorship also can change until the final claims are known. Failure to list the correct inventors can render a patent unenforceable.

Oftentimes inventors who were initially omitted are very difficult to track down later on, or if you do track them down they may not be very cooperative (or they might be cooperative, for a price).

Other Documents

Other items that are not required to be filed with the patent application but might be filed shortly thereafter include the Assignment, Power of Attorney, and Information Disclosure Statement. The Assignment is a legal document conveying ownership of the patent application from the inventors (the assignors) to the company or other owner (the assignee). Because inventors are the presumed owners of a patent application, an Assignment is typically filed to provide proof of a transfer of ownership to the company or other owner. You'll want to get your assignments signed by your inventors as soon as possible, because employees often leave and you could have problems chasing them down or getting them to sign without paying a price. The Power of Attorney is a document signed on behalf of the owner of the patent application (which may be the inventors themselves, if their rights have not been assigned), appointing an attorney as the agent to represent the owner before the USPTO on the particular patent application. The Information Disclosure Statement, or IDS, is described further in Chapter 11, and provides a listing of prior art references considered by the patent applicant to be relevant to the examination of the patent application. The Assignment, Power of Attorney, and Declaration are commonly referred to collectively as the "Formal Documents."

Requirements for Patentability

You've made your invention, kept it secret, paid $10,000 to a patent attorney to prepare the patent application, and finally got it on file. What's the worst that could happen now? The patent examiner rejects your patent application, telling you that someone has already previously invented the same thing. Or perhaps even worse, someone did something like what you did and your invention is different, but the examiner is still not going to give you a patent. To understand what could happen when your patent application gets examined, you'll need to understand what the examiner looks at to assess patentability (i.e., whether something is patentable).

Utility, Novelty, and Nonobviousness

For an invention to be patentable, it must have utility, novelty, and nonobviousness. The utility requirement (i.e., usefulness) is usually the most easily satisfied, because for most inventions the utility is readily apparent. However, in some areas like biotechnology, the utility requirement may pose a challenge because sometimes the compounds made in the course of research and development have no known therapeutic effect. In such cases, a patent application may be rejected for failing the utility requirement. For the umbrella invention, the utility requirement will be no problem.

Patent examiners will examine patent applications for issues such as utility, written description, and enablement as discussed above, but their primary focus is usually on reviewing the patent claims for novelty and nonobviousness over the "prior art." Prior art refers to the universe of references, such as prior patents, publications, or other information, that can be used by the examiner to reject an application. An explanation of the different types of prior art is provided further below.

> To be patentable, inventions must be useful, new, and nonobvious.

Anticipation

For an invention to be patentable, it must satisfy the novelty requirements of Section 102 of Title 35, as well as the nonobvious requirements of Section 103. A novelty-defeating reference (also known as a "102 reference") defeats patentability because it teaches, or includes, each and every limitation of the claim under examination. Such a reference is also said to "anticipate" the claimed invention, because it teaches every aspect of the claimed invention either explicitly or impliedly. An anticipation example for Claim 1 as discussed above is recited as follows:

1. An umbrella, comprising:
    an elongate shaft having a first end and a second end;
    a curved handle provided at the first end of the elongate shaft;
    a plurality of spokes connected to the second end of the shaft,
    the spokes being moveable from a collapsed configuration
    aligned with the shaft and an expanded configuration extending

away from the shaft; and

a covering supported by the spokes and forming a concave
surface facing toward the handle.

This claim would be anticipated by a reference, such as a patent, article, or other publication, that showed every feature described in the body of the claim. Thus, if the reference is a photo from a magazine showing an umbrella having the elongate shaft, curved handle, spokes, and covering as claimed, Claim 1 would be rejected under Section 102 as being anticipated by the photo from the magazine. However, if the photo showed only a straight handle, and not a curved handle, the rejection under Section 102 for anticipation would be inappropriate.

Obviousness

If a reference does not identically teach, or include, each and every limitation of a claim under examination, the reference may still defeat patentability if it renders obvious what is claimed. Put more simply, if the reference teaches most of what is being claimed, and what's missing from the reference would be obvious to include, an obviousness rejection may be appropriate. As stated in Section 103 of Title 35, an obviousness rejection may be made "if the differences between the subject matter sought to be patented and the prior art are such that the subject matter as a whole would have been obvious at the time the invention was made to a person having ordinary skill in the art to which said subject matter pertains."

Obviousness rejections may be based on a single reference, or a combination of references. For example, if a first reference teaches three out of the four limitations specified in a claim, a patent examiner might turn to a second reference teaching that fourth limitation and issue a rejection that the patent claim is obvious over the first reference in view of the second reference. Whether such a rejection is proper or not may turn on whether the examiner has articulated how a hypothetical person of skill in the art would have found proper motivation to combine the two references. If one skilled in the art would not have thought to combine the teachings of the two references, then an obviousness rejection may be improper.

The question of whether an invention is obvious or not often turns on the difficult question of how to define who is a person of ordinary skill in the art. When a patent examination is examined, the patent examiner herself typically fills the role of a person of ordinary skill in the art, and the applicant will try to convince the patent examiner that her skill level is higher than that which would be found in applicant's industry. To prove a case of nonobviousness, you will want the skill level to be as low as possible, in order to demonstrate that your invention would be beyond what anyone trained in your field would have thought to do.

In the previous example, Claim 1 would not have been anticipated by a magazine photo showing an umbrella having an elongate shaft, straight handle, spokes, and covering as claimed, because the umbrella in the photo lacked a curved handle as required by the claim. However, Claim 1 might still be unpatentable if substituting a curved handle for a straight handle would have been obvious. Simple modifications such as this as compared to the prior art are less likely to make a claim patentable.

On the other hand, consider Claim 5 from above:

5. The umbrella of Claim 1, further comprising an indicator displaying a weather condition.

It would be much more difficult for an examiner to argue that Claim 5 was obvious in view of the magazine photo, which provides no hint of including an indicator for displaying a weather condition. The examiner might then turn to a second reference, such as a prior patent describing an outdoor weather alarm, and argue that it would have been obvious to combine the umbrella in the magazine with the outdoor weather alarm to produce the invention of Claim 5. Your counter-argument might then be that one of ordinary skill in the art, who might be a traditional umbrella maker, would still not think to combine the two references together to produce your patented invention. More examples of obviousness are provided later in this chapter.

The Different Types of Prior Art

To figure out what can be used as prior art to reject or defeat your patent application, you should keep in mind that the United States is currently what is known as a "first-to-invent" country. This means that the U.S. patent system awards patents to the first person to invent, rather than the first person to file a patent application. In practical terms, this means that if two inventors come up with the same invention, the USPTO will award the patent to the first to actually invent the invention, regardless of whether he filed the application after the other. This differs from the rest of the world, which awards the patent to the first to file.

Because the patent examiner does not know the actual date that you invented your invention, she will instead presume that your filing date is the date of your invention. Based on this filing date, the examiner will search for prior art, such as patents, articles, publications, or other information, describing your invention filed or published prior to your filing date. Typically, a patent examiner will find mostly U.S. patents or patent publications, though many other types of information can also qualify as prior art. Table 11.1 provides a brief summary of different types of references and how they might be used to reject your application.

For many of the types of prior art listed above, whether a reference qualifies as prior art depends on whether it is prior to your date of invention. An examiner might cite a reference against you because it is prior to your filing date, but if you actually invented your invention prior to the date of the reference found by the examiner, you may be able to eliminate the reference as prior art. This is what's known as "swearing behind" the reference based on your earlier invention date.

If you want to be successful at swearing behind another party's prior art reference, you will want to make sure you keep good records. Proving an earlier invention date may require you to provide written documentation, such as lab notebooks or pictures of prototypes, that evidence that you actually are the first inventor. If you never made a prototype or only made a prototype recently, you may also need to demonstrate that you've been working diligently from the date that you first conceived of your invention to the date the prototype was completed or the date that you filed your patent application.

There are, however, limitations to your ability to swear behind a reference, and this is encompassed in the one-year grace period discussed in

TABLE 11.1. **Different Types of Prior Art References**

Type of Reference	What Is the Date of the Prior Art?	Whose Prior Art Is it?	Where Is the Prior Art From?	Statutory Section from Title 35	Example # (see examples pages 109-112)
Patent or printed publication	Issued or published prior to your invention	By anyone	Anywhere	102(a)	1, 2
	Issued or published more than one year prior to your filing	By anyone	Anywhere	102(b)	4
Patent application that later publishes or issues	Filed prior to your invention	By another	In the U.S.	102(e)	5, 6
Knowledge	Prior to your invention	By others	In the U.S.	102(a)	7
On sale	More than one year before your filing	Anyone	In the U.S.	102(b)	8
In public use	More than one year before your filing	Anyone	In the U.S.	102(b)	9
Invention made, and not abandoned, suppressed, or concealed	Prior to your invention	By Another	In the U.S.	102(g)	10

Chapter 10. If a reference such as a patent or article is published more than one year prior to your filing date, regardless of whether it is your own reference or that of someone else, the reference qualifies as an absolute bar to patentability, and the reference cannot be sworn behind. Such a reference is

commonly known as a Section 102(b) bar to patentability.

The following examples help to illustrate different types of prior art found in Table 10.1.

- *Example 1: Patent Issued Prior to Your Invention*
  You invent your new umbrella on January 1, 2006. A patent describing precisely the same umbrella was issued on December 31, 2005. Can you still obtain a patent?
  Answer: No. The patent predates your invention date, preventing you from obtaining your patent. It does not matter who owns the patent, nor does it matter if the patent is from the United States or a foreign country.

- *Example 2: Printed Publication Published Prior to Your Invention*
  You invent your new umbrella on January 1, 2006. An article is published in Argentina by someone else on December 31, 2005, describing your same umbrella. Can you still obtain a patent?
  Answer: No. The article was published prior to your invention date, so regardless of when you file your patent application, the article will always be prior art to your invention. It makes no difference that the article was not published in the United States, that the author of the article may never have filed a patent application, nor that the umbrella or the article in Argentina may never even have been made available in the United States

- *Example 3: Printed Publication Published After Your Date of Invention*
  You invent your new umbrella on November 1, 2005, and file your patent application on January 1, 2006. An article is published by someone else on December 31, 2005, describing your same umbrella. Can you still obtain a patent?
  Answer: Probably yes. Because the article was published prior to your filing date, an examiner may cite the article as prior art to your application. However, assuming you can provide sufficient evidence, you should be able to swear behind the article by proving an earlier invention date, thereby eliminating the article from being prior art.

- *Example 4: Patent Application Published More Than One Year Before Your Filing*
  You invent your new umbrella on January 1, 2005, but don't file your

patent application until February 1, 2006. A patent application describing your same umbrella is published on January 15, 2005. Can you still obtain a patent?

Answer: No. Even though you invented your umbrella prior to the date that the patent application published, because you waited too long to file your patent application your filing date is more than a year past the publication date of the patent application. The publication of the patent application counts as a printed publication, making this a 102(b) bar to patentability. The lesson to learn here is that the longer you wait to file your patent application, the more likely it is that someone else can make a publication or do some other act that will defeat your ability to obtain a patent. Note that even if the prior patent application is your own, this would still prevent you from obtaining the later patent.

- *Example 5: Patent Application Filed before Your Invention*
  You invent your new umbrella on January 1, 2005, and file your patent application on April 1, 2005. Someone else filed a U.S. patent application describing your same umbrella on November 1, 2004, though that application doesn't publish until May 1, 2006. Can you still obtain a patent?

  Answer: No. Even though the other party's patent application didn't publish until after you filed your patent application, it can still be used as prior art because it was filed before your date of invention. This is what's known as secret prior art, because you had no way of knowing about the patent application until it published. This rule applies only if the other party's application was filed in the United States (or is a PCT application designating the United States, described in Chapter 14).

- *Example 6: Patent Application Filed Before Your Filing Date but after Your Invention Date*
  Similar to Example 5, you invent your new umbrella on January 1, 2005, and file your patent application on April 1, 2005. Someone else filed a U.S. patent application describing your same umbrella on February 1, 2005, which published on August 1, 2006. Can you still obtain a patent?

  Answer: Maybe. Because you invented your umbrella before the filing of the other patent application, you may be able to swear behind the other patent application and obtain the patent, provided you have sufficient documentation to prove your invention to the patent examiner. However, if the other patent application claims the same umbrella, you may find yourself in an interference, where the patent will be awarded to the first party to invent the umbrella. See the interference discussion below.

- *Example 7: Your Product Is Known by Others Prior to Your Invention*
  You invent your new umbrella on January 1, 2006. The same umbrella was shown at a conference in Chicago by one of your competitors in November 2004, though it was never sold, published in a printed document, or patented. Can you still obtain a patent?
  Answer: No. The mere fact that the umbrella was publicly known prior to your invention date prevents you from being able to obtain a patent. Note that a different result might occur if the conference was in a foreign country, as "prior knowledge" prior art is limited to knowledge within the United States.

- *Example 8: Your Product Is on Sale More Than One Year Before Your Filing*
  You began selling your umbrella in the United States on April 16, 2005. If today is April 19, 2006, can you still file for a patent?
  Answer: No. As with Example 4, you waited too long to file your patent application. Your own prior sale operates as a 102(b) bar to patentability. You should have filed your patent application by April 16, 2006, if you wanted to preserve rights in the United States, and by April 16, 2005, if you wanted to preserve foreign rights.

- *Example 9: Your Product Is in Public Use More than One Year Prior to Your Filing*
  You invent your new umbrella on January 1, 2005, and begin using it publicly on March 1, 2005. If today is March 31, 2006, can you still file for a patent?
  Answer: No. As with Example 8, you waited too long to file your patent application, and your own public use of your umbrella prevents you from obtaining a patent.

- *Example 10: Someone Else Made Your Invention Prior to You*
  You invented your new umbrella on January 1, 2005, but unbeknownst

to you, another party, in the United States, made the same umbrella on August 1, 2004. However, that other party never filed for a patent application on the umbrella, and instead submitted an article for publication in September 2004 that didn't actually publish until February 2005. Can you still obtain a patent?

Answer: Probably not. The other party's invention of the umbrella, prior to yours, can qualify as prior art so long as the other party did not abandon, suppress, or conceal its invention. The fact that the other party submitted an article for publication describing the umbrella indicates that it was not trying to keep the umbrella secret. And even though the article didn't publish until after your invention date, the other party's making of the invention itself still predates you. This is another type of secret prior art in that it might have been very difficult for you to know that the other party had made the invention prior to you. This type of prior art only applies if the other party's invention was made in the United States, so inventions made in other countries, assuming that they don't otherwise become prior art such as by being published or becoming known, used, or on sale in the United States, will not count.

What Is an Interference?

When two or more inventors file a patent application for the same invention, the USPTO may declare what's called an "interference" to determine who can prove the earliest invention date. To that inventor, the patent will be awarded.

An interference resembles a mini-litigation, but it is conducted before a board of administrative judges rather than in a courtroom. Although the costs of conducting an interference are often substantially lower than litigation, interference proceedings are still quite expensive, in money and time, and may take several years to resolve.

The parties to an interference are referred to as the Senior Party and the Junior Party (or Junior Parties if there are more than two parties participating in the interference). The Senior Party is the party that has the earliest priority

Did You Know? Did you know that the United States is the only country in the world that has a first-to-invent patent system?

In the United States, even if you file a patent application on the same invention as another party after the other party, you can initiate an administrative proceeding in the USPTO to prove that you were the first party to invent the invention for which patent protection is sought. This USPTO proceeding is called an interference. Because the United States is the only country to follow a first-to-invent system, it is also the only country to allow interference proceedings to prove seniority of invention.

date (see Chapter 13 for a discussion of a patent's priority date versus its filing date). The Senior Party generally has a significant advantage in an interference proceeding. In fact, the Senior Party is presumed to be the winner of the interference unless the Junior Party can meet its burden of proof to show otherwise. Research indicates that Senior Parties prevail in interference proceedings the majority of the time. Some researchers claim they prevail in 67 percent of all interference proceedings. Therefore, filing your patent applications as early as possible could establish you as the Senior Party in an interference, which would improve the chances of success in an interference as well.

To provide an interference example, assume you invented and prototyped your new umbrella on January 1, 2006, and file your patent application on the umbrella on July 1, 2006. Your competitor invented and prototyped the same umbrella on February 1, 2006, and filed its patent application on the umbrella

Did You Know? Patent interferences are held before the Board of Patent Appeals and Interferences, and are decided by administrative patent judges (or APJs). Because interferences are often highly contentious, their costs can rival that of actual litigation, with some interferences costing from several hundred thousand dollars to over $1 million.

FIGURE 11.1 **Lab Notebook Page of Umbrella Invention**

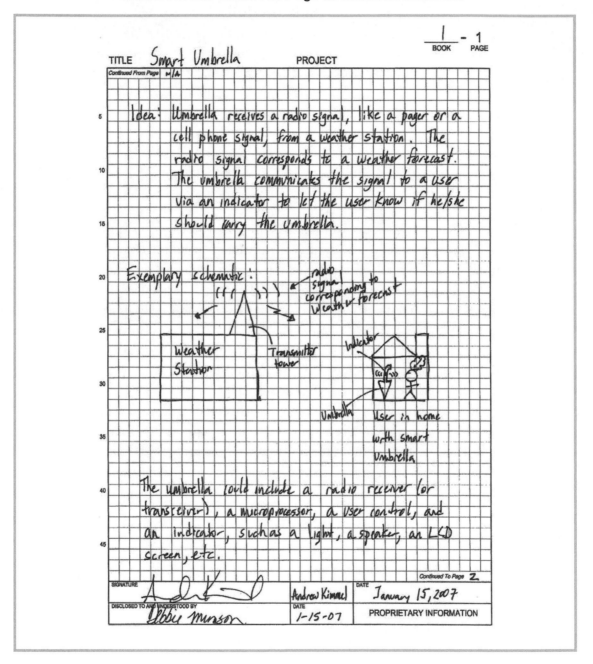

on June 1, 2006. Who will get the patent? You will, assuming that you can prove satisfactorily that you invented your umbrella prior to your competitor's date of February 1, 2006. This is a different result than in places like Europe, where your competitor would get the patent.

> Document your inventions in writing using lab notebooks, and have them dated and witnessed by others who are not also inventors.

This example simplifies some of the issues encountered in an interference, in that the example assumes that you not only invented your umbrella, but you also made a working prototype of the umbrella, prior to the date that your competitor invented the same thing. The issues become trickier if, for example, your prototype was not completed until after your competitor's invention date of February 1, 2006, or if you never made a prototype at all. If all you have is a sketch of your umbrella on January 1, 2006, you may then need to prove to the USPTO that you were diligent in either working toward building a prototype or preparing your patent application. This may require you to provide additional written documentation showing constant activity after you first came up with your original invention. This underscores the importance of maintaining good records in case you ever need to prove an early invention date.

Lab notebooks are still frequently used in the United States to document inventions. Because issues in interference often turn on the reliability of the invention documents, signing, dating, and witnessing lab notebooks may be invaluable to your likelihood of success in an interference. Figure 11.1 illustrates an example of a lab notebook page signed and witnessed for the umbrella invention. Ideally, you should have your lab notebook witnessed by someone who is not an inventor.

The Examiner and Prior Art

One of the patent examiner's main jobs is to search for prior art. Examiners have at their disposal a computerized searching system for searching prior patents and patent publications, and typically will use these types of references in rejecting your application. Examiners may also find foreign publications, articles, and other written documents. An examiner's universe of prior art is not limited to written documentation, however, and therefore, prior public use or offers for sale as discussed above may also be used by an examiner to reject an application.

You may wonder how an examiner would ever find out about a given piece of prior art, especially given that most examiners focus their searching on U.S. patent documents. The inventor, as well as the attorney and other parties associated with the application, are under an obligation to disclose to the USPTO any information that is "material to patentability." Such information is disclosed to the USPTO in the form of an Information Disclosure Statement or IDS, which provides a list to the examiner of the relevant pieces of prior art. Thus, if you or your patent attorney knows of a killer piece of prior art, whether it be a prior article or your own prior sales activity, you are required to disclose it to the examiner.

To give an example, let's say that after you file your patent application on the RAINGOD umbrella, one of your investors shows you a magazine published years ago in Japan showing an advertisement by a Japanese company for a very similar product, though instead of sounding an audible alarm on the handle like your umbrella, the Japanese umbrella sends a signal to a cell phone that flashes a message. You don't disclose the magazine ad to the examiner, figuring that the patent examiner will never find it. Your patent issues, and then the Japanese company releases in the United States a product just like yours with an audible alarm on the handle. You sue the Japanese company, and during the course of litigation, it is discovered that you knew about the magazine advertisement all along. The Court may find that you committed fraud on the Patent Office by failing to disclose a material reference, and your patent could be found unenforceable. Even though the Japanese umbrella in the ad was not

Strategy Tip If you want to do your own searching or find a copy of a U.S. patent or patent publication, you can go to the USPTO web site at www.uspto.gov/patft/. Other online databases, such as delphion.com or pat2pdf.org, also provide access to PDFs of patent documents.

the same as yours, it was close enough that an examiner would have considered it relevant.

Patent Searching

Because you're making a huge investment in the preparation and filing of your patent application, you may decide that you'd like to know what's out there before you file the patent application. No searching is required by the USPTO, but as discussed above, if you find something close, you should send it to the patent examiner. You can perform a patent search yourself, or you can have a patent attorney or professional search firm conduct one for you. Several online databases are available, including one at the USPTO web site (www.uspto.gov/patft/), which allows for searching of issued patents and published patent applications. Chapter 27 provides more information on patent searching.

Hiring a patent searcher is often a cost-effective way to assess patentability of your invention before investing in the cost of filing a patent application. For anywhere from a few hundred to a few thousand dollars, you can hire a search firm that will conduct a fairly comprehensive search of U.S. patents and publications. But be warned that patent searching is not perfect. Searchers do not typically search through scientific articles, and many patent documents that can be prior art to your patent application may not be published at the time the searcher performs the search. So while searching is beneficial, never consider it to be a guarantee of finding all the references relevant to your invention. In many cases, the patent examiner might still find other references in her own search that your search did not uncover.

CHAPTER 12

Examining a Patent Application

You've filed your patent application and now you're anxious to get your patent. But you wait, and you wait, and you wait, and then when you do finally hear from the USPTO, your patent application is rejected. Businesspeople and entrepreneurs often don't understand that it takes a long time to get a patent and that a lot goes on between the time that you file your application and when you finally get your patent. The process during that time period is known as "prosecution" of your patent application, and through this process you can turn that USPTO rejection into an allowance of your patent.

Figure 12.1 illustrates a typical patent prosecution timeline. Before a patent application even reaches an examiner, it sits in the USPTO queue, often for more than a year. Once the examiner picks up the application, she will examine it, and often issue a rejection in the form of an office action, setting forth the reasons for rejecting the application. Don't be discouraged if your patent application at first gets rejected, because it happens to most patent applicants, and you will have an opportunity (and likely several opportunities) to respond. The negotiation process with the examiner to try to get your patent allowed might take anywhere from a few months to several years. If you fail in your attempts to get the application allowed, you might choose to abandon your application. But more often than not your patent application will be allowed, at which time you will receive a Notice of Allowance. Hopefully within about six months of receiving this Notice, your patent will issue.

The Office Action

An examiner's office action may contain rejections based on the specification, drawings, or other formalities. The office action may also indicate that your

FIGURE 12.1 **Typical patent application prosecution timeline**

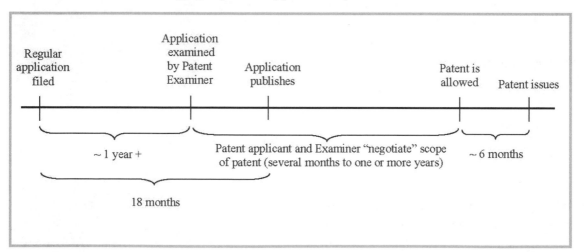

Did You Know? The written record of the communication between the patent applicant and the USPTO is known as the "file history" of the patent application. Sometimes it is helpful to obtain copies of a patent's file history, especially in litigation to learn whether the patent applicant said anything that might limit the scope of his invention. For most recently filed patent applications, file histories are available via the USPTO web site at http://portal.uspto.gov/external/portal/pair simply by entering information about the patent application or issued patent.

application contains more than one invention, and may require you to pick just one (called a "Restriction Requirement," described further in Chapter 13). But typically, the bulk of the office action is devoted to a rejection of the claims over prior art found by the examiner.

A conventional office action will set forth a period for response, typically three months, extendable to six months with payment of extension fees. Extension of time fees are not due until the response is filed, meaning that if you extend your response deadline to six months, the extension is paid at the sixth month. Therefore, you can extend the time period for response and not have to pay the extension fee until you finally respond.

For an office action that rejects the claims of the application, a typical response might include:

- Amending the claims to overcome the examiner's rejection
- Canceling some claims
- Adding new claims
- Arguing that the claims are patentable over the examiner's grounds for rejection

Anticipation Rejection

Assume that your patent application includes the following claim:

1. An umbrella, comprising:

an elongate shaft having a first end and a second end;

a handle provided at the first end of the elongate shaft;

a plurality of spokes connected to the second end of the shaft,
the spokes being moveable from a collapsed configuration
aligned with the shaft and an expanded configuration extending
away from the shaft;

a covering supported by the spokes and forming a concave surface facing toward the handle; and

an indicator on the handle for displaying a weather condition.

For fiscal year 2005, the USPTO reported that the average amount of time an applicant had to wait before receiving a first office action was 22.6 months. It took on average 31.1 months for the patent to either issue or go abandoned.

After waiting 12 months for an examination, you finally receive an office action from the USPTO. The first rejection in the office action states:

Claim 1 is rejected under 35 U.S.C 102(b) as being anticipated by U.S. Patent No. 8,123,456 to Jones et al.

As discussed above, because the rejection is made for anticipation, the examiner believes that each and every feature taught by your claim is found in the prior art reference (the Jones patent).

However, after you've reviewed the Jones patent, let's say that you disagree that Jones teaches an indicator on the handle for displaying a weather condition. Instead, Jones only teaches a light bulb in the handle that allows the umbrella to be used as a flashlight as well. You would probably then respond to the examiner's rejection by pointing out this difference, and arguing that Claim 1 is allowable as written.

On the other hand, perhaps the Jones patent teaches an umbrella having a display on the handle for showing the current temperature. This could be considered "an indicator on the handle for displaying a weather condition." You feel, however, that your invention is different because your preferred indicator doesn't tell the temperature, but it provides an audible alarm telling the user when it is going to rain. To overcome the examiner's rejection then, you might decide to amend Claim 1. In your response, you could present an amendment as follows:

1. (Currently amended) An umbrella, comprising:
an elongate shaft having a first end and a second end;
a handle provided at the first end of the elongate shaft;
a plurality of spokes connected to the second end of the shaft,
the spokes being moveable from a collapsed configuration
aligned with the shaft and an expanded configuration extending
away from the shaft;
a covering supported by the spokes and forming a concave surface facing toward the handle; and
an <u>audible alarm</u> ~~indicator~~ on the handle ~~for displaying a
weather condition~~ <u>that sounds when it is going to rain.</u>

Claims are amended by adding language (shown <u>underlined</u>) or delet-
ing language (shown with ~~strikethrough~~ or in brackets [ ]. By amending
Claim 1 as indicated above, you would then argue that this amended language is not found in the Jones patent, and for this reason amended Claim
1 is allowable.

You are permitted to make amendments to your claims, even well after
the filing of your application, so long as your amendments do not introduce
"new matter." As discussed in Chapter 10, this means that the language that
you put into your claims must satisfy the written description requirement and
be supported by your originally filed specification. With the Claim 1 example above, this amendment will be permitted as long as the specification
describes an audible alarm that sounds when it is going to rain. If the specification does not describe this feature, you cannot make this amendment.

Obviousness Rejection

As another example of a rejection that you might see, perhaps the same
Claim 1 above receives the following rejection:

Claim 1 is rejected as being unpatentable under 35 U.S.C.
103(a) as being unpatentable over Jones et al. (U.S. Patent No.
8,123,456 to Jones et al.) in view of Smith (U.S. Patent No.
8,543,121). Jones et al. teaches all of the limitation of Claim 1,
with the exception of an indicator on the handle for displaying

a weather condition. Smith teaches a portable thermometer. It would have been obvious to one of skill in the art to put the portable thermometer of Smith on the handle of the umbrella in Jones et al.

In this example, the examiner was not able to find a single reference teaching all of the limitations of your claim, so instead, she found two references which together include all of the features, and argues that it would be obvious to put them together.

One option for responding is to amend your claim as described above to recite an audible alarm that sounds when it is going to rain. Because neither the Jones patent nor the Smith patent discloses this feature, you would argue to the examiner that your claim is allowable even if the two references are combined.

But before making the amendment to the claim, you might also consider whether you can argue that the examiner's proposed combination of the references is improper. For example, you might argue that the portable thermometer found in the Smith patent is too large to be placed on the umbrella handle found in the Jones patent. You might also argue that a person of skill in the umbrella art would not have thought to use the Smith thermometer of an umbrella handle because neither the Jones patent nor the Smith patent suggests such a possibility.

Strategy Tip | For difficult obviousness rejections, you might consider submitting a declaration to the examiner presenting so-called "secondary considerations of nonobviousness." This type of declaration provides proof of other evidence, such as unexpected results, commercial success, long-felt need, failure of others, copying by others, and skepticism of experts, that could be useful in demonstrating the inventiveness of your invention. Such a declaration could be signed by an expert in the field, or even by the inventor himself. The examiner is required to consider this declaration in assessing patentability of your invention, and if successful, the examiner might remove the obviousness rejection.

Strategy Tip Because of the amount of time it takes to get a patent application examined, you might want to consider filing a Request for Accelerated Examination. The USPTO just implemented a new program in 2006 where it strives, but doesn't guarantee, to give you either an allowance or a final rejection within 12 months of filing. In order to take advantage of this program, you must satisfy a few additional requirements when filing your patent application, such as performing a prior art search and identifying limitations of your claims found in the prior art references. Especially in technology areas where the USPTO is taking several years to give you a first examination (such as with computer software or business methods patents), talk to your patent attorney about whether it might make sense to request accelerated examination.

In addition to the options above, your office action response also can cancel some or all claims if, for example, you believe that the examiner's rejections are actually correct, or if you are simply no longer interested in pursuing those claims. You might also add new claims for the same or even different features, although an examiner might refuse to examine your new claims if she believes they pertain to a different invention (see discussion of Restriction Requirements in Chapter 13).

A Final Rejection

You'll usually have at least one opportunity to respond to an examiner's rejection. However, if the examiner maintains her position and doesn't agree with the arguments you made in response to her office action, she may make a subsequent office action "final." A final office action closes substantive prosecution on your application, meaning effectively that you've reached the end of the line for the money that you paid to file the patent application. This doesn't mean that you're entirely out of options, but it does mean that you may have to pay more money or do more work to get your patent. It also may cause you to decide not to get a patent.

If your patent application has been finally rejected, you would have the following options.

Filing an Amendment after Final

An Amendment after Final is usually limited to minor issues not requiring substantive review, such as cleaning up typographical errors or canceling rejected claims to leave only allowed claims. In some instances, you may be able to convince an examiner of the patentability of your application through an Amendment after Final, although this can be difficult.

Filing a Request for Continued Examination (RCE)

Filing an RCE involves paying an additional fee to the USPTO (see Appendix B) to reopen prosecution, giving yourself another opportunity to convince the same patent examiner of the patentability of your invention. If this fails after another round or two of negotiations, the examiner may make the rejection final once more, and you might try to file another RCE, or you might at that time consider filing an appeal. Filing the RCE is usually the easiest way to continue the examination of your patent, because all you're doing is paying more money (the filing fee for an RCE is currently $810 for a large entity, and $405 for a small entity, plus the fees of your patent attorney).

Filing a Continuation Application

You might also consider filing a continuation application to continue prosecution of your invention, as discussed in Chapter 13. A continuation application is a brand new application, so it will require payment of additional fees

> **Strategy Tip** Filing a Request for Continued Examination is generally one of the easier ways to continue prosecution following a final office action rejection. But in tough cases, be sure to consider whether you might want to file an appeal instead.

for filing. The fee for filing a continuation is similar to that of filing an RCE, but normally an RCE will be examined much more quickly than a continuation application (usually within a few months). A continuation application, like a first-filed regular utility application, might take a year or more before being examined.

Filing an Appeal

If you find that you are not making progress with the examiner or if you feel that the examiner is taking an unreasonable position, you may appeal the examiner's rejections to the Board of Patent Appeals and Interferences, by filing a Notice of Appeal. In the appeal, you would present your arguments first in writing and then orally before the Board of Appeals. Sometimes the filing of the appeal causes the examiner to reconsider her position and withdraw the final office action rejection or invite you to make an amendment to make your application allowable. If you lose at the Board of Appeals, your case may then be appealed to federal court.

How Does My Patent Get Allowed?

Once your application is deemed allowable by the patent examiner (which means that the examiner believes that you have valid claims to your invention),

---

You Should Know   Appeals are not costly compared to lawsuits, but they will cost you a few thousand dollars in government fees (see Appendix B) and a few thousand more in attorneys' fees. But an appeal will take time, sometimes a few years from the filing of your Notice of Appeal (which starts the appeal process) to the final answer from the Board of Appeals. In the meantime, your competitors might be out there using your invention, without you having the ability to stop them. Therefore, you might consider filing a continuation application, discussed in Chapter 13, in addition to having your application on appeal, to seek additional claims to use against your competitors.

---

you will receive a Notice of Allowance, specifying a deadline (which will be three months from the date of the Notice of Allowance) for paying the Issue Fee for obtaining your patent. If you're lucky enough, you might even receive a Notice of Allowance as your first correspondence from the USPTO. The Issue Fee currently costs $1,440 for a large entity and $720 for a small entity. After you pay your Issue Fee, it might still take the USPTO a few months to issue your patent, because it takes time for the USPTO to properly print your issued patent.

CHAPTER 13

Continuing Applications, Provisional Applications, and Patent Publications

I f patents weren't confusing enough already, get ready for even more types of patents. This chapter explains (1) continuing applications (continuations, divisionals, and continuations-in-part), which are additional patents filed after you have filed a first, or a parent patent application, (2) provisional applications, which are informal, never-to-be-examined patent applications to save you money, and (3) patent application publications, which look deceptively like issued patents, but are not.

Continuation Applications

Continuation, divisional, and continuation-in-part (sometimes referred to as a "CIP") applications are patent applications that claim priority to an earlier-filed patent application. When one application claims priority to an earlier application, the earlier-filed patent application is often referred to as the "parent application," and the continuation, divisional, or CIP is often referred to as the child, or "continuing," application. If the continuing application is properly filed and certain requirements are satisfied, the claims in the continuing application will be treated as if filed in the parent. In other words, the USPTO will treat the continuing application's claims as if they had the filing date of the parent patent application. This "priority benefit" can help secure patent protection for later-filed claims that would not otherwise be patentable.

For example, consider a patent application filed in 2002 that describes several inventions in many different ways, lists various optional features, and combinations of features, in both broad and narrow terms. Later, in 2006, as the patent application is about to issue, you decide that you would like to pursue patent protection on different features and embodiments described in the original patent application. You may file a continuing application to pursue these features and embodiments. When assessing patentability of the 2006 application's claims, the USPTO will determine if those claims are entitled to the priority of the parent application (i.e., the 2002 application). If the USPTO determines that they are, it will determine patentability of the 2006 application's claims based only upon prior art in existence at the time the 2002 patent application was filed. In other words, "intervening prior art," that is, prior art coming into existence after the filing of the 2002 application, but prior to the filing of the 2006 application, is not available to defeat patentability of the claims in the 2006 patent application.

Continuations

Of the three types of continuing patent applications, the continuation and divisional applications are very similar. Their specifications do not include any new subject matter vis-à-vis the parent application, but they include different claims from the parent. The claims in continuation applications are generally directed to the same invention claimed in the parent (although they can be directed to a different invention); but the continuation might claim a different variation or seek a different scope of coverage than that claimed in the parent. In some cases, the continuation is directed to a different invention than that claimed in the parent.

For example, a patent might disclose several aspects or embodiments of a medical device and methods of using the medical device. The text and figures of the patent might describe the internal mechanical and electrical components, the external controls and patient interface, as well as methods of performing various procedures. The patent might also describe various possible combinations of components that could be provided in different situations. The patent might also provide broad, generalized descriptions of certain device and method embodiments, as well as several narrower, specific descriptions of similar devices and methods.

Even though the patent *describes* (i.e., in the text and figures) many different ideas and inventions, the patent will likely *claim* only one, or only closely related ideas and inventions. For example, the claims in the patent might be limited to the patient interface device. In this case, prior to your patent application issuing as a patent, you might want to consider filing a continuation. The continuation patent application's specification (i.e., text and figures) will be identical to the parent, but the claims will be directed to a different aspect of the invention claimed in the parent. For example, in the continuation, you may want to pursue claims directed to a broader or narrower patient interface device. Alternatively, in the continuation, you may want to pursue claims directed to a different one of the many inventions and ideas described in your patent application, such as the method of using the medical device or the particular configuration of internal electronic and/or mechanical assemblies.

Divisionals

The divisional application's claims are generally directed to an invention that is "patentably distinct" from that claimed in the parent. For example, if the claims in the parent patent are directed to a device (or devices), the divisional's claims may be directed to methods of using the device or systems that include the device as well as other devices or components. Divisional applications are filed as a result of a "restriction requirement" issued by the USPTO.

Restriction Requirements

If the patent examiner thinks that your patent application claims more than one patentably distinct invention, he can issue a restriction requirement and require you to select a single invention for examination. For example, if a patent application includes some claims to a novel bicycle and other claims to a novel toaster, the USPTO will issue a Restriction Requirement ordering the applicant to elect a single invention. This is because the patent laws provide that an inventor is entitled to only one patent per invention. Another reason the USPTO issues Restriction Requirements is that it would be too burdensome on the patent examiner to search the entire prior art database to assess patentability of both a bicycle and a toaster. Instead, the USPTO will require separate patent applications for the two distinct inventions.

The USPTO can also issue a Restriction Requirement when the difference between the claimed inventions is not so great. For example, the USPTO may issue a Restriction Requirement if a patent claims both a device and a method of using the device. The USPTO can also issue a Restriction Requirement if multiple "species," such as different alternatives, of an invention are described and claimed in the patent specification. The examiner may consider it burdensome to review and search for prior art on all of these species, and require you to pick or "elect" one for examination.

Whatever claims you elect in response to a Restriction Requirement will proceed to examination. The remaining claims are considered "withdrawn," and can be pursued by filing a divisional application containing those withdrawn claims.

Continuations-in-Part

Unlike the continuation and divisional applications, the continuation-in-part (CIP) application does include new subject matter vis-à-vis the parent application. Inventors often continue research and development and discover improvements to subject matter described in their patent applications. However, an inventor is not permitted to add new disclosure to a patent application once it is filed. Instead, the inventor can file another patent application that includes both the old and new subject matter as a continuation-in-part of the parent. Claims in the CIP that are directed solely to the old subject matter will be entitled to priority from the parent; otherwise, they will not.

As is discussed in Chapter 15, patent term is determined based upon the earliest date to which you claim priority—even if the claims in your patent

Warning! Think carefully before filing a continuation-in-part. If your CIP contains claims that are supported by a parent application, why wouldn't you file those claims in a continuation of the parent application? On the other hand, if the claims in the CIP are not supported by a parent application, consider filing those claims in an original application that does not claim priority from any parent. The reasoning is that claiming priority causes you to give up patent term (see Chapter 15), and it doesn't make sense to give up patent term if the claims in your application are not going to be entitled to priority anyway.

Some believe that if there is the slightest argument that even one claim is entitled to priority it makes sense to claim priority and file the application as a CIP, at least for technology areas in which patent term is not critical (e.g., in some technology areas, patented technology becomes irrelevant or obsolete after a few years, so losing a few years of patent term doesn't cause any real economic loss). In addition, filing a CIP can avoid the expense of having to file two patent applications—a continuation application to pursue claims supported by the parent application and a new application for the new matter. Consult a patent attorney to determine the best approach for you.

application are not entitled to the priority claimed. Therefore, you might want to consider the trade-off between patent term and priority date when filing a continuation-in-part patent application, and also consider whether it makes sense to claim priority or not.

Example

Consider your hypothetical company Rain Alert Inc. and the RAINGOD brand umbrella product that you are planning to manufacture. After meeting with your patent attorney and developing a comprehensive intellectual property strategy, you decide to file a patent application. This initial patent application describes your ideas of: (1) an umbrella that includes a radio transceiver for receiving weather information from a source and an indicator that lights up based upon the received weather information; (2) an umbrella that includes a wireless radio transmitter for sending an alarm to a cellular telephone; and (3) methods of using such umbrellas.

Did You Know? Did you know that claims in a patent do not necessarily all have the same priority date?

For example, the claims in a continuation-in-part are entitled to the priority date of its parent only if the parent patent can "support" the claims in the CIP. This means that the parent patent must describe, enable, and provide the best mode of practicing the claims presented in the CIP. All three requirements must be satisfied for a parent patent to provide support. If the parent patent does not support the claims in the CIP, the CIP's claims will not be entitled to the parent's priority date.

Claims should be analyzed individually because it is possible that some claims may be entitled to priority from a parent, while others may not. The USPTO often does not provide a clear assessment and determination of a particular claim's priority. A patent attorney can help you analyze claims in your or your competitors' patents to determine whether or not a claim is entitled to priority.

In this initial patent application, which we will refer to as the parent application, you write a complete description of these three aspects to your invention. This complete description forms the specification section of your patent application, and it includes both drawings and written text. In the claims section of your application, however, you decide to present claims only directed to the methods of using the umbrella, and not the umbrella device itself. You decide to file claims only directed to the methods because you think that you will have a better chance of having the method claims allowed quickly. You're trying to get a patent issued as quickly as possible because you think doing so will help you raise additional investment financing.

The USPTO eventually allows the method claims in the parent application and sends you a Notice of Allowance, which states that your patent application will be issued into a patent within the next few months. You decide that you would like to file additional patents that claim priority to this parent application. You decide that you would now like to seek patent protection for the umbrella device itself, which was described (but not claimed) in the parent application.

You also decide that you would like to seek patent protection for a new improvement that you've recently tested. You've figured out how to weave a conductive thread into the umbrella's canopy, which allows you to use the entire umbrella canopy as a giant antenna. This improvement not only improves the reliability of the umbrella's performance, but it requires less power to communicate.

Your attorney prepares two new patent applications. The first is a continuation of the parent application. The continuation's specification is an identical copy of the parent's, but the continuation includes claims directed to the umbrella device, and not the methods of using the umbrella. The second is a CIP of the parent application. The CIP's specification includes an identical copy of the parent's specification, but it also includes new figures and written description of the canopy antenna improvement. Most of the claims in the CIP are directed to the new improved umbrella. However, you've included a few claims in the CIP that you believe are broad enough to cover both the umbrella described in the parent application as well as the improvement described in the CIP.

> **Warning!** Your own earlier-filed patent applications and patents could be used as prior art against a later-filed continuation-in-part (CIP). In particular, if the earlier-filed applications (or patents) published (or issued) more than a year before you file the continuation-in-part, the examiner could assert either (1) the earlier-filed case fully describes (or anticipates) the invention claimed in the CIP, or (2) that the CIP is merely an obvious variant of the technology described in the earlier case.

Establishing Priority

There are generally four requirements that you must satisfy in order to establish priority to an earlier-filed, parent application: (1) continuity of inventorship, (2) continuity of pendency, (3) continuity of disclosure, and (4) a proper statement claiming priority. Each of these requirements is discussed below.

Inventorship

First, continuity of inventorship must exist between the cases. This means that there must be at least one common inventor named in both the parent and later-filed cases.

Pendency

Second, continuity of pendency must exist between the cases. This means that the earlier-filed case must still be pending in the USPTO (i.e., that the earlier-filed case must not have issued already) when the later-filed case is filed. However, if an earlier-filed case has issued, a later-filed case can still claim priority to it though an intervening case that was filed before the earlier-filed case issued and is itself pending at the time the later-filed case is filed.

Disclosure

Third, continuity of disclosure must exist between the cases. This means that the specification of the earlier-filed application must meet certain statutory requirements with respect to the claims of the later-filed application. For example, the earlier-filed application must meet the written description, enablement, and best mode requirements, as discussed in greater detail in Chapter 10.

Priority Claim

Finally, the later-filed application must include a proper "priority claim" to the earlier-filed application, which is generally a statement that appears as the first sentence or sentences in a patent application (although there are other, less common ways to present a priority claim). For example, a continuing application might provide, "This application is a continuation of U.S. Application No. 12/123,456, filed January 15, 2002, which claims priority from U.S. Provisional No. 60/123,111, filed January 15, 2001, and U.S. Provisional No. 60/123,222, filed February 2, 2001." Such a statement would indicate that the patent application is claiming the benefit of the filing date of a parent non-provisional patent application, as well as two provisional patent applications. Provisional applications are discussed in greater detail later in this chapter.

The USPTO provides formal requirements for presenting such priority claims. If the formal requirements are not satisfied, the priority claim will be deemed defective, and will require amendment for priority to be available. In addition, even if a priority claim is properly provided, priority will not be

> **Warning!** The USPTO provides strict time limits for presenting a proper priority claim. Priority claims must be provided by the later of 4 months from the filing of the later-filed application or 16 months from the filing of the earlier-filed application. Priority claims presented after the 4/16-month deadline must be accompanied by a petition to request acceptance of an unintentionally delayed claim for priority and a petition fee, which is currently $1,410. Although the USPTO offers a 50 percent discount on some fees to certain qualified small entities, the USPTO does not offer a discount on the petition to request acceptance of an unintentionally delayed priority claim fee.

granted unless the earlier-filed applications provide all of the statutory requirements vis-à-vis the later-filed claims. For example, the earlier-filed application must describe, enable, and provide the best mode for practicing the invention claimed in the later-filed application for priority to be granted. The statutory requirements are discussed in greater detail later in this chapter.

Multiple Continuing Applications

Some companies use multiple continuing applications to develop a comprehensive, intimidating patent portfolio. By implementing a "continuation practice" in this way, you can develop an entire patent portfolio based upon a single (or multiple) parent application.

"Continuation practice" is the strategy of filing multiple patent applications based upon one or more initial disclosures. Continuation practice allows an entrepreneur to develop an IP thicket or wall around her core technology. Continuing applications often provide claims of varying scope to provide both broad and narrow claim coverage. In some cases, continuing applications are filed with claims that are specifically drafted to cover a competitor's product. Continuation practice often leads to multiple patents and applications, which can increase a company's perceived dominance in the market, value, and leverage.

> **Warning!** The USPTO recently announced new rules that limit continuation practice. The rules limit the number of continuation applications (and RCEs) that can be filed off of an initial patent filing. Entrepreneurs should consult with their patent attorneys to understand how new rules may affect their overall patent portfolio development strategy.

Continuing Applications and Patent Term

As will be discussed in greater detail in Chapter 15, patents granted on applications filed after June 8, 1995, have a lifetime (or term) of 20 years from the earliest date from which priority is claimed. Therefore, although continuing applications can be filed sequentially, and spaced several years apart, the lifetime of the continuing application will be determined based upon the earliest filing date from which priority is claimed. For example, if the 2006 application claims priority from the 2002 application, the 2006 application's term will end in 2022 (not 2026).

A Provisional Patent Application

Sometimes you may be in a hurry to get a patent application on file. For example, perhaps there's a trade show coming up in two weeks that all the big umbrella manufacturers are going to attend, and you need to be there to show your umbrella to have a chance of making it a success. You know they won't sign a non-disclosure agreement, but you want to be protected. Is it possible to get a patent application filed that quickly?

In a bind, maybe your patent attorney can rush to get a utility patent filed. But you've heard other business people talk about filing a provisional patent application, often as a way to save money on getting patents. What are they? Are they worth filing?

> **You Should Know** Filing a continuation application does not entitle you to a patent term of 20 years from the filing of the continuation application. This is because the patent's term is based upon the earliest priority date claimed. Therefore, a continuation application filed in 2006, but claiming priority to an application filed in 2002, will expire in 2022 (not 2026).

> Consider filing a provisional patent application if you need to get something on file quickly, or if you're low on cash.

Provisional patent applications are informal utility patent applications filed instead of full utility applications for the purpose of obtaining an early filing date. Provisional applications will not be examined and will be accepted by the USPTO as long as they include a written description of the invention and any drawings if necessary. Claims are not required for a provisional application. The provisional filing fee, currently $210 for a large entity ($105 for a small entity), can even be paid after the filing of the initial application.

The filing of a provisional patent application on your product allows you to mark your product with "Patent Pending." Because the USPTO does not examine provisional applications, there is a lot of flexibility in what a provisional application may contain. Some provisional applications are written much like full utility applications, with claims (but they don't need to include claims). Other provisional applications contain no more than reproductions of lab notebook pages or a few paragraphs of description of the invention. The lab notebook page shown as Figure 11.1 in Chapter 11 could be filed as a provisional application, although you would likely remove the signatures and the dates from the filing. Thus, if you just want to say that you have a patent pending, you could file a very short provisional patent application that would cost you no more than a few hundred dollars.

However, filing a provisional application alone will not result in your getting a patent. To get a patent, you will still need to file a nonprovisional patent application. The advantage of a provisional application is that it provides you with one year from filing to file a nonprovisional application (the utility application discussed above) claiming priority to the provisional application. Any

> **Strategy Tip** The filing of a provisional application entitles the applicant to mark inventions disclosed in the provisional application with "Patent Pending." Many companies find that marking their products with Patent Pending can be valuable in marketing their products to prospective customers.

> **Did You Know?** Provisional applications remain confidential, at least for 18 months, after their filing. But if a regular application is filed later claiming priority to the provisional application and the regular application is published as discussed later in this chapter, the provisional application is also made available to the public (for example, at that point anyone can order the provisional application from the USPTO).

foreign filings (discussed in Chapter 14) must also be filed by the one year anniversary. Any claims in the later-filed nonprovisional application will be treated as though filed in the provisional application if they are supported by the information disclosed in the provisional application. Thus, a provisional application may be filed for relatively lower cost initially, and then by the one-year anniversary of the provisional filing date, the regular utility application may also be filed.

Despite the lack of formal requirements for a provisional application, for a claim in a later-filed nonprovisional application to be given the benefit of the earlier filed provisional application date, the provisional application must still satisfy the minimum requirements of written description, enablement, and best mode as described in Chapter 10. This is where you'll want to be careful, because if the disclosure of your provisional application is too sparse, you could lose your provisional application filing date, and any prior art uncovered between the filing of your provisional and your nonprovisional patent application could be used against you.

For example, assume that on December 1, 2005, you filed the page of disclosure in Appendix A as a provisional patent application. The disclosure shows and describes an umbrella with a flashing light on the handle. On December 1, 2006, you filed a regular patent application claiming priority to the provisional patent application. But in the regular patent application, you decide to claim an umbrella having an audible alarm. The examiner finds an article published on July 15, 2006, describing an umbrella with an audible alarm. Because your claim would only be entitled to the December 1, 2006, filing date, the examiner can use the article to reject your claim. You won't be able to rely on your provisional application to predate the article because it doesn't describe the audible alarm. While in this scenario you might be able to swear behind the article to prove an earlier invention date (described in Chapter 11), you would have been much better off if you had included more information when you first filed your provisional patent application.

After a Patent Application Publication

As discussed in Chapter 10, you can't file a patent application and expect to keep secret particular details of your invention. And because a patent takes so long to get issued, you're not sure if it makes sense to file a patent application, because your competitors might rip you off before you even get your patent. You would like to know—is there any way you can keep your patent secret?

18–Month Publication

Patents in the United States used to stay secret until they issued, but those days are mostly over. Now, at about 18 months after filing, the USPTO will publish almost all patent applications. Those 18 months are significant, because at least for 18 months, your patent will stay secret, giving you a head start on commercializing your product before anyone gets wind of what you're up to. The 18-month publication rule is the result of the USPTO wanting to be consistent with other countries in the world, which used the 18-month publication rule long before the United States adopted the policy. The

---

You Should Know | Most patent applications will publish 18 months from the earliest claimed priority date. These publications are *not* issued patents. The USPTO does not guarantee publication exactly 18 months after the earliest filing date, though they usually come pretty close. Most patent applications will publish within a week or two after the 18-month period.

18-month publication rule is measured from the date of the earliest claimed priority date. Therefore, for a regular utility application claiming priority to an earlier-filed provisional or non-provisional application, publication will occur as early as 18 months after the earliest filing date. For example, a utility application filed on January 5, 2006, claiming priority to a provisional application filed January 5, 2005, will publish on or shortly after July 4, 2006.

Patent publications are designated by the code "A" following the number, as opposed to the "B" code given for issued patents. A United States patent publication looks very similar to an issued United States patent, but it is not, so be sure to know the difference between the two. Figure 13.1 shows the cover page of a U.S. patent publication, and Figure 13.2 shows the cover page of the corresponding issued patent.

> If you don't want your patent application to publish until it issues, certify to the USPTO that you will not be seeking foreign patents.

Non-Publication Requests

Maybe you don't want your patent application to be published at all until it issues. For example, maybe you don't want your competitors to know what you're up to until you know if you're likely to get patent protection. If your patent application is published but the examiner ends up rejecting all of the claims, then you will basically have given to all of your competitors a road map to how to copy your invention. The only way for you to avoid the 18-month publication is if you're willing to give up your foreign patent protection. Specifically, you can avoid publication of your application if you certify to the USPTO that you will not be making a foreign filing for your invention. By doing so, your patent application will remain confidential until the date that the patent issues.

Because foreign patent protection might be too expensive, sometimes it might be to your advantage not to publish your patent application. If you have an invention that you think you can maintain as a trade secret, you might file your patent application with a request for nonpublication, and see whether the patent examiner will be willing to issue your patent. If the examiner is not willing to issue a patent, assuming you've taken the other appropriate steps to maintain your trade secrets (covered in Chapters 17 and 18), you can abandon

FIGURE 13.1 **Cover Page of a United States Patent Publication**

Note that no assignee is listed on the publication. Sometimes this information will be found here, but oftentimes the USPTO does not yet know who owns the patent application.

The "A" code following the number means that this is a patent publication, not an issued patent.

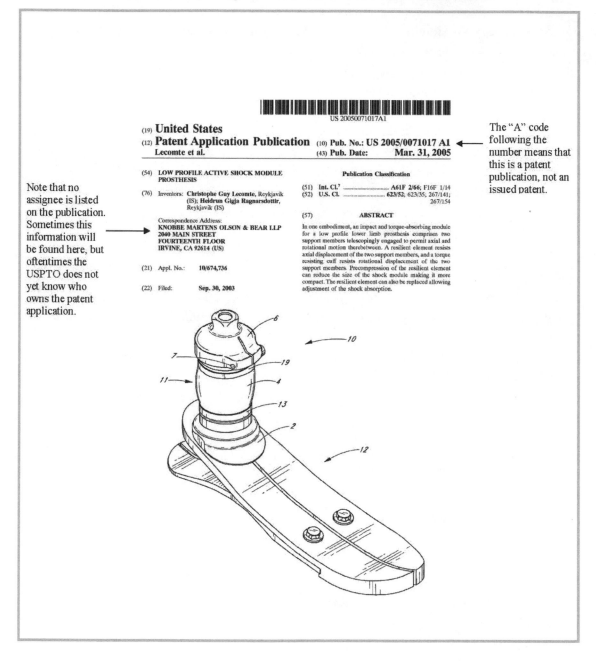

US 20050071017A1

(19) **United States**
(12) **Patent Application Publication** (10) Pub. No.: **US 2005/0071017 A1**
Lecomte et al. (43) Pub. Date: **Mar. 31, 2005**

(54) **LOW PROFILE ACTIVE SHOCK MODULE PROSTHESIS**

(76) Inventors: **Christophe Guy Lecomte**, Reykjavik (IS); **Heidrun Gigja Ragnarsdottir**, Reykjavik (IS)

Correspondence Address:
KNOBBE MARTENS OLSON & BEAR LLP
2040 MAIN STREET
FOURTEENTH FLOOR
IRVINE, CA 92614 (US)

(21) Appl. No.: **10/674,736**

(22) Filed: **Sep. 30, 2003**

Publication Classification

(51) Int. Cl.⁷ A61F 2/66; F16F 1/14
(52) U.S. Cl. 623/52; 623/35; 267/141; 267/154

(57) **ABSTRACT**

In one embodiment, an impact and torque-absorbing module for a low profile lower limb prosthesis comprises two support members telescopingly engaged to permit axial and rotational motion therebetween. A resilient element resists axial displacement of the two support members, and a torque resisting cuff resists rotational displacement of the two support members. Precompression of the resilient element can reduce the size of the shock module making it more compact. The resilient element can also be replaced allowing adjustment of the shock absorption.

FIGURE 13.2 **Cover Page of a Utility Patent**

US006969408B2

(12) **United States Patent**
Lecomte et al.

(10) **Patent No.:** **US 6,969,408 B2**
(45) **Date of Patent:** **Nov. 29, 2005**

(54) **LOW PROFILE ACTIVE SHOCK MODULE PROSTHESIS**

(75) Inventors: **Christophe Guy Lecomte**, Reykjavik (IS); **Heidrun Gigja Ragnarsdottir**, Reykjavik (IS)

(73) Assignee: **Ossur Engineering, Inc.**, Albion, MI (US)

(*) Notice: Subject to any disclaimer, the term of this patent is extended or adjusted under 35 U.S.C. 154(b) by 0 days.

(21) Appl. No.: **10/674,736**

(22) Filed: **Sep. 30, 2003**

(65) **Prior Publication Data**

US 2005/0071017 A1 Mar. 31, 2005

(51) Int. Cl.[7] **A61F 2/24**
(52) U.S. Cl. **623/55**
(58) Field of Search 623/55, 53, 52, 623/50, 47–49

(56) **References Cited**

U.S. PATENT DOCUMENTS

53,931	A	4/1866	Weston et al.
277,562	A	5/1883	Furrer
809,875	A	1/1906	Wilkins
817,340	A	4/1906	Rosenkranz
827,720	A	8/1906	Erwin
1,779,765	A	10/1930	Eichhorn
1,996,874	A	4/1935	Mascau
2,443,356	A	6/1948	Mathis
2,480,856	A	9/1949	Henschke et al.
2,570,735	A	10/1951	Weise
2,578,019	A	12/1951	Ryan
2,617,115	A	11/1952	Ellery
2,619,652	A	12/1952	Vesper
2,692,392	A	10/1954	Bennington et al.
2,699,554	A	1/1955	Comelli
2,843,853	A	7/1958	Mauch

2,899,685	A	8/1959	Bourcier de Carbon
3,663,967	A	5/1972	Vermillion
3,707,731	A	1/1973	Morgan
3,800,333	A	4/1974	Friberg
3,800,334	A	4/1974	Friberg
3,906,552	A	9/1975	Weber
3,956,775	A	5/1976	Moore
4,038,705	A	8/1977	Owens
4,161,042	A	7/1979	Cottingham et al.
4,216,550	A	8/1980	Thompson
4,370,761	A	2/1983	Serri
4,461,045	A	7/1984	Shorter et al.
4,463,459	A	8/1984	Shorter et al.
4,555,817	A	12/1985	McKendrick
4,605,417	A	8/1986	Fleischauer

(Continued)

FOREIGN PATENT DOCUMENTS

DE   328017   2/1919

(Continued)

OTHER PUBLICATIONS

Article entitled "Titanium Elastic Properties and Applications from Springs," Oct. 1987.

(Continued)

Primary Examiner—Alvin J. Stewart
(74) *Attorney, Agent, or Firm*—Knobbe Martens Olson & Bear, LLP

(57) **ABSTRACT**

In one embodiment, an impact and torque-absorbing module for a low profile lower limb prosthesis comprises two support members telescopingly engaged to permit axial and rotational motion therebetween. A resilient element resists axial displacement of the two support members, and a torque resisting cuff resists rotational displacement of the two support members. Precompression of the resilient element can reduce the size of the shock module making it more compact. The resilient element can also be replaced allowing adjustment of the shock absorption.

12 Claims, 5 Drawing Sheets

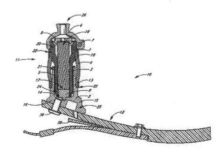

your patent application and it will never be published by the USPTO. Then you'll still have your trade secret rights, and not all will be lost.

Provisional Rights

One of the advantages of the patent publication is that it provides the patent owner with so-called provisional rights against potential infringers. What this means is that if your competitor is provided with actual notice of your patent publication (such as by your attorney writing a letter to the infringing competitor) and at least one claim infringed by your competitor in the published application is substantially identical to a claim in the issued patent, then after the patent issues, you will be entitled to receive a reasonable royalty from your competitor. That royalty would back-date to when your competitor received the notice of your patent publication.

Provisional rights often are not as helpful as they might seem, however, because patents are published based on the specification and claims as first filed with the USPTO. It is therefore likely that the claims of the application may change, especially after the application receives an office action from the examiner, and the usual back and forth results in amended claims (or no allowed claims at all). Once the claims are changed or amended, they may no longer be the same as the claims as originally filed and published.

For example, if you filed a patent application for your RAINGOD umbrella on January 1, 2005, your patent application would publish on or shortly after July 1, 2006. Perhaps your patent application publishes with Claim 1 above:

1. An umbrella, comprising:
   an elongate shaft having a first end and a second end;
   a curved handle provided at the first end of the elongate shaft;
   a plurality of spokes connected to the second end of the shaft,
   the spokes being moveable from a collapsed configuration
   aligned with the shaft and an expanded configuration extending
   away from the shaft; and
   a covering supported by the spokes and forming a concave surface facing toward the handle.

After your patent publishes, you send a letter to your competitor notifying them of your patent publication. If your patent ultimately issues with the same Claim 1 as in the publication, you will be entitled to obtain royalties from your competitor for infringement of Claim 1 back to the date that you sent your letter.

However, Claim 1 above is very broad and unlikely to be patentable. If you have to amend Claim 1 to make it patentable, for example by adding a limitation for an audible alarm on the handle, you will only be able to obtain royalties from your competitor if that amended claim were also in your patent publication.

Warning! Don't be alarmed if you find someone else's patent publication that has very broad claims. Quite often the claims of the publication have not been examined, and would never be issued. Most of the time you can keep track of a patent publication by obtaining its file history online via http://portal.uspto.gov/external/portal/pair. This way you can follow whether the patent examiner is willing to give that third party broad claims or not.

CHAPTER 14

Getting Worldwide Patent Protection

E ven though your business may be in the start-up phase, it may not be a bad idea to think big. Your market initially might be pretty local—your town, your metropolitan area, your state. But any successful entrepreneur understands that local success leads to national success and then to international success. For that reason, you should understand and think about getting patent protection outside of the United States.

Patents are generally specific to each country, and therefore, to obtain worldwide protection, a patent must be filed in every country where protection is desired. This can become an extremely costly

> **You Should Know** There is no single, worldwide patent. Each country has different patent laws, and therefore a patent is enforceable only in the country that issued the patent. For example, a U.S. patent can prevent an infringing product that is made overseas from being sold in the United States, but it will not prevent the product from being sold in a foreign country.

process—some companies spend over $100,000 doing international filings on just one invention. Thankfully, treaties are in place with most countries in the world to attempt to streamline the process of obtaining foreign patents.

Most countries in the world will recognize the filing of a U.S. patent application for the purposes of establishing a priority date in that country. To take advantage of the benefit of the U.S. filing date, the foreign patent application must be filed within one year of the U.S. filing date. Oftentimes, the foreign patent application is simply a reproduction (perhaps translated) of the U.S. application.

Most countries (with some notable exceptions such as Taiwan, Argentina, and Chile; see http://www.uspto.gov/web/offices/pac/dapp/pctstate.html) have signed the Patent Cooperation Treaty (PCT), which allows you to file a single application by the one-year anniversary of the U.S. filing to preserve your right to pursue patent applications in member countries. When you file a PCT application, the application designates all PCT member countries to preserve your right to file patent applications in some or all of those countries at a later date. Filing the PCT application usually buys you another 18 months, for a total of 30 months from the first U.S. filing, to decide whether to file individual applications in the designated foreign countries. If you decide at the 30-month date to file in individual foreign countries, you would then "enter the National Phase" of the PCT application, which means that you would file National Phase applications in each country where you decide to pursue foreign protection. Your U.S. patent attorney will be able to assist you by contacting lawyers in other countries who will do the filings for you. At the time of entering the National Phase, you will need to pay for the filing costs for each country you desire, but at least you will have deferred those costs for another 18 months after filing your PCT application. The PCT filing is useful if you are still testing the waters on your product in the United States, and aren't quite sure whether you are going to end up marketing it in other countries.

Many companies are particularly interested in Europe for their foreign patent protection. One mechanism for streamlining foreign prosecution is to take advantage of the European patent system, which allows for the filing of a single European patent covering most of the European countries. This European application can be filed at the one-year anniversary of your U.S. filing, or it can be filed at the National Phase stage of your PCT application. Filing and examination of a European patent application are centralized within the European Patent Office, so when your European patent is granted, you will have receive one European patent good for all of the member European countries. However, you will also need to validate your European patent in the individual countries where you may wish to enforce your patent, which basically means you'll need to pay a fee for each specific European country in which you want protection. Note that if you ever want to enforce your European patent against infringers, you will need to bring legal action in the courts of the individual countries, and not the European Patent Office.

PCT applications, like U.S. applications, publish at about 18 months after the earliest claimed priority date. An example of a PCT publication cover page is shown in Figure 14 .1. This PCT application is for the same invention found in the issued patent of Figure 13.2 and the U.S. publication of Figure 13.1.

The PCT process also offers the advantage of giving you an initial search and examination of your invention, often before the USPTO will get to your application. When you file a PCT application, you can choose from different searching authorities (such as the USPTO, European Patent Office, or Korean Patent Office) to examine your patent application. As the searches are conducted by actual patent examiners, the PCT process can often give you a decent idea of what kind of battle you might have ahead of you. Also, different searching authorities will provide different results. As you might expect, if the USPTO searches your application, it will likely find mostly

FIGURE 14.1 **Cover Page of PCT Application**

The publication date is about, but not exactly, 18 months from the earliest claimed priority date of September 30, 2003.

The international filing date will be within one year of the filing date of any applications to which the PCT application claims priority.

The priority data identifies the prior application to which the PCT application claims priority. In this case, it is a U.S. application, though PCT applications can claim priority to applications filed in other countries as well.

(12) INTERNATIONAL APPLICATION PUBLISHED UNDER THE PATENT COOPERATION TREATY (PCT)

(19) World Intellectual Property Organization
International Bureau

(43) International Publication Date
14 April 2005 (14.04.2005)   PCT

(10) International Publication Number
WO 2005/032436 A2

This is the PCT publication number.

(51) International Patent Classification[7]:   A61F 2/66

(21) International Application Number:
PCT/US2004/031515

(22) International Filing Date:
27 September 2004 (27.09.2004)

(25) Filing Language: English

(26) Publication Language: English

(30) Priority Data:
10/674,736   30 September 2003 (30.09.2003)   US

(71) Applicant (for all designated States except US): ÖSSUR ENGINEERING, INC. [US/US]; 10 Burstein Drive, Albion, MI 49224 (US).

(72) Inventors; and
(75) Inventors/Applicants (for US only): LECOMTE, CHRISTOPHE, GUY [FR/IS]; Snaelandi 7, IS-108 Reykjavik (IS). RAGNARSDOTTIR, Heidrun, Gigja [IS/IS]; Gardastraeti 17, IS-10 Reykjavik (IS).

(54) Title: LOW PROFILE ACTIVE SHOCK MODULE PROSTHESIS

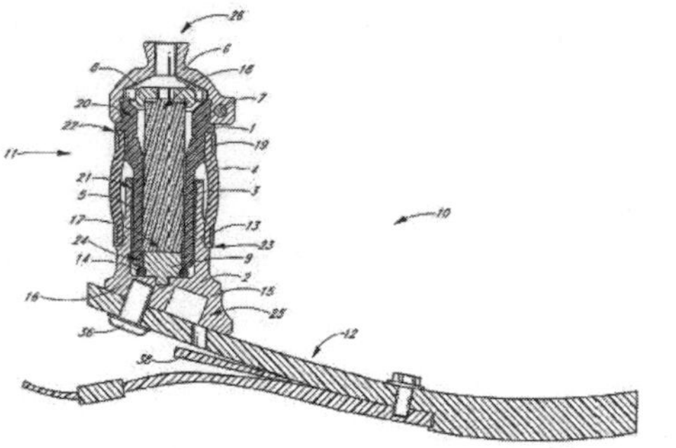

(74) Agent: ALTMAN?, Daniel, E.?; 2040 Main Street, Fourteenth Floor, Irvine, CA 92614 (US).

(81) Designated States (unless otherwise indicated, for every kind of national protection available): AE, AG, AL, AM, AT, AU, AZ, BA, BB, BG, BR, BW, BY, BZ, CA, CH, CN, CO, CR, CU, CZ, DE, DK, DM, DZ, EC, EE, EG, ES, FI, GB, GD, GE, GH, GM, HR, HU, ID, IL, IN, IS, JP, KE, KG, KP, KR, KZ, LC, LK, LR, LS, LT, LU, LV, MA, MD, MG, MK, MN, MW, MX, MZ, NA, NI, NO, NZ, OM, PG, PH, PL, PT, RO, RU, SC, SD, SE, SG, SK, SL, SY, TJ, TM, TN, TR, TT, TZ, UA, UG, US, UZ, VC, VN, YU, ZA, ZM, ZW.

(84) Designated States (unless otherwise indicated, for every kind of regional protection available): ARIPO (BW, GH, GM, KE, LS, MW, MZ, NA, SD, SL, SZ, TZ, UG, ZM, ZW), Eurasian (AM, AZ, BY, KG, KZ, MD, RU, TJ, TM), European (AT, BE, BG, CH, CY, CZ, DE, DK, EE, ES, FI, FR, GB, GR, HU, IE, IT, LU, MC, NL, PL, PT, RO, SE, SI, SK, TR), OAPI (BF, BJ, CF, CG, CI, CM, GA, GN, GQ, GW, ML, MR, NE, SN, TD, TG).

Declaration under Rule 4.17:
— of inventorship (Rule 4.17(iv)) for US only

[Continued on next page]

These are the country codes for all of the countries where the PCT application can be later filed.

(57) Abstract: In one embodiment, an impact and torque-absorbing module 11 for a low profile lower limb prosthesis 10 comprises two support members 1 and 2 telescopingly engaged to permit axial and rotational motion therebetween. A resilient element 3 resists axial displacement of the two support members 1 and 2, and a torque resisting cuff 4 resists rotational displacement of the two support members 1 and 2. Precompression of the resilient element 3 can reduce the size of the shock module 11 making it more compact. The resilient element 3 can also be replaced allowing adjustment of the shock absorption.

WO 2005/032436 A2

Strategy Tip Choosing the European Patent Office for PCT examination gives you the opportunity to get a second search of prior art, in addition to the U.S. search that will be done by the patent examiner during prosecution of your U.S. patent application. This can be an advantage—to try to identify more prior art that might be relevant to your application. That way, if you sue competitors in the future for infringing your patent, it would be less likely that your competitors would find prior art to invalidate your patent as a way of defeating your lawsuit. On the other hand, choosing Europe for the searching authority is more expensive (about $1,000 more), although those costs may be reimbursed to you if you ultimately do National Phase filings in Europe.

U.S. references. A European Patent Office search will often turn up U.S. and international publications.

As discussed in Chapter 10, to preserve most foreign patent rights, the U.S. application must be filed before any nonconfidential disclosure or offer for sale of the invention. Then as long as a foreign application, such as PCT application, is filed within one year of the filing of the U.S. application, foreign patent rights will be preserved. Because of the delay offered by the PCT

Warning! Obtaining foreign patents is expensive! A PCT filing may cost you around $5,000 but it does not give you foreign patent protection— it gives you 30 months from your earliest filing date to decide whether you want to spend your money on foreign patent filings. If you decide to do foreign patent filings, the filing in each country might cost you anywhere from a few thousand dollars to $10,000 or more, just for filing. This does not include foreign prosecution costs (the fees of your foreign attorney and the filing fees), grant fees, translation fees, validation fees (for Europe), and patent annuities (the cost to maintain a patent every year in the foreign country).

application process and because of the amount of time it may take for your individual foreign patents to get examined, it could be five, six, seven years or more from your U.S. filing date before your foreign patents will issue. While this may help defer costs, keep in mind that the term of your foreign patents will be measured from the earliest international filing date, such as the PCT filing date. Thus, by the time your foreign patents issue, you may have only a few years of patent protection left (which means that you will be able to prevent others from infringing your foreign patents for just a short period of time).

CHAPTER 15

Once Your Patent Issues

The day finally arrives when you receive your patent. Your company issues a press release, you go out to celebrate, you might even be ready to sue one of your competitors. But even though your patent has issued, you still need to watch out for a few things, like marking, correcting errors in your patent, and knowing how long your patent will last. You wouldn't want to have gone through all that trouble to get a patent only to forget something important afterwards.

Marking a Product with the Patent Number

> Mark your patented products with your patent number in order to collect damages against possible infringers.

Once your patent issues, you have the ability to enforce your patent against possible infringers. Ways to enforce your patent are described in Chapter 29. One decision you'll need to make is whether you want to mark your patent number on your product. A product is typically marked with a patent notice such as "Patent 5,000,000" or "Pat. 5,000,000" when the product, or the method used to produce the product, is patented. As discussed in Chapter 10, the term "Patent Pending" means a patent has been applied for, but has not yet issued.

You don't need to mark our patent number on your products to enforce your patent. However, to collect damages against an infringer, you may need to give the infringer notice of the issued patent. One way to give notice is by providing the infringer with actual notice of the infringement (for example, by sending a letter telling the infringer about your patent). The other way is to mark your products with the patent notice provided above.

The law on patent marking requires you to place the marking directly on the patented product itself. Sometimes your product is so small that it's difficult to place a label or inscription directly on your product. If that's the case, you can put a label on the packaging of the product, rather than the product itself. The patent law is not entirely clear as to whether other types of notice, such as a loose leaflet in a package or a web site notice, are sufficient marking for the purposes of preserving your right to collect damages. Although you may also provide patent notices on these types of materials, it's always best, where possible, to mark the product directly or at least its packaging.

Errors in an Issued Patent

There are a few ways to correct errors in issued patents. For minor typographical errors, either made by the patentee or by the USPTO, a Certificate of Correction may be filed to correct the errors. If the mistake is your own, you'll have to pay a fee (currently $100). If it's the USPTO's mistake, then there is no charge for filing the Certificate of Correction.

> **Warning!** Be careful when marking patent numbers, or even Patent Pending, on your products. False marking, such as marking an unpatented product, can carry with it penalties of up to $500 per offense.

More significant errors can be cured by filing a reissue application, which reopens prosecution of the patent application in order to have the error corrected. Errors to be corrected by reissue include instances where:

- The claims are too narrow or too broad.
- The specification contains inaccuracies.
- The applicant failed to claim or incorrectly claimed foreign priority.
- The applicant failed to make or incorrectly made reference to other applications that were pending at the same time.

Because filing a reissue application reopens prosecution of the application, you run the risk that the examiner (who could be the same or a different examiner) will reject your application on some other grounds not addressed in the previous prosecution. Prosecution of a reissue application is much like prosecution of a regular patent application (discussed in Chapter 12). You may receive one or more office actions from the examiner and will have the opportunity to respond to an examiner's rejections. If the USPTO corrects the error and re-allows the application, a new patent will issue and be given a reissue number, for example, Re. 39,089, shown in Figure 15.1. Any language added to your original patent in the reissue patent will be shown in *italics*, and any language deleted will be shown [in brackets]. Figure 15.2 shows, for example, the limitations added and deleted from some of the claims of the reissue patent.

> **Warning!** Be sure to review your issued patent carefully for errors. Sometimes the USPTO will make printing errors in transcribing the patent application to the issued patent, and you'll need to file a Certificate of Correction to fix these errors.

FIGURE 15-1 **Cover Page of a Reissue Patent**

The "RE" tells you this is a reissue patent.

The original patent, now surrendered, is shown here. ➡

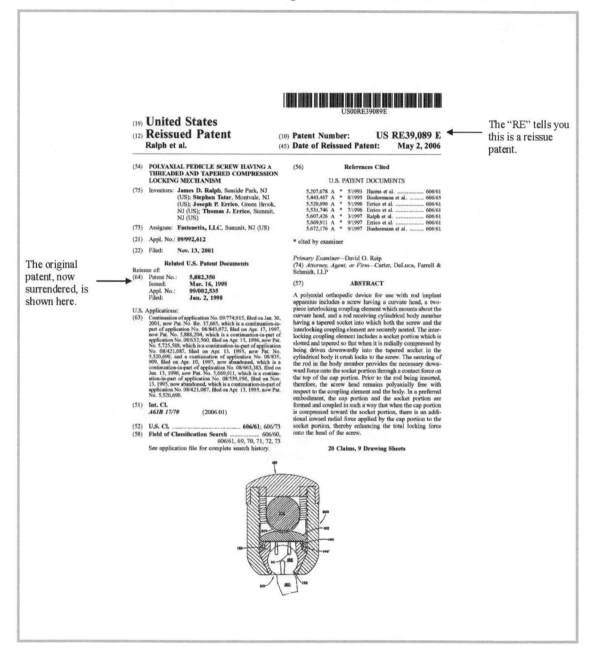

FIGURE 15-2 **Claims of Reissue Patent, Showing Claims Deleted and Claims Added**

US RE39,089 E

11

portion of the axial bore, and locks the screw, coupling element and body relative to one another.]

[8. The apparatus as set forth in claim 7, wherein said threading on said top end is on the interior surface of said channel.]

[9. The apparatus as set forth in claim 8, wherein said cap portion further includes a threading and wherein said cap portion needs to be threadably advanced along the threading to be seated in the bore into its initial position.]

[10. The apparatus as set forth in claim 7,

wherein said socket portion further comprises a substantially constant diameter upper section having an outwardly annular extending lip at an extreme end thereof,

wherein said opening in the bottom of the cap portion comprises an inwardly directly annular lip, and

wherein at least one of said vertical slots in the upper section of said socket portion renders the upper section thereof to be expandable and contractable such that the upper section of the socket portion may be forceably inserted into the opening in the bottom of the cap portion so that it may be retained in the interior chamber therein by mutual interference engagement of the inwardly directed annular lip of the cap portion and the outwardly extending annular lip of the socket portion.]

[11. The apparatus as set forth in claim 10, wherein the interior chamber of the cap portion comprises a tapered surface such that advancement thereof into the socket portion causes an inwardly directed force against the upper section of the socket portion, therein causing the at least one of said vertical slots in the upper section to narrow and causes the upper section to contract and further lock the head of the screw within the interior semi-spherical volume of the socket portion.]

12. An orthopedic device for securing immobilizing structures to sequences of bone, comprising:

a screw having a semi-spherical head and a threaded shaft;

a coupling element having an axial hole extending therethrough, a portion of the axial hole defining an interior volume for receiving therein the semi-spherical head of the screw that the threaded shaft may be moved through a variety of angles relative to the axial hole, the coupling element further including at least one slot rendering at least the interior volume deformable, the coupling element further including a tapered exterior surface, the coupling element further comprising a two-part interlocking coupling element including:

a socket portion containing the interior volume, the interior volume being semi-spherical shaped, the socket portion further including upper and lower sections, and at least one vertical slot formed in each of the upper and lower sections, at least one of the slots rendering the interior volume deformable, the lower section having the tapered exterior surface; and

a cap portion having an opening in a bottom thereof and an interior chamber extending upwardly therefrom for joining with, and slideably retaining therein, the upper section of the socket portion;

a receiving member including a through hole having an interior wall surface, a portion of the interior wall surface of the through hole being shaped to receive the coupling element and the screw when the semi-spherical head of the screw is mounted within the coupling element; and

wherein advancement of the screw through the through hole relative to the receiving member when the exterior

12

surface of the coupling element engages the interior wall surface of the through hole prevents the coupling element from further advancement through the hole, preventing the semi-spherical head of the screw from advancing further through the through hole, and causing locking of the screw relative to both the coupling element and to the receiving member thereby locking the angle of the screw relative to the axial hole.

13. The assembly as set forth in claim 12 wherein the semi-spherical head of the screw further includes a recess formed therein for receiving therein a screwdriving tool such that the screw may be advanced into a vertebral bone.

14. The assembly as set forth in claim 12, wherein the cap portion further includes a threading.

15. An orthopedic implant apparatus comprising:

a fixation element having a semi-spherical head and a shaft extending therefrom;

a receiving member including an axial bore defined by an interior surface wall, a portion of the axial bore having a tapered portion;

a socket portion having a semi-spherical interior volume for receiving therein the semi-spherical head, and an exterior surface capable of nesting against the interior surface wall of the tapered portion, the socket portion being located in the axial bore of the receiving member, the socket portion further including:

upper and lower socket sections, and at least one vertical slot formed in at least one of the upper or lower sections, the at least one slot rendering the spherical interior volume deformable, where he exterior surface of the socket portion is tapered and located on the lower section; and

a cap portion having an opening in a bottom hereof and an interior chamber extending upwardly therefrom for joining with, and slideably retaining therein, the upper socket portion;

wherein the semi-spherical head is rotationally freely mounted within the semi-spherical interior volume of the socket portion prior to the socket portion being forcibly advanced against the interior surface wall of the tapered portion, and whereby after forcible advancement of the socket portion causes the fixation element, the socket portion and the receiving member to be locked relative to one another.

16. The assembly as set forth in claim 15 wherein the semi-spherical head of the fixation element further includes a recess formed therein for receiving therein a screwdriving tool such that the fixation element may be advanced into a vertebral bone.

17. The assembly as set forth in claim 15 wherein the cap portion further includes a threading.

18. An orthopedic implant apparatus comprising:

a fixation element having a semi-spherical head, having a lower and upper curvate surface, and a threaded shaft extending from the semi-spherical head;

a receiving member including an axial bore defined by an interior surface wall, the axial bore having a lower portion and an upper threaded portion;

a socket portion containing the semi-spherical head of the fixation element therein and having a lower socket portion and a threaded upper socket portion, the socket portion being moveably located in the axial bore;

wherein the lower socket portion has an interior volume defined by an interior surface which receives the lower curvate surface of the semi-spherical head, such that the threaded shaft is inserted through a hole in the

> **Strategy Tip** One particular type of error that can be corrected by a reissue application is the error that the claims are too narrow. A claim that you deem to be too narrow in and of itself qualifies as an error suitable for reissue. This type of reissue is known as a broadening reissue, and is filed to attempt to broaden the scope of the claims of the already issued patent. A broadening reissue application must be filed within two years of the issuance of the patent, or else it will be too late.

If your reissue application is allowed and issued, the original patent will be surrendered and no longer be in force. Therefore, the original patent of Re.39,089 shown in Figure 15.1, U.S. Patent No. 5,882,350, will no longer be in force. If you decide to abandon your reissue application during prosecution, your original patent will continue to be in force.

A Reexamination

Sometimes after your patent has issued, you find a new piece of prior art that you wish the examiner had considered. Or you might find that your competitor received a patent that you think it shouldn't have because of some piece of prior art that you know about. In either case, one option you might consider is filing for reexamination of the patent.

> **You Should Know** Reexaminations can only be requested based on prior patents or printed publications. Therefore, if you believe that a competitor's patent should be invalidated because he sold his product more than a year before he filed for the patent, this would not be a ground for reexamination. However, if you ever were involved in litigation with this competitor, you could attempt to invalidate the patent in court based on the prior art that you found.

A reexamination gives you the opportunity to send to the USPTO prior art patents or printed publications that you believe impact the patentability of either your own patent or your competitor's patent. If the USPTO agrees that the prior art that you send it raises "a substantial new question of patentability," it will reopen prosecution and reexamine the patent application. Thus, in a reexamination the claims that were previously issued could be amended, canceled, or even be reaffirmed as still being patentable.

There are two options for reexamining a patent: *ex parte* reexamination and *inter partes* reexamination. In an ex parte reexamination, the requestor of the reexamination, who may be the patent holder himself or a third party, asks the USPTO to conduct the reexamination based on the prior art patents or printed publications sent to the USPTO. If the requestor of the reexamination is a third party, the requestor will not participate in the reexamination after filing the request for examination. The USPTO will consider the information it receives and conduct the reexamination with only the patent holder himself. A reexamination is conducted like prosecution for a regular utility patent application. At the end of the reexamination, a reexamination certificate will be issued. Figure 15.3, for example, shows a reexamination certificate where all of the claims were confirmed to be patentable. The reexamination certificate becomes part of the issued patent and can normally be found with the issued patent in the USPTO records.

> **Warning!** Reexamination can be an expensive process. The filing fee for an *ex parte* reexamination is currently $2,520, and for an *inter partes* reexamination it's $8,800. This doesn't even include attorneys fees or other costs that will be incurred during the prosecution of the reexamination. If you find a competitor's patent that you think is invalid, sometimes it's better to wait to see if you get sued on the patent, and if you do, raise your arguments that the patent is invalid in court. This also reduces the risk that you might make the competitor's patent even stronger if it survives the reexamination process with the patentability of all of the claims confirmed.

FIGURE 15.3 **Sample Pages of a Reexamination Certificate**

US004828483B1

REEXAMINATION CERTIFICATE (2249th)

United States Patent [19]

Finke

[11] **B1 4,828,483**

[45] Certificate Issued **Mar. 22, 1994**

[54] **METHOD AND APPARATUS FOR SUPPRESSING NOX FORMATION IN REGENERATIVE BURNERS**

[75] Inventor: Harry P. Finke, Pittsburgh, Pa.

[73] Assignee: Bloom Engineering Company, Inc., Pittsburgh, Pa.

Reexamination Request:
No. 90/002,830, Sep. 4, 1992

Reexamination Certificate for:

Patent No.:	4,828,483
Issued:	May 9, 1989
Appl. No.:	198,739
Filed:	May 25, 1988

[51] Int. Cl.⁵ F23D 11/44; F23L 15/00; F27D 17/00

[52] U.S. Cl. 431/11; 431/181; 431/215; 432/28; 432/180

[58] Field of Search 110/204, 205, 206, 207; 202/139, 141, 142, 151; 431/11, 5, 207, 328, 181, 215; 165/4; 432/28, 181, 182, 180

[56] **References Cited**

U.S. PATENT DOCUMENTS

1,492,674	5/1924	Chapman .	
1,814,567	7/1931	Merkt .	
2,110,209	3/1938	Engels	158/1
2,188,133	1/1940	Hepburn	126/91
2,285,036	6/1942	Kneass, Jr.	263/43
2,346,991	4/1944	Otto	202/142
2,512,326	6/1950	Harrison	263/19
2,863,807	12/1958	Van Ackeren	202/142
3,146,821	9/1964	Wuetig	158/1
3,186,694	6/1965	Beggs	263/3
3,581,679	6/1971	Jansen et al.	107/63
3,760,776	9/1973	Durrant	122/459
3,801,267	4/1974	Okuno et al.	432/171
3,839,156	10/1974	Jakobi et al.	202/139 X
3,880,570	4/1975	Marshall	431/4
3,920,382	11/1975	Hovis et al.	432/209
3,957,418	5/1976	Sata	431/9
3,994,665	11/1976	Young	431/116
4,004,875	1/1977	Zink et al.	431/9
4,030,874	6/1977	Vollerin	431/9

4,077,761	3/1978	Dollinger et al.	431/8
4,100,741	7/1978	Michels	60/517
4,135,874	1/1979	Tsuzi et al.	431/115
4,218,211	8/1980	Caplan	432/219
4,338,074	7/1982	Johansson	431/6
4,355,973	10/1982	Bailey	432/54
4,357,134	11/1982	Katsushige et al.	431/9
4,424,754	1/1984	Coleman et al.	110/190
4,439,137	3/1984	Suzuki et al.	431/8
4,445,843	5/1984	Nutcher	431/115
4,453,913	6/1984	Gitman	431/8
4,467,779	8/1984	Kreinin et al.	126/91
4,493,309	1/1985	Wedge et al.	126/91
4,496,306	1/1985	Okigami et al.	431/8
4,515,553	5/1985	Morimoto et al.	431/8
4,522,588	6/1985	Todd et al.	432/131
4,531,904	7/1985	Sato et al.	431/10
4,585,161	4/1986	Kusama et al.	236/15
4,588,372	5/1986	Torborg	431/78
4,601,655	7/1986	Riley et al.	431/116
4,604,051	8/1986	Davies et al.	126/91 A X
4,619,604	10/1986	Pickering	431/353
4,631,022	12/1986	Ferri et al.	431/90
4,645,450	2/1987	West	431/12
4,659,305	4/1987	Nelson et al.	431/9
4,673,348	6/1987	Riley et al.	431/115

(List continued on next page.)

FOREIGN PATENT DOCUMENTS

0141594 5/1985 European Pat. Off. .

(List continued on next page.)

Primary Examiner—Carl D. Price

[57] **ABSTRACT**

A method and apparatus for repressing NOx formation in twinned regenerative burner pairs includes inducing a stream of hot flue gas, preferably containing enriched products of combustion, from the main hot flue gas exhaust stream and vitiating the preheated combustion air with the hot flue gas in the firing burner. An interconnecting duct communicating with the twinned burner pair includes a coaxial gas nozzle for injecting a high kinetic energy gas stream into the exhausting hot flue gas to induce a portion of the hot flue gas into the interconnecting duct to pass the hot flue gas to the firing burner for vitiation purposes.

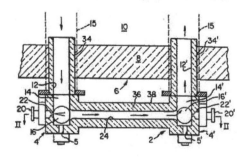

FIGURE 15.3 **Sample Pages of a Reexamination Certificate, cont.**

B1 4,828,483

1

REEXAMINATION CERTIFICATE
ISSUED UNDER 35 U.S.C. 307

THE PATENT IS HEREBY AMENDED AS INDICATED BELOW.

Matter enclosed in heavy brackets [ ] appeared in the patent, but has been deleted and is no longer a part of the patent; matter printed in italics indicates additions made to the patent.

AS A RESULT OF REEXAMINATION, IT HAS BEEN DETERMINED THAT:

Claims 1, 3–12 and 14–19 are cancelled.

Claims 2 and 13 are determined to be patentable as amended.

New claims 20–28 are added and determined to be patentable.

2. A method of repressing NOx formation in a twinned pair of regenerative burners *communicating with a radiant tube extending into and exiting from a furnace and* of the type having heat regeneration beds associated therewith for alternately withdrawing heat from a flue gas exiting [a furnace] *the radiant tube* and heating a combustion air stream being fed therethrough, comprising the steps of:
  withdrawing a stream of hot flue gas from the [furnace] *radiant tube;*
  injecting a stream of gas *separate from the combustion air stream* into said flue gas stream;
  entraining a portion of said hot flue gas within said injected gas stream;
  passing said stream of injected gas and said entrained portion of hot flue gas to a burner chamber; and
  vitiating a combustion process in said burner chamber with said portion of hot flue gas whereby NOx formation is repressed.
13. An improved regenerative burner apparatus of the type comprising a pair of first and second spaced-apart burners, each of said burners comprising a chamber for mixing a fuel and a stream of preheated combustion air supplied from a regenerative heat storage bed associated with each of said burners, said burners adapted to operate cyclically wherein a first of said burners is in a firing mode directing hot gases into a furnace interior while a flue gas stream exits the furnace and passes through the second burner chamber and then passes to the regenerative heat storage bed associated therewith said second burner, wherein the improvement comprises[.]:
  a radiant tube extending into the furnace interior and communicating with each of the first and second burners;
  an interconnecting duct communicating with the chambers of said first and second burners; and
  nozzle means adapted to inject a gas stream *separate from the combustion air stream* for inducing a flow of a portion of the hot flue gas exiting the [furnace] *radiant tube* into said interconnecting duct to enter the burner in the firing mode to vitiate the combustion air therein, whereby NOx formation *within the radiant tube* is repressed.

20. A method of repressing NOx formation in a twinned pair of regenerative burners of the type having heat regeneration beds associated therewith for alternately withdrawing heat from a flue gas existing a furnace and heating a combustion air stream being fed therethrough, comprising the steps of:
  withdrawing a stream of hot flue gas from the furnace;
  injecting a stream of gas into said flue gas stream;
  aligning the injected gas stream in a tangential direction relative to said hot flue gas stream whereby a swirling motion is imparted to the flue gas to create an enriched layer of products of combustion in said hot flue gas for entraining a portion of said hot flue gas within said injected gas stream;
  passing said stream of injected gas and said entrained portion of hot flue gas to a burner chamber; and
  vitiating a combustion process in said burner chamber with said portion of hot flue gas whereby NOx formation is repressed.
21. A method of repressing NOx formation in a twinned pair of regenerative burners of the type having heat regeneration beds associated therewith for alternately withdrawing heat from a flue gas exiting a furnace and heating a combustion air stream being fed therethrough, comprising the steps of:
  withdrawing a stream of hot flue gas from the furnace;
  injecting a stream of gas into said flue gas stream, wherein the injected gas stream is flue gas containing products of combustion;
  entraining a portion of said hot flue gas within said injected gas stream;
  passing said stream of injected gas and said entrained portion of hot flue gas to a burner chamber; and
  vitiating a combustion process in said burner chamber with said portion of hot flue gas whereby NOx formation is repressed.
22. A method of operating a heat regenerative burner pair operably connected to a furnace, comprising the steps of:
  (a) withdrawing a stream of hot flue gas from the furnace;
  (b) inducing a portion of the hot flue gas to flow to a first of said burner pair when said first burner is in a firing mode, said inducing step comprising injecting a high velocity gas stream tangentially into said hot flue gas stream whereby said injected stream possesses sufficient kinetic energy to flow to said firing burner;
  (c) flowing a balance of said hot flue gas through a first regenerative bed associated with the second of said burner pair when said second burner is in an exhaust mode;
  (d) preheating a combustion air stream in a second regenerative bed associated with said first burner;
  (e) vitiating said preheated combustion air with said portion of said induced portion of hot flue gas in said first burner;
  (f) whereby upon introduction of a fuel, a resulting combustion process taking place contains a repressed NOx level; and
  cycling said process steps of (a)-(f) to said second burner wherein said second burner is in a firing mode and said first burner is in an exhaust mode.
23. The method of claim 22 wherein the injected high velocity gas stream is one selected from the group consisting of air, flue gas, gaseous fuel and mixtures of two or more thereof.
24. The method of claim 22 wherein the injected high velocity gas stream is flue gas.

An *inter partes* reexamination is where both the requestor of the reexamination and the patent holder have the opportunity to file documents before the USPTO. This is the only proceeding available before the USPTO where a third party might be able to invalidate a patent (although patents can be invalidated in court, as discussed in Chapters 29 and 30). The USPTO will receive documents filed by both sides and decide, based on these filings, whether the patent claims should remain as is, be amended, or be canceled. As with the *ex parte* reexamination, a reexamination certificate will issue indicating any changes versus the original patent.

Patent Term

An old English proverb states "All good things must come to an end," which is certainly true for patents. As a general rule, utility and plant patents last 20 years from filing, while design patents last 14 years from issuance. Once the patent expires, the invention is placed into the "public domain." This means that when a patent expires, the public is free to make, use, sell, and offer for sale the claimed invention. However, determining the specific term of a patent, especially a utility patent, is not always an easy calculation to make. Unfortunately, a utility patent does not show on its cover when the patent will expire. Complicating factors that can alter the term of a patent are when the patent was filed, whether the patent is related to other applications, whether the USPTO unreasonably delayed in examining or issuing the patent, and whether all patent maintenance fees have been paid. A few of these factors are explained in more detail below:

Did You Know? The amount of time that a patent lasts, known as its patent term, is different for utility patents and design patents. A utility patent's term is usually calculated as 20 years from filing, whereas a design patent's term is 14 years from issuance.

FIGURE 15.4 **Example of Utility Patent Expiring 20 Years from Filing**

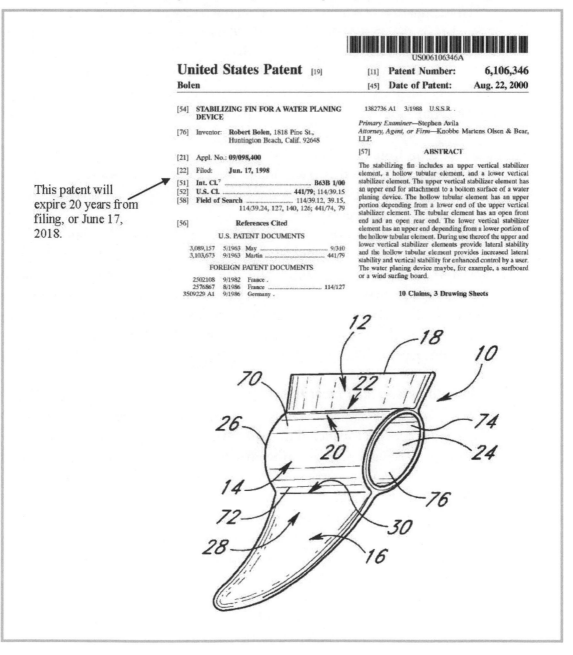

This patent will expire 20 years from filing, or June 17, 2018.

United States Patent [19]

Bolen

[11] **Patent Number:** **6,106,346**

[45] **Date of Patent:** **Aug. 22, 2000**

US006106346A

[54] **STABILIZING FIN FOR A WATER PLANING DEVICE**

[76] Inventor: **Robert Bolen**, 1818 Pine St., Huntington Beach, Calif. 92648

[21] Appl. No.: **09/098,400**

[22] Filed: **Jun. 17, 1998**

[51] Int. Cl.⁷ **B63B 1/00**

[52] U.S. Cl. **441/79; 114/39.15**

[58] Field of Search 114/39.12, 39.15, 114/39.24, 127, 140, 126; 441/74, 79

[56] **References Cited**

U.S. PATENT DOCUMENTS

3,089,157 5/1963 May 9/310
3,103,673 9/1963 Martin 441/79

FOREIGN PATENT DOCUMENTS

2502108 9/1982 France .
2576867 8/1986 France 114/127
3509229 A1 9/1986 Germany .

1382736 A1 3/1988 U.S.S.R .

Primary Examiner—Stephen Avila
Attorney, Agent, or Firm—Knobbe Martens Olsen & Bear, LLP.

[57] **ABSTRACT**

The stabilizing fin includes an upper vertical stabilizer element, a hollow tubular element, and a lower vertical stabilizer element. The upper vertical stabilizer element has an upper end for attachment to a bottom surface of a water planing device. The hollow tubular element has an upper portion depending from a lower end of the upper vertical stabilizer element. The tubular element has an open front end and an open rear end. The lower vertical stabilizer element has an upper end depending from a lower portion of the hollow tubular element. During use thereof the upper and lower vertical stabilizer elements provide lateral stability and the hollow tubular element provides increased lateral stability and vertical stability for enhanced control by a user. The water planing device maybe, for example, a surfboard or a wind surfing board.

10 Claims, 3 Drawing Sheets

Measuring Terms

In the simplest case, a utility patent's term can be calculated by looking for the filing date on the cover of the patent, and adding 20 years. In Figure 15.4, the patent shown was filed on June 17, 1998, and therefore, will expire on June 17, 2018.

But as discussed in Chapter 13, many patents claim priority to earlier filed applications. In those cases, the 20-year term is measured from the earliest claimed nonprovisional priority date. So for the patent shown in Figure 15.5, you will need to find the earliest claimed filing date, and calculate the patent term from that date. The patent shown will expire 20 years from January 19, 2000. Note that even though the patent claims priority to a provisional application, the filing of the provisional application does not count against the 20-year term.

For older patents, that is, those filed before June 8, 1995, patent term calculations are even more complicated. Prior to June 8, 1995, all patents had a term of 17 years from issuance. The 20-year term came into effect June 8, 1995, but with that change, any patents already filed received the longer of the 17 years from issuance or 20 years from earliest claimed priority date. So in Figure 15.6, this patent will expire on January 26, 2010, whereas in Figure 15.7, this patent will expire on February 28, 2011.

Ways to Extend the Patent Term

Some patents can have their terms extended beyond the normal 20-year term if, for example, the issuance of the patent was delayed due to interference proceedings, a secrecy order (e.g., when patent issuance is withheld for reasons of national security), or successful appellate review (e.g., if you have to appeal a rejection of your application to the federal courts and you win the appeal). The USPTO also has procedures where, if the USPTO itself delayed excessively in sending you an office action or issuing the patent, the term can be extended. For example, you may be entitled to a patent term adjustment if the USPTO took more than three years from filing to issue your patent, or more than 14 months to send you an office action. Generally, for every day of USPTO delay, you can get one additional day of patent term. However, you will lose these extra days for every day that you yourself delayed in taking

FIGURE 15.5 **Example of Utility Patent Claiming Multiple Priorities (Including to a Provisional)**

US006644711B2

(12) **United States Patent**
Leitner et al.

(10) **Patent No.:** US 6,644,711 B2
(45) **Date of Patent:** Nov. 11, 2003

(54) **VEHICLE BED STORAGE BOX**

(75) Inventors: **Horst Leitner**, Laguna Beach, CA (US); **Jonathan E. Weisel**, Norco, CA (US)

(73) Assignee: **American Moto Products, Inc.**, Irvine, CA (US)

(*) Notice: Subject to any disclaimer, the term of this patent is extended or adjusted under 35 U.S.C. 154(b) by 0 days.

(21) Appl. No.: **10/282,954**

(22) Filed: **Oct. 28, 2002**

(65) **Prior Publication Data**

US 2003/0098591 A1 May 29, 2003

Related U.S. Application Data

(63) Continuation of application No. 09/846,577, filed on May 1, 2001, now Pat. No. 6,471,278, which is a continuation of application No. 09/488,207, filed on Jan. 19, 2000, now Pat. No. 6,257,640.

(60) Provisional application No. 60/117,098, filed on Jan. 25, 1999.

(51) Int. Cl.[7] B60N 3/12
(52) U.S. Cl. 296/37.6; 296/37.5; 224/404
(58) Field of Search 296/37.6, 37.5, 296/57.1, 180.1; 224/404, 402, 403, 543

(56) **References Cited**

U.S. PATENT DOCUMENTS

1,764,615 A	6/1930	Edwards	
4,451,075 A	5/1984	Canfield	
4,635,992 A	1/1987	Hamilton et al.	
4,749,226 A	6/1988	Heft	
4,750,773 A	6/1988	Chapline et al.	
4,789,195 A *	12/1988	Fletcher	296/37.6
4,828,312 A	5/1989	Kinkel et al.	
5,037,153 A	8/1991	Stark	
5,169,200 A	12/1992	Pugh	
5,201,561 A	4/1993	Brown	
5,722,714 A	3/1998	Vallerand	
5,736,567 A	4/1998	Mora, Sr.	
5,743,589 A	4/1998	Felker	
5,853,116 A	12/1998	Schreiner	
5,961,173 A	10/1999	Repetti	
6,305,730 B1 *	10/2001	Stone	296/37.6
6,543,829 B2 *	4/2003	Brown	296/37.6

* cited by examiner

Primary Examiner—Joseph D. Pape
(74) *Attorney, Agent, or Firm*—Knobbe Martens Olson & Bear, LLP

(57) **ABSTRACT**

A collapsible storage device includes a first panel and a second panel, with one end of the first panel rotatably secured to one wall of a vehicle bed. One end of the second panel is rotatably secured to the opposite end of the first panel. The device has a deployed or storage position in which the first panel is generally horizontal and the second panel is generally vertical so that the two panels, in cooperation with the existing walls of the bed, form an enclosed container. The device also has a folded position in which the second panel is folded against the first panel, and the first panel together with the second is folded against a wall of the vehicle bed. The collapsible storage device has means for locking the device in the deployed and/or the folded position. Alternatively, the device may have means for locking the two panels together during deployment and/or retraction, or the device may be interposed between two storage bins along a wall of the vehicle bed. A track or tracks may be provided on one or both sides of the storage device to coact with a track follower on one or both sides of the second panel to provide easier collapse or deployment of the device.

15 Claims, 21 Drawing Sheets

This patent will expire 20 years from the first non-provisional filing date, or January 19, 2020. The provisional application does not count against the 20 year term.

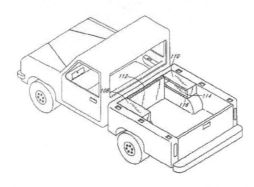

FIGURE 15.6 **Example of Utility Patent Filed before June 8, 1995 Expiring 17 Years from Issuance.**

This patent was filed before June 8, 1995, so it gets the longer of 20 years from filing or 17 years from issuance. 20 years from filing in this case is April 13, 2009. Note that if the patent claimed priority to earlier-filed non-provisional applications, the 20 year term would be measured from the filing date of the earliest -filed non-provisional application.

17 years from issuance in this case is January 26, 2010, longer than 20 years from filing. Therefore, the patent will expire on January 26, 2010.

US005181932A

United States Patent [19]

Phillips

[11] Patent Number: **5,181,932**

[45] Date of Patent: **Jan. 26, 1993**

[54] FOOT PROSTHESIS HAVING AUXILIARY ANKLE CONSTRUCTION

[76] Inventor: Van L. Phillips, 4702 San Jacinto Ter., Fallbrook, Calif. 92028

[21] Appl. No.: 337,374

[22] Filed: Apr. 13, 1989

[51] Int. Cl.⁵ A61F 2/66
[52] U.S. Cl. 623/52; 623/55
[58] Field of Search 623/47–56

[56] References Cited
U.S. PATENT DOCUMENTS

809,875	1/1906	Wilkins	623/49
817,340	4/1906	Rosenkranz	623/49
2,075,583	3/1937	Lange .	
3,335,428	8/1967	Gajdos .	
3,699,554	1/1955	Comelli	623/49
3,707,731	1/1973	Morgan	623/49 X
3,754,286	8/1973	Ryan	623/55
3,833,941	9/1974	Wagner .	
3,874,004	4/1975	May .	
3,890,650	6/1975	Prahl .	
4,091,472	5/1978	Daher et al. .	
4,177,525	12/1979	Arbogast et al. .	
4,180,872	1/1980	Chaikin .	
4,225,982	10/1980	Cochrane et al. .	
4,302,856	12/1981	May .	
4,306,320	12/1981	Delp .	
4,328,594	5/1982	Campbell et al. .	
4,360,931	11/1982	Hampton .	
4,370,761	2/1983	Serri	623/47 X
4,547,913	10/1985	Phillips	623/27
4,636,220	1/1987	Ziegelmeyer	623/53
4,645,509	2/1987	Poggi et al.	623/55
4,721,510	1/1988	Cooper et al.	623/55

4,792,340	12/1988	Autie et al.	623/49
4,822,363	4/1989	Phillips	623/27
4,865,612	9/1989	Arbogast et al.	623/55
4,938,776	7/1990	Masinter	623/49
4,959,073	9/1990	Merlette	623/55

FOREIGN PATENT DOCUMENTS

0308671	10/1918	Fed. Rep. of Germany	623/55
1179328	10/1964	Fed. Rep. of Germany	623/51
1211354	2/1966	Fed. Rep. of Germany	623/49
0800547	7/1936	France	623/55
2626463	8/1989	France	623/53
0621576	4/1949	United Kingdom	623/55
2202448	9/1988	United Kingdom	623/53

Primary Examiner—Randall L. Green
Assistant Examiner—D. Willse
Attorney, Agent, or Firm—Knobbe, Martens, Olson & Bear

[57] **ABSTRACT**

A prosthetic foot characterized by a foot portion having an ankle portion demountably and interchangeably connected thereto. The foot portion and ankle portion are fabricated from polymer impregnated and encapsulated laminates, including such laminates as carbon fibers and/or fiberglass or synthetic fibers such as Kevlar. The demountable connection of the ankle portion permits interchangeability of ankle and foot portions to match the weight, stride and activity schedule of the wearer utilizing the prosthetic foot. Auxiliary ankle members and wedge blocks between the foot portion and the ankle portion provide additional adjustability. A split sleeve is provided for assembling the various components.

19 Claims, 4 Drawing Sheets

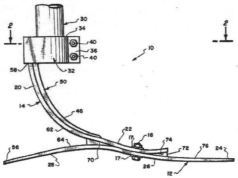

FIGURE 15.7 **Example of Utility Patent Filed before June 8, 1995**
Expiring 20 Years from Filing

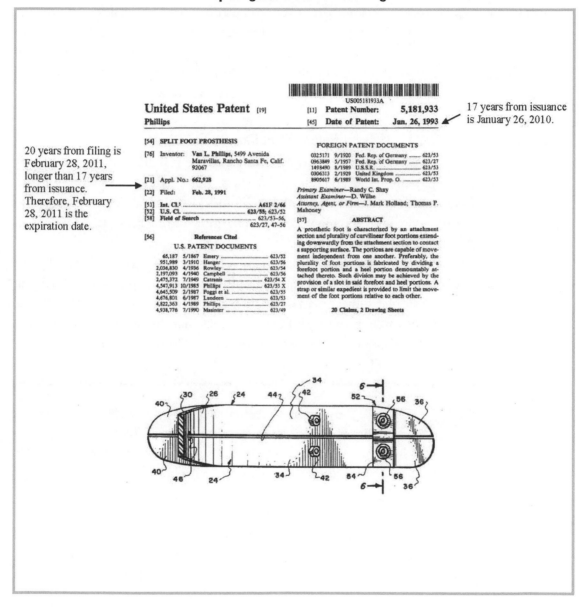

20 years from filing is February 28, 2011, longer than 17 years from issuance. Therefore, February 28, 2011 is the expiration date.

17 years from issuance is January 26, 2010.

In some industries, like that for prescription drugs, even a patent term extension of a few days can mean millions of dollars in additional profits.

certain actions before the USPTO, such as by waiting more than three months to respond to an office action.

The patent term adjustment will normally show on the cover of the patent. Figure 15.8 shows a patent that receives 393 days of patent term adjustment. Therefore, instead of expiring on July 1, 2023 (20 years from filing), this patent will expire 393 days later on July 28, 2024.

Ways a Patent Term Can Be Cut Short

A patentee is only entitled to the full 20-year term if it continues to pay the required maintenance fees. For a patent to remain in force, maintenance fees must be paid at 3½, 7½ and 11½ years (each extendable by six months through payment of a surcharge). These fees are specified in Appendix B.

Patent term can also be cut short by a "terminal disclaimer" filed by the patent holder. Sometimes a patent applicant may file two applications claiming the same or similar subject matter. Because an applicant is only entitled to one patent per invention, if the USPTO determines that the inventions claimed in the two applications are too similar, it may issue a "double patenting rejection."

Strategy Tip Before your patent issues, you normally will receive with your Notice of Allowance an indication from the USPTO of how much patent term adjustment your patent will receive. The rules for calculating whether you might be entitled to a patent term adjustment are often complicated, so your patent attorney might ask you whether you want him to confirm that the USPTO's calculation is correct. Most of these corrections can only be made before the patent issues, so you will need to decide quickly whether to pay for this additional expense. You may just decide that the risk of the USPTO miscalculating your patent term adjustment does not justify paying for your patent attorney's review, especially if the useful life of your patent is within the next ten years or so.

FIGURE 15.8 **Example of Patent Having Patent Term Adjustment**

This patent receives an extra 393 days of patent term beyond the normal 20 year term of July 1, 2023.

US007022054B2

(12) **United States Patent**
Contreras

(10) **Patent No.:** US 7,022,054 B2
(45) **Date of Patent:** Apr. 4, 2006

(54) **LEG-STRETCHING DEVICE AND METHOD**

(76) Inventor: **Isaiah G. Contreras**, P.O. Box 18406, Anaheim, CA (US) 92817

(*) Notice: Subject to any disclaimer, the term of this patent is extended or adjusted under 35 U.S.C. 154(b) by 393 days.

(21) Appl. No.: **10/611,124**

(22) Filed: **Jul. 1, 2003**

(65) **Prior Publication Data**

US 2004/0029689 A1   Feb. 12, 2004

Related U.S. Application Data

(60) Provisional application No. 60/393,062, filed on Jul. 1, 2002.

(51) **Int. Cl.**
A61H 1/02   (2006.01)
A63B 21/002   (2006.01)

(52) **U.S. Cl.** **482/131**; 482/79; 482/91; 482/907

(58) **Field of Classification Search** 482/23, 482/24, 34, 79, 91, 92, 95, 96, 131, 132, 482/143, 907; 601/35; D21/673
See application file for complete search history.

(56) **References Cited**

U.S. PATENT DOCUMENTS

3,117,782 A	*	1/1964	Johnston 482/95
4,205,839 A	*	6/1980	Best 482/131
4,277,062 A		7/1981	Lawrence
4,411,426 A	*	10/1983	McCoy et al. 482/131
4,988,096 A	*	1/1991	Jones 482/94
5,067,709 A	*	11/1991	Christianson 482/95
5,261,865 A	*	11/1993	Trainor 482/95
5,324,245 A	*	6/1994	Fontana et al. 482/131
5,405,306 A		4/1995	Goldsmith et al.
5,407,411 A	*	4/1995	Trainor 482/95
5,885,190 A	*	3/1999	Reiter 482/69
6,110,083 A	*	8/2000	Riser 482/142
6,113,564 A	*	9/2000	McGuire 602/32

FOREIGN PATENT DOCUMENTS

DE	296 06 156	6/1995
WO	WO 2005009319 A1 *	2/2005

OTHER PUBLICATIONS

International Search Report mailed Sep. 8, 2004.

* cited by examiner

Primary Examiner—Jerome W. Donnelly
Assistant Examiner—Victor K. Hwang
(74) *Attorney, Agent, or Firm*—Knobbe, Martens, Olson & Bear, LLP

(57) **ABSTRACT**

Disclosed is a device to aid in spreading a person's legs to increase the flexibility of the groin and thigh muscles. The device employs a bar having a central curved segment that engages the lower back region. Each end of the bar has a pulley through which a cord extends with a handgrip and a stirrup at opposite ends of the cord. The user sits on the floor and places their feet through the respective stirrups, and pulls on the handgrips which pull the feet to spread the legs.

14 Claims, 5 Drawing Sheets

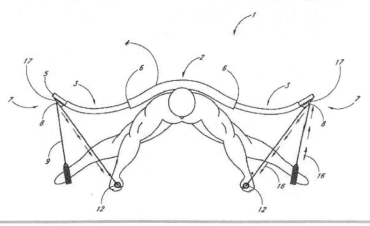

There are two types of double patenting rejections: same invention or statutory double patenting, and obviousness-type double patenting. A same invention double patenting rejection is made when two patents or applications claim substantially the same thing. This usually happens when the claims between the two patents or applications are identical. Same invention double patenting is prohibited, so if you receive one of these rejections, you will likely need to cancel your claims from one of the applications.

An obviousness-type double patenting rejection is made when the claims of two patents or applications are not identical, but they are considered to be merely obvious over one another. Obviousness in this context relates to the language of the claims, that is, whether the invention defined by one claim makes obvious the invention defined by the other claim. Obviousness-type double patenting is not prohibited, and may be overcome if the applicant agrees to shorten, or disclaim, the term of one patent relative to the other. This is what's called a "terminal disclaimer." The terminal disclaimer requires that for the applicant to hold both patents, it can only do so if it expressly agrees that both patents will remain commonly owned and will expire on the same day. Thus, a terminal disclaimer ties the term of one patent to another patent. This will be noted on the cover of the patent (see Figure 15.9).

If you receive an obviousness-type double patenting rejection, this does not automatically mean that you'll need to file a terminal disclaimer. You will still have the option of arguing to the examiner that the rejection is incorrect, perhaps because you do not agree that the claim of one application is obvious over the claim of the other. Oftentimes, however, filing a terminal disclaimer is an easier way to go, and will not significantly affect your scope of patent protection. This is because double patenting rejections are frequently made in

---

Did You Know? The reason that a terminal disclaimer requires that both patents remain commonly owned is to prevent the possibility that two patents become owned by two different parties, making a potential infringer subject to multiple lawsuits by the different parties.

FIGURE 15.9 **Example of a Utility Patent with a Terminal Disclaimer Noted**

The cover of the patent will typically indicate whether a terminal disclaimer was filed, though it will not indicate the other patent that this patent is tied to.

US006842999B2

(12) **United States Patent**
Russell

(10) **Patent No.:** **US 6,842,999 B2**
(45) **Date of Patent:** *Jan. 18, 2005

(54) **SOLE CONSTRUCTION FOR ENERGY STORAGE AND REBOUND**

(75) Inventor: **Brian A. Russell**, Littleton, CO (US)

(73) Assignee: **Britek Footwear Development, LLC**, Littleton, CO (US)

(*) Notice: Subject to any disclaimer, the term of this patent is extended or adjusted under 35 U.S.C. 154(b) by 0 days.

This patent is subject to a terminal disclaimer.

(21) Appl. No.: **10/435,945**

(22) Filed: **May 12, 2003**

(65) **Prior Publication Data**

US 2004/0006891 A1 Jan. 15, 2004

Related U.S. Application Data

(63) Continuation of application No. 09/948,174, filed on Sep. 5, 2001, now abandoned, which is a continuation of application No. 09/313,778, filed on May 17, 1999, now Pat. No. 6,327,795, which is a continuation-in-part of application No. 08/903,130, filed on Jul. 30, 1997, now Pat. No. 5,937,544, and a continuation-in-part of application No. 09/135,974, filed on Aug. 18, 1998, now Pat. No. 6,330,757.

(51) Int. Cl.[7] A43B 13/18

(52) U.S. Cl. 36/28; 36/27; 36/29

(58) Field of Search .... 36/28, 28 R, 30 R, 36/32 R, 30 A, 31, 35 R, 37, 29, 27

(56) **References Cited**

U.S. PATENT DOCUMENTS

904,891 A	11/1908	Olderstedt
1,382,180 A	6/1921	Emery
1,778,089 A	10/1930	Pomerantz
2,058,975 A	10/1936	Gray
2,549,343 A	4/1951	Stoiner
2,811,791 A	11/1957	Cox
3,086,532 A	4/1963	Mistarz
3,100,354 A	8/1963	Lomard et al.
3,290,801 A	12/1966	Bente
3,402,485 A	9/1968	McMorrow
3,834,046 A	9/1974	Fowler

(List continued on next page.)

FOREIGN PATENT DOCUMENTS

WO	WO 90/12518	11/1990
WO	WO 92/03069	3/1992
WO	WO 93/03639	3/1993
WO	WO 96/39061	12/1996
WO	WO 99/35928	7/1999

OTHER PUBLICATIONS

International Search Report for PCT/US99/18670 dated Dec. 13, 1999.

Primary Examiner—Ted Kavanaugh
(74) *Attorney, Agent, or Firm*—Knobbe Martens Olson & Bear LLP

(57) **ABSTRACT**

A sole construction for supporting at least a portion of a human foot and for providing energy storage and return is provided. The sole construction includes a generally horizontal layer of stretchable material, at least one chamber positioned adjacent a first side of the layer, and at least one actuator positioned adjacent a second side of the layer vertically aligned with a corresponding chamber. Each actuator has a footprint size smaller than that of the corresponding chamber, and is sized and arranged to provide individual support to the bones of the human foot. The support structure when compressed causes the actuator to push against the layer and move the layer at least partially into the corresponding chamber. In one embodiment, dual action energy storage and rebound is provided by using a plurality of actuators that move both upwardly and downwardly into corresponding chambers. In another embodiment, lateral stability is improved by using tapered actuators having a convex shape to accommodate the natural rolling movement of the foot.

23 Claims, 30 Drawing Sheets

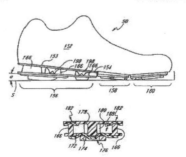

continuation applications that claim priority to an earlier-filed application, and therefore, they would have the same term and would remain owned by the same party anyway.

Unfortunately, even though most patents with a terminal disclaimer will have this noted on the cover of the patent, the cover of the patent will not identify the other patent to which the terminal disclaimer ties the patent term. To determine this, you will need to obtain the file history of the patent to find a copy of the terminal disclaimer.

CHAPTER 16

IP Audits and Developing a Patent Strategy

Congratulations! You're now well-versed in the foundations of patent law, procedure, and policy. This chapter concludes Part Two, Subpart B, on protecting a patent by discussing some topics of interest to the advanced reader. In particular, this chapter introduces the related concepts of conducting an intellectual property audit of your company and developing a comprehensive patent strategy to make sure you are taking your patent planning in the right direction.

A comprehensive patent strategy provides a framework for all patent issues relevant to your business. A patent strategy generally consists of three prongs: (1) an offensive plan, (2) a defensive analysis, and (3) an ownership review. Preparing and reviewing a patent strategy will allow you to plan for patent-related expenses and to budget appropriately. In addition, your patent attorney may be able to conduct an IP audit to give you an overview of your patent strategy and to let you know where it might make sense to implement changes or additions.

IP Audits

If your company has already begun executing a patent strategy or developing intellectual property, you might consider conducting an IP audit. An IP audit is an internal auditing procedure designed to help you assess what you have, what you need, and the direction in which you're heading. An IP audit also involves double checking to make sure the company owns all of the IP that it thinks it owns.

An IP audit should involve not only the technical people at your company but also the corporate executive, the sales and marketing team, regulatory affairs personnel (if it is a medical device company), and other senior managers. An audit will address the three prongs of a patent strategy: offensive strategies, defensive strategies, and ownership review.

For example, as part of an offensive analysis, the IP audit may compare the issued and pending claims in your patent portfolio to the products and technologies that you are developing and planning to market, and may also analyze products of your competitors. As part of a defensive analysis, the IP audit may consider the impact of third party patent rights on the products you are selling and hoping to develop and sell in the future. Finally, as part of the ownership analysis, the IP audit may review all the assignment agreements for each of the patents in your portfolio as well as research, consulting, contractor, and employment agreements that may also exist. The IP audit may also determine if copyrights in software and other creative works have been assigned properly to the company.

A review of internal procedures may also performed. For example, the review may cover process controls regarding establishing IP-related agreements, establishing and defining the duties of your company's Patent Review Committee, and prior art screening. The IP audit may also include preparing a series of graphical representations of your company's patent portfolio so you can quickly determine the interrelationship of the patents and applications within each of your company's patent families.

The Offensive Plan: Developing a Patent Portfolio

The first prong of a comprehensive patent strategy involves planning to develop your patent portfolio. It is important that you consider not only whether or not to file patent applications on your company's technologies, but also which technologies to protect, as well as when and where to apply for patent protection. Several factors to consider in deciding whether, which, when, and where to patent, include:

- *Excluding competition*. Would a patent allow you to exclude others from practicing your core technology as well as commercially viable, competitive alternatives?
- *Providing leverage*. Would a patent provide you with leverage to negotiate with others?
- *Improving strategic relationships*. Would a patent help you establish or expand relationships with your strategic partners?
- *Increasing licensing revenues*. Would a patent entitle you to receive additional licensing revenue?
- *Enhancing company value*. Would a patent enhance the company's value?
- *Attracting capital*. Would a patent help the company attract capital?
- *Developing a defensive shield*. Would a patent provide defensive support, e.g., would it pose a threat to your competition?

Whether to Patent

One of your first strategic decisions will be whether or not to pursue patent protection for your inventions, or whether you will try to keep you inventions as company secrets. As discussed in Chapter 1, the underlying policy behind the U.S. patent system is to stimulate innovation. The patent system tries to achieve this goal by granting inventors a limited term of exclusive rights in exchange for the inventor sharing the details of her invention with the public.

In other words, the inventor receives a patent in exchange for a complete written disclosure of a new, nonobvious, and useful invention. Therefore, the patent system requires a full disclosure of your invention in exchange for patent protection. If you do not want to disclose your technology to the public, you might want to consider keeping the technology as a trade secret.

Maintaining Inventions as Trade Secrets

A patent's disclosure is considered complete as long as the inventor provides a detailed written disclosure of her invention and explains (or enables) the invention in enough detail that a person familiar with the field of the technology ("one of skill in the art") could perform it. The disclosure must also provide the best manner (or mode) of performing the invention known to the inventor. In other words, the inventor is not allowed to disclose only the second-best manner known to perform the invention while keeping the best manner a secret.

An important factor to consider when deciding whether or not to seek patent protection is whether you are willing to provide this complete written disclosure. If an invention relates to secret methods, algorithms, or constructions that could not be reverse engineered from your commercial product or independently created, then patent protection may not be the best form of intellectual property to use. However, relatively few technologies *could not* be reverse engineered or independently created—after all, you independently created the technology yourself. If your invention could be reverse engineered, then patent protection might be appropriate. Therefore, it might make sense to evaluate the probability or likelihood that a competitor would reverse engineer or independently create your invention during the time that the product (or method) will have a valuable market lifetime.

Searching to Assess Patentability

One option to help you decide whether to seek patent protection or not is to commission a patentability search. A patentability search involves hiring a professional patent searcher to search for existing patents and other public documents (e.g., scientific papers, journal articles, etc.) that describe technologies similar to your invention. The patentability search should inform you of the closest "prior art" relevant to your invention. You and your patent attorney can review the patents and other references identified through the patentability search to determine a patent drafting strategy and to give you a sense of the scope of patent protection that may be available. For more information on how to conduct a search, see Chapters 11 and 27.

A patentability search is generally a search for patents, patent applications, and any other published documents that describe (in the body of the document, not just in a patent's claims) the features of your invention for which patent protection is sought. There are some strategic advantages to performing a patentability search prior to preparing and filing a patent application. For example, if a patentability search is performed and uncovers prior art that seems directly related to the technology you have developed, you may determine that the probability of the USPTO issuing a patent to you on your invention is so low that the cost of filing a patent application is not justified. On the other hand, reviewing prior art can help you and your attorney write a clearer, more focused patent application on your technology by identifying features of your technology not included in the prior art and focusing the description of your invention on those features that are patentable over the references identified by the patentability search. Articulating these differences in your patent application can lead to a stronger position when distinguishing your invention from the prior art during the patent examination process.

Considering the Useful, Marketable Life of Your Technology

Another consideration in determining whether or not to seek patent protection is the useful, marketable life of your invention. For example, depending upon the type of technology that you seek to patent, it can take several years to receive a patent. If the useful, marketable life of the technology will end before the USPTO is likely to grant a patent, the costs of filing and pursuing patent protection may not be justified.

Requesting Nonpublication of Your Patent Application

Another strategic decision is whether or not to request nonpublication of your patent application. Unless nonpublication is requested, your patent application will publish for the world to see, regardless of whether the application ever issues into a patent. Approximately 18 months from your patent's priority date (refer to the Continuing Applications Section for a discussion of priority), the USPTO will send you a published version of your patent application, which will be publicly available on the USPTO's web site, for review. You can instruct the USPTO not to publish your patent application by filing a request for nonpublication with the filing of your patent application. However, if you request nonpublication, you have to agree that you will not seek foreign patent protection for your invention. See Chapter 13 for an additional discussion on nonpublication requests.

What to Patent

One of the fundamental goals of an offensive patent strategy is to protect the company's revenue stream. For many, the most important technology to protect may not be the most technical or innovative aspect of a company's product line. Instead, patent protection can sometimes provide the most value when it protects a consumable or disposable component. Protecting the revenue stream can be more challenging than protecting a company's core technology, especially when the revenue stream involves only minor innovations over currently existing technologies.

> **Strategy Tip** One reason that you might want to consider nonpublication is that companies typically monitor the publications of their competitors to try to understand what their competitors have been working on and what they're planning to develop and introduce into the market in the future. It could take many additional months, often years, before the USPTO issues a patent, if ever, from a published application.

Another goal of an offensive patent strategy is to protect the company's core technology. By protecting the core technology, the entrepreneur can provide an offensive weapon against copycat competitors and reverse engineering. Even though protecting the core technology may not prevent others from developing improvements or competitive alternatives, it provides some assurance that the company's key innovations remain exclusively their own.

Patenting competitive or less-competitive alternative technologies makes up another aspect of an offensive patent strategy. It may be useful to have patents that not only cover your core technology, but also less optimal yet competitive alternatives. A competitor analyzing your patent portfolio will try to determine possible "design-arounds" that avoid patent infringement but allow the competitor to compete in your market. Therefore, brainstorming alternative technology possibilities and pursuing patents directed to these alternatives can provide you and your company additional strategic benefit.

It sometimes makes sense to seek patent protection on improvements to competitors' technologies as well. For example, even if a competitor holds patents on its core technology, if you develop improvements, you might be entitled to patents on those improvements. By building a wall of patents around your competitors' core technologies, you may be able to lock competitors into early generations of their products and prevent your competitors from developing and releasing next-generation, advanced technologies.

Finally, patents directed to a competitor's or a potential acquirer's technologies can make your company more attractive as a licensing partner or as an acquisition. If your company owns patents that are directed to improvements on their technologies, the competitor might consider it more economically efficient to partner with or acquire your company than to try to seek their own patents, to try to work around your patents, or to defend against your patents if you decide to assert them.

When to File Your Patent Applications

To assure that you or your company will have the best chance of receiving patent protection for your inventions, you should try to file patent applications as early as possible. Some companies wish to defer the expenses associated with

> **Did You Know?** Did you know that it is simple to establish a competitor monitoring program? Online services, such as Delphion (www.delphion.com) allow you to establish an account and set up a periodic search for particular patents and publications. For example, you could set up a search to identify patents and publications issued and published during a certain time period (e.g., weekly, monthly, every six months, etc.) that include certain keywords, inventor names, assignee (patent owner) names, and combinations of these parameters. Alternatively, you can do it yourself using free sources such as the USPTO's web site at www.uspto.gov. Your patent attorney should be able to help you set up such service, or provide searching through her own service.

seeking patent protection as long as possible, and so they delay preparing and filing patents. However, delaying patent filings can lead to loss of patent rights, both in the United States and abroad. See Chapter 10 for an additional discussion on when to file your patent applications.

Deciding when to file for patent protection also involves considering how to best preserve limited resources. For example, a company might find it difficult to justify allocating limited resources to developing a patent portfolio when engineering, manufacturing, sales and marketing, and other departments all need greater budget allocations. In addition, it often makes sense to defer patent prosecution costs as long as possible so you can determine market acceptance and demand for your new technologies. For example, you might want to conduct market studies, or test market a product, or review clinical results associated with a new technology prior to investing to develop an extensive patent portfolio. Fortunately various strategies can be employed to provide the benefit of filing early while deferring patent portfolio development costs for a limited time.

Filing Provisional Patent Applications to Defer Costs

One way to defer costs of patent prosecution is to file a provisional application. Provisional patent applications are discussed in greater detail in Chapter 13.

The USPTO currently only charges about $210 to file a provisional patent application compared to $1,030 for a nonprovisional patent application (the fees are reduced by 50% to $105 and $515 for small entities). In addition, provisional patent applications are not examined, which means that the USPTO does not send any communications (often referred to as office actions). Because the USPTO doesn't send office actions in provisional patent applications, you will not need to incur the expense of having a patent attorney respond to such communications.

On the other hand, as discussed in the Chapter 13, a provisional patent application does not confer any patent rights to the patentee; it merely serves as a filing date placeholder for a later-filed nonprovisional patent application. Also, provisional patent applications expire after one year from the date they are filed. Therefore, within a year of filing a provisional patent application, you will need to file a nonprovisional U.S. patent application and foreign patent applications if you wish to take advantage of the priority, or earlier filing date, of the provisional. There may be some inefficiency associated with having a patent attorney prepare your provisional patent application and then, one year later, file another application (i.e., a nonprovisional patent application) that is based upon the provisional. However, even so, provisional patent applications do provide one mechanism for deferring the costs associated with patent prosecution, even if for only one year.

Filing Under the Patent Cooperation Treaty to Defer Costs

Another strategy for deferring costs of seeking patent protection is to file a patent application under the terms of the Patent Cooperation Treaty, or PCT, discussed in greater detail in Chapter 14. PCT patent applications can help defer costs of seeking both U.S. and foreign patents. A PCT application currently costs approximately $5,000 to file, and it essentially delays the costs of filing U.S. or foreign patent applications, which can be several tens of thousands of dollars, or more, for 18–31 months. The PCT application can be converted into multiple national patent applications prior to the PCT application's expiration. The procedure for converting a PCT application into national patent applications is often referred to as "entering the national stage." The deadline for entering the national stage varies from country to country, but most countries have a deadline of 30 months from the earliest claimed priority date. Some other countries (and regions, which will be discussed below) have a 31–month deadline. However, not all countries have signed the Patent Cooperation Treaty. Therefore, not all countries allow PCT applications to be converted into national applications.

To make things more complicated, a PCT application can claim priority from a U.S. provisional, a U.S. nonprovisional, or a PCT country's national patent application (for example, a patent application filed in Germany) as long as the PCT application is filed within 12 months of the earlier-filed application. Therefore, you can delay patent prosecution costs beyond 12 months (which is the delay provided by filing only a provisional) by also filing a PCT patent application after filing the provisional. In other words, instead of filing a provisional application first and a nonprovisional application (United States or foreign) 12 months later, you could file a provisional application first, a PCT application 12 months later, and then a nonprovisional application (United States or foreign) 18 months after filing the PCT application.

Deferring the expenses associated with patent preparation, filing, and prosecution are often desired. For example, deferring expenses allows you to develop a market for your products and analyze whether market demand

---

Did You Know? Did you know that because the United States is a signatory to the Patent Cooperation Treaty you may "enter the national stage" within the United States, just as you are permitted to do with respect to other, foreign countries?

This means that it is not necessary to file a patent application initially with the USPTO. Instead, you are permitted to file a patent application under the PCT procedures, and then 30 months from your PCT application's priority date, your patent application may enter the United States. This provides one strategic possibility for deferring costs associated with the prosecution of a U.S. patent application, as will be discussed in greater detail below.

TABLE 16.1 **Filing Strategies**

	Timing	Filing sequence	
Fastest Patent Track	File as early as possible.	(1) U.S. nonprovisional filed simultaneously with foreign national patent applications.	Immediate Expenses
	File U.S. provisional as early as possible and U.S. nonprovisional and foreign national applications within 12 months.	(1) U.S. provisional first, then (2) U.S. nonprovisional with foreign national patent applications.	
Slowest Patent Track	File U.S. provisional as early as possible, and U.S. nonprovisional and PCT applications within 12 months. Foreign national applications must be filed within 30 (in some cases 31) months from filing of U.S. provisional.	(1) U.S. provisional first, then (2) U.S. nonprovisional with PCT application, then (3) foreign national applications.	Deferred Expenses
	File U.S. provisional as early as possible and PCT application within 12 months. U.S. nonprovisional and foreign national applications must be filed within 30 (in some cases 31) months from filing of U.S. provisional.	(1) U.S. provisional first, then (2) PCT application, then (3) U.S. nonprovisional and foreign national applications.	

justifies patent expenses. Deferring expenses permits you to study the likelihood of favorable patent examination. Another benefit provided by deferring expenses is that doing so provides more time to analyze clinical results and effectiveness before deciding whether to pursue patent protection. The primary disadvantage of deferring expenses is that doing so generally delays patent examination and issuance. Table 16.1 summarizes a few of the filing timing options discussed in this chapter.

Where to Apply for Patent Protection
Patent protection, and especially foreign patent protection, can be very expensive. Therefore, although it would be nice to have worldwide patent protection for your inventions, the benefits often do not justify the costs. You may

want to consider several factors in determining where to seek foreign patent protection, including:

- *Market size.* Patent costs may not be justified in a country with a small market size.
- *Manufacturing.* Patents can help if you want to be able to prevent others from manufacturing product in the country.
- *Enforceability.* Patents may not help if the country has a poor patent enforcement track record.
- *Negotiating leverage.* Patents could help if perceived as valuable to a potential licensee or acquirer.
- *Necessity.* Remember, you do not need a patent in a country in order to sell product into that country.

Cost Considerations

The total costs of securing patent protection in the United States can be broken down into three general categories: preparation, prosecution, and maintenance. Preparation includes the costs associated with the drafting, review, and filing a patent application. Prosecution includes the costs associated with communicating with the USPTO and amending your patent application. Maintenance includes the costs of issuing your patent and keeping it alive after it issues. Additional possible costs include those associated with appealing a USPTO decision to refuse to grant a patent as well as costs of interference proceedings.

Although a single worldwide patent does not exist, many companies find that individual patent protection in the United States, Europe, Japan, Canada, Australia, and China provides adequate protection.

Patent preparation costs include those associated with your patent attorney's time to interview you or your inventors and to draft your patent application. In addition, the USPTO charges certain government fees to file a patent application (currently $1,030 per application for large entities or companies and $515 per application for small entities or companies) and additional fees depending upon the number and types of claims and total pages in the patent application. You should also consider the time you and your employees spend to provide the initial invention description (sometimes called an invention disclosure) to your patent attorney and to review drafts patent applications as part of the patent preparation costs. The attorney time component of patent preparation costs varies widely but is generally in the range of about $5,000 to $15,000, and potentially much more depending upon the complexity of the invention, number of variations or embodiments described, and claims prepared.

Patent prosecution includes the time that your patent attorney spends reviewing communications from the USPTO and responding to those communications. In some cases, your patent attorney might recommend conducting an interview with the examiner to help the examiner understand your invention and the differences between your invention and the prior art. In addition, you also should consider the time you and your employees spend discussing the prior art and reviewing the USPTO communications (i.e., office actions) as part of patent prosecution costs.

Although prosecution costs vary widely and will depend upon the complexity of the office actions received from the USPTO, patent prosecution costs can fall within the range of an additional $1,500 to $5,000 for each office action received. A typical patent application generates at least two office actions, so total prosecution costs can often fall within the range of about $3,000 to $10,000, and sometimes much more.

Finally, once the USPTO determines that your patent application is ready to issue as a patent, you must pay additional issue fees before the patent will issue. Then, once the patent issues, maintenance fees are due at 3½, 7½, and 11½ years after issuance. The current patent issue fee is $1,440, and the 3½-, 7½-, and 11½-year maintenance fees are $930, $2,360, and $3,910, respectively. However, issue and maintenance fees are reduced by 50 percent for qualifying small entities.

Additional costs are required to secure patent protection abroad. For example, for each foreign country in which you file a foreign patent application you must hire a local patent attorney. U.S. patent attorneys are generally not licensed to practice patent law outside of the United States. However, U.S. patent attorneys often have networks of foreign associates that they commonly use to pursue foreign patent protection on behalf of their clients.

Foreign jurisdictions often require translations of patent applications in the local language. Translation costs can be significant, especially for very long patent applications. Finally, many foreign jurisdictions offer administrative proceedings whereby a third party can challenge the patentability of the claims in a patent application prior to issuance. These proceedings, often called opposition proceedings, allow a third party to appear before a foreign country's patent office and formally oppose the granting of a patent application. Unfortunately, you must participate in (and fund the costs of) an opposition proceeding if an action is brought against your patent application; otherwise, your patent application will probably be denied.

Defensive Analysis: How to Avoid Infringing Someone Else's Patents

Prior to investing in development of a new product or technology, your company may wish to understand whether patents related to the new product already exist. If so, you can assess the likelihood of receiving a patent itself and the likelihood of being sued for infringing the patent, and you can identify patent holders with whom the company might seek a licensing or patent purchase agreement.

One way to identify such patents is to conduct a search, sometimes called a "market clearance search," a "freedom-to-operate search," a "right to practice search," or an "infringement search." A market clearance search is designed to identify patents that might pose infringement risk. Unlike a patentability search, a market clearance search only identifies unexpired, issued patents having claims that appear to cover (or "read upon") the product that you plan to develop.

A market clearance search is typically performed by a professional patent searcher. The searcher is given a brief description of the technology to be developed and typically returns a list of patents having claims that may be related to the described technology. However, there are currently over 7 million issued nonprovisional utility patents in the United States. Therefore it is not possible to guarantee that all such patents will be identified. Indeed, the thoroughness of a market clearance search is directly related to the time (and money) spent conducting the search. For more information on patent searching, see Chapters 11 and 27.

Once the searcher returns the search results, your patent attorney can review the claims of the patents with you and provide an assessment of risk associated with each patent identified by the searcher. If a patent looks like it is particularly problematic, either because it seems close to your technology or because the patent owner is a competitor or known to file patent infringement lawsuits, you can request that your attorney study the patent and determine whether it is possible to prepare a formal written favorable opinion regarding the patent. An attorney's written opinion often concludes that either (1) a court would likely determine that your product, as described, would not be found to infringe the patent (or particular claims of the patent), (2) the patent (or particular claims of the patent) could likely be proven to be invalid (for example, due to prior art not presented to the USPTO during prosecution of the patent application) and should not have been issued, (3) the patent is unenforceable (for example, due to improper or fraudulent conduct committed by the patent applicant or her attorney), and/or (4) a combination of the above. See Chapter 27 below for a discussion of opinions of counsel.

A formal, competent written opinion by a patent attorney can be helpful if you are ever charged with infringing the patent for which an opinion was rendered. The written opinion can be important in avoiding a charge of "willful infringement" (discussed in Chapter 27), as a court can increase a patent damages award (up to three times) for a finding of willful infringement. For example, patent holders often assert not only that an accused infringer infringed the patent holder's patent, but that the infringement was "willful." This means that the accused acted with reckless disregard for another's patent rights, and went forward to infringe a patent even though he knew that his actions were infringing.

Finally, in addition to assessing infringement risk, a defensive patent strategy often also includes filing a large number of patent applications as a deterrent to potential plaintiffs. Just as the nuclear arms race was thought of as providing a deterrent to war, building a patent arsenal can have the same effect. For example, a patent holder might be less likely to sue you if it believes that doing so would cause you to assert your patents against the patent holder. Similarly, if your competitor is infringing even just one of your patents, it might decide not to come after you for infringing your competitor's patents.

Establishing Ownership

The final element of a patent strategy is to make sure that you or your company will own, or at least understand the ownership status of, the IP developed by your employees, contractors, consultants, vendors, distributors, etc., during the course of business. For example, paying an employee's salary, or a consultant's fees, often does not alone establish the company's ownership in patented inventions that name employee or consultant inventors.

As discussed in Chapter 10, unless otherwise provided by an agreement, *inventors* "jointly" own the patent. Because the inventors are not necessarily the employer or the party that paid for the invention, it is important to make sure your company protects its rights. Joint ownership means that each inventor has an undivided interest and right to the patent and cannot prevent the other from practicing the claimed inventions. In addition, the ownership interest is perfectly equal among *all* inventors, regardless of how much each inventor actually contributed to the inventions claimed.

For at least these reasons, it is very important that you make sure that all employees, consultants, etc., assign all invention and patent rights to you or your company. Even if you are an inventor on the patent and therefore would have the right to practice and sue for patent infringement, you should still make sure that all other inventors assign to you or the company. If you fail to do so, the inventors could grant rights and/or licenses to your competitors without your permission. In addition, joint ownership creates a cloud of uncertainty over the patent, which makes it much less desirable to licensees, acquirers, and investors.

Patent rights are typically assigned via employment agreements and specific assignment instruments. Employment agreements generally create an obligation to convey rights to all inventions conceived and worked on during, and related to employment. Specific assignment instruments convey

> **Warning!** Intellectual property assignments should be signed with consultants and contract employees prior to disclosing confidential information. If such agreements are not put into place, there is a risk that your consultant could file patents on your technologies and demand payments. For example, consider a consultant hired to solve a particular technical problem. You disclose the problem to the consultant, and she develops a solution to the problem at the company's expense. However, the consultant then turns around and files one or more patent applications on the solution. When the patent applications issue as patents, the consultant may try to stop the company from implementing the solution unless it pays additional fees, royalties, etc.

rights to a particular patent or family of related patents (e.g., a U.S. patent, all continuations, divisionals, and related foreign applications).

Once an assignment is signed, it should be recorded with the USPTO as soon as possible. In fact, if an assignment is not recorded with the USPTO within three months of execution, in some situations, it can be deemed void against a subsequent purchaser of the assigned patents, who did not have express knowledge of the assignment.

For example, if a consultant assigns rights to a patent to you, you never record the assignment with the USPTO, and the consultant later assigns the same patent to one of your competitors, your assignment would be deemed unenforceable against your competitor, and your competitor could wind up owning the patent (although the competitor would have had to have paid valuable consideration for the subsequent assignment, and the competitor could not have known about the prior assignment to you).

Similarly, if a consultant assigns patent rights to you and a week later assigns the same patent rights to your competitor, and your competitor records his assignment immediately, you must record your assignment within three months of the assignment to you; otherwise, your assignment will be held unenforceable against the competitor, and the competitor will receive the patent rights.

Purchasing Patent Protection

There are other, and sometimes much more efficient, ways to obtain patent protection, other than by filing patent applications. For example, patents can be purchased and/or licensed. One strategy for acquiring patent protection is to purchase patents without disclosing the identity of the purchaser.

One of the difficulties in purchasing patents is identifying suitable targets. However, various searches, such as patentability searches, market clearance searches, and competitor-specific searches, can often reveal potential patent acquisition targets. Finally, one relatively new method of purchasing patent protection is through an intellectual property auction.

Purchasers often wish to keep their identity hidden from a potential patent seller. For example, if the company is well known, public, and/or profitable, the seller might increase the asking price. In addition, companies often wish to "stay off the seller's radar." Otherwise, the company could become a target and possibly accused of infringing the seller's patents.

Did you know that the USPTO's assignment records are available and searchable online? You can access the USPTO's assignment records at http://assignments.uspto.gov/assignments/?db=pat.

To avoid these complications, patent purchasers often use a straw man to facilitate a patent purchase or to inquire into the terms and availability of a patent license. The straw man is generally a third party who is unrelated to the purchaser or his patent attorney. In fact, the straw man often does not know the identity of the purchaser. The company's patent attorney usually asks a trusted colleague from a different law firm, perhaps from a different city or state, to contact the potential seller to inquire regarding the availability of a patent license or purchase. In some cases, the patent can be transferred first to the straw man and then to the company. In other cases, an escrow-type exchange is used.

Generating Licensing Revenue from Your Patent Protection

Once you receive a patent, you might want to use it to generate an ongoing revenue stream. Some people call this "monetizing" your patent portfolio.

One way to generate revenue from patents is to grant one or more licenses to your patented technologies. Although an entire book could be written just on strategic issues related to licensing, it is important to remember to think about your ultimate exit strategy prior to granting a license. For more discussion on licensing your patents, see Chapter 27.

For example, if you ultimately hope to sell your company, you should think about whether it makes sense, in the long run, to grant a patent license. Acquirers generally prefer that all rights to patented technologies be held exclusively by the company. The revenue stream generated by a license could potentially be much less than the value given to the exclusivity otherwise available to the company.

One of the difficulties in generating licensing income from your patent portfolio is identifying suitable licensees. However, as with purchasing patent protection, patent searches can often reveal potential targets. In addition, you may be able to identify potential targets by searching the USPTO database for all patents that refer to your patent. For example, if a patent examiner cites one of your patents against another party's patent application, your patent may be relevant to both that party's patents and possibly its products, as well. You also could consider retaining an investment banker or other brokers to find buyers or licensees, if your patents appear to be particularly valuable in your market. Finally, an intellectual property auction can be used to sell off IP, as well.

Protecting Company Secrets

Subpart C

CHAPTER 17

Trade Secrets

T rade secrets are one of the four basic types of intellectual property. They are very different from the other because as is suggested by the name, trade secrets are information that gains its value from remaining secret from your competitors.

As a starting point, you can think of trade secrets as being the opposite of patent rights. With patent rights, you are required to tell the public just about everything you know about your idea or invention—what it is, what makes it work, what it's made of, etc. In contrast, trade secrets require that no one know what your idea or invention is, how it works, what it's made of, etc. Because of those differences, it is

A trade secret gains its value from remaining secret. This is almost the opposite of patents, which require a complete disclosure of your invention to the USPTO.

difficult, if not impossible, to treat and protect an idea or invention as a trade secret, and at the same time try to protect it with a patent. Therefore, one of the first decisions that you, as an inventor/entrepreneur, must make is whether to protect your ideas and inventions with patents, or treat and protect them as trade secrets.

Another basic principle with trade secrets is simple: If you start selling your product, and your innovative new feature is easy to figure out or reverse engineer, then your new feature will not be a trade secret. At that point, everyone will know what your idea is and how it works.

Let's look at our umbrella example. Are there any trade secrets to protect? Certainly as your business starts to grow and flourish, you will develop a list of premium suppliers, distributors, and retailers, so your lists of those parties may be trade secrets. The pricing that you set for various versions of your umbrella may also be trade secrets.

As to the actual umbrella itself, your trade secrets would be those things that you are not seeking patent protection on and that can't be reverse engineered or figured out by someone. For example, there might be a special water repellent spray formula that you put on the umbrella fabric that cannot be reverse engineered. There might be software that you use with

Myth vs. Reality

Myth: I can get a patent on something I want to keep as a trade secret.

Reality: A patent is a limited government-granted monopoly for an idea that must be disclosed to the world in order to earn the monopoly (assuming the idea is patentable to begin with). In order to obtain a patent on an inventive idea, you must set forth all of the relevant details. You can probably guess why that same idea cannot be protected as a trade secret. A trade secret depends upon the idea being maintained strictly in confidence. The minute you obtain patent protection on your idea, you've lost the idea as a trade secret.

the weather transmission feature that you could keep as a trade secret. You might even have a special machine that you've developed that's used behind closed doors in your factory to stitch the umbrella fabric to the spokes.

Of course, you might be able to do some of both. In other words, you could protect some of your ideas via patents and some of your ideas as trade secrets, just not the same idea. What's the advantage of one over the other? Each has their own advantages and disadvantages, but as you may gather after reading this chapter, the decision to choose one over the other has more to do with the type of idea it is and the type of business you are in rather than any other factor.

The Legal Requirements for Trade Secrets

Not all confidential information or secrets that you might use in your business are automatically trade secrets under the law. However, if your information meets all of the legal requirements of a trade secret, you are entitled to take action against others who might be misappropriating (stealing or misusing) your trade secrets (see Chapter 18). If your information does not meet the legal requirements of a trade secret, you will not have this right. Therefore, it is in your best interests to take steps to ensure that your information meets the trade secret requirements.

Under the law, the confidential information you use in your business can be a trade secret if it

(1) provides *economic benefit* to your business;

(2) is *not generally known* by others; and

(3) is *maintained in secret using reasonable measures* to keep it secret.

There is no minimum amount of economic benefit that your trade secret must provide to your business. In fact, you don't have to figure out how much benefit the information provides to you as compared to how much that information would benefit your competitors or others if they were aware of it. It just means that the information must provide some business advantage to you over your competitor because they don't have that information. A typical example of a trade secret is a customer list or a vendor list. Other examples of trade secrets are recipes for your materials, manufacturing processes, chemical formulas, etc. Each of those provides an economic benefit or competitive advantage to you over your competitor.

The second requirement for a trade secret is that the information is not generally known by others, which is what you would expect with a secret. It does not mean that *no one* outside of your company knows your secret, but it does mean that your secret cannot be generally known. It's not an objective requirement, so there's no hard and fast rule as to when information is generally known and when it is not. However, the fewer people who know your secret, the better. As a practical matter, this makes sense. If your competitors had information that you considered a trade secret, the information wouldn't provide much economic benefit to you over your competitor.

That leads to the last and most difficult requirement for a trade secret—using reasonable measures to keep the information confidential enough to be a secret. With a one-man show, it's probably easy to keep the information secret. As your business grows, however, even secret information that you share with your employees on a need-to-know basis has a way of leaking out of your business. It's human nature for people to want to discuss things they are involved in at work. It's not so much that employees intentionally leak sensitive information to outsiders, but that they inadvertently disclose the information, and these inadvertent slips are difficult to control. People sometimes have trouble separating the information that they can discuss from the information they cannot discuss. That is why it is imperative that you set up procedures in your business to control the flow of your sensitive information, both within your company and outside it.

CHAPTER 18

Protecting and Enforcing Your Trade Secrets

O bviously, the challenge with trade secrets is keeping them secret. There are steps that you can take, both with your employees and with your suppliers and other outsiders, that will help you protect your trade secrets. This chapter discusses steps you can take with your employees. It also discusses non-disclosure agreements (NDAs) with outside third parties.

There are a number of measures you can take with your employees to protect your trade secrets. The goal of these measures is to limit the number of employees having access to your secrets and minimize the flow of secrets among your employees. The key is that you must set up *reasonable* measures. Simply telling your employees to keep confidential everything that they see and hear at work may not be reasonable. It may be unrealistic to expect employees never to talk about anything that happens at work. Simply telling your employees to keep confidential all of the confidential information they see and hear at work may not be reasonable either, because that may put too much of a burden on employees to figure out what is and what isn't confidential. So how do you develop reasonable measures to keep your trade secrets confidential?

What Information Should Be Secret

The first step in developing measures to protect your trade secrets is to figure out what information your business has that is a secret. You should ask yourself: "What information do I have that needs to remain secret? What secrets do I have that help my business because my competitors don't have them?" You also need to train your managers to ask the same questions so that they will be able to recognize newly acquired confidential information and protect it right away.

Inform Employees About Your Confidential Information

Once you determine what your confidential information is, you'll need to identify it to your employees. You can label or stamp confidential written information with the word "CONFIDENTIAL" or some other wording that your employees can easily see. Important documents, drawings, specifications, files, customer lists, secret formulas, and the like can be marked as confidential.

Another way to identify confidential information is to store it in a place that allows limited access to employees. Maybe it's a locked safe or filing cabinet that contains selected documents and files. Maybe it's an electronic database that is accessible only to authorized employees with passwords. Maybe it's a laboratory in your facility that is accessible only to certain employees. Each of these measures accomplishes two things: (1) it helps identify to employees that the information is intended to be confidential, and (2) it limits access to such information and therefore safeguards it from free dissemination.

Employee Entrance Interviews

Many companies conduct entrance interviews with new employees. An entrance interview is a private meeting that you or your HR manager has with a new employee when the employee starts work. During the entrance interview, you would explain to the new employee his obligations to keep secret your company's confidential information. You would explain how he can identify confidential information (for example, documents that are stamped "CONFIDENTIAL"). You might take him on a tour of the facilities to identify which areas are accessible and which areas are off limits. When you set the new employee up on your company's computer network, you would tell the employee the types of information that are confidential and have restricted access. You would not need to specify each tidbit of information that is confidential, but you would identify it by category at least, unless the employee needs to know the specific information in order to carry out his work responsibilities.

Reminders

The courts will not require you to closely police your employees to prevent them from stealing or inadvertently disclosing trade secrets, but the courts will require that you take reasonable steps to identify, secure, and maintain

---

Strategy Tip Use employee entrance interviews as an opportunity to explain your company's confidentiality requirements to your new employees. In the interview, ask your new employees to sign an employee confidentiality agreement. By signing an agreement, your new employee is agreeing to keep secret your confidential information.

An entrance interview is also a good opportunity to make clear that you do not want the new employee to disclose to you or use any trade secrets that she may have learned while at her former employer. Make a written record of that warning, and be careful not to assign the new employee to a situation where it will be difficult for her not to disclose or use trade secrets learned at her former employer.

---

information as confidential so that your employees are aware of their obligations. Many companies send periodic reminders to their employees about their continuing obligations to keep the company's secrets confidential.

Confidentiality Agreements

One of the things many companies do to protect their trade secrets is to have new employees sign employee confidentiality agreements. Your IP lawyer can help you prepare an agreement suitable for your company. By signing an employee confidentiality agreement, the new employee acknowledges what business information is confidential and agrees to keep it secret. This makes the employees aware of their confidentiality obligations at the very beginning of their employment. A good time to give the employee the confidentiality agreement is in the entrance interview. Even after the entrance interview, you should give your employees periodic reminders about their obligation to keep secret your company's confidential information.

Exit Interviews

When an employee has given notice of her intent to leave or if she has been terminated from her job, it is important that you conduct an exit interview. An exit interview is a private meeting you would hold with the employee just before she leaves your company. The meeting should be held to ensure that all of your confidential information in the employee's possession has been returned to the company and all copies destroyed. You should also use this as an opportunity to remind the employee of what categories of information the company still considers to be company trade secrets and to reinforce the employee's confidentiality obligations in the employment agreement. You also may want to consider sending a letter to the departing employee's new employer, advising the new employer that the employee had access to your company's trade secrets, and that you expect that that new employer will take all necessary precautions to prohibit your trade secrets from being disclosed or used. See Chapter 29 on enforcement of your trade secrets.

Using Technology to Safeguard Your Trade Secrets

The electronic age has made it increasingly difficult for businesses to safeguard their trade secrets. Employees can easily download files to portable media or e-mail documents outside of the company. This poses a threat to your trade secrets, and may mean that you will need to use technology reasonably available to you to protect your trade secret information.

Losing Trade Secret Protection

A trade secret loses its value when the "cat's out of the bag." In other words, the information no longer offers a competitive advantage if others generally know about it. So if you have failed to keep visitors from seeing your secret manufacturing process, then these visitors now know the secret. The same is true if all of your ex-employees were not made aware that you considered certain information they learned while at the company to be confidential. You may have intended the information to be secret, but you didn't take steps to ensure that others knew it was supposed to be secret.

What if your sales of the RAINGOD™ umbrella have taken off, you have developed a prized customer list of premium distributors and retailers and a detailed price list as your trade secrets, and then one of your employees steals the lists and posts them on the internet? Then what? Are these situations hopeless?

As to the unintended visitors, maybe not. If the unintended visitors make no use of that information outside of your company, eventually the information will be lost from their minds and your secret information may grow once again to be "not generally known" by others. In other words, if with the passage of time your information again puts you in an economic advantage over your competitors because it is not generally known, then that information may again be protected as a trade secret.

On the other hand, the internet-posted customer list and price list may spell doom for that information, at least if the lists get into the hands of your competitors and others who could take advantage of that information. Your only relief against the one who stole your secrets may be money damages

> **Did You Know?** Can I sue someone for independently developing my trade secret information?
>
> No. Someone can be liable for trade secret misappropriation only if they have access to your trade secrets and use them without authority. If others figure out the information that you consider to be trade secrets on their own, there is no liability for trade secret misappropriation. Trade secret misappropriation, unlike patent infringement, requires that the offender had access to your confidential information and took it or used it without your authority to do so. Creating the information independently is permissible under the law. Think about it like this: If you have spent years creating a great customer list that you consider to be a trade secret but your competitor has spent years generating the same or a similar list, your competitor is not liable for trade secret misappropriation. On the other hand, if an employee of yours takes your customer list and uses it to start his own company, that is misappropriation, and you can sue the employee.

(that is, if you can locate the ex-employee who stole the lists). You may also be able to stop your competitors from using the stolen lists by obtaining an injunction in court.

Enforcing Your Trade Secrets

If someone misappropriates your trade secrets, you have a legal claim. You have a right to seek relief in court just as if someone had infringed your patents, trademarks, or copyrights. For more discussion on enforcing your intellectual property rights, see Chapter 29. If you discover that someone has taken your confidential information that you worked hard to develop and keep secret, you can file a lawsuit and seek one of two things: (1) an injunction against that person using or disclosing the information or (2) money damages for the loss of business caused by the misappropriation. Unlike patent and copyright infringement, and many forms of trademark infringement, which are claims you can make based on federal law, trade secret misappropriation is a claim under state law. So you would have to sue the defendant in state court unless you met other requirements for being in federal court.

On a preventative level, you could enforce your trade secrets before they become misappropriated. In other words, be proactive to minimize the risk of losing your trade secrets, particularly with regard to employees who are leaving your company. This tactic is particularly useful in highly competitive industries and with ex-employees who had access to your most sensitive information. One way to do so is to send a warning letter to the next employer of your departing employee. It need not be a nasty-gram, but you are certainly entitled to notify the company that you have trade secrets that your ex-employee had access to and that you expect that that company will take all necessary precautions to prohibit your trade secrets from being disclosed or used. Indeed, it would not be surprising if your company receives such a letter from time to time when you hire new employees.

Non-disclosure Agreements with Third Parties

In the course of your business, you will meet with possible suppliers and customers and may hear the term "NDA" tossed around. What is that, and do you need one?

A non-disclosure agreement, or NDA for short, is an agreement between parties that governs how the parties will handle the transfer of confidential information between them. It doesn't need to be a very long agreement, and often the best ones are fairly short and succinct. In its simplest form, an NDA obligates the recipient of confidential information to keep it confidential and to use it only for the limited purpose set forth in the agreement, and for nothing else. The limited purpose is usually to determine whether the parties should enter into a business relationship. If the parties decide not to enter into a business relationship, the recipient of the information is usually required to destroy all copies of the information and not use the information for any purpose. Of course, NDAs can be part of a much larger, more complex and ongoing business relationship (for example, as part of a supplier relationship in which there is a steady stream of information that is exchanged). Either way,

NDAs, whether they stand alone or are incorporated into larger agreements, provide some comfort to those who want or need to disclose confidential information and want to ensure that it remains confidential, even if the relationship goes nowhere. Obviously, making routine use of NDAs to protect your trade secret information will help support your position that you have used reasonable measures to protect your confidential information.

So when do you need an NDA? As noted above, you should use an NDA when you talk with potential suppliers, distributors, and/or customers about your product and there is a need to provide those parties with your trade secrets (such as specifications, formulas, etc.). If you end up having a business relationship with any of them, you should include a non-disclosure/confidentiality provision in your contract with that party.

Another situation in which you might use an NDA is when you believe you have an inventive idea and do not want to lose potential patent rights, but you need to share your ideas with those outside your company to further develop or test your idea. Under the U.S. patent laws, an inventor may file a patent application on an invention so long as his idea was not publicly disclosed more than one year prior to the filing date of the patent application. The one-year grace period was set by Congress to give inventors a short opportunity to see if the product, material, or methodology has commercial

---

Myth vs. Reality

Myth: As long as I have a non-disclosure agreement in place, I can sell my idea more than one year before I file a patent application.

Reality: A non-disclosure agreement only buys time for an inventor if the disclosure of information made under the agreement is for purposes of furthering the development or testing of the invention. Any commercial exploitation of the invention, whether or not it is done under a non-disclosure agreement, starts the one-year clock ticking. This is an important lesson that gets lost on many inventors, with the unfortunate result of losing their patent rights.

> **Strategy Tip** | **Does filing a patent application mean that I don't need an NDA?**
>
> Essentially yes, with respect to preserving your patent rights. You can publicly disclose your invention, at least to the extent described in the patent application, without fear of losing your patent rights. However, recommended practice is always to disclose information on a need-to-know basis under an NDA. It is prudent to do so because a patent may not issue for a couple of years, during which time you have nothing to enforce. Or, you may decide to abandon your patent application before it publishes. At least with an NDA, the other party has contractually obligated itself not to use or disclose your invention.

value before investing in the patent protection effort. To avoid triggering the clock on the one-year period, inventors who are still in the development or testing stage may need to disclose the idea to others in order to further the development or testing. Under such a situation, using an NDA to provide sufficient information to achieve the goal of furthering development or testing is appropriate and is good practice. As long as the reason for disclosing information was not for purposes of exploiting the invention (i.e., selling the invention or product of the invention), an NDA will generally prevent the one-year grace period from ticking. Any exploitation of the invention, however, regardless of whether it is done under an "NDA" arrangement, starts the clock ticking. So that means, unless you're prepared to file a patent application within a year, refrain from selling the invention or from selling a product that embodies the invention.

Unlike the United States, most countries do not have a one-year grace period. That means any public disclosure whatsoever before the filing of your patent application will cause a loss of patent rights in most countries even if the disclosure was in another country. Because the United States is a member of a global patent treaty (the PCT), most other countries recognize the U.S. filing date for purposes of public disclosure. In other words, once a U.S. application is on file, then the invention may be disclosed publicly, even if the corresponding patent application in foreign countries is not filed for another year. The only requirement is that the application be filed in the desired foreign countries within one year of the U.S. filing date. So if you want to seek foreign patent protection on your invention, you may want to have an NDA in place at least until you file your U.S. patent application.

Protecting Catalogs and Marketing Materials

Subpart D

Copyrights and How They Can Protect Your Marketing Materials, Web Sites, and Other Artistic Expressions

Copyright is a means of protecting creative works, such as books, songs, photographs, paintings, and other expression of ideas. Almost every business has products and/or materials that are entitled to copyright protection. For instance, you will probably develop marketing and promotional materials, a web site, and maybe some software in connection with your business. All of these are works that can be protected from copying by copyright. Copyright is different from other forms of intellectual property. Copyrights protect original expression, while patents protect novel inventions or discoveries, trademarks protect the names and logos that identify the source

> Copyright protection is provided by the laws of the United States to authors of "original works of authorship."

of a product, and trade secrets protect confidential information. The next few chapters will walk you through the basics of what copyright is and how you can use it to protect your valuable intellectual property.

Overview of Copyrights

Copyright is a form of protection provided by the laws of the United States to authors of "original works of authorship." It protects a wide variety of works, including art, music, technical and architectural drawings, books, computer programs, photographs, and advertisements.

Protection exists in any original *expression* of an idea as soon as the expression is fixed in any physical medium, such as on paper, electronic discs or tapes, or videotape. For instance, if you write a poem, sketch a drawing, record yourself singing a song, or write some computer code, each of those works of original expression is protected by copyright from the moment the work is in a fixed form. You do not have to register your copyright to have copyright rights, and there is no requirement that you include a copyright notice on your work (for works first published after March 1, 1989).

Copyright protection gives the copyright owner the exclusive right to do the following and to authorize others to do the following:

- Reproduce the copyrighted work
- Make derivative works based on the copyrighted work
- Distribute copies of the copyrighted work by sale, lease, or rental
- Publicly perform certain types of copyrighted works, such as music plays, or audiovisual works.
- Publicly display certain types of copyrighted works, such as paintings or sculptural works.

Ownership of copyright in a work is distinct from ownership of the material object (e.g., the copy of the painting, the music CD, or the software program on your computer). If you buy Microsoft Excel software, you get a copy of the program and a license to use it. You do not get ownership of any copyright in the program. Similarly, if a painter sells her painting, she does not automatically sell the copyright in the painting. What that means is that you can hang the painting on your wall or donate it to a museum, but you cannot exercise the other rights that belong only to the copyright owner, such as make copies of the painting to sell as posters or postcards.

CHAPTER 20

What Can Be Protected by Copyright

Any original work of authorship that is fixed in a tangible form of expression is entitled to copyright protection. A copyright will protect many types of works, including:

- Literary and textual works, such as books, software, and any other written work
- Musical works and accompanying lyrics
- Dramatic works, such as plays
- Pictorial, graphic, and sculptural works, such as photographs, graphics, and paintings
- Audiovisual works, such as motion pictures
- Architectural works, such as houses and office buildings

> Copyright protection can give you the right to stop others from copying the content of your marketing materials, web site, software, and other creative works.

You should consider copyright protection for your marketing materials, the content on your web site, and software so that you can stop others from copying the content of these things.

Expression That Is Not Copyrightable

Not every written expression is copyrightable. There must be some minimal amount of originality included in the work. The following things are considered not to have the minimal amount of originality and are generally not entitled to copyright protection:

- Titles and names (like RAINGOD)
- Short phrases and slogans
- Blank forms used to collect and record information, such as the patient information forms you fill out in a hospital
- Familiar symbols or designs, such as circles, triangles, or a happy face
- Mere variations of fonts, lettering, or coloring
- Listings of ingredients and contents
- Facts or news, although a particular article or other writing can be copyrightable (for example, the fact that Hurricane Katrina hit the Gulf Coast in August 2005 is not copyrightable, but the text of a magazine article describing the destruction and personal stories can be protected by copyright).
- Standard measurements and tables, such as calendars, and height and weight charts
- Works that are not "fixed," like a live performance that is not recorded

The Minimal Amount of Originality Requirement

You can easily meet the amount of originality required for copyright protection. The requirement that the work be "original" does not mean that your work must represent something entirely new. Rather, all that is needed is a very small amount of creative expression that constitutes something more than just a copy of another work. You must actually have created something that did not already exist. If your work is nothing more than a copy of another work, it will not be entitled to copyright protection.

It is possible for two people to have copyright in works that are nearly identical to one another, as long as each person independently created their work. For instance, if you ask a classroom of kindergarten children to paint a dog, each of the children will own the copyright in their painting, even if several of them end up looking substantially similar to one another.

Copyright in Your RAINGOD Umbrella

Your RAINGOD umbrella potentially includes several types of copyrightable expression. The entire umbrella is probably not entitled to copyright protection, but features of the RAINGOD umbrella might be. The thatched roof design on the umbrella fabric may be entitled to copyright protection. The software incorporated into the RAINGOD umbrella for providing weather alerts is probably copyrightable subject matter. Finally, the design of the tiki on the umbrella handle might be entitled to copyright protection.

Not every feature of the RAINGOD umbrella will be entitled to copyright protection. Purely functional parts of the umbrella, such as the shape of the umbrella or the spring mechanism that allows you to open and close the umbrella, would not be entitled to copyright protection because they are useful articles that do not include creative expression.

Copyright Only Protects the Expression of an Idea

Once you disclose to the public your idea for a product or a story, you cannot stop others from using that idea. You can only prevent others from copying your particular expression of that idea. An example of this distinction between your ideas and your expression of those ideas might be a television proposal. You give a sales pitch to a television studio for a revolutionary new television show that will take a group of people from all walks of life and force them to live together and compete against everyone else in the group to win a significant prize at the end of

> Copyright protects expression of ideas, not the idea itself.

the game. The show will be even more interesting because one player will get kicked off in every episode. That idea cannot be protected. You later film your show, called *Survivor*, and someone else films a show called *The Apprentice*. You might say that *The Apprentice* copied your "idea." But the expression of that idea in *The Apprentice* is entirely different, and there is unlikely to be any violation of your copyrightable expression in *Survivor*.

The RAINGOD umbrella encompasses the *idea* of an umbrella having a Hawaiian theme that gives its owner an alert when rain is likely. Your particular expression of that idea is that the top of the umbrella uses a fabric having a thatched roof design and the handle of the umbrella looks like a tiki carving with eyes that light up when rain is likely.

Let's say that your competitor, Copycat Inc., wants to capture part of the market demand for the RAINGOD umbrella by selling a competing Hawaiian-themed umbrella with alert features. Copycat creates and sells an umbrella with a floral Hawaiian print fabric. Instead of a handle that looks like a tiki carving, Copycat makes the handle in the shape of a hula girl. Copycat has clearly copied your idea. But have they violated your copyright rights? Looking only at the design of the umbrella, the likely answer is that Copycat has not infringed your copyrights. Copycat has copied your idea, but not your expression of that idea. Copycat has used an entirely different fabric design and an entirely different handle design. If, however, Copycat creates and sells an umbrella with a thatched roof fabric design and a tiki carving handle, it may have infringed upon your copyright, should the Copycat umbrella look substantially similar to the RAINGOD umbrella.

Copyright Protection Limited to Artistic Expression

Copyright protects original creative or artistic expression. Useful articles are generally not entitled to copyright protection. A "useful article" is something that has an intrinsic useful function and is not merely decorative. If a product has a function, such as a lamp or clothing, and also has decorative features, can there be copyright protection in the product? Maybe. The answer to that question depends on whether the decorative features of the product can be identified separately from the utilitarian function of the product.

For example, a lamp has a base, an electrical socket for the light bulb, and a shade, and each of those things performs a function and would generally not be entitled to copyright protection. But what if the base of the lamp looks like a statuette of a Balinese dancer? That artwork can receive copyright protection. So can a coin bank in the shape of a dog or a pencil sharpener that looks like an antique telephone. As another example, a common, straight-backed chair will not be copyrightable because there is nothing about it that is artistic expression. But if the chair has a carving of a dragon on its back, the dragon carving is conceptually separate from the chair, and is copyrightable. This is a difficult concept, and there is no clear answer if artwork included in any product is obviously entitled to copyright protection. But there is certainly the possibility that it is, and if so, it can be valuable protection for any company.

Consider the handle of the RAINGOD umbrella. It has a function as the handle of the umbrella. A standard umbrella handle will not be entitled to copyright protection. But like the dragon carving on the back of the chair, the tiki carving design on the handle is probably entitled to copyright protection.

Copyrighting a Web Site

A web site may contain many works that could be protected by copyrights. For example, protected works may include individual graphic images within web pages, textual content of web pages, or the visual appearance of entire web pages. Copyrights also may protect certain selections or arrangements of data or images contained in the web site, such as a library of thumbnail graphical images of tikis or a database of recipes to prepare authentic Hawaiian dishes.

Other copyrightable subject matter includes original sequences of computer instructions that: (1) format web page content; (2) hyperlink to other web pages; (3) prompt users for input; (4) respond to user input; and/or (5) carry out other related processes. Examples may include sequences of markup language (e.g., HTML) instructions, CGI scripts, or JAVA modules.

As with any other copyrightable subject matter, web site–related works can only receive copyright protection if they are original works of authorship and include the independent expression of the author. Generally, copyright protection arises automatically upon fixing such expression in a tangible medium such as computer memory. While copyright protection is automatic and does not *require* copyright notice, the owner of copyrights related to a web site might discourage copying by including a copyright notice on protected features.

If you create copyrighted works available for downloading via the internet, you should be careful to use appropriate copyright notice as explained in Chapter 25 (© 2007 Rain Alert Inc.). If you do not, you might be granting an implied license to do more than simply download the work for viewing. To limit the scope of an implied license, a copyright owner should include an express limitation in addition to a standard copyright notice. For example, if the copyright owner intends that the work be viewed only and not copied, then the owner may wish to include the following notice: "The recipient may only view this work. No other right or license is granted."

CHAPTER 21

Who Can Claim Copyright?

Copyright can be claimed by any number of persons or companies. These include authors, independent contractors, corporations, and other employers.

Author's Rights

Only the author, or someone who has obtained rights from the author, can claim copyright. This is the general rule, subject to a few exceptions, such as "work made for hire" discussed later in this chapter. The author of a work owns the copyrights regardless of who pays for the work to be created.

> The general rule is that the author or creator of the work owns the copyrights in the work.

If you have created your marketing materials, including taking the photographs, writing the text, and creating the graphics, then you own the copyright in those materials. If you obtain photographs or other materials from other sources or you hire others to create materials for you, then you do not automatically own the copyright in the work even though you paid for the copy. You might have even given the author detailed instructions about what you wanted them to create, but that does not change the result that the author or creator of a work owns the copyright in the work. It is very important to understand the consequences of author's copyrights. That is something we discuss in more detail later in this chapter.

Contract Workers

Every time you hire an independent contractor, such as a software programmer, graphic artist, or photographer, you should consider entering into a written agreement to transfer the ownership of any copyrights to you after the work is completed. Your payment for the work done for you does not transfer ownership of the copyright to you.

Without a written agreement transferring the copyright rights, the independent contractor will own the copyright and you will have only limited rights to use the copyrightable work they create for you. In most instances,

> **Warning!** An independent contractor you hire to create marketing materials, write software, take photographs, or create some other work for you, will own the copyright in that work even though you pay for the work to be done. If you want to own the copyrights, you must have a written agreement with the independent contractor to transfer the copyrights to you when the work is completed.

that means that you can use the copyrighted work for its intended purpose when you had it created. But you may not be able to use it for other purposes. For instance, if you hire someone to design and create the fabric for your RAINGOD umbrella and you later want to transfer that design to canvas and make canvas bags out of it, the designer may be able to stop you. In addition, you may not be able to modify the fabric design in the future without permission of the author/independent contractor that created it for you.

The other consequence of the independent contractor owning the copyright is that he can re-use what he created for you for other purposes. For instance, if he took photographs for you to include in your product brochure, he can use those same photographs in materials he creates for other clients.

Ownership of copyrights is something you should consider each time you request someone to do work for you or your company. Any transfer of the copyrights in a work must be in writing. It is best to have a written agreement about copyright ownership *before* any work is started, such as an agreement in which the independent contractor agrees to assign to you all copyrights in the work being created for you. After the work is finished, you should confirm the assignment of copyright by having the independent contractor sign another agreement describing what was created and confirming that she assigns all copyrights to you. Ownership issues are often complex and you should consult an experienced copyright lawyer on such issues.

Work Made for Hire

In most instances, an employer owns the copyrights in works created by its employees. This is the primary exception to the general rule of copyright ownership and is called "work made for hire." Under the work-made-for-hire rule, an *employer* owns the copyrights in works created by full-time employees. It is the employer, and not the employee, that is considered to be the author of the work.

Ownership of copyrights is an important topic to discuss with your existing and new employees. Your employees need

> The primary exception to the general rule that an author owns the copyrights is that an employer owns the copyrights in works created by its employees. This is called the "work-made-for-hire" doctrine.

to understand that they don't own the rights in the works they create for the company. They can't take their works with them when they leave.

The "work-made-for-hire" rule does not cover things that your employees develop on their own time or that are outside of the scope of their employment with you. For instance, if you have an employee whose job is to market and promote the RAINGOD umbrella and that employee spends his weekends writing song lyrics for his rock band, your company will not own the copyright in his song lyrics.

You should beware of a prospective employee who offers to bring to your company the rights to some product or work she previously created. For example, you are hiring a computer programmer who has already developed some basic programming that you will want to use in developing your own software. You need to find out who owns the rights to that software. If the prospective employee developed that software on her own time, she likely owns the copyrights and can transfer them or license them to your company. On the other hand, if she developed the software while working for a former employer, her former employer likely owns all of the copyrights in that software. If you use that software, you might be infringing on the copyrights of the former employer.

Other Works Made for Hire

In addition to works prepared by employees, copyright law defines other specific types of works created by independent contractors that can be treated as works made for hire. That means you will automatically own these works and you do not need to have the rights assigned to you by the independent contractor. This other category of works made for hire is limited and must meet specific requirements. This category of works includes:

- Contributions to a collective work, such as a periodical or encyclopedia
- A part of a motion picture or other audiovisual work
- A translation
- A supplementary work to another work, such as a forward to introduce a book or illustrations

- A compilation
- An instructional text
- A test
- Answer material for a test
- An atlas

In addition to falling within one of these categories, you must also have a written agreement with the author before the author starts creating the work. That agreement must expressly state that you and the author agree that the work to be created for you is a "work made for hire."

Co-Authors of Copyright

If a work is created by two or more authors with the intent that their works be merged into one work, the work is considered a "joint work," and the authors are co-owners of the copyright. For example, this book you are reading was written by several people who intended for their contributions to become inseparable parts of one book. If they did not have a written agreement to the contrary, they would be co-owners of the copyright in the entire book. Unlike co-owners of a piece of real estate, though, each copyright owner can do whatever they want to with the copyrighted work, but all of the other owners are entitled to a portion of whatever profits are made.

Copyright Ownership in Your RAINGOD Umbrella

Let's consider ownership of the copyrightable subject matter in your RAIN-GOD umbrella. A typical scenario might be the following:

- You develop the idea for the new umbrella.
- You and your full-time employees develop the overall design of the RAINGOD umbrella.
- Your employee has a book about hand-carved Hawaiian tiki masks and totems and finds one that you really want to use for the handle of the RAINGOD umbrella.

- For the fabric of the umbrella, you know what you want and you hire a screen printing shop to design the fabric to your specifications.
- You do not have the expertise or time to develop the software to operate the RAINGOD umbrella so you hire a software developer who can use some standard programming code and add to it to operate the RAINGOD umbrella alert features. The software developer will charge you a flat fee for the project and will work out of his home on his own computer.

Copyright in the Overall Umbrella Design

As we have discussed, the idea for RAINGOD umbrella is not protected by copyright.

The overall design of the umbrella was developed by you and your full-time employees. Any copyrightable subject matter created by your full-time employees belongs to Rain Alert Inc. under the work-made-for-hire doctrine. Rain Alert Inc. is actually considered to be the author of that work. Whether or not there is something that is copyrightable in that design depends on what you create. If you have product sketches, those sketches are likely copyrightable expression.

Copyright in the Handle Design

Copyright in the design of the tiki handle for the RAINGOD umbrella raises some difficult issues. Rain Alert based the design of the RAINGOD umbrella handle on a design of a tiki totem found in a book. That means the umbrella handle design is a derivative work based on the design shown in the book. If someone owns copyright in the tiki totem shown in the book, you might be infringing on that copyright unless you get permission of the copyright owner. If the tiki totem design in the book was created before 1923, the design is in the public domain. In that event, you are free to copy or modify the design. Before using another work as a source of inspiration for your design, you should research that other work to find out whether you need permission to use it.

Because your design of the tiki handle is a derivative work, you will only own copyright in the creative expression you added to the tiki design from the book.

Copyright in the Fabric Design

What about rights in the fabric design? You knew what you wanted the fabric to look like and instructed the screen printer to create the design to your specifications. So does Rain Alert Inc. own the copyright in the fabric design, or is the copyright owned by the screen printer that actually created the design using your idea? It depends. Remember, the screen printer is not your employee, so to the extent the screen printer creates copyrightable subject matter, the screen printer will own the copyright in that work unless it agrees in writing to transfer those rights to you. If you don't own the copyright, you might be limited in your right to later change the fabric design or use the fabric design for another product or purpose. If you only told the screen printer to create a fabric design that looks like a thatched roof, the screen printer probably owns all of the copyright in the resulting fabric design. If you were significantly more involved, for instance, you spent time with the screen printer and made specific suggestions about the fabric design, you and the screen printer might jointly own the copyright in the fabric design. Again, this is something you need to consider when you hire an outside company or person to create work for you.

Copyright in the Software

Ownership of the rights in the software also might be complicated. It probably will be important for Rain Alert to own all of the copyrights in the software so that you are free to modify and update the software over time. You might also want to license the software to others for other uses. The software developer is probably not your employee because you have hired him only for one project, and he will work when he wants and at home using his own computer. Whether a person is your employee or an independent contractor is something you should discuss with your lawyer. Assuming this software developer is not your employee, he will own the copyright in any code he writes. You must obtain a written assignment of those copyrights. This is something you should agree to in writing at the time you first hire the software developer.

In our example, the software developer is going to start with some software code that he did not develop. You need to know who owns the copyright in that software and whether the software developer has the right to use it and the right to incorporate it into your software. Will including that code in your software limit your ability to use your software in any manner? Again, these are complicated issues that must be thoroughly researched and analyzed with the help and advice of a copyright lawyer.

Copyright in Your Marketing Materials

Ownership issues regarding marketing materials also will arise if Rain Alert hires an advertising agency to develop a marketing brochure. If the marketing company does not assign the copyrights in the brochure to Rain Alert, Rain Alert will obtain a license to use the brochure for its intended purpose, but may be limited in its ability to revise the brochure in the future without permission from the copyright owner. If you decide to hire a new advertising agency in the future, you might not be able to get permission to re-use materials that your original advertising agency created for you. In addition, if the advertising agency uses photographs or other materials obtained from a third party, you need to make sure they obtained the appropriate rights in those photographs so that you can use them as you want to.

Getting Ownership of Copyrights You Do Not Own

As you now know, if you hire an independent contractor to develop something for you, you may need an upfront written agreement that the independent contractor will assign the copyrights to you. In addition, you might find a work that has already been created, and you want to purchase the copyrights in that work so that you can use it and change it freely without any restrictions. These transfers of copyrights must be in writing. For example, an agreement transferring copyright in the fabric design can include language similar to:

> Screen Printing Inc. hereby assigns to Rain Alert Inc. all of its rights, title, and interest to all copyrights and copyrightable subject matter in the thatched roof fabric design created for Rain Alert Inc. Screen Printing Inc. represents that it did not engage any individual or entity, other than its own employees working within the scope of their employment, to assist Screen Printing Inc. in the creation of the fabric design.

This is just an example. You might need additional terms included in your agreements.

CHAPTER 22

Copyright Protection and How Long It Lasts

It is illegal for anyone to violate any of the rights provided by copyright law. Remember, copyright protection is a bundle of exclusive rights giving the copyright owner the exclusive right to do the following and to authorize others to do the following:

- Reproduce the work
- Make derivative works based on the copyrighted work
- Distribute copies of the copyrighted work by sale, lease, or rental
- Publicly perform certain types of works, such as plays or audiovisual works
- Publicly display certain types of works, such as pictorial or sculptural works

Copyright protection stops others from exercising any of these exclusive rights. If someone copies your copyrighted work, makes a derivative work based on your copyrighted work, or distributes copies of your copyrighted work without permission, they have violated your copyrights.

Derivative Works

A derivative work is a work that is *based upon* one or more preexisting works. For example, a translation of a book is a derivative work because it is based on the original book. A screenplay for a movie that was adapted from a book is also a derivative work of the original book. The handle of your RAINGOD umbrella, if it was based on an actual tiki design, is a derivative work. All works borrow from preexisting works to some degree, but a derivative work is based on, or is a substantial copy of, a preexisting work.

The Test for Copyright Infringement

It is unlikely that you would be able to prove that someone actually copied your copyrighted work. For that reason, proof of copying is usually circumstantial, and is proven by showing that

- the infringer had access to your copyrighted work, and
- the infringer's work is substantially similar to your copyrighted work.

Whether or not a work is "substantially similar" generally means that the infringer has copied a substantial and material amount of your protected expression.

Remedies for Copyright Infringement

If your work is infringed, there are a number of remedies:

- *Injunctions*. The most common remedy for someone infringing your copyright is for the court to issue an order prohibiting the infringer from infringing your copyright in the future. That order is called an "injunction."

- *Impounding and destruction of infringing items.* A court can order that all products that infringe your copyright be impounded and destroyed. The court can also order that manufacturing equipment designed specifically to copy your copyrighted work (such as tapes or film negatives) be destroyed.
- *Money damages.* A copyright infringer is generally liable for either: (1) the copyright owner's actual damages or the infringer's profits, or (2) statutory damages.
- *Actual damages and profits.* If you are seeking money damages, you will have to choose between seeking your own actual damages or the infringer's profits. You cannot recover both, because that would be considered a double recovery. Your actual damages are generally measured by your lost sales—that is, sales you lost because the infringer copied your work and sold the infringing items. If you cannot prove that you actually lost sales, you can instead seek to recover the profits that the infringer made from sale of the infringing items (gross sales less deductible expenses).
- *Statutory damages.* Statutory damages are money damages that are awarded by the court instead of actual damages. It can be difficult and very expensive for you to prove in court that you suffered actual monetary damages as a result of the infringement. Similarly, it can be very difficult to prove that the infringer made profits as a result of the infringement. If you registered your copyright before the infringement occurred, though, you have the option of asking the court to award you statutory damages in the amount the court believes are fair and just.

    If you choose to seek statutory damages instead of actual damages or profits, you will not have to prove any actual damages or profits. The amount of the statutory damages is within the discretion of the court, but under current law, cannot be less than $750 or more than $30,000 for infringement of each work involved in the lawsuit. If the infringement was willful, the court can decide to increase the award of statutory damages to not more than $150,000. Again, your copyright must have been registered before the infringement occurred to recover statutory damages.

- *Costs and attorney's fees.* The court can order the infringer to pay your reasonable attorney's fees and your costs incurred in bringing a lawsuit. An award of attorney's fees and costs is not automatic. It is within the court's discretion. Your copyright must have been registered when the infringement occurred to recover attorney's fees (but not costs).

- *Criminal Penalties.* The government can bring a criminal action against someone that is willfully infringing copyright. An action by the government can subject the infringer to criminal penalties.

Length of a Copyright

Copyright protection under U.S. law is for a limited term, but it does last for a long time. The idea behind the government granting copyright protection is to promote creation of original works of authorship and to allow the author or creator a sufficient period of time to collect royalties for his efforts. When the copyright expires, the work becomes part of the public domain and can be used, copied, and modified freely.

The U.S. laws that fix the term of copyright protection have changed many times. Because of those changes, it is often very difficult to figure out whether a work is still protected by copyright or has fallen into the public domain. The length of copyright protection can depend on when the work was first created, when it was first published, whether it was first published with copyright notice, and whether the copyright registration was renewed.

Works Created on or After January 1, 1978

Generally, copyright protection for works created on or after January 1, 1978, will last for the life of the author plus 70 years. The term of copyright always runs to the last day of the year in which it expires. If you create copyrightable works in 2006, 2007, and 2010, and you die in 2040, all of these works will enter into the public domain on the same date, the day after December 31, 2110.

If the work was created for an employer by an employee within the scope of his or her employment (i.e., a work made for hire), the copyright protection will last for 95 years from the date the work was first published, or 120 years from the date of creation, whichever is shorter.

For works first published in the United States between 1978 and 1989, the failure to include a copyright notice when the work was first published could result in the loss of copyright protection unless certain steps were taken in a timely manner. For works first published before 1978, omission of a copyright notice from published works usually resulted in the loss of any copyright protection.

Works Created and Published or Registered Before January 1, 1978

If a work was published in the United States before January 1, 1978, with copyright notice, the author's copyright can last for a total of 95 years. If a work was published in the United States before 1978 without copyright notice, the copyright in that work was invalid. The author could not claim copyright protection, and the work became part of the public domain.

Works Created Before January 1, 1978,
But Not Published or Registered Before January 1, 1978

Generally, the copyright in a work that was created before January 1, 1978, and not published or registered before January 1, 1978, will last for the life of the author plus 70 years. In the case of a work made for hire (in which the copyright is owned by the employer), the copyright protection will last for 75 years from the date the work was first published, or 100 years from the date of creation, whichever is shorter.

Other Factors Affecting the Term of Copyright

The length of the copyright term will also depend on whether the author filed the necessary renewals in a timely manner. Renewals are no longer necessary.

Appendix C might help you determine the term of the copyright in a particular work. Determining precisely when the term of a copyright ends, and who owns any renewal rights, is complicated. You may need to consult with a lawyer who specializes in this area.

Publication

The concept of "publication" of a work, as that term is used in the Copyright Act, is worthy of brief mention here. "Publication" in general is the distribution of copies of a work to the public by sale or other transfer of ownership, or by rental, lease, or lending. A public performance or public display of a work does not necessarily constitute publication. It can be difficult to figure out whether or not a work has been published. If you have a question about a specific work, you may want the advice of a copyright lawyer.

The Public Domain

Certain works are old enough that it is easy to determine that they are in the public domain. If a work was published before 1923, it is in the public domain.

Similarly, if a work was created on or after January 1, 1978, it is fairly easy to establish that the copyright will still be valid for many years. For works published on or after January 1, 1923, and prior to January 1, 1978, you must go through the process of determining the term of the copyright under the copyright law in effect at the time and whether that copyright is still valid. Refer to Appendix B for a chart that provides an overview of when works are likely to pass into the public domain.

CHAPTER 23

Using Copyrighted Work Owned by Others in Your Business

You may wonder whether you can use copyrighted work owned by others. Most uses require the permission of the copyright owner, while some do not.

Using Derivative Work

As discussed above, a work that is *based upon* one or more preexisting works is a derivative work. Only the copyright owner has the exclusive right to authorize someone to make a derivative work based on a copyrighted work.

If you want to change that preexisting work, you must first figure out if anyone owns the copyright in the preexisting work. If the preexisting work is in the public domain, you don't need permission. If someone else owns the copyright, you must get their permission in order to create a derivative work.

Another issue to consider when you create a derivative work is what rights do you have in the derivative work? A derivative work is a combination of the original preexisting work and of the new material you have added to the original preexisting work. If you did not create the preexisting work, you do not own the copyright in it. You only own the copyright in the material you have added to the original work. This can make things very complicated if you want to do something with the derivative work that you didn't anticipate when you obtained permission from the owner of the original preexisting work.

Using Copies of Works

Copying the works of others is increasingly easy to do. Many people do not realize that they may be infringing the author's copyrights when they download works from the internet and distribute copies or incorporate them into another work. For instance, if you want to download a photograph for use in an advertisement, you will need the permission of the copyright owner to do so. Similarly, if you want to reprint an article in your company newsletter, you should obtain the permission of the copyright owner to both copy and distribute the article. Both of these rights are exclusive rights of the copyright owner.

Using Only a Small Portion of a Copyrighted Work

You may have heard that you can use portions of a work created by someone else as long as you don't use more than 10 percent. There is no such rule

> Did you know that copying even 10 percent of a work can be copyright infringement?

under U.S. copyright law. In certain instances copying 10 percent of a work created by someone else can be an infringement. The test for copyright infringement is whether the accused work is copied from and is "substantially similar to," the copyrighted work. If the portion you take from a copyrighted work created by someone else is the "heart" of the copyrighted work or is a widely recognized part of that copyrighted work, then you might infringe even though you copied less than 10 percent of the copyrighted work. There is no single rule or fixed amount regarding the portion of a work that you must change in order to avoid infringement. If you have concerns about specific situations, you should consult with an experienced copyright lawyer.

Obtaining Permission

The owner of copyright in any work has the right to give you permission to exercise any of the exclusive rights: to copy, make derivative works, distribute, perform, and/or display the work. If you get permission from the copyright owner to use their copyrighted work, that permission is generally called a license. The terms of the license are determined through your negotiations with the copyright owner.

If you want to own the copyright in the work, you must get an assignment of the copyright from the copyright owner. Transfer of ownership of copyrights must be in writing.

It can sometimes be difficult to identify the copyright owner, particularly of older works. If you have a copy of the work, the owner should be listed in the copyright notice. The Copyright Office maintains records of registrations that are open to public inspection. The Copyright Office also has a searchable database of copyright registrations on its web site that will give you basic information about registrations issued since January 1, 1978. Sometimes you have to go to the Library of Congress and conduct a manual search of the records to find out if the copyright has been transferred or has expired. There are services located in Washington, D.C., that will help you do this.

Fair Use

There may be instances when you can use a copyrighted work owned by someone else without getting permission. You may have heard the term "fair use." The doctrine of fair use gives you the right to make certain uses of copyrighted works without getting permission and without being liable for infringement. The United States copyright law provides fair use guidelines, but whether or not a particular use of a copyrighted work is a "fair use" is evaluated on a case-by-case basis.

For a particular use to qualify as a fair use you must be able to show that the use was for purposes such as criticism, comment, news reporting, teaching (including multiple copies for classroom use), scholarship, or research. In addition, you have to consider the following four factors:

- The purpose and character of the use, including whether the use is a commercial use or is for nonprofit educational purposes. If the use is for a nonprofit educational purpose, it is more likely to be a fair use. If it is for a commercial purpose, it is less likely to be a fair use.
- The nature of the copyrighted work. If you use portions of a scientific, biographical, or historical work, your use is more likely to be fair use. If you use portions of a work of entertainment, your use is less likely to be a fair use.
- The amount and substantiality of the portion of the work used. If you use only so much of the work as is necessary to make your comment or criticism, then your use is more likely to be a fair use. Excessive copying is less likely to be a fair use.
- The effect of your use upon the potential market for, or value of, the copyrighted work. If your use is likely to harm the market for the copyright owner's work, your use is less likely to be a fair use.

As an example, let's say you write an article for a newsletter that is distributed throughout your industry. In your article this month, you want to comment on a recently published book written by someone else titled *The 10 Most Important Things to Consider before Manufacturing Your Goods in China*. You want to encourage everyone in your industry to read that book. You think it would be great to include the list of the 10 most important things directly from that book in your article. But would doing so be a fair use? If not, you might infringe the copyright in that book. Your use of portions of that book is not for commercial purposes, and you are encouraging people to read the book. That certainly seems fair. The author or publisher of that book, however, might disagree with you. They might think that you have copied the "heart" of the book and that your readers will be less likely to purchase the book because you have given them the entire list of the 10 most important things.

These are issues you should consider whenever you are using any material you did not create. You should consult with a copyright lawyer on whether a particular use is likely to be a fair use.

CHAPTER 24

Registering Your Copyright

Copyrights exist immediately upon creation of an original work of authorship. Under current law, you do not have to register a copyright to have copyright rights. You must, however, have a copyright registration before you can sue anyone for copyright infringement in federal court. In addition, early registration of your copyright offers you significant advantages. Most significantly, if you register your work before an infringement occurs, the infringer may have to pay you statutory damages and reimburse your attorney's fees and costs.

> ### You Should Know
>
> You do not have to register your copyright with the U.S. Copyright Office to have copyright rights. Registration does give you certain significant advantages, including the right to file a copyright infringement lawsuit in federal court, and the right to obtain "statutory damages" and reimbursement of your attorneys' fees and costs.

Advantages to Registering a Copyright

The most obvious advantage of registration is that you must have a copyright registration to sue for copyright infringement in federal court. There are also other significant advantages to registering your copyright. One of the other advantages is that the defendant in a lawsuit for infringement of your copyright might have to pay your attorney's fees and costs. Whether or not to award you your attorney's fees and costs is within the discretion of the court. You might also be able to get the court to order the defendant to pay you statutory damages to compensate you for the infringement, instead of having to prove actual damages. Another significant advantage to registration is it allows you to record your registration with U.S. Customs Service for protection against the importation of infringing copies.

> Copyright registrations can be recorded with U.S. Customs Service to stop importation of infringing copies.

When to Register a Copyright

You can register the copyright in your work at any time during the life of the copyright, but there are significant advantages to early registration. Registration can take up to eight months and if you do not yet have a registration for your work, your ability to file an infringement lawsuit could be delayed.

There is a three-month grace period for registering a copyright after the work is first published. This means that if you submit an application for copyright registration within three months of first publication of the work, you are entitled to the benefits of registration from that first publication date. This is true even if the registration does not actually issue until several months later. The term "publication" in this context, means when you first distributed copies of your work to the public by sale or other transfer of ownership or when you first offered to distribute copies to a group for purposes of further distribution.

If you register your copyright after the three-month grace period, the registration date will be the date your complete application was received by the U.S. Copyright Office.

> You should register copyrights in works that are important to your business within three months of first publishing the works.

The Importance of Registration

Let's say that you discover that a former employee has copied portions of your software program for the RAINGOD umbrella and incorporated those portions into her own products. She is now selling her products with an alert system similar to the alert system in your RAINGOD umbrella. You contact your attorney and want to sue her right away for copyright infringement.

The first thing you must do before you can sue your former employee for copyright infringement is to register the copyright in your software. If you diligently registered your copyright within three months of first publication and have already received your registration from the U.S. Copyright Office, you can file the lawsuit for copyright infringement and can seek statutory damages and attorneys' fees and costs.

If you have not yet registered your copyright, you can file an application with the Copyright Office and seek a registration on an expedited basis (currently requiring a $540 fee in addition to the regular filing fee). You should receive your copyright registration within a few weeks, and you can then file a lawsuit for copyright infringement. Because you didn't have a registration when she copied your software, you can seek recovery of only your actual damages. You are not entitled to seek statutory damages. This means that you will have to prove that you lost profits because of her infringement or that she received profits from using your software. In addition, you are not entitled to seek recovery of your attorneys' fees incurred in the lawsuit, although you might be able to recover some of your costs.

> **Strategy Tip** You should develop a system to timely register the copyright in your products and written materials. One way might be to put a reminder in your calendar every three months to check whether to register any of your copyrights.

This is just an illustration of a likely scenario and one that should encourage you to diligently register copyrights in your valuable property. Issues relating to your right to sue for copyright infringement, and the legal remedies available to you, are complex matters and must be discussed with your legal counsel.

The Process and Cost of Registering

Copyright registration is a legal formality that gives you certain rights and benefits, but is not required for copyright protection. Copyright registration also creates a public record of the basic facts of a particular copyright.

Copyright registration is obtained from the U.S. Copyright Office, Library of Congress in Washington, D.C. Registration of copyright is a relatively simple process. The current filing fee charged by the Copyright Office is only $30 per application (nonrefundable). You must be careful to follow the instructions and properly complete the application form. In some instances, registration of your copyright in a particular work can be complicated, particularly if the work is a derivative work based on earlier works, or if you do not own the copyright in the entire work. An attorney specializing in copyright matters can help you through the registration process.

The Mechanics

To register a work, you must send the following three things to the Copyright Office:

1. A properly completed application form
2. The filing fee for the application
3. A copy of the work being registered

Application Forms

The application forms are available on the Library of Congress web site at www.copyright.gov. There are several forms available (see Appendix C), so the proper form to use depends on the type of work you are registering. The currently available forms include:

- *Form TX.* For written (textual) works, including books, poems, song lyrics, computer programs, automated databases, and other written works.
- *Form VA.* For works of the visual arts, including photographs, graphic works and sculptural works.
- *Form SR.* For sound recordings.
- *Form PA.* For works of the performing arts, including musicals and dramatic works, motion pictures, musical compositions, and multimedia works (if the predominating material is performance).
- *Form SE.* For periodicals, newspapers, magazines, and other serials issued in successive parts and intended to be continued indefinitely.

Using the correct form is not critical. The Copyright Office will transfer the application to a different form if they determine that you used the wrong form.

Sometimes a work might be part written text (Form TX), part software (also form TX), part audiovisual (Form PA), and part sound recording (Form SR), such as a video game. If so, you should try to determine whether most of the copyrightable subject matter is written text or audiovisual, and choose the form on that basis.

The Fees

The current fees for copyright registration are posted on the Copyright Office web site at www.copyright.gov. See Appendix C for the current fees.

The Deposit Copy Requirement for Registration

Along with the completed application and the filing fee, you are required to send a copy of the "best edition" of the work being registered. This copy is called a "deposit copy" and it will not be returned to you. The requirements for what you send in as the deposit copy are different depending on the type of work being registered. The general rules are as follows:

- If the work is unpublished, send one complete copy of the best edition of the work.
- If the work is published, send two complete copies of the best edition of the work.

The "best edition" of the work also varies depending on the type of work. If two or more editions of the same work have been published, best edition means the highest quality edition.

There are numerous exceptions to these general rules, including special rules for submitting computer software source code. An acceptable deposit for registration of software is two copies of the first 25 pages and the last 25 pages of source code with trade secrets blocked out.

The Copyright Office deposit regulations do not specifically address works that are only transmitted online. Until such regulations are adopted, one form of deposit acceptable to the Copyright Office is a computer disk containing the entire work and representative portions of the work in a format that the examiner at the Copyright Office can examine.

The Copyright Office web site includes detailed instruction sheets for completing the application forms and other information particular to registering certain types of works, and for determining the proper deposit.

The Mandatory Deposit Requirement

If you published a copyrightable work in the United States, you are obligated to provide a copy of the work to the Library of Congress. This is true even if you never seek registration of the work. Although this is a separate requirement from the deposit made for registration of your copyright claim, generally the deposit made with your copyright application will satisfy the mandatory deposit requirement.

Marking Catalogs and Marketing Materials with Copyright Notice: Foreign Copyright Protection

For works first published in the United States after March 1, 1989, you do not have to include a copyright notice to maintain copyright protection. Using a copyright notice, however, has advantages. It might deter people from copying your work. In addition, it makes it difficult for other people to claim that they are "innocent" infringers who were misled by the fact you did not have a copyright notice on your work.

Copyright notice is still required for protection in some countries, so you might lose rights by publishing your works with no notice. For works first published in the United States between 1978 and 1989, the omission of a copyright notice from published

You Should Know   Although it is no longer required, you should include a copyright notice on all published works.

works could result in the loss of copyright protection entirely unless certain steps were taken in a timely manner. For works first published in the United States before 1978, omission of a copyright notice from published works usually resulted in the automatic loss of any copyright protection.

A copyright notice should include: the copyright symbol ©, the year the work is first published, and the name of the copyright owner, (*e.g.*, ©2007 Knobbe, Martens, Olson & Bear, LLP). The © symbol is particularly recommended if you want to protect your rights in foreign countries. But if you are only concerned about protection in the United States, you can also use "Copyright" and "Copr." If you are publishing a sound recording, use ℗ instead of ©. You should still include the first publication date and copyright owner name. Many companies like to add "All Rights Reserved" after their copyright notice. This does not add any additional protection under the copyright statute, but it does sound good.

A common question is: What year should you include in your copyright notice if you release a new revised version of your book, video game, or other work? Because the new version is really a new work, you can use the year you publish the new version, and you do not need to include the year of the earlier version. Some people prefer to include the year the first version was released and the year the new version was released, which is acceptable. The name in your copyright notice should be the full name or an abbreviation that can be recognized.

> Proper copyright notice includes three elements: the copyright symbol (©), the year of publication, and name of the owner of the copyright.

There is no strict rule about where the copyright notice should be placed on your work. The purpose of the copyright notice is just that, to give people notice of your copyright claim. So you should place the notice on the work in a place that it is reasonably likely to be seen and give notice of your claim of copyright.

Protecting Copyrights in Foreign Countries

The United States is a member of the Universal Copyright Convention, which gives U.S. copyright owners copyright protection in many foreign countries. In 1988, the United States joined the Berne Convention, which extends copyright protection in U.S. works to the vast majority of foreign countries. Obtaining and enforcing copyrights in foreign countries requires compliance with the laws and treaties of each individual country. You should consult a lawyer knowledgeable in copyright law about your specific needs.

Registration of Patents, Trademarks, and Copyrights

Subpart E

Registering your IP
Does Not Give You the
Right to Sell Your Product

CHAPTER 26

The Benefits of IP Protection

L et's say you obtain patents on the novel features of your umbrella, you register your clever trade-marks, and you even get your copyrights registered. Are you good to go? Do you now have a guaranteed right to sell your umbrella?

After reading the above chapters, you should now know that the answer to these questions is no. Patents, trademarks, and copyrights are very different animals—they offer different types of protection, scope of protection, and rights. This chapter provides a recap of what your patents, trademarks, and copyrights give you and perhaps more importantly, what they don't.

The Myth About Patents: Getting a Patent on Your Product Guarantees That You Can Sell It Freely

As discussed previously, one of the more common myths about patents is that getting patent protection on one or more aspects of your product guarantees that you can sell your product at will. In other words, there is the misperception that if you obtain a patent on a new device that you want to commercialize, you are free to sell that product without worry about infringing other people's patents. Unfortunately, that is not the case. A patent only provides the right to exclude others from practicing the invention protected in the patent. The patent does not provide the right to the patent owner to use what is protected.

As discussed in Chapter 9, even if you come up with an improved umbrella with lots of nifty bells and whistles, the patent obtained may protect only one feature or a couple of features on the improved umbrella. But a previous patent owned by a separate company may cover the core technology in the umbrella; for example, the mechanism for effectively and efficiently opening and closing the umbrella arms. So while your patent may provide you with the right to stop others from using certain features of an improved umbrella, you may not, without authority of the earlier patent holder, use the core technology incorporated in the umbrella.

So it is important when bringing a new product to market that you distinguish between seeking to protect improved features or core technology in the new product from assessing whether the new product can be commercialized without infringing the patent rights of others. Seeking patent protection on the improved features or core technology serves a very different strategy than ensuring that another's patent is not infringed by the commercialization of that product. Taking steps to ensure a certain level of "market clearance" is discussed in Chapter 16 and again in Part Three.

> Because your patent may only cover improved features and not core technology, you might need the permission of another patent holder to sell your product.

The Rights Provided by a Trademark Registration

Unlike patents, trademarks have a more direct relationship with your right to use them. In other words, the more you use a trademark, the more likely it is that you have a right to use that mark. It is not a guarantee, as explained in Chapter 5, but it does have some bearing. Trademarks reflect use of a word, logo, and/or slogan unique to the user for those goods or services. The more a trademark is identified with a single user, the stronger the right to use that mark. So in that regard a trademark is very different from patents.

> Registering a trademark may permit you to continue using the registered mark.

A trademark registration can be obtained only when you have used the mark in a manner that is, at least according to the USPTO, not likely to cause confusion with any other mark being used in the marketplace. In other words, in order to obtain a trademark registration, you must show that you are using a word, a slogan, a logo, or some combination of words and designs, that is uniquely different and not confusing with respect to any other marks, logos, or slogans in the marketplace. By the very nature of that assessment, the issuance of her trademark registration permits the owner to continue to use the registered mark. So, unlike patents, the obtaining of the trademark registration serves two purposes: (1) to show evidence of ownership in, and the right to use, a particular trademark; and (2), to preclude others from using a confusingly similar mark. Of course, even if you have the right to use a particular trademark on your product, that is no guarantee that you have the right to sell your product at all. Your product may infringe another party's patent.

The Rights Provided by a Copyright Registration

A copyright registration can only be obtained on works that actually have been created and that are original and creative. Unlike the examination process for trademark registration applications and patent applications by the USPTO, the copyright registration application review by the Copyright Office does not involve substantive analysis. In other words, the Copyright Office is not making an assessment of whether there is legitimate copyright protection in the work created. While the test for copyrightability is both originality and creativity (i.e., sufficiently new and creative), the Copyright Office does not determine whether the test is satisfied. The Copyright Office serves mostly to

> **Did You Know?** | Can someone else challenge my copyright registration?
>
> In most cases, yes. The issuance of a copyright registration provides not only evidence of your ability to continue to use and copy the protected work but also a vehicle for excluding others from copying the protected work. However, if you accuse another person or company of infringing your copyright registration, the alleged infringer can challenge whether or not your copyrighted work is sufficiently original and creative to permit you to assert it against someone else. So while the copyright registration looks like it gives you the right to continue to use and copy the protected work, it is far from a guarantee.

ensure that the copyright registration application has been filled out correctly. So that means that a copyright applicant will almost always get a copyright registration, even if he shouldn't be entitled to one under the copyright laws.

Protecting Yourself from Infringing the IP Rights of Others

How to Make Sure You Can Sell and/or Continue to Sell a New Product

Because obtaining a patent on an improved feature or on core technology will not guarantee you the right to sell those features or technologies in the marketplace, one of the things you might do before going to market with your product is to assess whether other patents exist or are likely to issue that protect features or technology that you may use in your product. These predesign and pre-launch product evaluations are often referred to as "right to practice" or "freedom to operate" studies or analyses. We've touched on some of these subjects in Chapter 16. This part of the guide provides some helpful guidance on how to take those steps. We won't touch upon trademarks or copyrights in Part Three because we assume that you have done adequate trademark searching to ensure that you can use your trademark with your product and we also assume that you already have confirmed your right to use copyrighted material in your marketing materials.

CHAPTER 27

Protecting Yourself from a Patent Infringement Claim

O ne of the worst things that can happen in launch-ing your new product is to be hit with a claim or lawsuit from a patent holder that your product infringes the patent holder's claim. A lawsuit could force you to stop selling your product and/or drain your business of the cash it needs to market your prod-uct. This chapter discusses the ways in which you can guard against a patent infringement claim or lawsuit.

The First Step: Focus on the New Features

In taking the steps to assess whether a proposed design or finished product may infringe a patent or patents owned by someone else, it's first important to consider what technology is at issue. Almost all products are combinations of old elements with potentially new elements. For example, even with an improved umbrella that has a new mechanism that more effectively and reliably opens and closes the umbrella, the fabric attached to the arms may be the same water-impervious material that's been used for decades. Thus, the improved umbrella may comprise old fabric covering a new mechanism.

In terms of prioritizing the step of ensuring your right to market a product, it makes sense to focus on the new features, separate from materials or mechanisms that are fairly old. Because patents only last for 17 years from issuance or 20 years from the original filing date (see Chapter 15), you can take some comfort in being able to use technology or materials that are older than 20 years. This is not a guarantee, of course. But it does help from a cost and timing standpoint in helping you to prioritize.

But let's assume for the moment that your inventive umbrella product includes not only your inventive mechanical features (for which you may be seeking your own patent protection) but also a new waterproof membrane material that is especially made for cold environments. Let's assume that the membrane is made through a chemical engineering process that was developed by a company called Fabricorp, which specializes in developing impervious membrane materials. If your supplier of the membrane material has used a similar process, or if you attempt to fabricate the membrane material yourself following the same or similar process then it is important to assess whether Fabricorp has a patent on the new membrane material. So what does that involve?

> Conduct a patent search to identify patents owned by other companies that you might infringe. You can search the USPTO database yourself at www.uspto.gov.

Conducting a Technology/Patent Search: Figuring Out What Is Unprotected and What Is Protected

In assessing whether any features, processes, or methodology you are using may be protected by patents owned by other companies, a first step is a technology search or a patent search. What is a technology/patent search? It is a search of the database of the patents that have issued and the patent applications that are pending at the USPTO.

Like any database, the USPTO database is searchable. Historically, before electronic databases were instituted, patents were kept in individual "shoes" at the USPTO. Those shoes were essentially boxes of related patents categorized by classes of technology and subclasses of particular features or methodology. Until recently, a search of the patent database required manual searching of shoes of patents relating to the technology at issue.

Thankfully, today, with the institution of electronic databases and continuously updated software, searching efficiency has improved. With the ability to effectively search through the electronic database with appropriate word searches (called "queries"), it is a much more efficient task to search for patents on related technology. The modernization of the USPTO and its connection to the internet now enable you to search both issued patents and pending applications from your home computer. The web site is www.uspto.gov. Once there, you will find links to trademarks and patents, among other information about the USPTO. On the web page that permits patent searches, you will find separate links for issued patents and pending applications.

You can also search for patents by patent owner. One very common strategy is to search for your competitors' patents because they are the parties most likely to sue you and most likely to have relevant patents. However, this strategy alone is rarely sufficient to locate all relevant patents and should be combined with other search strategies.

Hire a Professional Patent Searcher

Don't want to do your own searching? No problem. There are plenty of professional patent searchers throughout the United States and the world whom you can hire to conduct searches. Many have obtained copies of most (if not all) issued patents in the last 50 to 60 years, although with the PTO storing patents electronically, saving hard copies is no longer necessary. Some search services have created text searchable databases for others to use for a subscription fee. Hiring a service to provide a search of the relevant database is not necessarily an expensive endeavor. Depending upon the scope of the technology searched and how comprehensive you want the search to be, professional search services will typically cost between $200 and $2,000. It is a time-based cost, so the more time necessary to conduct a thorough and wide-ranging search, the more expensive. A search of a single feature would probably cost in the lower range. Electronic searches, of course, are not perfect, and for an additional fee many professional searchers will hand search the USPTO's records to reduce the risk that relevant patents will be overlooked.

So what happens if a competitor filed a patent application two years ago, but it has not yet issued? Will your patent search reveal patent applications? The answer is yes, as long as the patent application was filed at least 18 months prior to the search. That is because the USPTO has adopted a rule that most countries around the world have followed for years: a patent application will be published after 18 months unless the applicant chooses to give up his right to file corresponding patent applications outside the United States. As explained in Chapter 12, the patent application examination process historically has been conducted in secret. That created an unfair disadvantage to competitors who had adopted the same or similar technology in parallel to the examination process and then were hit with a lawsuit the day the patent issued. The unfairness resulted from the investment of time and money into tooling and marketing for a product that may now be infringing a competitor's newly issued patent.

To remedy the situation, the PTO now publishes applications after 18 months. That permits you to learn what inventions your competitors are

---

Warning! When hiring a patent searcher, be sure you know what you want the searcher to find. If you're only concerned with patentability of your own invention, you want a patentability search (discussed in Chapter 11). But if you're trying to find patents that you might infringe, you want an infringement search that will identify potentially relevant claims (since you're mainly concerned with infringing someone else's patent claims). You can discuss these distinctions with your patent searcher or patent attorney, though often it's better to let your patent attorney sort through the search details.

---

developing and seeking to protect with a patent even before the patent issues. Once a patent application is published, it can be discovered in a patent/technology search.

Reliability of Patent Searches

The search itself is usually not that difficult, and it can be an informative learning process if you do it yourself. Simply conducting the search will expose you to patented technology that would surprise you. With the search complete, the more difficult task is reviewing the results of the patent search. Like modern day internet searches, you often get more information than you really want. In other words, patents may be discovered in the search that share some common element, but really don't apply to your situation. Likewise, it is still possible that relevant and important information may have been missed in the search. That is because the particular words that are selected as part of the search inquiry may not always be the appropriate words used by others for the same technology. For example, you might conduct a search for patents on a

---

You Should Know | Why would patents use different words for the same technology?

It's an interesting question that often confounds lawyers as well as patent holders. The USPTO permits a great deal of flexibility in how patents are written. The writer of a patent application can choose to use his own language to describe technology, as long as it is clear to the reader. So, in theory, but thankfully not too often in practice, an inventor could call a hammer a saw if he wanted to, as long as he makes that seemingly nonsensical word choice clear. More often, however, since there are many synonyms in the English language—think "null" and "void," "cease" and "desist," etc.—there almost always is an unintentional interchange of word choices. So one inventor might refer to a device for holding liquid as a cup, a container, a holder, a bowl, a tank, etc. Because of the freedom of inventors to choose their own words to describe their invention, any patent search must take that into consideration. So whenever you do a patent search, you should search for concepts using multiple word choices.

"widget," but an early patent holder may have described his widget as a "gadget" instead, even though they are the same or similar technology. So if you search for all patents on widgets, you may in fact have missed patents on the identical technology because the word "gadget" was not included in your search query.

Nonetheless, with improving search technology, patent searches provide fairly reliable results. If you conduct the search yourself, then it would be helpful to understand that reliable searching often requires that you try different types of word searches to cover as much ground as possible.

Analyze the Results of Your Patent Search

Once your search is complete, then you can begin the process of reviewing the patents and patent applications to find out whether any of them creates potential obstacles to the marketing of your new product. To prioritize your review, you might want to review your competitors' patents first. Read the specification and claims in each patent, and if they seem relevant to your product, also review the file history for the patent (see the discussion below on file histories).

If you do this assessment yourself, it is important to remember that a patent protects only what is specified in the claims of the patent. The claims are the numbered paragraphs at the end of a patent and they define, with words, the scope of the "invention." In other words, the claims describe what the public is not permitted to do for the life of the patent.

An assessment of claims in a patent involves "claim interpretation" or "claim construction"—an analysis of what the words mean and thus the scope of protection provided by a patent. If you are not used to reading and interpreting claims of patents, it can be pretty daunting to figure out what is protected by the claims, what is protectable even if not claimed, and what cannot be protected. Indeed, an entire body of law has developed over just how to interpret claims in a patent. Entire lawsuits can revolve around what a single word in a claim means.

As a general first principle, the law states that the words used in claims should be given their normal meaning unless the patent applicant expressly

> **You Should Know** Your search might uncover published applications that are still pending (meaning that they have not issued yet). With respect to pending applications, you should know that the claims at the end of the applications are not enforceable because the application has not issued as a patent. It is also important to keep in mind that claims may change during the patent examination process at the PTO. So there is no assurance that the claims in a published application will ever issue or issue without revision. Nonetheless, the assessment of claims in a pending application is still useful in that they serve as an indicator of what the applicant it seeking to protect. Therefore, once you discover a published pending patent application that seems relevant, you should continue to monitor the application as it is examined to see if it issues and whether changes have been made by the applicant to the claims.

explains in his application that he intends otherwise. However, in deciding how to interpret a patent claim, you must look at the specification of the patent carefully to see if the patent applicant redefined the terms of the claim. The redefinition can be subtle or implicit, and many cases have been litigated over whether a claim term has been implicitly redefined.

Look at the File History

In interpreting the meaning of the patent claims, you should consider not only the patent specification but also the file history associated with the examination of the patent application at the PTO. All of the paperwork and communications exchanged between the applicant (or his attorney) and the PTO make up the "file history" of a patent. The file history is important to claim interpretation because the applicant and/or the examiner may have provided explanations, or definitions, or clarifications not found in the patent specification itself. It is important in assessing the scope of protection of any claim to see what statements were made during prosecution of that patent that may shed light on whether the claim is actually narrower or broader than the claim may appear at first glance.

Did You Know?	How can I see the file history of someone else's patent?

You can order a copy of the file history from the USPTO. You can do so directly or by hiring an outside service to obtain a copy for you. Indeed, many of the individuals or companies that provide patent/technology searches also provide file history copies if requested. Whether you order it yourself or through an agency, the cost is usually about a couple of hundred dollars, unless the file history is really long. File histories for more recently issued patents are available at http://portal.uspto.gov/external/portal/pair. The file history usually consists of the initial application (including the drawings and transmittal papers), office actions sent by the examiner explaining her assessment of the patentability of the pending application, and responses to the office actions by the patent applicant. The file history will also include a notice of allowance that is provided once examination has concluded, which also may provide comments by the examiner as to reasons for allowance.

The file history can also be the source of "prosecution history estoppel." This is where the patent applicant says something or makes an amendment that comes back to bite them. The common case is where the patent applicant makes an amendment to narrow his claims to overcome some prior art reference. This prevents the patent applicant from later arguing under the doctrine of equivalents that his claim should be broader than what's literally in the claim. The doctrine of equivalents is discussed further on page 273.

After the Patent Search

OK, you've conducted the search and looked at the patents discovered in the search. Now what? Well, it depends. Are you early in the design process for your product, or are you ready to launch the product? If you're early in the design process, then the patents you reviewed may provide a road map, although maybe a difficult one, to a design that is both marketable and noninfringing. In other words, the issued patents and pending applications should guide you on what types of features or materials that you can include in your product or process that would not infringe the patent of another, thus providing some level of comfort that you have removed one or more barriers to market entry (i.e., launching your product). If you are later in the design process (i.e., you're ready to launch), then you still have options—it's just that a change in design may not be one of them.

If the results of the technology/patent search make you comfortable that the product you want to bring to market is *not* protected by other patents, then it may be appropriate to proceed to the marketplace. Depending upon how risk-averse you are, however, you may want to have your analysis confirmed by a patent attorney.

If the search results suggest that there may be patent obstacles to bringing your product to market, what can you do? Well, there are several options, as described in the next chapter.

Design-Arounds

Sometimes an inventor who does patent searching almost wishes he had never done any searching, because he finds patents that cover the innovation that he thought he was the only one clever enough to invent. Not only do those patents mean that the inventor didn't invent his innovation, the

> If you find problem patents in your search, consider designing around the patents.

patents might block him from marketing his product that incorporates the innovation. In that case, all is not lost.

One option at that point is to "design around" the problematic patents. The term "design around" means to change one or more aspects of the design to avoid the patent(s) owned by someone else. If you successfully design around a patent, then a judge or jury is likely to find that you do not infringe the patent.

For example, if the material you've selected for your umbrella membrane is covered by the patent of your competitor, one simple way to design around that patent is to select a different material for your umbrella's membrane. Of course, the choice of alternative materials will be limited by the perceived marketability of the alternative design. Would the expected sales be sufficient to justify the investment in the alternative design route? Your goal should be to strike the appropriate balance between marketability of your product and non-infringement (via a design-around). If you can design around a patent and still come up with a marketable product, then you will reach your goal of reducing the risk of infringing someone else's patent and increase the chance of achieving commercial success.

The Need for an Opinion of Counsel

It is difficult to assess whether your design may infringe someone else's patent. It is not easy to come to a meaningful and reliable conclusion as to whether any patents create potential barriers to going to market with your product, especially if you have little experience with patents.

However, as an entrepreneur with little experience dealing with patents, your initial assessment can still be very valuable in eliminating those patents that have little or no relevance to the technology in your new product. If you're not sure you did a satisfactory search or if you aren't sure whether or not the patents you found actually present obstacles to launching your product, then you should consider hiring a patent attorney to help you.

But why? There are a number of reasons, one or more of which may be applicable to your situation: (1) patents are complicated, (2) your investors may insist that you hire a patent attorney, and (3) a patent attorney can help you guard against an accusation of willful infringement.

Patents Are Complicated

The obvious reason to hire counsel is that the assessment of the scope of protection provided by a patent is not only a technical assessment but also a legal one. Patent law has developed over hundreds of years, and continues to evolve today. At least a couple of times a year, the U.S. Supreme Court is asked to clarify one or more important patent law issues. Claim interpretation alone is often a sufficiently complex legal analysis to warrant seeking

> **You Should Know** | **What is the "doctrine of equivalents"?**
> Talk to your patent lawyer about this one, but generally, the doctrine of equivalents means that you can infringe someone else's patent even if you don't do exactly what the claims of that patent say. Infringement in this case is based on whether there are merely insubstantial differences between your product and the claims of the patent.

confirmation by a patent attorney. Even if your product doesn't literally infringe the claims of a patent, your product may still infringe the patent based on the "doctrine of equivalents," and so you will want to do a careful infringement analysis. A patent lawyer can perform this analysis for you.

Your Investors Insist on It

Another reason to hire a patent lawyer is that your investors or management may require that an opinion of counsel be obtained before launching the product. By doing so, the investors or management are seeking to reduce the risk of liability for patent infringement. If you are seeking to be acquired by another company, that other company will conduct "due diligence" on your company and your product line. As part of that due diligence, the potential acquirer will almost certainly seek the advice of independent patent counsel to assess both the patentability of your products and the risk of your products infringing other patents. On some occasions, a potential acquirer will find it sufficient if you have obtained an opinion of counsel yourself, confirming that your products don't infringe the patents belonging to others.

Protect Yourself from an Accusation of Willful Infringement

A third reason for seeking an opinion of patent counsel is because patent lawsuits almost always involve allegations by the patent holder that the accused infringer willfully infringed the patent. By way of background, the patent law

> **Warning!** If you know about someone else's patent and it's close to what you're doing, consider obtaining an opinion of counsel to avoid being accused of willful infringement. This can avoid you being liable for enhanced damages if you're later found to infringe.

states that you could be liable for patent infringement, whether or not you knew of the patent. In other words, no intent to infringe is necessary to be liable for patent infringement (assuming, of course, that the patent covers your product). However, if a judge or jury also finds that you made and/or sold your product knowing it to be an infringement of a third party's patent, the law permits damages to be increased by up to three times (sometimes called "treble damages"). This is called "willful infringement."

Traditionally, the courts have required a written opinion of competent patent counsel to show good faith. That opinion had to comprehensively and sufficiently explain why the patent was either invalid or not infringed by your product. That added an almost necessary expense to selling a new product because of the need to hire a patent attorney to give such an opinion. The courts have recently recognized that an attorney's written opinion may not always be necessary. Still, it is highly advisable to have a counsel's opinion because patent analysis is inherently complex.

The court decisions mean that sophisticated people who understand patent law may take good-faith steps to avoid infringement without the need to hire patent counsel. In other words, if you launch a product or service and are sued for patent infringement and charged with willful infringement, acceptable evidence to rebut such charges of willful infringement may include the comprehensive assessment of a patent by a layperson that the patent is not infringed or is invalid. It's not an easy assessment, and it still brings some risk that the analysis may not be considered sufficiently reliable to rebut allegations of willful infringement because it must reflect a correct understanding of the law. But it does provide some leeway for those who have undergone this type of analysis in the past to consider whether an investment in seeking an opinion of counsel is truly necessary.

In deciding whether to hire an attorney, you should weigh the cost of hiring one versus the potential cost of being found to be a willful infringer. A patent attorney's analysis will more than likely cost several thousands of dollars and varies depending upon how complex the technology is and the number of patents at issue. So whether or not you hire an attorney to do a non-infringement analysis isn't an easy decision, unless the risk of infringement is high. If the relevant market is highly competitive and your competitors are sophisticated about patents, the risks of being accused of infringing patents of others may be high.

The Cost of an Opinion of Counsel

The decision as to whether to obtain a formal opinion of counsel about "market clearance" issues is really a cost-benefit analysis. Do the expected revenues warrant the investment in attorney services? If you decide to obtain a written opinion of counsel, you can expect to spend anywhere between $5,000 and $20,000, possibly more, depending again upon the complexity of the technology, the number of patent references that are red flags, or the number of differing technologies at issue. If you expect that your product will generate profits in the six figures or greater, the cost of getting a competent written opinion of patent counsel may easily be justified as an added expense in your profit analysis. In the end, it's simply a matter of how risk-averse you are in proceeding to launch a product. The big risk takers play the odds, and hope that they don't get sued for infringement down the road. The risk-averse individuals give themselves greater comfort by retaining counsel to do a patent analysis and prepare formal written legal opinions.

> **You Should Know** | ## What does "market clearance" mean?
>
> The term "market clearance" is an often over-used term that basically means that no known patents pose meaningful risks of patent infringement. It implies that an analysis has been done to give you a comfort level that the patent(s) of another do not cover your product or service. The term may imply to an unsophisticated person, however, that no patent in existence covers your product or service. Rarely does it really mean that. A lawyer can only make a determination of non-infringement or invalidity of a patent if she knows about the patent. A lawyer cannot make such assessments for other patents that may exist that she did not analyze. So a "market clearance" opinion is only reliable as to the patents analyzed and should not be read to provide clearance as to other unknown patents.

Being Sued—And the Chances of Winning

The question we are often asked by a client considering whether to launch a new product or new service is: "Am I going to get sued?" That's a fair question to ask. Unfortunately, it's not a legal question, so it cannot be answered with any reliability by a lawyer. Lawsuits are almost always filed because of the economic impact of the accused infringer in the marketplace. It's not always a logical decision to file a lawsuit—it can be an emotional or irrational decision. That is one reason why lawsuits are sometimes filed against accused infringers whose product or service isn't covered by the patent(s) at issue. So it's not a matter of whether you're right or wrong—you may get sued anyway.

It is even difficult to answer the question: "If I'm sued, will I win?" A lawyer worth his salt should have no trouble telling you whether you **should** win or lose, but would have trouble telling you whether you **will** win or lose. That is because the outcome of a lawsuit depends heavily upon two things: one, whether you have enough money to remain in the lawsuit long enough to get to a decision on the merits, and two, whether the judge and/or jury understands the technology and the law well enough to reach the correct

| Strategy Tip | What does being risk-averse have to do with whether to seek an opinion of counsel? |

Lawsuits are not necessarily about right or wrong. That is because in the law there is rarely a right or wrong answer. Two reasonable judges or juries can come to opposite conclusions on the facts. And lawsuits can be expensive. Even if a company believes strongly that it is right, it still requires lawyers to prove them right in court. Given all of that, tackling legal decisions takes on the need for a cost-benefit analysis. Not only should you think about whether your position is correct, you should also think about the odds of getting sued and the odds of the judge and/or jury getting it right. If you expect to make a big impact in the market with your product, the risk of getting sued goes up, even if you reasonably believe your product does not infringe anyone else's patent. That is because lawsuits are most often economic decisions. For the same reason, the decision to seek an opinion of counsel is an economic decision—does the expected benefit of launching the product justify the cost (real or imagined)? Do this analysis, and then decide what's best for your business.

conclusion. If your legal "war chest" is small, the likelihood of being able to sustain a lawsuit long enough to have the judge rule on the merits is low. You would have to hope that your adversary's war chest is also small.

Likewise, if the judge assigned to the case does not like patent cases or has a docket of cases that is very long, he may not invest the time necessary to truly understand the patent issues. Or if the available jury pool where the case is filed is not very sophisticated, there is a risk that the jury would not fully understand the technology or applicable patent law, or both. That is not intended as a slight against juries or judges—it is simply the recognition that no one has expertise in all things. Indeed, there is at least one judge who is known for requiring CEOs of large companies in lawsuits against each other to attend the jury selection process, particularly when there are large potential damages at stake. It is an eye-opening experience to see who will be making the decision of whether your company will pay $100 million in

> **Strategy Tip** | How risk-averse are you?
>
> That's a difficult question to answer because it often depends upon the circumstances. If we told you that if you launch this product, you may be found liable to a patent holder for $3 million in damages, plus paying the other side's attorneys' fees, you may become suddenly very risk-averse even if you've always considered yourself to be a risk taker. On the hand, even those entrepreneurs who are generally not willing to take much risk should not necessarily retain patent counsel prematurely. In the end, it may be a necessary expense, but it is worth doing a cost-benefit analysis initially, even if your analysis is rough.

damages or not. Almost invariably, the CEOs agree to settle the case then and there, before the opening statements even begin.

Other factors you should consider are how likely your competitors are to sue you (i.e., have they sued others before), how competitive the marketplace is, the profits you expect to generate versus the cost of litigation, and whether the technology involved is the type on which people would get patents. If you are just entering this market, those factors may be difficult to assess without the guidance and advice of a patent lawyer or someone who knows your market. On the other hand, if you've been entrenched in the industry for a long time, you already may be well aware of those considerations, which may make it easier to assess how risk-averse you are.

Patent Trolls

Historically, it was competitors that brought patent lawsuits to drive infringers out of the market. More recently, a trend has emerged in which "trolls" are suing companies for patent infringement. A troll is usually a company that doesn't have operations or sales, but that buys patents for the sole purpose of suing deep pockets to extract settlements. With the emergence of trolls, it may no longer be sufficient to search only for competitors' patents when conducting a patent search. Even patents on similar technology to yours that are issued to individual inventors may still pose a risk if a troll comes across the patent and buys it from the individual for the purpose of suing you or others. Thankfully, smaller companies usually do not have to worry about patent trolls because there's usually not enough gold at the end of the rainbow for a troll to spend its time on you.

Risk-Aversion and Problematic Patents

If you're risk-averse, you may find it better to design around the problematic patent. You or someone you worked with to develop your product may be able to analyze the patent and alter your design to avoid the scope of the patent.

There also may be unexpected advantages to doing a design-around. One is that you may come up with an improved design or methodology that is actually superior to the patented design. As they say, necessity is the mother of invention. Avoiding patents by others is certainly considered by some to be a "necessity." In this way, you may turn a defensive situation into an offensive situation. Instead of facing the risk of infringing patents of another, you may find that you can patent technology that is not only marketable but technologically advantageous. By patenting or seeking to patent these new advantages (think "patent pending"), you may find that your competitors will start worrying about your patents. In that regard, you may want to refer back to Part Two, Subpart B (starting at Chapter 9).

But what happens if design-around options are very limited or do not exist? There may still be other viable business options. Not all may be lost.

> **Warning!** While many engineers and scientists know how to analyze patents, many do not. Therefore, before you allow an engineer or scientist to take charge of your design-around, you need to make sure that they know how to analyze patents. That's not always easy to determine, but it certainly helps if they've been through the drill before and, even better, have worked with patent lawyers for a long enough time to have a general understanding of when to ask for help.

Obtaining Rights to the Problematic Patent

You could obtain rights to the problematic patent by either buying the patent or by obtaining a license under the patent to make, use, and/or sell the invention covered by the patent. In many cases, particularly those that don't involve competitors, the problematic patent may be owned by an entity that would be interested in money in return for selling or licensing to you the patent. If the invention covered by the patent is not being used by the patent owner, the patent owner may be interested in selling the patent for the right price. Or, the patent holder may be willing to grant to you a license under the patent, very likely for a lower price.

Buying the Patent vs. Obtaining a License Under the Patent

The advantage of owning the patent is that you get to call all the shots. It is a potentially valuable asset just like any other asset in your business. You could

Did You Know?	What is a license?

A license is essentially an agreement by the patent owner that she will not sue you for patent infringement as long as the terms of the license agreement are met. A patent holder can grant a license to a patent in a variety of different arrangements. For example, a license could be either exclusive (which means that the holder agrees not to license the patent to anyone else) or non-exclusive (which means that the holder has licensed or is reserving the right to license the patent to others in addition to you). A license could be limited to certain permissible activities (e.g., to only make the licensed product or to only sell the licensed product). A license could be limited to a certain region or to a certain time period. A license could grant rights to all possible products covered by the patent, or only to select products covered by the patent. Many different arrangements are possible depending upon what works best from a business standpoint for each party and based upon the negotiating leverage of each party. The party with more negotiating leverage can demand more favorable terms.

enforce it to block your competitors from the marketplace or to recover past infringement damages, you could license it to generate a future stream of revenues, or you could resell it in the future for profit. As an asset, however, it is only as valuable as the invention described and claimed in the patent. Thus, its value depends upon how inventive the idea and how broadly it is protected. See Chapter 11 above for more information on the patentability of your ideas. Importantly, there is no requirement that you manufacture the patented item in order to enforce the patent against someone else.

> Consider buying or licensing problem patents if you can't get around them.

If you can't buy the problematic patent, you could try to obtain a license under the patent from the patent holder. One advantage is that you're likely to obtain a license for much less than if you were to buy the patent. That is particularly true if the rights you want under the license are limited and permit the patent holder to grant patent rights to others in the field.

If the patent owner is willing to grant a license under the patent, you should note that there are several approaches under which a license can be granted. One may be an exclusive license in which, for a higher price, the patent owner agrees not to license the patent to anyone else. If the patent owner is not willing to grant an exclusive license and is willing only to grant a non-exclusive license (which means the owner has licensed or is reserving the right to license the patent to others in addition to you), the price will be lower but you may have to compete with the other licensees.

Patent Licenses vs. Product Licenses

There are generally two main types of licenses granted under patents; in this chapter, we'll call them "patent" licenses and "product" licenses. Although these terms are sometimes used interchangeably, we will treat them distinctly here for purposes of explaining the difference. Traditionally, a patent license is one that grants rights to practice any and all products covered by the patent. Let us explain. While a patent can only protect one "invention," it may be possible to make numerous versions or "embodiments" of that invention.

For example, suppose you have a patent on an improved umbrella with a new mechanism for opening and closing the umbrella more easily. One embodiment might be an umbrella with the new mechanism that also has a retractable handle. Another might have a clear waterproof skin. You probably can imagine numerous other variations on the general theme. The only thing they would necessarily have in common is the mechanism for opening and closing the umbrella. Even that mechanism could be built in one of several different ways or with different materials. So a patent license typically grants the licensee the right to make all embodiments covered by the patent, free from a lawsuit by the patent holder.

A product license, on the other hand, is traditionally limited to a particular version or embodiment, or a particular methodology. So in our example above, the patent holder might agree to grant a license so long as the licensee makes and sells only nonretractable umbrellas, or umbrellas with an opaque waterproof membrane. In that case, the agreement by the patent holder not to sue the licensee is limited to the licensee making and selling only the agreed-upon products. If the licensee were to make a retractable umbrella using the patented opening/closing mechanism, then the patent holder could sue the licensee for going outside the license rights.

If you have developed an umbrella for a particular market and you think that it would be important to be able to sell multiple versions of the umbrella or that it would be important to incorporate modifications into the umbrella that you might design in the future, then you would want to seek a patent license from the patent holder. A patent license provides more flexibility to vary your product without fear of going outside the bounds of the license agreement. You should expect to pay more for a patent license than a product license because you are getting greater legal rights under the license agreement. On the other hand, a product license may be sufficient to carry out your business strategies. In other words, it may be acceptable for you to simply limit yourself to one product that you know will enjoy commercial success on its own. In that case, a product license would suffice. And you can very likely get a product license for a cheaper royalty rate.

Obtaining a License Under Someone Else's Patent

If you want a license to someone else's patent, can you do it yourself or do you need a lawyer? The easy answer is either way. A license is like any other business deal. It can be negotiated and drafted by you or with the help of counsel. Indeed, it is often more cost-effective to approach the patent holder without lawyers getting involved just to test the waters, much like you would if you were making a pitch to a particular customer or if you were trying to strike a deal with a well-established distributor. As long as you know what terms are important to you, you can negotiate a license yourself.

The trickier part is drafting a document that accurately reflects your understanding of the deal and does not leave gaping holes for the other party to step through. Almost invariably, even if an attorney has not negotiated the license deal, an attorney should draft the license agreement—or at least review the agreement before it is signed. If you're not sure what important terms should be in the license agreement, then it also makes sense to seek advice from an attorney on negotiating the terms of the license.

Either way, there is no magic to obtaining a license. In a highly contentious situation between strong competitors, it may make sense to bring in patent lawyers from the start. Where the situation is much less contentious, and you believe that you already have (or would expect to have) a cordial and professional relationship with the patent holder, it is sometimes simpler to call him up and put your cards on the table. But, as the analogy suggests, there are strategies to negotiating any deal. You should think about how to play your cards—would it better to put them all on the table up front, or maybe hold some back so that you don't look too anxious? The personal dynamics involved in negotiating any deal, particularly a license agreement, means that there is no one best way to approach it.

The Terms of a Patent License

Whether you buy or obtain a license under the problematic patent, you should recognize that any agreement entered into is like any other agreement: The terms can vary dramatically from situation to situation. Also, the terms of compensation (what you pay) for the license or purchase can vary from situation to situation. For example, if you buy the patent or obtain a license under the patent, the compensation could be a one-time, lump-sum payment. Or it could be an ongoing future stream of royalties based on the number of your products that you sell in the future. Or it could be a combination of up-front money for past sales and ongoing royalties for future sales.

What You Pay for a Patent License

Compensation need not necessarily be in the form of money. It could also be provided in the form of a cross-license under your own patents (meaning that you grant a license under your own patent to the other party), or it could be provided in the form of a commitment to purchase components from the other party at a set price. Or the terms of compensation could include any combination of these forms of compensation. The same is true whether you purchase the patent or obtain a license under it. Indeed, the same is true in almost any business agreement; the compensation for the rights obtained can be paid in cash, stock, or in-kind services.

Invalidating the Problematic Patent

If a design-around would be difficult or too expensive and if the patent owner does not want to part with any rights under her patent, another available option would be to determine whether the patent can be invalidated.

Telling If a Patent Is Invalid

A patent must meet certain requirements in order to be valid. If one or more of these requirements is not met, then the patent is invalid. These requirements include novelty, nonobviousness, written description, enablement, and best mode.

Show That the Invention Is Not Novel or Is Obvious

As discussed in Chapter 11, an invention is patentable over the prior art only if it is both novel (new) and nonobvious to a person of ordinary skill in the art. If you can show that the invention is really not patentable over the prior art,

> **Strategy Tip** Patents can be invalidated. So if you find a problem patent, but know of some killer prior art, you might be able to avoid your problems by relying on patent invalidity. Typically, though, you would not file a lawsuit just to invalidate your competitor's patent. Rather, you would wait until you were accused of infringement or sued, and at that point, counter with the argument that the patent is invalid.

then the patent could be invalidated in court or in a PTO proceeding known as a re-examination. In other words, you can invalidate a patent by showing that the invention is either not new or would have been obvious to a person of ordinary skill in the art at the time the patent application was filed. Keep in mind that patents issued by the PTO are presumed to be valid, so it would your burden to prove that the patents are invalid.

Show Insufficient Written Description, No Enablement, No Best Mode, and/or the Claims Are Indefinite

The USPTO also requires that the patent specification satisfy certain description requirements. The specification must meet the written description, enablement, and best mode requirements described in Chapter 11. These requirements ensure that the public gets its end of the bargain, that in exchange for a limited monopoly, it gets the benefit of understanding the invention completely. Nothing important can be held back by the patent applicant or he'll risk losing his patent.

Any one of these prior art requirements and specification requirements could be a basis for attacking the validity of a patent. If you are accused of infringing a patent (or you are worried about infringing a patent), you may rely upon one or more of these requirements to expose a deficiency in the patent. The most common basis for invalidating a patent is to uncover a prior art patent or publication that the patent examiner did not have before him when the patent was originally examined and which describes the same invention as the problematic patent, or a very similar one.

> **Did You Know?** How could a patent that was examined by the USPTO be invalid?
>
> It's simple. A USPTO examiner is a mere mortal. The examiner may have simply made a mistake. He might have missed some important prior art reference in his search. He might have had the best reference but misread the portion that shows the applicant's invention. He might have simply misunderstood the technological improvement offered by the applicant. Or, as it sometimes happens, the applicant may have misled the examiner in a way that leads to the issuance of a patent that should never have issued. Another possible reason is that the USPTO has limited resources. Several hundred thousand applications are filed each year at the USPTO. Examiners, therefore, have only limited time to examine each patent application. It is not that they are rushed, but they are required to balance a heavy load.

Legal Opinions on Patent Invalidity

Should you ask your patent lawyer to give you an opinion of counsel that the patent is invalid? It depends. Like the question of infringement, the question of invalidity can be a complex analysis. Thus, it is often advisable to obtain the advice of patent counsel on this subject. Once you become aware of a potentially problematic patent, obtaining a written opinion of counsel (that the patent is likely to be held invalid by a court or jury if a lawsuit is ever filed) can be used to rebut allegations of willful infringement. The same cost-benefit analysis should be followed as discussed in this chapter.

CHAPTER 28

Cease-and-Desist Letters and Infringement Suits

The term "cease-and-desist" letter could mean many things. It literally refers to a demand by the sender that the recipient stop doing whatever it is that is the subject of the letter. However, the term "cease and desist" has evolved into an umbrella term (no pun intended) that covers any letter from a patent holder or patent licensee that puts the recipient on notice of the patent, accompanied by some request for desired action. That action may be, in fact, to stop the allegedly offending activity (namely, selling your product). Or the action may simply be to contact the sender about negotiating a potential license under the patent. In some cases, the desired action may be nothing more than for the recipient to evaluate the patent before selling the recipient's product. If you receive such a letter, particularly if you've have never received one before, there are several options that you can pursue.

Assess the Seriousness of the Threat

The first step is to assess the seriousness of the threat. For example, has the letter been sent by a lawyer or the patent owner himself? If the letter is sent directly by the patent owner, it may indicate that the patent owner doesn't have much money or isn't very sophisticated, or both. It does not always mean that the letter should not be taken seriously, but it usually tells you that the matter is less urgent (meaning that you are less likely to be sued the next day). If the letter is sent by a lawyer, however, it usually means that the patent owner considers the issue significant and serious enough to pay a lawyer to handle the matter. In addition, the letter may be a serious threat if the sender is a direct competitor who has a history of suing people or companies for patent infringement. If the letter is from someone who isn't making any product, then perhaps it is a less serious threat. Is the sender an individual, with potentially limited funds to bring a lawsuit against you, or is the sender a company, with greater financial resources available? The sophistication in the wording of the letter is also often a clue as to how serious the threat is.

In any case, letters should be taken seriously enough to look at the patent and consider its impact on the activities of your business (particularly, selling your product), regardless of whether the particular activities are identified specifically in the letter. That is because the letter, in whatever form it is or from whomever it is sent, could be considered by a court to be formal notice of infringement, which the patent owner can later rely upon to charge you with willful infringement. While there are formal requirements that must be in place before an alleged infringer is on formal notice, it is often subject to debate in court. To be safe, however, it is best to ensure that the patent does not pose obstacles to selling your product, even if you don't think the threat is serious.

Options in Responding

You have several options if you receive a cease-and-desist letter. Although you could decide to ignore the letter, it is not advisable to do so unless you know the sender well enough to know the threat is not real or urgent. If you conclude that a lawsuit is not likely to be filed and you are satisfied that you don't infringe the patent, it may be sufficient to either not respond at all or send a response that just acknowledges receipt of the letter and doesn't address the substance of the cease-and-desist letter. There are times when you can tell that the sender of the letter is "trolling" for anyone to bite. But if you're not sure, it's best to seek advice of counsel as to what to do.

Even if you don't respond, can you do nothing? Not likely. If nothing else, a cease-and-desist letter puts you on notice of the existence of the patent. You can't later say in court that you weren't aware of the patent. Because a patent owner in any future lawsuit is likely to allege that you willfully infringed, you had better be prepared to show that you proceeded in good faith, as we discussed above in Chapter 27. It is prudent for you to take some action in good faith under the circumstances. Good faith is measured differently from situation to situation, but a good first step is for you to determine whether the patent is applicable to your product or business.

Whether or not patent counsel should be retained depends on a cost-benefit analysis discussed above. If the threat is real and your product generates a great deal of revenue, the risk of enhanced damages may be too high not to seek the advice of counsel. If your company has sophisticated in-house engineers or scientists, they may be able to engage in a sufficient analysis to determine whether the patent poses potential problems or not. If the conclusion is clearly that the patent does not apply, it may be safe to take no further steps.

The problem, however, is that nonlawyers can misinterpret patent claims, and that gets businesses into trouble more times than not. There have been many times when a client tells us that a patent has no relevance to their product or business—and then it turns out that they have not looked at the right materials in making the assessment. Often they will have looked merely at the description in the patent, but not the claims (numbered paragraphs) at the end of the patent that define the scope of the invention. Nor are they likely to have looked at the file history of the patent. The claims and the file history are critical to the analysis.

Stopping Competitors from Sending Cease-and-Desist Letters

You can stop competitors from sending you and your customers cease-and-desist letters. While one should not take on litigation lightly, the law permits a party faced with a reasonable fear of being sued to sue first. Such an action is called a "declaratory judgment action," or "DJ action" for short. It is a lawsuit that has all the look and feel of a lawsuit by the patent holder against the accused infringer, but it is brought by the accused infringer against the patent holder. The purpose of the DJ action is to ask the court for an order declaring that you are not infringing the patent holder's patent, either because the accused product or service doesn't infringe and/or because the patent is invalid or unenforceable.

A DJ action permits a person or company being harassed by letters—particularly if the letters are being sent to customers and possibly driving customers away—to strike first. This usually means that the lawsuit will be in a court that is located near you, as opposed to a court located near the patent holder. The courts do not provide advisory orders, so the law requires that the cease-and-desist letter be worded so as to give you a real sense that you or your customers are going to be sued anyway. In other words, if all a patent holder has done is put you on notice that he has a patent that you should be aware of, then the law would not permit you to bring a DJ action. That is because the courts want parties to resolve their disputes without using the court system, if possible. However, when the cease-and-desist letter threatens legal action, either expressly or impliedly, then you are more likely to be permitted to proceed with a DJ action.

The value of a DJ action is to remove the "cloud" over your head or your customers' heads. Cease-and-desist letters are powerful tools that can rattle cages and scare away customers without the patent holder actually filing a lawsuit. The DJ action is an accommodation to persons and businesses to clear title, so to speak, to the right to make and sell a product or service. A

DJ action is filed in court and will proceed almost as if the patent holder had brought suit first, except you would be officially listed as the plaintiff and the patent holder listed as the defendant. But, otherwise, the issues would generally be the same—whether the patent is valid, infringed, and/or enforceable. So, like all litigation, it can be a powerful tool to bring the other side to the bargaining table, but it can also be expensive if not properly controlled. For that reason, you should consult with your IP litigation attorney about the risks and benefits of filing a DJ action.

What To Do If You Are Sued for Infringing Patents, Trademarks, or Copyrights

Unlike a cease-and-desist letter, a lawsuit cannot be ignored. In almost all cases, lawsuits based upon violations of patents, trademarks, or copyrights are filed in federal district court (which are United States courts, unlike state courts that are governed by the individual states). There are federal district courts throughout the United States, each of which is authorized to preside over patent, trademark, and copyright cases. Each state has at least one district court, although the larger states have multiple districts. For example, California has four districts (Northern, Central, Southern and Eastern Districts). Even the smaller states with one district still have multiple courtrooms scattered throughout the state for the convenience of the parties. For example, the District of New Jersey has courtrooms in Newark, Trenton, Camden, and elsewhere.

So what should you do if you get sued for infringement in district court?

Move Quickly—Time's-a-Tickin'

In federal court, a response to a complaint (known as the "answer") must be served on the plaintiff within 20 days after the complaint has been served on the defendant. That doesn't give the defendant much time to react. Occasionally, the defendant will have 60 days to respond, but that is only where the plaintiff has provided a written request for waiver of personal service. Personal service usually involves a person (known as a "process server") who

> **Did You Know?** **What happens if I ignore a lawsuit filed against me or my company?**
>
> The court could enter a default judgment against you. That means that you are legally liable for the damages sought by the plaintiff and any injunction requested by the plaintiff. You also may be required to pay the other side's attorneys fees. The plaintiff could take steps to collect the judgment, including seizing your assets. While it's possible to later retain a lawyer and file a paper with the court asking the judge to set aside the default judgment, you better have a good excuse.

finds you and physically hands you a copy of the complaint and the accompanying summons. In other words, if the plaintiff asks you to waive personal service, he is asking you to allow him to skip hiring a formal process server to serve the complaint upon you, which gives you an extra 40 days to respond. Under such circumstances, it is usually advisable to waive personal service to buy additional time to respond.

Even if you do not receive the complaint by personal service, you should act as if you have been formally served, just in case. Courts sometimes are not very sympathetic to a defense that you were not served properly with a complaint, if you had notice of the complaint and obtained a copy of it via fax, e-mail, or letter.

So the best advice is to get a lawyer as quickly as possible.

Options

If you are sued for patent infringement, you will have options. The first thing you should do is hire a lawyer. Your lawyer can then help you evaluate your options—filing the lawsuit, stopping the sale of your product, or negotiating a settlement with the plaintiff.

Hire a Lawyer

There are lots of ways to find an attorney, but recommendations from people you trust are the best way. Finding a lawyer in the telephone book is not the best way. You could always call the local county bar association, which usually keeps a list of attorneys you could call.

Depending upon the particular circumstances, a defendant may be able to obtain an extension of time to respond to the complaint. Professional courtesy often rules the day when defendant's counsel asks plaintiff's counsel for an extension of time. In other words, a lawyer is more likely to provide an extension of time when requested simply because she knows there may come a time where she'll ask for a courtesy extension from your counsel. What goes around comes around!

Strategy Tip | If I get sued for infringement, should I hire a lawyer who specializes in intellectual property (i.e., patents, trademarks, and copyrights)?

We certainly think so. Theoretically, a lawyer can litigate almost any issue for which a client retains him, regardless of whether that lawyer has expertise in that area (of course, that lawyer would have a duty to become competent in that area). There are many lawyers who describe themselves as IP lawyers but who are not registered patent attorneys or who do not have experience obtaining trademark and/or copyright registrations. In fairness, some non-IP lawyers are successful at litigating IP cases. But as between two equally effective litigators, the one who is an experienced IP lawyer almost invariably provides greater value to his client. That is particularly true when there is technology involved in the lawsuit, or where the lawyer also has experience obtaining patents, trademark registrations, or copyright registrations.

For example, in a patent case involving electronics or biotechnology, a patent lawyer who has a degree in that technology will likely be able to assess the patent issues more quickly than a trial lawyer who does not. Likewise, a trademark lawyer who has experience prosecuting trademark applications in the USPTO adds greater value in a trademark infringement lawsuit because she better understands the intricacies of the trademark registration process. For that reason, while it is not necessary that a lawyer prosecuting or defending an IP litigation case be an IP lawyer, it certainly helps to have an IP lawyer on the case.

Assess the Allegations in the Complaint

Once you have hired legal counsel and you have confirmed that you have sufficient time to respond to the complaint, the next step is to assess the allegations in the complaint. A typical infringement complaint sets forth a series of allegations and claims, whether those claims are of patent infringement, trademark infringement, or copyright infringement. A complaint will identify the IP at issue and the products and services that are accused of infringement, although some attorneys have a practice of not identifying the product in the complaint.

It is important early in the case to determine whether the asserted IP is infringed and/or whether it is valid. Every week that goes by where your products or services continue to be sold or provided is another week in which the plaintiff could allege that you were willfully infringing, and seek money damages. Thus, your situation may justify obtaining an opinion of counsel, as discussed in Chapter 27. Likewise, where your sales are generating significant daily revenues, potential damages also accrue quickly. So in that case there would be some urgency in deciding whether the significant sales and/or services should be discontinued or altered. Of course, if product sales are fairly small, then the urgency may be lower.

Do a Cost-Benefit Analysis of Fighting Vs. Settling the Case

In any cost-benefit analysis that involves considering how to respond to allegations of infringement, you should begin by considering what your business goals are with the product in particular and the entire market more generally. The more important that long-term, healthy sales of a single product are, the more important it is for you to invest in legal fees to defend your case.

The cost-benefit analysis must take into consideration a number of important points:

- The amount of forecasted revenue you expect
- The length of time that you expect the product or service to be available in the marketplace
- The impact on your company if sales or services are enjoined or halted (i.e., the court grants an injunction against you to stop selling the accused product)

- The impact on your company's reputation if you are enjoined
- The potential damages you could be found liable for
- The anticipated legal fees that you will spend in your defense
- Whether you obtained opinions of counsel or design-around advice

Each of these factors can have a big impact on whether to litigate, whether to settle, or what strategy you should adopt for either litigation or settlement.

While it is natural for defendants to inject emotion and ego into the equation, this tendency should be avoided if possible. When it comes to legal issues, emotion and ego can only serve to drive up legal costs.

Think About the Intrusion of Litigation into Your Business

Another thing you should consider, besides the cost of legal services and possible damages, is the potential intrusion into your business. In order to participate in a lawsuit, you'll have to assign someone the task of working with your lawyer to discuss strategy, to apprise your lawyer of the relevant facts, and to gather documents and witnesses as needed. Depending upon the case, that intrusion can become quite burdensome even if managed properly. As discussed in Chapter 29, all lawsuits involve "discovery," the process by which one party seeks information from the other parties in the lawsuit. Discovery taken during litigation can be burdensome and time-consuming and can distract employees from revenue-generating activities. On the other hand, if your sales are significant, your reputation is strong, and the plaintiff's case is weak, continued litigation may be justified. Chapter 30 discusses the out-of-pocket costs normally associated with IP litigation.

Almost certainly with any litigation, the ultimate goal should be to get out of litigation and get back to business. Litigation should be viewed as a business tool that a company engages in only when the cost-benefit analysis warrants it. The same applies when you are in a position to enforce your own patents, trademarks, or copyrights.

Stopping Others from Infringing Your IP Rights

Enforcing Your IP

Before you consider filing a lawsuit against those whom you believe are copying your intellectual property rights, you should first decide what business goals would be achieved by your asserting (enforcing) your intellectual property rights. You should not enter into litigation lightly because it is intrusive and time consuming, and can be expensive even if you closely monitor and control it. Again, litigation should be viewed solely as a business tool to accomplish a business goal or strategy. If you believe that litigation is the necessary path to achieving your goals, it is still wise to revisit your strategy from time to time to ensure that your goals continue to be met or to consider whether your goals should be revised. What was good for your business in year seven when the lawsuit was filed may not be good for your business in year nine, two years into the lawsuit. Below are some of the things you might consider in developing your strategy for enforcing your IP.

The Copier: Individual, Group of Individuals, and/or Company or Companies

Much like assessing the opposing team in a sports match, you should consider who the opposing party (or parties) is likely to be when enforcing your IP. As the saying goes, "Know the face of your enemy." Naturally, the amount of money you have to use for your lawsuit against the infringer affects how you will conduct it. An individual infringer is less likely to have great financial and personnel resources, although that is not always the case. Likewise, a group of individuals, a partnership, or an established company is more likely to have greater financial and personnel resources at their disposal, although again that is not always the case. The more financial and personnel resources that the infringer has, the more likely the infringer will be able to absorb and withstand the burdens and costs associated with litigation. On the other hand, the size of the alleged infringer can greatly impact their ability to hurt your market share because of their continued infringement. Whether the alleged infringer is a direct competitor also greatly influences how the infringer will respond when you sue them.

Do You Need the Infringer to Stop?

One of the key questions to ask yourself in establishing a strategy for IP enforcement is: "What outcome would I like from the enforcement?" Depending upon the market dynamics and whether the alleged infringer is a direct competitor, it may not be necessary to obtain an injunction (a court order for the infringer to stop the infringing conduct). It may be more beneficial to you to receive a continuing future stream of royalties from the infringer to help with your bottom line. It could very well be that the infringer owns one or more patents, trademarks, or copyrights that would be of interest to you; so a viable outcome might be a cross-license of IP rights (meaning you license your IP to the infringer and he licenses his IP to you and you both win, or at least call a truce).

As part of this analysis, it is important to consider your own product line. Are you a one-trick pony (one business with one product), do you have a line of various products, or do you hope to expand into a variety of diverse products and technologies? If the alleged infringer is not competing with you directly (i.e., taking potential sales away from you), it may be advantageous to encourage the infringer to continue by giving him a license in exchange for his paying you a stream of royalties over time or a lump sum payment now. In some cases, having a larger company with greater resources stand behind a competing infringing product can be advantageous because the larger company continues to educate and draw attention to the market in which you sell your product. In other words, by selling the product that incorporates your invention, the infringer is creating a market demand for your invention. That

---

Strategy Tip | ## Should I let my competitor infringe my patent?

There may be a business advantage in doing so, for the right price. While you don't want to let an infringer escape scot-free, you should consider whether you're better off letting the competitor pay you a fair royalty and continue to sell a great deal of product, provided the market is big enough for the both of you. Too often, companies jump to the conclusion that the market in which their product is sold can only accommodate one supplier—them. But that may not be true. If the market has growth potential, then one supplier can actually benefit from a competing supplier because the competition raises consumer awareness and helps expand the market to a greater degree than you might achieve on your own. Think Pepsi and Coca-Cola. Think Apple and Microsoft. The competition draws attention to the products. If your situation does fit that equation, then maybe seeking an injunction against your competitor is not the right answer. You should simply consider the alternatives.

---

latter point is a nuance that is often missed in the emotions and egos sometimes associated with IP enforcement strategy.

It is particularly useful to consider the positive impact of an infringer when the market is not yet developed. New technologies are often met with wildly different perceptions in the market—overwhelming success based upon the sheer novelty of a product or significant pushback from the marketplace. The infringer may want to take a license from you based upon his reluctance to shift courses midstream. Allowing an alleged infringer to continue to sell his product, for a price, especially when he has the ability to develop the market in a way that benefits you, ultimately may result in long-term sales that are critical to your business strategy.

For many of these reasons, getting an injunction to stop the infringer may not be the best course for you. Thus, an important part of litigation and enforcement strategy is to recognize that a favorable outcome can include

---

Did You Know? Is there ever a situation in which I have to make the patented product in order to enforce the patent against someone else?

Yes, where you are trying to stop the importation of an infringing product into the United States, and the importer of the product cannot be sued in the United States. In federal courts throughout the country, a patent infringement lawsuit can only proceed if the court has jurisdiction over the accused infringer/defendant. U.S. law prohibits lawsuits against foreign persons or companies that have no contact with the United States. But there is one tribunal—the International Trade Commission ("ITC") in Washington, D.C.—that permits patent infringement lawsuits against the importation of products into the United States. In that case, the foreign exporter or manufacturer of the product is not technically a party to the lawsuit (although as a practical matter, the company is represented by legal counsel in the case). In ITC cases, the law requires that the patent holder make or sell the patented product. That is the only tribunal that requires that the patent holder use his invention as a condition to filing a lawsuit.

---

granting a royalty-bearing license to the infringer. You can make the license limited, both by technology and by time. As explained above in Chapter 27, the license may be restricted to a particular product configuration or service methodology. Such a license is often referred to as a product license because it is limited to a particular product or particular methodology. If desired, however, a license could be technologically broad enough to encompass any and all products or methods covered by the claims of the patent. Equally important are the time restrictions, which may be advantageous to you. For example, the license could be limited to a defined period of time or until certain milestones or thresholds are reached. That way, the infringer can legally sell his product and compete with you for only a limited period of time. On the other hand, you could grant a license to the infringer until the expiration or termination of the IP that is the subject of the license.

Available Resources

Of course you know that you will have to pay your lawyers to engage in meaningful IP enforcement. Everyone knows lawyers cost money. In considering litigation, however, it is also important to consider the disruption to you and your company during the course of litigation. In other words, before litigation begins, you need to consider which employee or employees may need to support the litigation periodically or more continuously as litigation proceeds.

The Costs of Discovery

An important part of IP litigation in the United States is "discovery." "Discovery" is the process in litigation through which the parties are entitled to collect information from each other. You will be asking for information from your opponents, and they will be asking for information from you. That information can be in the form of documentary evidence (hard copy or electronic documents) or testimonial evidence (things that are said verbally). That means that you and/or your company will have to be prepared to dedicate at least some time and personnel to gathering information requested by the other party, and possibly helping your attorney sort through the mounds of documents you will get from the other side.

The requesting party will serve the other party with a subpoena or request for production of documents or a request for a deposition. Sometimes the parties will argue over whether the document request is relevant to the case or too wide-sweeping and burdensome on the party with the documents. The party served with the subpoena or request must respond to it by either producing (giving) documents to the other side, objecting to the request and explaining why, or showing up at the deposition.

You should assume that all information relevant to the issues in the case will be subject to discovery. That means that someone in your company will have to take the time to search through hard copy and electronic (computer) archives and files for the documents that the other side is requesting. If you have an organized and effective document management system in place, you can minimize the intrusion that discovery will have on your business.

The other party may also request the deposition of one or more of your key employees, or your deposition. A deposition is a procedure by which a party to a lawsuit can obtain testimony from a witness, whether it

Warning! If you are thinking about enforcing your patent against a competitor, but haven't yet filed a lawsuit, watch carefully what you say to your competitor. You might be planning to send a letter to your competitor to inform him of your patent. But if your letter blatantly threatens your competitor by saying that he infringes your patent and that you're going to sue him, your competitor could file a declaratory judgment lawsuit against you asking a judge to declare that your patent is either not infringed or invalid. This could force you into litigation prematurely, and because this lawsuit would likely be filed in your competitor's home state, could put you at a significant geographical disadvantage. Also watch what your employees are saying to your competitors. Even an oral statement as simple as "You infringe my company's patent" to a competitor at a trade show can cause you problems if you're not ready to sue.

is a witness from an opposing party or from a person who is not a party to the lawsuit. Basically, the other side sits in a room with you and your attorney, and asks you questions about the IP that you are trying to enforce. Unless your attorney has legal grounds to object to the questions, you will be required to answer.

If the other party asks for your deposition or for the deposition of one of your employees, it will be necessary to invest time to prepare for the deposition and to participate in the deposition. Before you testify in a deposition, your attorney will want to meet with you to get you to practice answering questions that the other side will most likely ask you. This can eat up dozens of hours that could be otherwise spent focusing on your business. Can you or your employees afford to participate in the deposition process? Most often the answer is yes, but you should still consider the time drain when deciding whether to enforce your intellectual property.

The Nature and Cost of IP Litigation: Going to Trial

An intellectual property lawsuit is not much different than most lawsuits in that it begins with a complaint and concludes (if not settled or dismissed earlier) with a trial and possible appeal. Figure 30.1 is a flow chart that illustrates the typical progress of litigation in the federal courts. Referring to the chart will make it easier to understand the cost and timing of a lawsuit. This chapter will discuss the items that are highlighted in the flow chart. To make things simple, the rest of the chapter will refer to one of the most common types of IP litigation—patent infringement, where a patent holder accuses someone else of infringing their patent.

FIGURE 30.1 **Litigation Flowchart**

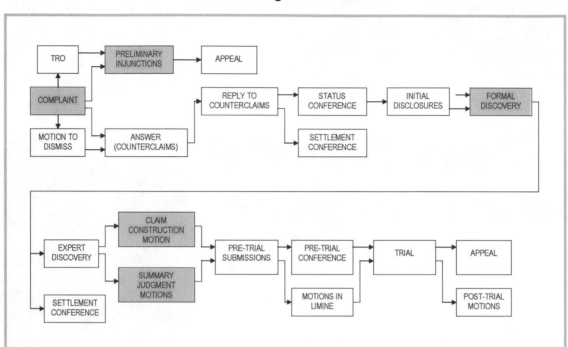

Using a typical patent infringement case as an example, we will illustrate how a lawsuit proceeds, with a rough estimate of the typical costs associated with the various stages in the lawsuit. Let us assume that you have obtained a patent on your invention and that you believe that another company is infringing your patent. While the law does not require that you have sufficient evidence to prove infringement when you file a lawsuit, the law does require that you have done a sufficient investigation to conclude in good faith that you will likely be able to prove infringement once you have gathered all of the relevant facts during the lawsuit. If you have requested that your attorney first generate an oral opinion as to whether the accused product or process infringes your patent, then that analysis is likely to cost about $5,000 to $10,000 per patent.

The Complaint

Once you and your attorney have at least a good faith belief that there is infringement, even if you still need to gather evidence to prove it, you can have your attorney prepare a complaint. In preparing a complaint, the lawyer's goal is to understand the facts sufficiently to (1) set forth appropriate allegations of infringement, and (2) assess where the case can be properly brought.

Location of the Lawsuit

Federal law permits a patent infringement case to be brought in any district court in the United States as long as the facts show that infringement occurred in that district and/or that the accused infringer has sufficient contacts with that district. A national company that sells products in all 50 states normally can be sued in any district in any state in the country. A regional or local company with only regional sales would not be subject to suit throughout the country, but could only be sued in those regions.

Once the possible district courts have been identified, then selecting which one of those in which to file the lawsuit in calls for some strategic thinking. It is important to consider the expertise of the judges in that district in IP law, the procedural rules adopted by those judges that litigants must follow, the speed at which cases proceed from beginning to end, and the sophistication of the jury pool that exists in that district. There are different schools of thought as to which of these factors is the most important in deciding where to file a lawsuit, but suffice it to say that you should consider these factors when developing your litigation strategy with your counsel.

Whom Should You Sue?

Another strategic decision is whom to sue. The patent law identifies two types of infringers: (1) direct infringers who do one or more of the following acts: import, manufacture, use, sell, and/or offer to sell a product covered by a patent; and (2) indirect infringers who either induce another person (or company) to directly infringe or who make or sell a component that can be used only in an infringing product.

Suppose in our umbrella example that you have patented both a mechanical device (that permits an umbrella to open and close more effectively) and the umbrella with the mechanical device built in. Suppose also that there is a company, ACME, that assembles components into umbrellas for distribution to retailers, but that purchases the mechanical opening/closing device from a supplier. ACME then sells its assembled umbrellas to a national distributor who then sells the umbrellas to various retailers throughout the country. Should you sue just ACME, the company that assembles the umbrellas? Should you also sue the supplier of the mechanical opening/closing device? What about the distributor or the retailers?

The answer is—you guessed it—it depends. It depends upon your litigation goals. If you also are selling your umbrella device through these same retailers, it wouldn't make much sense to sue your own customers. Similarly, if you use the same distributor or if you don't but want to preserve the ability to use that distributor in the future, then it may not make good business sense to sue the distributor either. You certainly don't want to sue the end users who take your product home. So who's left? The device supplier and ACME, the umbrella assembler. While both may be fair game, you may have determined that the supplier does not have a great deal of cash from which to recover a meaningful damages judgment or settlement, but that the umbrella assembler is a deep-pockets company flush with cash. It may make sense to sue only the deep pockets assembler, unless you want an injunction against the supplier. In that case, suing both the supplier and the assembler makes sense.

If you don't sell through the infringer's retailers and have no intention of doing so (maybe because your umbrella is a higher end product and your competitor sells a cheaper version through discount stores), then suing those retailers would be a viable option as well. Retailers typically put a great deal of pressure on their suppliers to get the case dismissed against the retailers. That often causes the defendant suppliers to try to work with the plaintiff to settle the case. These are examples of the strategic thinking that goes into choosing whom to sue.

Allegations in the Complaint

So you've decided whom to sue and where to sue, and you've confirmed that you have a good-faith basis for infringement. Now what? Prepare and file the complaint. The cost of preparing and filing a complaint that contains at least one allegation of patent infringement is usually about $3,000 to $5,000. Each patent that is asserted against a product or process is considered a legal claim. A plaintiff bringing a lawsuit is permitted to make several claims, whether it is several patent claims (each reflecting a different patent being asserted) or a patent infringement claim along with one or more trademark infringement claims, unfair competition claims, or other claims.

The Answer of the Defendant Infringer

Once the complaint is filed and assuming the defendant has not agreed to settle the case immediately, the defendant will file an answer to the complaint. An answer is a document that responds point by point to the complaint, either denying or admitting the factual allegations made in the complaint.

Affirmative Defenses

Typically, the defendant will set forth one or more affirmative defenses. For example, in a typical patent case, affirmative defenses include invalidity and various equitable defenses that may or may not be applicable. An example of an equitable defense is laches, a defense that the patent holder waited too long to sue. Estoppel is also an equitable defense that is based upon reliance by the defendant upon the plaintiff's inaction over a long period of time or communications from the plaintiff to the accused infringer that the infringer's conduct was not a problem. Without getting into the details of these affirmative defenses, suffice it to say that the defendant likely will have spent about $5,000 to $10,000 in preparing the answer, which necessarily includes the time spent by the lawyer to investigate the allegations and claims made in the complaint.

Counterclaims

If the defendant believes that they have their own claims against the plaintiff, they can file their own claims in the answer in the form of "counterclaims." Counterclaims are simply claims by the defendant against the plaintiff. For example, if the defendant believes that you are infringing his patents, he could assert his patents against you in a counterclaim. In addition, the courts recognize that certain defenses can be asserted as counterclaims in a patent case. For example, asking the court to rule that your patent is not infringed by the defendant or that your patent is invalid may be considered a counterclaim as well. If a defendant wants to assert counterclaims in the case, he should do so in the answer that he files. Depending upon which counterclaims he asserts, the cost of preparing the answer could still be in the same range identified above.

The Plaintiff's Reply to Counterclaims

If, in response to the complaint, the defendant files an answer with counterclaims, then you would be required to file a reply, which is in essence your answer to his counterclaims. Such a reply can be prepared for about $1,500, or much more depending on the number of counterclaims and whether the counterclaims are essentially defenses to your original patent claims. If the defendant files an answer without counterclaims, then there is no need for a reply.

The Pleadings

The complaint, answer, and reply are all referred to as the "pleadings." The pleadings identify the claims and high-level issues that the parties will litigate in the case. If either party discovers new claims, the courts usually allow the new claims to be added to the case so long as it would not prejudice the other side and the new claims relate to those already in the case. For example, if the technology already at issue in the case is umbrella mechanisms, a later discovered legal claim dealing with umbrellas would likely be added to the case as long as there is still plenty of time left in the case to do so. However, if the newly discovered legal claim relates to entirely different technology or if the new claim is not discovered until late in the case, the court will not likely add the new claim to the case. That claim would have to be asserted in a separate lawsuit instead.

The Case Management Conference

Once the pleadings (complaint, answer, reply) are filed, the court will set a case management conference. This is a first opportunity for the parties to educate the judge on the big picture issues in the case and tell the court a little bit about the parties and where they expect the case to go. It's also an opportunity for the court to set dates for the case; for example, discovery dates, trial date, etc. Before the case management conference, the federal rules require that the lawyers for each party meet ahead of time to discuss certain mandatory topics, including what each believes a proposed schedule should be for the case. They are also required to discuss how information will be produced and exchanged from one party to the other. Just before the conference with the court, the lawyers are required to prepare a joint report to the court identifying areas of agreement and disagreement and proposed dates for the case. Based upon that report and the actual conference with the judge, deadline dates will be set that the parties have to live by.

The cost of preparing for a case management conference, as well as conducting the initial meeting with the opposing lawyer and creating the joint report, should be about $5,000 to $12,000. The wide variation in cost reflects that, in some cases, there are numerous issues and dates to be addressed, and that sometimes opposing counsel can be very contentious, which requires more time to work through issues. On that issue, while being contentious is perceived by some clients to be an effective way to wear down a legal opponent, it is also a more costly way to litigate. You should avoid needless legal battles that reflect mere chest-beating because they tend to lead to more costly litigation. If you carefully pick your battles, the litigation can be carried out at a more reasonable cost. It is critical to communicate well with your lawyer so that he knows your strategy. Lawyers should not normally be given a blank check and free rein to run the case as they see fit.

The Discovery Process

Once the court has set a schedule for the case, discovery then starts. In all cases, formulating a discovery strategy with your attorney early is key to obtaining the evidence you need to prove your case while managing litigation costs.

In many cases, each party will produce several thousand documents. In larger cases, tens of thousands or hundreds of thousands of documents may be exchanged. Regarding the number of depositions, until a few years ago each party in theory could take an unlimited number of depositions, each for as many days as was necessary. Today, the courts limit each party to ten depositions, and each deposition can only last seven hours. While there are certain exceptions, the courts usually hold the parties to those limits. So that is a good thing from a cost standpoint, although it may inhibit a "turn-over-every-stone" strategy.

Did You Know?	Discovery? You mean I have to turn over everything to the other side?

Not quite. Yes, discovery is the process in which the parties in litigation have an opportunity to learn facts from the other side. Discovery usually includes an exchange of documents requested by one party of the other. One party can also ask to take testimony from witnesses employed by or working with the other party. Discovery also consists of an exchange of written questions to each other directed toward learning specific facts. While the courts permit fairly broad discovery, the information requested must still be "relevant" to the issues and claims in the case. So if the lawsuit is a patent case about umbrella technology, it's not likely the court would require you to produce information (documents and/or testimony) about historical sales of tables and chairs.

If there are few issues and the patent infringement claim is focused and narrow, the discovery process may cost about $100,000 to $200,000 in attorneys' fees the first year. That would include your lawyer assisting you in gathering and reviewing documents to produce to the other side, as well as your lawyer reviewing all of the documents produced by the other side. It would also likely include preparing for and taking depositions of the other side's witnesses or in preparing and defending you or your employees who are deposed by the other side. Fees could be less or more than that range depending upon many factors, but you should be prepared to spend somewhere in that range. For larger, more contentious cases, you should expect to spend more in the first year on discovery.

In addition, there are the intangible costs of lost employee and management time, discussed above. What impacts discovery costs the most is the number of documents produced by both sides, the number of depositions taken by both parties, and how many discovery disputes arise that require time-consuming attention and possible motions before the court concerning discovery disputes. Even if you decide not to fight every issue, the other side might not be as reasonable as you, so you may still end up with expensive discovery disputes.

If there are several parties in the case and each party takes its allotment of depositions, including third party witnesses (for example, witnesses who will testify about prior art that might invalidate the patent), and there are repeated discovery disputes, including a few discovery motions to the court, discovery costs can escalate by another $200,000 to $400,000 within a year. Discovery disputes occur when the parties disagree over whether or not a document must be produced, or whether or not a witness has to testify about a certain subject. For example, documents that show advice given by the attorney to her client normally would be considered privileged and not something that a party is required to produce to the other side.

Again, spending those kinds of costs would not be recommended if your goals can be achieved by focused and noncontentious discovery approaches. To some degree you can control the contentiousness of a case by simply authorizing your lawyer to ignore the unmeritorious challenges often raised by contentious adversaries. However, if the opposing counsel becomes impossibly difficult to deal with, your lawyer may be forced to make repeated trips to the judge to resolve disputes. This would make it more difficult for you to control costs. In those situations, you should expect your legal fees to increase significantly.

Another thing that affects discovery costs is where the case is filed. There are some courts (for example, the Eastern District of Virginia and Western District of Wisconsin) that set very short discovery periods. That can be advantageous in lowering costs because there isn't enough time to engage in time-consuming discovery battle sideshows. Also, in many places throughout the country, there are judges who have little tolerance for games played by the lawyers and keep a close tab on lawyers' conduct. That is very helpful in keeping costs down because parties are less likely to go to the court about unresolved disputes for fear of angering the judge. In some courts, like Los Angeles, the judges are so backlogged with criminal cases that discovery can sometimes drag on for two or more years. Any time discovery drags on, there are sure to be added discovery costs because there is more time for issues to arise and be addressed.

On the other hand, if delay is one of the goals of the plaintiff, filing the case in Los Angeles can be advantageous. Why might you, as a plaintiff, want to delay your case? A couple of reasons. One is that your cash flow may be limited at first, and so you would want to postpone paying for some of the litigation costs. The lawsuit may be a business necessity from your standpoint, but your war chest may be a bit light. Another is the timing of the market. Maybe you want the accused infringer to have built up more sales under his belt before trial so that it makes his exposure higher and your negotiating leverage better. Yet another is pure endurance. Suppose that the emotions are running too high from both sides. A lawsuit moving quickly will not help to quell those emotions very easily. However, a lawsuit that drags out for a long time can start to wear on the accused infringer and eventually bring them to the bargaining table in a better frame of mind. Of course, all of these factors could yield a different result (as they say in the commercials, "results may vary"), depending upon the particular personalities involved.

Claim Construction and Markman Hearings (aka Markman Proceedings)

You might have heard about "Markman hearings" in patent litigation. A Markman hearing is a proceeding held by the judge in a patent case for the sole purpose of determining what the words in the patent claims mean. Determining the meaning of words in a patent claim is often difficult. Indeed, the English language is full of ambiguities and double meanings. Lawyers refer to the process of interpreting words in a claim as "claim construction." Markman hearings require that the parties file papers with the court explaining what they think the words in the claims mean. Sometimes the judge will listen to expert witnesses hired by the parties to help the judge decide how the claims should be interpreted.

Years ago there were no Markman hearings because the claim construction process was simply part of the overall process. About 15 years ago the trend changed to segregate that part of the process and address it separately (although still part of the main lawsuit). Now, after several years, Markman proceedings are in a state of flux. More and more courts are resisting the need for a formal Markman proceeding as it sometimes adds more burden to the parties and the court and often is inefficient. Those courts are instead trying to address claim construction issues in the context of summary judgment motions in which one party or the other is asking the court to construe the claims and find infringement or non-infringement as a matter of law.

So what is a summary judgment motion? It a set of papers filed with the court by one party for the purpose of asking the court to rule in favor of that party without need for trial. Trial is for purposes of resolving factual

> **You Should Know** | A Markman hearing is a hearing for the purpose of determining what a claim means. Markman hearings are often the most important phase of a patent case because once the meaning of a claim is determined, it might become much easier to determine whether or not your competitor infringes.

questions. However, if, after sufficient discovery, there is no longer any debate about the facts, the court can decide the case in favor of one party or the other on the papers without need for a trial. The party bringing the motion is telling the judge that there is no need to go to trial—the parties agree on the facts and the judge can simply apply the law to the facts and decide whether infringement has occurred.

Sometimes the court will agree with the party bringing the motion and decide the case on the papers and dismiss either the case or at least one or more of the claims in the case. Summary judgment is cost-efficient because it has the benefit of possibly avoiding trial, which is an expensive part of litigation. If the court decides there is still some genuine debate about the facts, the court will deny the motion and ask the parties to proceed to trial (assuming they do not settle before then). A party against whom a summary judgment is granted can typically appeal from the order. If the court denies the motion on the grounds that there still remain questions of fact for trial, that decision is not appealable.

Sometimes claim construction issues are resolved during the summary judgment motion proceedings. There are still some judges, though, who prefer to address claim construction proceedings separately from summary judgment motion proceedings. Depending upon the number of claim construction issues and whether or not expert testimony is required to resolve those issues, claim construction proceedings can cost anywhere between $50,000 to $125,000. If the court is amenable, it may be preferable to recommend to the court that any claim construction issues be resolved as part of summary judgment motions because it is more cost efficient and provides an opportunity to dispose of the case at the same time, if possible. It is difficult to estimate the cost of a summary judgment motion because there are so many variables, but you should expect to spend in the range of $75,000 to $150,000.

Expert Witnesses

In a patent infringement lawsuit, the parties might hire expert witnesses. These witnesses help the judge or jury understand complicated technology and things such as how much damages the plaintiff has suffered because of the alleged infringement. Sometimes the judges freely allow experts to be designated by the parties; sometimes they don't. If the court allows experts, the parties will be involved in expert discovery, which means that each party may take depositions of the other side's experts.

Expert discovery does not need to be expensive, but it can be and usually is very expensive depending upon the number of experts selected by both parties. If the lawsuit is what lawyers like to call a "plain vanilla" patent infringement case, a single technical expert and a single damages expert may be all that is required. While it is difficult to predict how much time each expert would need to spend preparing his/her opinions, the expert discovery costs associated with a plain vanilla patent infringement case are likely to be about $50,000 to $100,000, including depositions. If there are more experts and tests are required to be conducted and analyzed by any of the experts in order to help them conclude whether or not the claims are infringed, expert discovery can be two to three times higher or more.

The Trial

Only three percent of patent infringement cases in the United States go to trial. That is good for businesses from an economic standpoint, because trial is often the most expensive part of a patent infringement case. Again, depending upon your goals, you should be looking to resolve the case long before trial, preferably via a preliminary injunction motion that could bring the opposing party to the bargaining table or a summary judgment motion that leads to the judge resolving the case favorably to you.

If a case is heading to trial, it means that the parties were unable to obtain any legal leverage during the course of the case to exert pressure on the other party to agree to an acceptable settlement. In some cases, however, the judges are simply not willing to cooperate with the parties' interest in resolving the case earlier rather than later. For example, there are times where a party has submitted a summary judgment motion that is well-prepared and postured to permit the court to rule and dismiss the case. However, sometimes the judge either doesn't like summary judgment motions in general or is simply too busy with his/her docket to devote sufficient time to the motion. In those cases, the judge denies the motion and requires the parties to go to trial. Thankfully, that occurs in the minority of cases.

Pre-trial Proceedings

With that said, if a case is headed to trial, then there are pre-trial matters that need to be addressed first. The judge is going to want the parties to confer about what issues truly remain in debate. All of the procedural and substantive disputes must be identified and explained in papers submitted before trial.

Witness Lists, Summaries of Testimony, and Exhibit Lists

The court also requires that a list of all witnesses and exhibits be prepared by both parties. The list will not only identify the witnesses but also give a short summary of the expected testimony. In addition, the court requires the parties to exchange lists identifying all of the exhibits they will use at trial, including documents and product samples. By exchanging a list of witnesses and exhibits with each other before trial, both parties will have an opportunity to identify their objections.

Trial Briefs

The court is also likely to require a trial brief by each party. A trial brief is a comprehensive presentation to the court of all of the claims and issues, including an explanation of why the submitting party should win on these facts and under the applicable law.

Pre-trial Costs

The pre-trial process can take weeks or on occasion months and reflects a large investment of time "crystal-balling" what will be necessary at trial. If it's not in the pre-trial papers, it's not likely to be admissible at trial. That is why the lawyers tend to throw in the kitchen sink, just in case (meaning that they will be overbroad in telling the judge what the trial will include). The pre-trial costs are likely to be about $150,000 to $300,000, depending upon the number of issues remaining to be tried, the number of witnesses, and the number of exhibits that the parties want to introduce as evidence in the trial.

Jury Focus Groups and Jury Experts

If a jury will be deciding the fact issues at trial, pre-trial efforts could also include jury focus groups and jury experts assisting in assessing how to present the case to a jury. Such jury focus efforts can cost $50,000 to $150,000, depending upon how comprehensive you and your lawyer want to be.

Jury Instructions

There are also jury instructions that become necessary when a jury is involved, which can add to the cost of the pre-trial papers that are filed. Jury instructions typically cost about $25,000 to $50,000 because each party proposes jury instructions to the judge, and then the parties try to agree upon a joint set of instructions to be submitted to the jury, which often requires that the court resolve the differences. If a lot of "motions in limine" (motions to exclude evidence at trial) are required, then the cost of the pre-trial proceedings is likely to increase by about $10,000 per motion.

Trial Costs

Trial itself is likely to cost about $100,000 to $300,000 a week. Those high costs reflect that there is typically a team of lawyers and paralegals working 12-plus hour days during trial. Even smaller cases typically require three lawyers and two paralegals. Where there are lots of witnesses and issues to be tried, the number of trial team members needs to increase, because each lawyer will focus on certain issues or certain witnesses. We have participated in hundreds of patent trials at our firm, and have found that most patent trials last about two to three weeks.

For a jury trial in a patent case, the same "voir dire" (jury selection), opening statements, testifying and examining of witnesses, closing statements, jury deliberations, and reading of the jury verdict are involved as they are with most other trials.

Post-trial Proceedings

Whether or not the trial involves a jury, there can be and most likely will be post-trial papers, either in the form of a post-trial brief (where there is no jury) or a motion for judgment as a matter of law (where there is a jury). With post-trial briefs, each party sets forth all of the evidence that was presented at trial and argues why they should win. Not all of the evidence presented in the pre-trial papers gets used during trial, so the post-trial briefs argue only what was used at trial.

Sometimes trial comes out differently than expected or planned, in which case the post-trial briefs may differ significantly from the pre-trial papers. The reason is that each party jostles for position during trial and reacts to how the testimony comes out. No matter how well you prepare a witness, you don't always know what will come out during cross-examination (the questioning of your witness by the other side). Also, the judge may decide to exclude certain evidence during trial that she believes is either too prejudicial or not relevant. That, of course, can affect your strategy and change your approach for the post-trial briefs. Part of the reason that trial is expensive is that plans must be adjusted and redeveloped frequently to accommodate daily changes in testimony and evidence as played out in the courtroom.

Where a jury is involved, post-trial briefing is usually limited to asking the court to rule differently than the jury did. Obviously, the only party filing that type of paper is the one who lost before the jury. In effect, the law permits a judge to overrule a jury by ruling as a matter of law that no reasonable jury could conclude the way that this particular jury did. There are times when the jury simply gets it wrong and the judge can save the day for the losing party. Such a paper is called a motion for judgment as a matter of law (aka "JMOL")—you are asking the judge to rule in your favor even though the jury ruled against you.

The Costs of Post-trial Proceedings

Post-trial papers could be very focused (covering just one or a few issues) or they could be very comprehensive (covering all issues), depending upon what the judge wants to hear or what the parties want the judge to consider. Thus, the range of costs is quite wide, anywhere from $50,000 to $200,000. As with most motions filed with the court, in filing a post-trial motion you will get two bites of the apple: an initial moving paper, and a reply to the other side's opposition. In each bite you will be trying to convince the judge of your position. The cost associated with post-trial papers includes the evaluation and presentation of all the relevant evidence from trial, the preparation and submission of at least two papers in support of your position, and often a lengthy hearing.

Appealing Your Case

If you are not satisfied with the outcome of the trial, you may decide to appeal the verdict to a higher court. With patent cases, all appeals go to a special appeals court in Washington, D.C. That court, known as the Federal Circuit Court of Appeals, is the only appellate court that can hear patent cases. The preparation of appeal briefs and argument usually costs about $100,000 to $300,000, depending upon the number of issues addressed.

The Overall Costs of Litigation

In light of the above costs, laying out a litigation strategy early is absolutely key to managing litigation costs. We have litigated fairly straightforward patent infringement cases that ended up costing about $250,000 through appeal, without trial. We also have litigated complex patent cases involving numerous patents and contentious opposing counsel that have ended up costing $5 million through trial and appeal. So it is very difficult to give meaningful estimates without knowing more about the facts of a particular case and your goals and strategies. It is also important that you recognize that hardheaded aggressiveness in pursuing litigation will always make litigation more expensive.

Appendix A

Umbrella Patent

Smart Umbrella
Background of The Invention

Field of the Invention

[0001]   The field relates to umbrellas, and in one embodiment, wireless communication with an umbrella.

Description of the Related Art

[0002]   Conventional umbrellas are well suited to shield users from rainfall. However, conventional umbrellas are completely passive devices that fail to warn their users when rainfall is predicted. Since users are generally too busy to check the weather forecast before leaving shelter, it would be useful for the umbrella to inform the user whether or not rain is predicted, and therefore, whether or not the user should bother carrying the umbrella.

Summary of the Invention

[0003]   In one embodiment, an umbrella includes: an elongate shaft having a first end and a second end; a handle provided at the first end of the elongate shaft; a plurality of spokes connected to the second end of the shaft, the spokes being moveable from a collapsed configuration aligned with the shaft and an expanded configuration extending away from the shaft; a covering supported by the spokes and forming a concave surface facing toward the handle; and an indicator configured to display a weather condition, wherein the indicator is located near the first end.

[0004]   In another embodiment, a method of transmitting information to an umbrella includes: transmitting weather information from a weather station to a receiver on an umbrella; and activating a signal on the umbrella when the receiver receives weather information indicating that it is going to rain.

[0005]   In yet another embodiment, a method of receiving information with an umbrella includes: receiving a weather signal indicative of a weather condition; generating an indicator signal with a microprocessor carried by the umbrella, wherein the indicator signal corresponds to the weather signal; and activating an indicator with the indicator signal.

Brief Description of the Drawings

[0006]   FIG. 1 provides a front schematic view of an umbrella in accordance with one embodiment of the present invention;

[0007]   FIG. 2 provides a front schematic view of a weather forecast communication system that can include the umbrella of FIG. 1;

[0008]   FIG. 3 provides a block schematic diagram of an umbrella, such as the umbrella of FIG. 1; and

FIGURE 1

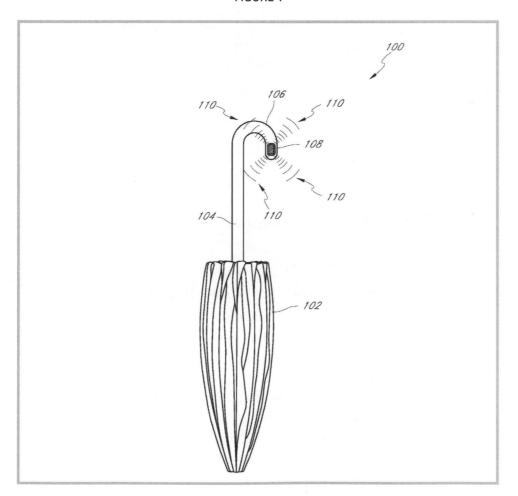

FIGURE 2

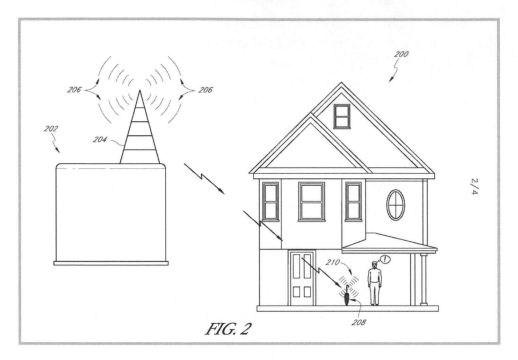

FIG. 2

[0009] FIG. 4 provides a flow chart describing a method of communicating with an umbrella.

Detailed Description
of the Preferred Embodiments

[0010] **FIG. 1** illustrates an umbrella 100 in accordance with one embodiment of the present invention. The umbrella 100 includes a canopy 102 attached to an elongate shaft 104 at one end. The opposite end of the elongate shaft 104 includes a handle 106. Struts (not shown) extend from the end of the elongate shaft 104 towards the handle 106. The canopy 102 attaches to the elongate shaft 104 with the struts. The struts (and canopy 102) can be moved from a first, collapsed position, in which they are generally parallel to the elongate shaft 104 (as shown in FIG. 1) to a second, expanded position, in which they extend away from the elongate shaft 104.

FIGURE 3

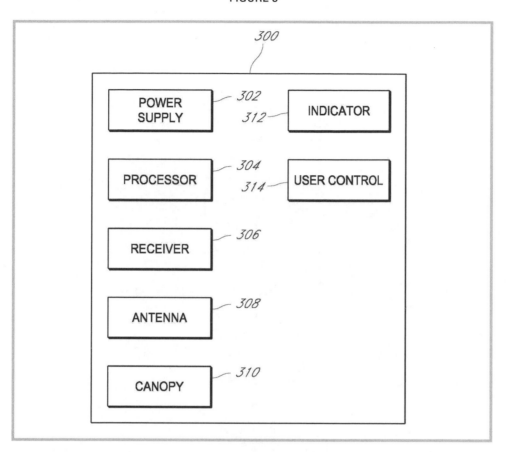

[0011]   In some embodiments, the umbrella 100 includes 4, 8, or 10 struts. The struts, as well as the elongate shaft 104 can be made from a variety of materials, including metal, wood, and/or plastic. The canopy 102 can be made from a woven fabric. In some embodiments, the canopy 102 is made from plastic, polyurethane, polytetrafluoroethylene, or expanded polytetrafluoroethylene (ePTFE). In other embodiments, the canopy 102 includes TEFLON, RAYON, DACRON, polyester, or GORE-TEX.

[0012]   The handle 106 is curved in an arc. In other embodiments, the handle 106 is not curved, and is coaxially aligned with the elongate shaft 104.

FIGURE 4

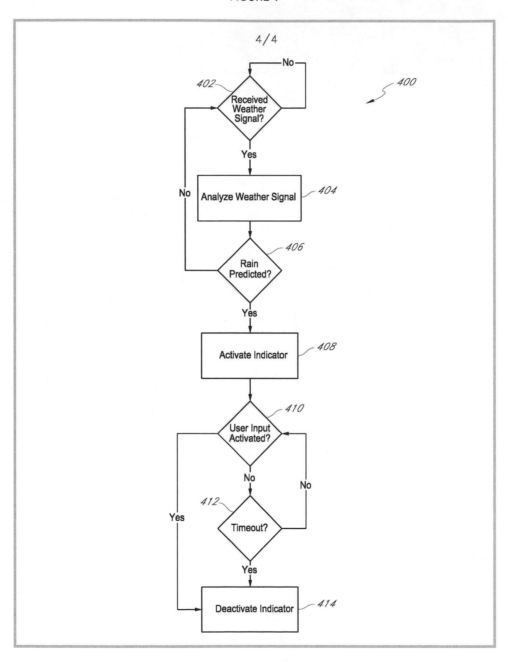

An indicator 108 is positioned on the handle 106. In other embodiments, the indicator 108 is located adjacent or near the handle 106. For example, the indicator 108 can be located at a portion of the elongate shaft 104, within, or attached to the elongate shaft 104. The indicator 108 can include a visual indicator, an audio indicator, or both. For example, the indicator 108 can include a light, LED, LCD, and/or a speaker.

[0013]   The umbrella 100 can include other components not shown on FIG. 1. For example, the umbrella 100 can also include a power supply, microprocessor, radio receiver, antenna, and user control, such as described with respect to FIG. 3, below. The antenna can extend through the elongate shaft 104. In some embodiments, the antenna extends through at least one strut. In yet another embodiment, the canopy 102 includes the antenna. In some embodiments, the umbrella 100 also includes a radio transmitter. In others, the receiver includes a transceiver.

[0014]   In operation the umbrella 100 receives a radio signal with its receiver and antenna (not shown). The radio signal can be generated by a weather forecast source, and the radio signal can correspond to a weather forecast for a predetermined period. A microprocessor analyzes the radio signal and determines if rain is predicted. If so, the microprocessor provides an indicator signal to the indicator 108. The indicator signal causes the indicator 108 to activate or not. For example, if the radio signal indicates that rain is predicted in the next 24 hours, the microprocessor can cause the indicator 108 to illuminate, or flash. A power supply supplies power to the electronic components of the umbrella 100.

[0015]   A user can activate a user control (not shown) to turn off, or "snooze" the indicator, similar to an alarm clock snooze. The user control can be any device configured to allow the user to communicate with the microprocessor, including a switch or a sensor. In some embodiments, when the user holds the handle 106, the indicator 108 is automatically deactivated for a predetermined period of time (e.g., 2, 6, 12, 24, or 48 hours).

[0016]   In some embodiments the umbrella 100 includes a weather sensor (not shown), such as a barometer, thermometer, and/or humidity sensor. The umbrella 100 uses information received by the weather sensor to provide a corroboration or inconsistency determination with the received radio signal. The microprocessor can generate a confidence value associated with the weather forecast based upon whether the radio signal and weather sensor signals are consistent (e.g., both indicate the same weather forecast), or inconsistent with each other.

[0017]   FIG. 2 illustrates a weather forecast communication system 200 in accordance with another embodiment of the present invention. The weather forecast communication system 200 includes a weather station 202 and a transmitter 204. The transmitter 204 transmits a radio signal 206 from the weather station to an umbrella 208, which in some embodiments, is the umbrella 100 described above with respect to FIG. 1. The radio signal 206 corresponds to a weather forecast provided by the weather station 202.

[0018]   The umbrella 208 receives the weather signal 206 and provides a user notification signal 210 to the user. The user notification signal 210 can be a visual or audio signal that informs a user the forecasted weather conditions, and whether it is recommended to carry the umbrella or not.

[0019]   FIG. 3 illustrates components of an umbrella 300, such as the umbrella 100, 208 of FIGs. 1 and 2. The umbrella 300 includes a power supply 302, microprocessor 304, receiver 306, antenna 308, canopy 310, indicator 312, and user control 314. The components of the umbrella 300 work together as discussed above with respect to FIG. 1.

[0020]   The receiver 306 can be a wireless receiver, such as the receiver found in a pager or cellular telephone. In some embodiments, the receiver 306 is configured to communicate in accordance with the IEEE 802 standard, such as 802.11(a), (b), or (g). In other embodiments, the receiver 306 is configured to communicate in accordance with an IEEE 802.15 standard, such as any known BLUETOOTH. The receiver 306 can receive a wireless signal directly from a weather station, a transmitter, or from an intermediate station (not show), such as a repeater, or from a local source. For example, in some embodiments, a user's computer or cellular telephone communicate receive information from a weather station (or any source of weather-related information) and provide a weather forecast signal to the umbrella 300.

[0021] In other embodiments, the receiver 306 is a VHF (very high frequency) or UHF (ultra high frequency) receiver, as is used with over-the-air television signal broadcasts. In some embodiments, the receiver 306 is configured to receive a weather signal from the National Weather Service (NWS). For example, the receiver 306 can be configured to receive a Specific Area Message Encoded (SAME) broadcast from the NWS, or other source. In other embodiments, the receiver 306 receives XML-based data, such as data provided according to the Common Alerting Protocol. In addition, the receiver 306 can be configured to receive data through the California Irrigation Management Information System (CIMIS), a system maintained by the California Department of Water Resources, or any other irrigation management information system.

[0022] **FIG. 4** illustrates a method 400 of communicating with an umbrella. At step 402 the method 400 determines if a weather signal has been received. If not, the method continues to monitor whether a weather signal has been received. If a weather signal is received, the method 400 continues to step 404. At step 404, the method 400 analyzes the weather signal to determine if rain, snow, or other weather suitable for umbrella use is predicted. If adverse weather is not predicted, the method 400 returns to step 402; otherwise, it continues to step 408.

[0023] At step 408, the method 400 activates an indicator. For example, in some embodiments, the method 400 turns on a visual or audible indicator, such as a light or lights, LED, or LCD. In other embodiments, the method 400 causes an audible alarm to sound. In other embodiments, the method 400 sends a wireless signal to another device, such as a cell phone, pager, computer, PDA or computing device.

[0024] At step 410, the method 400 checks whether the user has activated an input. For example, in one embodiment, the method 400 determines if the user has pressed a button or activated a switch or sensor. The input could be a pressure switch, temperature switch, level switch, or galvanic sensor. For example, in some embodiments, the method 400 determines if the user has picked up the umbrella. Impedance measurements across the umbrella's handle, or a level switch, could be used to determine if the umbrella has been picked up.

[0025] If the user has activated an input, the method proceeds to step 414, where the indictor is deactivated; if not, the method continues to step 412. At step 412 the method 400 determines if a timeout period has passed. For example, the method 400 determines if a predetermined period of time has passed since the indicator is activated (e.g., the timeout period). The predetermined period of time could be any suitable period, such as minutes, hours, or days. In one embodiment, the predetermined period of time is about 30 minutes, about 1 hour, about 6 hours, about 12 hours, about 24 hours, or about 2 days.

[0026] If the timeout period has not passed, the method returns to step 410; if it has, the method 400 continues to step 414. At step 414 the indicator is deactivated. For example, at step 414 the method 400 turns off the visual or audible indicator previously activated at step 408.

[0027] Although this invention has been disclosed in the context of certain preferred embodiments, it will be understood by those skilled in the art that the present invention extends beyond the specifically disclosed embodiment to other alternative embodiments and/or uses of the invention and obvious modifications and equivalents thereof. In particular, while the present smart umbrella device, system, and methods have been described in the context of particularly preferred embodiments, the skilled artisan will appreciate, in view of the present disclosure, that certain advantages, features and aspects of the information communication system, device, and method may be realized in a variety of other applications and software systems. Additionally, it is contemplated that various aspects and features of the invention described can be practiced separately, combined together, or substituted for one another, and that a variety of combination and sub-combinations of the features and aspects can be made and still fall within the scope of the invention.

[0028] Those of skill in the art will understand that information and signals can be represented using a variety of different technologies and techniques. For example, data, instructions, commands, information, signals, bits, symbols, and chips that can be referenced throughout the above description may be represented by voltages, currents, electromagnetic waves, magnetic fields or particles, optical fields or particles, or any combination thereof.

[0029]   Those of skill in the art will further appreciate that the various illustrative logical blocks, modules, circuits, and algorithm steps described in connection with the embodiments disclosed herein can be implemented as electronic hardware, computer software, or combinations of both. To illustrate this interchangeability of hardware and software, various illustrative components, blocks, modules, circuits, and steps have been described above generally in terms of their functionality. Whether such functionality is implemented as hardware or software depends upon the particular application and design constraints imposed on the overall system. Skilled artisans can implement the described functionality in varying ways for each particular application, but such implementation decisions should not be interpreted as causing a departure from the scope of the present invention.

[0030]   The various illustrative logical blocks, modules, and circuits described in connection with the embodiments disclosed herein can be implemented or performed with a general purpose processor, a digital signal processor (DSP), an application-specific integrated circuit (ASIC), a field programmable gate array (FPGA) or other programmable logic device, discrete gate or transistor logic, discrete hardware components, or any combination thereof designed to perform the functions described herein. A general purpose processor can be a microprocessor, but in the alternative, the processor can be any conventional processor, controller, microcontroller, or state machine. A processor can also be implemented as a combination of computing devices, e.g., a combination of a DSP and a microprocessor, a plurality of microprocessors, one or more microprocessors in conjunction with a DSP core, or any other such configuration.

[0031]   The steps of a method or algorithm described in connection with the embodiments disclosed herein can be embodied directly in hardware, in a software module executed by a processor, or in a combination of the two. A software module can reside in RAM memory, flash memory, ROM memory, EPROM memory, EEPROM memory, registers, hard disk, a removable disk, a CD-ROM, or other form of storage medium known in the art. A storage medium is coupled to the processor, such that the processor can read information from, and write information to, the storage medium. In the alternative, the storage medium can be integral to the processor. The processor and the storage medium can reside in an ASIC. The ASIC can reside in a user terminal. The processor and the storage medium can reside as discrete components in a user terminal.

[0032]   The previous description of the disclosed embodiments is provided to enable a person skilled in the art to make or use the present invention. Various modifications to these embodiments will be readily apparent to those skilled in the art, and the generic principles defined herein can be applied to other embodiments without departing from the spirit or scope of the invention. Thus, the invention is limited only by the claims that follow. Thus, it is intended that the scope of the present invention herein disclosed should not be limited by the particular disclosed embodiment described above, but should be determined only by a fair reading of the claims that follow.

What is claimed is:

1. An umbrella, comprising:
   an elongate shaft having a first end and a second end;
   a handle provided at the first end of the elongate shaft;
   a plurality of spokes connected to the second end of the shaft, the
   spokes being moveable from a collapsed configuration aligned with
   the shaft and an expanded configuration extending away from the shaft;
   a covering supported by the spokes and forming a concave surface fac
   ing toward the handle; and
   an indicator configured to display a weather condition, wherein the
   indicator is located near the first end.
2. The umbrella of Claim 1, further comprising a receiver configured to receive a radio signal indicative of the weather condition.
3. The umbrella of Claim 2, further comprising a microprocessor, wherein the microprocessor is configured to activate the indicator based upon the radio signal.

4. The umbrella of Claim 2, wherein the receiver comprises a BLUE-TOOTH receiver.
5. The umbrella of Claim 2, wherein the receiver comprises a radio transceiver.
6. The umbrella of Claim 1, wherein the indicator comprises a visual display.
7. The umbrella of Claim 6, wherein the indicator comprises an LED.
8. The umbrella of Claim 1, wherein the indicator comprises an audible alarm.
9. A method of transmitting information to an umbrella, comprising: transmitting weather information from a weather station to a receiver on an umbrella; and
    activating a signal on the umbrella when the receiver receives weather information indicating that it is going to rain.
10. A method of receiving information with an umbrella, comprising: receiving a weather signal indicative of a weather condition; generating an indicator signal with a microprocessor carried by the umbrella, wherein the indicator signal corresponds to the weather signal; and activating an indicator with the indicator signal.

SMART UMBRELLA
Abstract of the Disclosure

An umbrella includes an elongate shaft having a first end and a second end; a handle provided at the first end of the elongate shaft; a plurality of spokes connected to the second end of the shaft, the spokes being moveable from a collapsed configuration aligned with the shaft and an expanded configuration extending away from the shaft; a covering supported by the spokes and forming a concave surface facing toward the handle; and an indicator configured to display a weather condition, wherein the indicator is located near the first end.

Appendix B

USPTO Selected Patent Fees, effective September 30, 2007, Page 1

Description	Fee	Small Entity Fee (if applicable)
Patent Application Filing Fees		
Basic filing fee - Utility *filed on or after December 8, 2004*	310.00	155.00
Basic filing fee - Utility (electronic filing for small entities) *filed on or after December 8, 2004*	n/a	75.00
Basic filing fee - Utility *filed before December 8, 2004*	810.00	405.00
Independent claims in excess of three	210.00	105.00
Claims in excess of twenty	50.00	25.00
Multiple dependent claim	370.00	185.00
Surcharge - Late filing fee, search fee, examination fee or oath or declaration	130.00	65.00
Utility Application Size Fee - for each additional 50 sheets that exceeds 100 sheets	260.00	130.00
Basic filing fee - Design *filed on or after December 8, 2004*	210.00	105.00
Basic filing fee - Design *filed before December 8, 2004*	360.00	185.00
Design Application Size Fee - for each additional 50 sheets that exceeds 100 sheets	260.00	130.00
Basic filing fee - Plant *filed on or after December 8, 2004*	210.00	105.00
Basic filing fee - Plant *filed before December 8, 2004*	570.00	285.00
Plant Application Size Fee - for each additional 50 sheets that exceeds 100 sheets	260.00	130.00
Basic filing fee - Reissue *filed on or after December 8, 2004*	310.00	155.00
Basic filing fee - Reissue *filed before December 8, 2004*	810.00	405.00

USPTO Selected Patent Fees, effective September 30, 2007, Page 2

Description	Fee	Small Entity Fee (if applicable)
Reissue independent claims in excess of three	210.00	105.00
Reissue claims in excess of twenty	50.00	25.00
Reissue Application Size Fee - for each additional 50 sheets that exceeds 100 sheets	260.00	130.00
Provisional application filing fee	210.00	105.00
Provisional Application Size Fee - for each additional 50 sheets that exceeds 100 sheets	260.00	130.00
Surcharge - Late provisional filing fee or cover sheet	50.00	25.00
Non-English specification	130.00	
Patent Search Fees		
Utility Search Fee	510.00	255.00
Design Search Fee	100.00	50.00
Plant Search Fee	310.00	155.00
Reissue Search Fee	510.00	255.00
Patent Examination Fees		
Utility Examination Fee	210.00	105.00
Design Examination Fee	130.00	65.00
Plant Examination Fee	160.00	80.00
Reissue Examination Fee	620.00	310.00
Patent Allowance Fees		
Utility issue fee	1,440.00	720.00
Design issue fee	820.00	410.00
Plant issue fee	1,130.00	565.00
Reissue issue fee	1,440.00	720.00
Publication fee for early, voluntary, or normal publication	300.00	
Publication fee for republication	300.00	
Patent Maintenance Fees		
Due at 3.5 years	930.00	465.00

USPTO Selected Patent Fees, effective September 30, 2007, Page 3

Description	Fee	Small Entity Fee (if applicable)
Due at 7.5 years	2,360.00	1,180.00
Due at 11.5 years	3,910.00	1,955.00
Surcharge - 3.5 year - Late payment within 6 months	130.00	65.00
Surcharge - 7.5 year - Late payment within 6 months	130.00	65.00
Surcharge - 11.5 year - Late payment within 6 months	130.00	65.00
Surcharge after expiration - Late payment is unavoidable	700.00	
Surcharge after expiration - Late payment is unintentional	1,640.00	
Miscellaneous Patent Fees		
Request for continued examination (RCE) (see 37 CFR 1.114)	810.00	405.00
Request for voluntary publication or republication	130.00	
Request for expedited examination of a design application	900.00	
Submission of an Information Disclosure Statement	180.00	
Petition to revive unavoidably abandoned application	510.00	255.00
Petition to revive unintentionally abandoned application	1,540.00	770.00
Acceptance of an unintentionally delayed claim for priority	1,410.00	
Filing an application for patent term adjustment	200.00	
Request for reinstatement of term reduced	400.00	
Extension of term of patent	1,120.00	
Patent Post-Issuance Fees		
Certificate of correction	100.00	
Request for ex parte reexamination	2,520.00	
Request for inter partes reexamination	8,800.00	
Reexamination independent claims in excess of three and also in excess of the number of such claims in the patent under reexamination	210.00	105.00

USPTO Selected Patent Fees, effective September 30, 2007, Page 4

Description	Fee	Small Entity Fee (if applicable)
Reexamination claims in excess of twenty and also in excess of the number of claims in the patent under reexamination	50.00	25.00
Statutory disclaimer	130.00	65.00
Patent Extension of Time Fees		
Extension for response within first month	120.00	60.00
Extension for response within second month	460.00	230.00
Extension for response within third month	1,050.00	525.00
Extension for response within fourth month	1,630.00	815.00
Extension for response within fifth month	2,220.00	1,110.00
Patent Appeals		
Notice of appeal	510.00	255.00
Filing a brief in support of an appeal	510.00	255.00
Request for oral hearing	1,030.00	515.00

Declaration for Utility or Design Patent Application, Page 1

PTO/SB/01 (06-07)
Approved for use through 06/30/2007. OMB 0651-0032
U.S. Patent and Trademark Office; U.S. DEPARTMENT OF COMMERCE
Under the Paperwork Reduction Act of 1995, no persons are required to respond to a collection of information unless it contains a valid OMB control number.

DECLARATION FOR UTILITY OR DESIGN PATENT APPLICATION (37 CFR 1.63)

Attorney Docket Number	
First Named Inventor	
COMPLETE IF KNOWN	
Application Number	
Filing Date	
Art Unit	
Examiner Name	

☐ Declaration Submitted With Initial Filing **OR** ☐ Declaration Submitted after Initial Filing (surcharge (37 CFR 1.16 (e)) required)

I hereby declare that:

Each inventor's residence, mailing address, and citizenship are as stated below next to their name.

I believe the inventor(s) named below to be the original and first inventor(s) of the subject matter which is claimed and for which a patent is sought on the invention entitled:

(Title of the Invention)

the specification of which

☐ is attached hereto

OR

☐ was filed on (MM/DD/YYYY) _____ as United States Application Number or PCT International

Application Number _____ and was amended on (MM/DD/YYYY) _____ (if applicable).

I hereby state that I have reviewed and understand the contents of the above identified specification, including the claims, as amended by any amendment specifically referred to above.

I acknowledge the duty to disclose information which is material to patentability as defined in 37 CFR 1.56, including for continuation-in-part applications, material information which became available between the filing date of the prior application and the national or PCT international filing date of the continuation-in-part application.

I hereby claim foreign priority benefits under 35 U.S.C. 119(a)-(d) or (f), or 365(b) of any foreign application(s) for patent, inventor's or plant breeder's rights certificate(s), or 365(a) of any PCT international application which designated at least one country other than the United States of America, listed below and have also identified below, by checking the box, any foreign application for patent, inventor's or plant breeder's rights certificate(s), or any PCT international application having a filing date before that of the application on which priority is claimed.

Prior Foreign Application Number(s)	Country	Foreign Filing Date (MM/DD/YYYY)	Priority Not Claimed	Certified Copy Attached? YES	NO
			☐	☐	☐
			☐	☐	☐
			☐	☐	☐
			☐	☐	☐

☐ Additional foreign application numbers are listed on a supplemental priority data sheet PTO/SB/02B attached hereto.

[Page 1 of 2]

This collection of information is required by 35 U.S.C. 115 and 37 CFR 1.63. The information is required to obtain or retain a benefit by the public which is to file (and by the USPTO to process) an application. Confidentiality is governed by 35 U.S.C. 122 and 37 CFR 1.11 and 1.14. This collection is estimated to take 21 minutes to complete, including gathering, preparing, and submitting the completed application form to the USPTO. Time will vary depending upon the individual case. Any comments on the amount of time you require to complete this form and/or suggestions for reducing this burden, should be sent to the Chief Information Officer, U.S. Patent and Trademark Office, U.S. Department of Commerce, P.O. Box 1450, Alexandria, VA 22313-1450. DO NOT SEND FEES OR COMPLETED FORMS TO THIS ADDRESS. **SEND TO: Commissioner for Patents, P.O. Box 1450, Alexandria, VA 22313-1450.**
If you need assistance completing the form, call 1-800-PTO-9199 and select option 2.

Declaration for Utility or Design Patent Application, Page 2

PTO/SB/01 (06-07)
Approved for use through 06/30/2007. OMB 0651-0032
U.S. Patent and Trademark Office; U.S. DEPARTMENT OF COMMERCE
Under the Paperwork Reduction Act of 1995, no persons are required to respond to a collection of information unless it contains a valid OMB control number.

DECLARATION — Utility or Design Patent Application

Direct all correspondence to:	☐ The address associated with Customer Number:		OR ☐ Correspondence address below

Name

Address

City	State	ZIP

Country	Telephone	Email

WARNING:

Petitioner/applicant is cautioned to avoid submitting personal information in documents filed in a patent application that may contribute to identity theft. Personal information such as social security numbers, bank account numbers, or credit card numbers (other than a check or credit card authorization form PTO-2038 submitted for payment purposes) is never required by the USPTO to support a petition or an application. If this type of personal information is included in documents submitted to the USPTO, petitioners/applicants should consider redacting such personal information from the documents before submitting them to the USPTO. Petitioner/applicant is advised that the record of a patent application is available to the public after publication of the application (unless a non-publication request in compliance with 37 CFR 1.213(a) is made in the application) or issuance of a patent. Furthermore, the record from an abandoned application may also be available to the public if the application is referenced in a published application or an issued patent (see 37 CFR 1.14). Checks and credit card authorization forms PTO-2038 submitted for payment purposes are not retained in the application file and therefore are not publicly available.

I hereby declare that all statements made herein of my own knowledge are true and that all statements made on information and belief are believed to be true; and further that these statements were made with the knowledge that willful false statements and the like so made are punishable by fine or imprisonment, or both, under 18 U.S.C. 1001 and that such willful false statements may jeopardize the validity of the application or any patent issued thereon.

NAME OF SOLE OR FIRST INVENTOR:	☐ A petition has been filed for this unsigned inventor
Given Name (first and middle [if any])	Family Name or Surname

Inventor's Signature	Date

Residence: City	State	Country	Citizenship

Mailing Address

City	State	Zip	Country

☐ Additional inventors or a legal representative are being named on the _____ supplemental sheet(s) PTO/SB/02A or 02LR attached hereto.

[Page 2 of 2]

U.S.P.T.O. Trademark Search, Page 1

 United States Patent and Trademark Office   **TRADEMARKS**

Home | Site Index | Search | FAQ | Glossary | Guides | Contacts | eBusiness | eBiz alerts | News | Help

Trademarks

Check NEWS & NOTICES for the latest advisories and Trademark news

Electronic forms for submitting Madrid-Protocol related documents

Madrid Protocol: Tips for Paper Filers ▶▶ be sure to check for more Madrid guidance

Basics...	*eBusiness* *What you can do online ...*
Where do I start? << START HERE!	**Use Trademark Electronic Business Center** to file, search, check status, view documents, and more...
Basic Facts about Trademarks	
PTDLs - Depository Libraries search resources & support near you	*Get a Trademark Registration ...*
Public Search Facilities at USPTO	**Search**
Where to send mail ...	**File**
Who to call ...	**Fees, pricing and payments**
Border Enforcement ...	**Forms** - all USPTO forms
Record Trademarks With Customs and Border Protection (CBP)	*Correspondence:*
Madrid Protocol ...	Respond to office actions Respond to Notice of Allowance Amendments after publication Appeals: *(TMEP-1500)* or *(TBMP-1200)* Petitions guidance
Madrid Protocol for **International Registration of Marks** basics, procedures and guides, rules, and laws Madrid Protocol Fee Change - Effective May 2, 2005	**Petitions forms**
Manuals & Publications ...	**Opposition to registration** (*TMEP-1503*) *or (TBMP)*
About Trademarks, Patents & Copyrights	**Abandoned Applications - Revival of**
Geographical Indications	*Keep a Trademark Registration ...*
Internet Domain Names, registration as trademark - TMEP 1209.03(m)	**Assignment (change) of Ownership**
Types of Marks	FILE Assignment documents
Acceptable Identification of Goods and Services Manual	SEARCH Assignments
Design Search Code Manual	**Changes & Correction of information (TMEP)**
Official Gazette - Trademarks marks published for opposition & registration certificates	**Documents to file**
	Maintaining a registration
Trademark Examination Guides, Notes and Announcements ----- Change in Co-Pending Application Policy (20MAR2006) ----- Modifications to Design Search Codes (06DEC2006)	**Registration**
	Trademark Trial and Appeal Board (TTAB) ...
	About TTAB decisions, documents, fees, procedures
	TTAB Manual of Procedure Second Edition published 11 June 2003

http://www.uspto.gov/main/trademarks.htm

U.S.P.T.O. Trademark Search, Page 2

Trademark Manual of Examining Procedure TMEP 4th Edition, rev. April 2005

Laws & Regulations ...

US Trademark Law: Rules of Practice & Federal Statutes ⚖ 30 May 2007

Trademark Law on *GSA FedLaw* **site** ⚖

Trademark Law Treaty Implementation Act ⚖

Trademark Law Treaty (International) ⚖

Fastener Quality Act insignia

OG Notices (Official Gazette)

Rulemaking/Federal Register Notices:

Correspondence With the Madrid Processing Unit of the United States Patent and Trademark Office (16Apr2007) *[PDF]* ⚖

Changes in the Requirements for Filing Requests for Reconsideration of Final Office Actions in Trademark Cases (14Feb2007) *[PDF]* ⚖

>> More trademark-related rulemaking/notices

Table of Authorities added 6 November 2003

See **Trademark Electronic Business Center** for online filing, searching and viewing of TTAB proceedings

Resources ...

FAQs - questions & answers

Forms

Global / International Intellectual Property

Glossary

Locate **Native American Tribal Insignia**

Locate **FQA Register of Active Fastener Insignia**

Products and Services Catalog

Related non-USPTO links

Statistics

USPTO employment

Download PDF Viewer

KEY: =online business system ❀=fees =forms =help ⚖=laws/regulations =definition (glossary)

Call the **Trademark Assistance Center** *at* 1 800 786-9199 *for help on trademark matters. Send questions about USPTO programs and services to the* **USPTO Contact Center (UCC).** *You can suggest USPTO webpages or material you would like featured on this section by E-mail to the webmaster@uspto.gov. While we cannot promise to accommodate all requests, your suggestions will be considered and may lead to other improvements on the website.*

Last Modified: 05/30/2007 10:25:26

Madrid Protocol Schedule of Fees, Page 1

Home   IP Services   Madrid System for the International Registration of Marks   Fees / Fee Calculator

Schedule of Fees prescribed by the Common Regulations under the Madrid Agreement and the Madrid Protocol

(in force on January 1, 2006)

	Swiss francs
1. International applications governed exclusively by the Agreement	
The following fees shall be payable and shall cover 10 years:	
1.1 Basic fee (Article 8(2)(a) of the Agreement)[1]	
1.1.1 where no reproduction of the mark is in color	653
1.1.2 where any reproduction of the mark is in color	903
1.2 Supplementary fee for each class of goods and services beyond three classes (Article 8(2)(b) of the Agreement)	73
1.3 Complementary fee for the designation of each designated Contracting State (Article 8(2)(c) of the Agreement)	73
2. International applications governed exclusively by the Protocol	
The following fees shall be payable and shall cover 10 years:	
2.1 Basic fee (Article 8(2)(i) of the Protocol)[1]	
2.1.1 where no reproduction of the mark is in color	653
2.1.2 where any reproduction of the mark is in color	903
2.2 Supplementary fee for each class of goods and services beyond three classes (Article 8(2)(ii) of the Protocol), except if only Contracting Parties in respect of which individual fees (see 2.4, below) are payable are designated (see Article 8(7)(a)(i) of the Protocol)	73
2.3 Complementary fee for the designation of each designated Contracting Party (Article 8(2)(iii) of the Protocol), except if the designated Contracting Party is a Contracting Party in respect of which an individual fee is payable (see 2.4 below) (see Article 8(7)(a)(ii) of the Protocol)	73
2.4 Individual fee for the designation of each designated Contracting Party in respect of which an individual fee (rather than a complementary fee) is payable (see Article 8(7)(a) of the Protocol): the amount of the individual fee is fixed by each Contracting Party concerned	

Madrid Protocol Schedule of Fees, Page 2

3. International applications governed by both the Agreement and the Protocol

The following fees shall be payable and shall cover 10 years:

3.1 Basic fee[1]	
3.1.1 where no reproduction of the mark is in color	653
3.1.2 where any reproduction of the mark is in color	903
3.2 Supplementary fee for each class of goods and services beyond three classes	73
3.3 Complementary fee for the designation of each designated Contracting Party in respect of which no individual fee is payable	73
3.4 Individual fee for the designation of each designated Contracting Party in respect of which an individual fee is payable (see Article 8(7)(a) of the Protocol), except where the designated State is a State bound (also) by the Agreement and the Office of origin is the Office of a State bound (also) by the Agreement (in respect of such a State, a complementary fee is payable): the amount of the individual fee is fixed by each Contracting Party concerned	

4. Irregularities with respect to the classification of goods and services

The following fees shall be payable (Rule 12(1)(b)):

4.1 Where the goods and services are not grouped in classes	77 plus 4 per term in excess of 20
4.2 Where the classification, as appearing in the application, of one or more terms is incorrect	20 plus 4 per incorrectly classified term

provided that, where the total amount due under this item in respect of an international application is less than 150 Swiss francs, no fees shall be payable

5. Designation subsequent to international registration

The following fees shall be payable and shall cover the period between the effective date of the designation and the expiry of the then current term of the international registration:

5.1 Basic fee	300
5.2 Complementary fee for each designated Contracting Party indicated in the same request where an individual fee is not payable in respect of such designated Contracting Party (the fee covers the remainder of 10 years)	73
5.3 Individual fee for the designation of each designated Contracting Party in respect of which an individual fee (rather than a complementary fee) is payable (see Article 8(7)(a) of the Protocol): the amount of the individual fee is fixed by each Contracting Party concerned	

6. Renewal

The following fees shall be payable and shall cover 10 years:

6.1 Basic fee	653
6.2 Supplementary fee, except if the renewal is made only for designated Contracting Parties in respect of which individual fees are payable	73
6.3 Complementary fee for each designated Contracting Party in respect of which an individual fee is not payable	73
6.4 Individual fee for the designation of each designated Contracting Party in respect of which an individual fee (rather than a complementary fee) is payable (see Article 8(7)(a) of the Protocol): the amount of the individual fee is fixed by each Contracting Party concerned	
6.5 Surcharge for the use of the period of grace	50% of the amount of the fee payable under item 6.1

Madrid Protocol Schedule of Fees, Page 3

7. *Miscellaneous recordings*

7.1 Total transfer of an international registration	177
7.2 Partial transfer (for some of the goods and services or for some of the Contracting Parties) of an international registration	177
7.3 Limitation requested by the holder subsequent to international registration, provided that, if the limitation affects more than one Contracting Party, it is the same for all	177
7.4 Change of name and/or address of the holder of one or more international registrations for which recordal of the same change is requested in the same request	150
7.5 Recording of a license in respect of an international registration or amendment of the recording of a license	177

8. *Information concerning international registrations*

8.1 Establishing a certified extract from the International Register consisting of an analysis of the situation of an international registration (detailed certified extract),	
up to three pages	155
for each page after the third	10
8.2 Establishing a certified extract from the International Register consisting of a copy of all publications, and of all notifications of refusal, made with respect to an international registration (simple certified extract),	
up to three pages	77
for each page after the third	2
8.3 A single attestation or information in writing	
for a single international registration	77
for each additional international registration if the same information is requested in the same request	10
8.4 Reprint or photocopy of the publication of an international registration, per page	5

9. *Special services*

The International Bureau is authorized to collect a fee, whose amount it shall itself fix, for operations to be performed urgently and for services not covered by this Schedule of Fees.

---

[1] For international applications filed by applicants whose country of origin is a Least Developed Country, in accordance with the list established by the United Nations, the basic fee is reduced to 10% of the prescribed amount (rounded to the nearest full figure). In such case, the basic fee will amount to 65 Swiss francs (where no reproduction of the mark is in color) or to 90 Swiss francs (where any reproduction of the mark is in color).

Appendix C

Form TX, Page 1

 # Form TX

Detach and read these instructions before completing this form.
Make sure all applicable spaces have been filled in before you return this form.

BASIC INFORMATION

When to Use This Form: Use Form TX for registration of published or unpublished nondramatic literary works, excluding periodicals or serial issues. This class includes a wide variety of works: fiction, nonfiction, poetry, textbooks, reference works, directories, catalogs, advertising copy, compilations of information, and computer programs. For periodicals and serials, use Form SE.

Deposit to Accompany Application: An application for copyright registration must be accompanied by a deposit consisting of copies or phonorecords representing the entire work for which registration is to be made. The following are the general deposit requirements as set forth in the statute:

Unpublished Work: Deposit one complete copy (or phonorecord)
Published Work: Deposit two complete copies (or one phonorecord) of the best edition.
Work First Published Outside the United States: Deposit one complete copy (or phonorecord) of the first foreign edition.
Contribution to a Collective Work: Deposit one complete copy (or phonorecord) of the best edition of the collective work.
The Copyright Notice: Before March 1, 1989, the use of copyright notice was mandatory on all published works, and any work first

published before that date should have carried a notice. For works first published on and after March 1, 1989, use of the copyright notice is optional. For more information about copyright notice, see Circular 3, *Copyright Notices.*

For Further Information: To speak to a Copyright Office staff member, call (202) 707-3000 (TTY: (202) 707-6737). Recorded information is available 24 hours a day. Order forms and other publications from the address in space 9 or call the Forms and Publications Hotline at (202) 707-9100. Access and download circulars, forms, and other information from the Copyright Office website at *www.copyright.gov.*

PRIVACY ACT ADVISORY STATEMENT Required by the Privacy Act of 1974 (P.L. 93-579)
The authority for requesting this information is title 17 *USC*, secs. 409 and 410. Furnishing the requested information is voluntary. But if the information is not furnished, it may be necessary to delay or refuse registration and you may not be entitled to certain relief, remedies, and benefits provided in chapters 4 and 5 of title 17 *USC.*
The principal uses of the requested information are the establishment and maintenance of a public record and the examination of the application for compliance with the registration requirements of the copyright code.
Other routine uses include public inspection and copying, preparation of public indexes, preparation of public catalogs of copyright registrations, and preparation of search reports upon request.
NOTE: No other advisory statement will be given in connection with this application. Please keep this statement and refer to it if we communicate with you regarding this application.

LINE-BY-LINE INSTRUCTIONS

Please type or print using black ink. The form is used to produce the certificate.

 ## SPACE 1: Title

Title of This Work: Every work submitted for copyright registration must be given a title to identify that particular work. If the copies or phonorecords of the work bear a title or an identifying phrase that could serve as a title, transcribe that wording *completely* and *exactly* on the application. Indexing of the registration and future identification of the work will depend on the information you give here.

Previous or Alternative Titles: Complete this space if there are any additional titles for the work under which someone searching for the registration might be likely to look or under which a document pertaining to the work might be recorded.

Publication as a Contribution: If the work being registered is a contribution to a periodical, serial, or collection, give the title of the contribution in the "Title of This Work" space. Then, in the line headed "Publication as a Contribution," give information about the collective work in which the contribution appeared.

 ## SPACE 2: Author(s)

General Instructions: After reading these instructions, decide who are the "authors" of this work for copyright purposes. Then, unless the work is a "collective work," give the requested information about every "author" who contributed any appreciable amount of copyrightable matter to this version of the work. If you need further space, request Continuation Sheets. In the case of a collective work, such as an anthology, collection of essays, or encyclopedia, give information about the author of the collective work as a whole.

Name of Author: The fullest form of the author's name should be given. Unless the work was "made for hire," the individual who actually created the work is its "author." In the case of a work made

for hire, the statute provides that "the employer or other person for whom the work was prepared is considered the author."

What Is a "Work Made for Hire"? A "work made for hire" is defined as (1) "a work prepared by an employee within the scope of his or her employment"; or (2) "a work specially ordered or commissioned for use as a contribution to a collective work, as a part of a motion picture or other audiovisual work, as a translation, as a supplementary work, as a compilation, as an instructional text, as a test, as answer material for a test, or as an atlas, if the parties expressly agree in a written instrument signed by them that the works shall be considered a work made for hire." If you have checked "Yes" to indicate that the work was "made for hire," you must give the full legal name of the employer (or other person for whom the work was prepared). You may also include the name of the employee along with the name of the employer (for example: "Elster Publishing Co., employer for hire of John Ferguson").

"Anonymous" or "Pseudonymous" Work: An author's contribution to a work is "anonymous" if that author is not identified on the copies or phonorecords of the work. An author's contribution to a work is "pseudonymous" if that author is identified on the copies or phonorecords under a fictitious name. If the work is "anonymous" you may: (1) leave the line blank; or (2) state "anonymous" on the line; or (3) reveal the author's identity. If the work is "pseudonymous" you may: (1) leave the line blank; or (2) give the pseudonym and identify it as such (for example: "Huntley Haverstock, pseudonym"); or (3) reveal the author's name, making clear which is the real name and which is the pseudonym (for example, "Judith Barton, whose pseudonym is Madeline Elster"). However, the citizenship or domicile of the author *must* be given in all cases.

Dates of Birth and Death: If the author is dead, the statute requires that the year of death be included in the application unless the work is anonymous or pseudonymous. The author's birth date is optional but is useful as a form of identification. Leave this space blank if the author's contribution was a "work made for hire."

Form TX, Page 2

Author's Nationality or Domicile: Give the country of which the author is a citizen or the country in which the author is domiciled. Nationality or domicile *must* be given in all cases.

Nature of Authorship: After the words "Nature of Authorship," give a brief general statement of the nature of this particular author's contribution to the work. Examples: "Entire text"; "Coauthor of entire text"; "Computer program"; "Editorial revisions"; "Compilation and English translation"; "New text."

 ## SPACE 3: Creation and Publication

General Instructions: Do not confuse "creation" with "publication." Every application for copyright registration must state "the year in which creation of the work was completed." Give the date and nation of first publication only if the work has been published.

Creation: Under the statute, a work is "created" when it is fixed in a copy or phonorecord for the first time. Where a work has been prepared over a period of time, the part of the work existing in fixed form on a particular date constitutes the created work on that date. The date you give here should be the year in which the author completed the particular version for which registration is now being sought, even if other versions exist or if further changes or additions are planned.

Publication: The statute defines "publication" as "the distribution of copies or phonorecords of a work to the public by sale or other transfer of ownership, or by rental, lease, or lending." A work is also "published" if there has been an "offering to distribute copies or phonorecords to a group of persons for purposes of further distribution, public performance, or public display." Give the full date (month, day, year) when, and the country where, publication first occurred. If first publication took place simultaneously in the United States and other countries, it is sufficient to state "U.S.A."

 ## SPACE 4: Claimant(s)

Name(s) and Address(es) of Copyright Claimant(s): Give the name(s) and address(es) of the copyright claimant(s) in this work even if the claimant is the same as the author. Copyright in a work belongs initially to the author of the work (including, in the case of a work made for hire, the employer or other person for whom the work was prepared). The copyright claimant is either the author of the work or a person or organization to whom the copyright initially belonging to the author has been transferred.

Transfer: The statute provides that, if the copyright claimant is not the author, the application for registration must contain "a brief statement of how the claimant obtained ownership of the copyright." If any copyright claimant named in space 4 is not an author named in space 2, give a brief statement explaining how the claimant(s) obtained ownership of the copyright. Examples: "By written contract"; "Transfer of all rights by author"; "Assignment"; "By will." Do not attach transfer documents or other attachments or riders.

SPACE 5: Previous Registration

General Instructions: The questions in space 5 are intended to show whether an earlier registration has been made for this work and, if so, whether there is any basis for a new registration. As a general rule, only one basic copyright registration can be made for the same version of a particular work.

Same Version: If this version is substantially the same as the work covered by a previous registration, a second registration is not generally possible unless: (1) the work has been registered in unpublished form and a second registration is now being sought to cover this first published edition; or (2) someone other than the author is identified as copyright claimant in the earlier registration, and the author is now seeking registration in his or her own name. If either of these two exceptions applies, check the appropriate box and give the earlier registration number and date. Otherwise, do not submit Form TX. Instead, write the Copyright Office for information about supplementary registration or recordation of transfers of copyright ownership.

Changed Version: If the work has been changed and you are now seeking registration to cover the additions or revisions, check the last box in space 5, give the earlier registration number and date, and complete both parts of space 6 in accordance with the instructions below.

Previous Registration Number and Date: If more than one previous registration has been made for the work, give the number and date of the latest registration.

 ## SPACE 6: Derivative Work or Compilation

General Instructions: Complete space 6 if this work is a "changed version," "compilation," or "derivative work" and if it incorporates one or more earlier works that have already been published or registered for copyright or that have fallen into the public domain. A "compilation" is defined as "a work formed by the collection and assembling of preexisting materials or of data that are selected, coordinated, or arranged in such a way that the resulting work as a whole constitutes an original work of authorship." A "derivative work" is "a work based on one or more preexisting works." Examples of derivative works include translations, fictionalizations, abridgments, condensations, or "any other form in which a work may be recast, transformed, or adapted." Derivative works also include works "consisting of editorial revisions, annotations, or other modifications" if these changes, as a whole, represent an original work of authorship.

Preexisting Material (space 6a): For derivative works, complete this space *and* space 6b. In space 6a identify the preexisting work that has been recast, transformed, or adapted. The preexisting work may be material that has been previously published, previously registered, or that is in the public domain. An example of preexisting material might be: "Russian version of Goncharov's 'Oblomov.'"

Material Added to This Work (space 6b): Give a brief, general statement of the new material covered by the copyright claim for which registration is sought. *Derivative work* examples include: "Foreword, editing, critical annotations"; "Translation"; "Chapters 11–17." If the work is a *compilation*, describe both the compilation itself and the material that has been compiled. Example: "Compilation of certain 1917 speeches by Woodrow Wilson." A work may be both a derivative work and compilation, in which case a sample statement might be: "Compilation and additional new material."

SPACE 7, 8, 9: Fee, Correspondence, Certification, Return Address

Deposit Account: If you maintain a Deposit Account in the Copyright Office, identify it in space 7a. Otherwise leave the space blank and send the fee with your application and deposit.

Correspondence (space 7b): Give the name, address, area code, telephone number, fax number, and email address (if available) of the person to be consulted if correspondence about this application becomes necessary.

Certification (space 8): The application cannot be accepted unless it bears the date and the *handwritten signature* of the author or other copyright claimant, or of the owner of exclusive right(s), or of the duly authorized agent of author, claimant, or owner of exclusive right(s).

Address for Return of Certificate (space 9): The address box must be completed legibly since the certificate will be returned in a window envelope.

Form TX, Page 3

Copyright Office fees are subject to change. For current fees, check the Copyright Office website at *www.copyright.gov*, write the Copyright Office, or call (202) 707-3000.

Form TX
For a Nondramatic Literary Work
UNITED STATES COPYRIGHT OFFICE

REGISTRATION NUMBER

_____

TX _____ TXU _____
EFFECTIVE DATE OF REGISTRATION

_____

Month _____ Day _____ Year _____

DO NOT WRITE ABOVE THIS LINE. IF YOU NEED MORE SPACE, USE A SEPARATE CONTINUATION SHEET.

1

TITLE OF THIS WORK ▼

PREVIOUS OR ALTERNATIVE TITLES ▼

PUBLICATION AS A CONTRIBUTION If this work was published as a contribution to a periodical, serial, or collection, give information about the collective work in which the contribution appeared.   **Title of Collective Work ▼**

If published in a periodical or serial give: Volume ▼   Number ▼   Issue Date ▼   On Pages ▼

2 **a**

NAME OF AUTHOR ▼

DATES OF BIRTH AND DEATH
Year Born ▼   Year Died ▼

Was this contribution to the work a "work made for hire"?
☐ Yes
☐ No

AUTHOR'S NATIONALITY OR DOMICILE
Name of Country
OR { Citizen of ▶ _____
Domiciled in▶ _____

WAS THIS AUTHOR'S CONTRIBUTION TO THE WORK
Anonymous?   ☐ Yes ☐ No
Pseudonymous?   ☐ Yes ☐ No

If the answer to either of these questions is "Yes," see detailed instructions.

NATURE OF AUTHORSHIP Briefly describe nature of material created by this author in which copyright is claimed. ▼

NOTE

Under the law, the "author" of a "work made for hire" is generally the employer, not the employee (see instructions). For any part of this work that was "made for hire" check "Yes" in the space provided, give the employer (or other person for whom the work was prepared) as "Author" of that part, and leave the space for dates of birth and death blank.

b

NAME OF AUTHOR ▼

DATES OF BIRTH AND DEATH
Year Born ▼   Year Died ▼

Was this contribution to the work a "work made for hire"?
☐ Yes
☐ No

AUTHOR'S NATIONALITY OR DOMICILE
Name of Country
OR { Citizen of ▶ _____
Domiciled in▶ _____

WAS THIS AUTHOR'S CONTRIBUTION TO THE WORK
Anonymous?   ☐ Yes ☐ No
Pseudonymous?   ☐ Yes ☐ No

If the answer to either of these questions is "Yes," see detailed instructions.

NATURE OF AUTHORSHIP Briefly describe nature of material created by this author in which copyright is claimed. ▼

c

NAME OF AUTHOR ▼

DATES OF BIRTH AND DEATH
Year Born ▼   Year Died ▼

Was this contribution to the work a "work made for hire"?
☐ Yes
☐ No

AUTHOR'S NATIONALITY OR DOMICILE
Name of Country
OR { Citizen of ▶ _____
Domiciled in▶ _____

WAS THIS AUTHOR'S CONTRIBUTION TO THE WORK
Anonymous?   ☐ Yes ☐ No
Pseudonymous?   ☐ Yes ☐ No

If the answer to either of these questions is "Yes," see detailed instructions.

NATURE OF AUTHORSHIP Briefly describe nature of material created by this author in which copyright is claimed. ▼

3 **a**

YEAR IN WHICH CREATION OF THIS WORK WAS COMPLETED This information must be given in all cases.
◀ Year

b DATE AND NATION OF FIRST PUBLICATION OF THIS PARTICULAR WORK
Complete this information ONLY if this work has been published.
Month▶ _____ Day▶ _____ Year▶ _____
◀ Nation

4

See instructions before completing this space.

COPYRIGHT CLAIMANT(S) Name and address must be given even if the claimant is the same as the author given in space 2. ▼

TRANSFER If the claimant(s) named here in space 4 is (are) different from the author(s) named in space 2, give a brief statement of how the claimant(s) obtained ownership of the copyright. ▼

DO NOT WRITE HERE OFFICE USE ONLY

APPLICATION RECEIVED

ONE DEPOSIT RECEIVED

TWO DEPOSITS RECEIVED

FUNDS RECEIVED

MORE ON BACK ▶   • Complete all applicable spaces (numbers 5-9) on the reverse side of this page.
• See detailed instructions.   • Sign the form at line 8.

DO NOT WRITE HERE
Page 1 of _____ pages

Form TX, Page 4

FORM TX

EXAMINED BY	
CHECKED BY	

❑ CORRESPONDENCE
Yes

FOR
COPYRIGHT
OFFICE
USE
ONLY

DO NOT WRITE ABOVE THIS LINE. IF YOU NEED MORE SPACE, USE A SEPARATE CONTINUATION SHEET.

PREVIOUS REGISTRATION Has registration for this work, or for an earlier version of this work, already been made in the Copyright Office?

☐ Yes ☐ No If your answer is "Yes," why is another registration being sought? (Check appropriate box.) ▼

a. ☐ This is the first published edition of a work previously registered in unpublished form.

b. ☐ This is the first application submitted by this author as copyright claimant.

c. ☐ This is a changed version of the work, as shown by space 6 on this application.

If your answer is "Yes," give: **Previous Registration Number** ▶   **Year of Registration** ▶

5

DERIVATIVE WORK OR COMPILATION

Preexisting Material Identify any preexisting work or works that this work is based on or incorporates. ▼

a

6

See instructions
before completing
this space.

Material Added to This Work Give a brief, general statement of the material that has been added to this work and in which copyright is claimed. ▼

b

DEPOSIT ACCOUNT If the registration fee is to be charged to a Deposit Account established in the Copyright Office, give name and number of Account.

Name ▼   **Account Number** ▼

a

7

CORRESPONDENCE Give name and address to which correspondence about this application should be sent.   Name/Address/Apt/City/State/Zip ▼

b

Area code and daytime telephone number ▶   Fax number ▶

Email ▶

CERTIFICATION* I, the undersigned, hereby certify that I am the

Check only one ▶

☐ author
☐ other copyright claimant
☐ owner of exclusive right(s)
☐ authorized agent of _____

of the work identified in this application and that the statements made
by me in this application are correct to the best of my knowledge.

Name of author or other copyright claimant, or owner of exclusive right(s) ▲

8

Typed or printed name and date ▼ If this application gives a date of publication in space 3, do not sign and submit it before that date.

Date ▶ _____

Handwritten signature ▼

Certificate
will be
mailed in
window
envelope
to this
address:

Name ▼

Number/Street/Apt ▼

City/State/Zip ▼

9

YOU MUST:
• Complete all necessary spaces
• Sign your application in space 8

SEND ALL 3 ELEMENTS
IN THE SAME PACKAGE
1. Application form
2. Nonrefundable filing fee in check or money
order payable to *Register of Copyrights*
3. Deposit material

MAIL TO:
Library of Congress
Copyright Office
101 Independence Avenue SE
Washington, DC 20559-6222

*17 *USC* §506(e): Any person who knowingly makes a false representation of a material fact in the application for copyright registration provided for by section 409, or in any written statement filed in connection with the application, shall be fined not more than $2,500.

Form TX – Full   Rev. 11/2006   Print: 11/2006 — 30,000   Printed on recycled paper

U.S. Government Printing Office: 2006-xx-xxx/60,xxx

Form VA, Page 1

 Form VA

Detach and read these instructions before completing this form.
Make sure all applicable spaces have been filled in before you return this form.

BASIC INFORMATION

When to Use This Form: Use Form VA for copyright registration of published or unpublished works of the visual arts. This category consists of "pictorial, graphic, or sculptural works," including two-dimensional and three-dimensional works of fine, graphic, and applied art, photographs, prints and art reproductions, maps, globes, charts, technical drawings, diagrams, and models.

What Does Copyright Protect? Copyright in a work of the visual arts protects those pictorial, graphic, or sculptural elements that, either alone or in combination, represent an "original work of authorship." The statute declares: "In no case does copyright protection for an original work of authorship extend to any idea, procedure, process, system, method of operation, concept, principle, or discovery, regardless of the form in which it is described, explained, illustrated, or embodied in such work."

Works of Artistic Craftsmanship and Designs: "Works of artistic craftsmanship" are registrable on Form VA, but the statute makes clear that protection extends to "their form" and not to "their mechanical or utilitarian aspects." The "design of a useful article" is considered copyrightable "only if, and only to the extent that, such design incorporates pictorial, graphic, or sculptural features that can be identified separately from, and are capable of existing independently of, the utilitarian aspects of the article."

Labels and Advertisements: Works prepared for use in connection with the sale or advertisement of goods and services are registrable if they contain "original work of authorship." Use Form VA if the copyrightable material in the work you are registering is mainly pictorial or graphic; use Form TX if it consists mainly of text. **Note:** Words and short phrases such as names, titles, and slogans cannot be protected by copyright, and the same is true of standard symbols, emblems, and other commonly used graphic designs that are in the public domain. When used commercially, material of that sort can sometimes be protected under state laws of unfair competition or under the federal trademark laws. For information about trademark registration, write to the U.S. Patent and Trademark Office, PO Box 1450, Alexandria, VA 22313-1450.

Architectural Works: Copyright protection extends to the design of buildings created for the use of human beings. Architectural works created on or after December 1, 1990, or that on December 1, 1990, were unconstructed and embodied only in unpublished plans or drawings are eligible. Request Circular 41, *Copyright Claims in Architectural Works*, for more information. Architectural works and technical drawings cannot be registered on the same application.

Deposit to Accompany Application: An application for copyright registration must be accompanied by a deposit consisting of copies representing the entire work for which registration is to be made.

Unpublished Work: Deposit one complete copy.

Published Work: Deposit two complete copies of the best edition.

Work First Published Outside the United States: Deposit one complete copy of the first foreign edition.

Contribution to a Collective Work: Deposit one complete copy of the best edition of the collective work.

The Copyright Notice: Before March 1, 1989, the use of copyright notice was mandatory on all published works, and any work first published before that date should have carried a notice. For works first published on and after March 1, 1989, use of the copyright notice is optional. For more information about copyright notice, see Circular 3, *Copyright Notice*.

For Further Information: To speak to a Copyright Office staff member, call (202) 707-3000 (TTY: (202) 707-6737). Recorded information is available 24 hours a day. Order forms and other publications from the address in space 9 or call the Forms and Publications Hotline at (202) 707-9100. Access and download circulars, forms, and other information from the Copyright Office website at *www.copyright.gov*.

LINE-BY-LINE INSTRUCTIONS

Please type or print using black ink. The form is used to produce the certificate.

 SPACE 1: Title

Title of This Work: Every work submitted for copyright registration must be given a title to identify that particular work. If the copies of the work bear a title (or an identifying phrase that could serve as a title), transcribe that wording *completely* and *exactly* on the application. Indexing of the registration and future identification of the work will depend on the information you give here. For an architectural work that has been constructed, add the date of construction after the title; if unconstructed at this time, add "not yet constructed."

Publication as a Contribution: If the work being registered is a contribution to a periodical, serial, or collection, give the title of the contribution in the "Title of This Work" space. Then, in the line headed "Publication as a Contribution," give information about the collective work in which the contribution appeared.

Nature of This Work: Briefly describe the general nature or character of the pictorial, graphic, or sculptural work being registered for copyright. Examples: "Oil Painting"; "Charcoal Drawing"; "Etching"; "Sculpture"; "Map"; "Photograph"; "Scale Model"; "Lithographic Print"; "Jewelry Design"; "Fabric Design."

Previous or Alternative Titles: Complete this space if there are any additional titles for the work under which someone searching for the registration might be likely to look, or under which a document pertaining to the work might be recorded.

SPACE 2: Author(s)

General Instruction: After reading these instructions, decide who are the "authors" of this work for copyright purposes. Then, unless the work is a "collective work," give the requested information about every "author" who contributed any appreciable matter of copyrightable matter to this version of the work. If you need further space, request Continuation Sheets. In the case of a collective work, such as a catalog of paintings or collection of cartoons by various authors, give information about the author of the collective work as a whole.

Name of Author: The fullest form of the author's name should be given. Unless the work was "made for hire," the individual who actually created the work is its "author." In the case of a work made for hire, the statute provides that "the employer or other person for whom the work was prepared is considered the author."

What Is a "Work Made for Hire"? A "work made for hire" is defined as: (1) "a work prepared by an employee within the scope of his or her employment"; or (2) "a work specially ordered or commissioned for use as a contribution to a collective work, as a part of a motion picture or other audiovisual work, as a translation, as a supplementary work, as a compilation, as an instructional text, as a test, as answer material for a test, or as an atlas, if the parties expressly agree in a written instrument signed by them that the work shall be considered a work made for hire." If you have checked "Yes" to indicate that the work was "made for hire," you must give the full legal name of the employer (or other person for whom the work was prepared). You may also include the name of the employee along with the name of the employer (for example: "Elster Publishing Co., employer for hire of John Ferguson").

"Anonymous" or "Pseudonymous" Work: An author's contribution to a work is "anonymous" if that author is not identified on the copies or phonorecords of the work. An author's contribution to a work is "pseudonymous" if that author is identified on the copies or phonorecords under a fictitious name. If the work is "anonymous" you may: (1) leave the line blank; or (2) state "anonymous" on the line; or (3) reveal the author's identity. If the work is "pseudonymous" you may: (1) leave the line blank; or (2) give the pseudonym and identify it as such (for example: "Huntley Haverstock, pseudonym"); or (3) reveal the author's name, making clear which is the real name and which is the pseudonym (for example: "Henry Leek, whose pseudonym is Priam Farrel"). However, the citizenship or domicile of the author *must* be given in all cases.

Dates of Birth and Death: If the author is dead, the statute requires that the year of death be included in the application unless the work is anonymous or pseudonymous. The author's birth date is optional but is useful as a form of identification. Leave this space blank if the author's contribution was a "work made for hire."

Form VA, Page 2

Author's Nationality or Domicile: Give the country of which the author is a citizen or the country in which the author is domiciled. Nationality or domicile *must* be given in all cases.

Nature of Authorship: Categories of pictorial, graphic, and sculptural authorship are listed below. Check the box(es) that best describe(s) each author's contribution to the work.

3-Dimensional sculptures: fine art sculptures, toys, dolls, scale models, and sculptural designs applied to useful articles.

2-Dimensional artwork: watercolor and oil paintings; pen and ink drawings; logo illustrations; greeting cards; collages; stencils; patterns; computer graphics; graphics appearing in screen displays; artwork appearing on posters, calendars, games, commercial prints and labels, and packaging, as well as 2-dimensional artwork applied to useful articles, and designs reproduced on textiles, lace, and other fabrics; on wallpaper, carpeting, floor tile, wrapping paper, and clothing.

Reproductions of works of art: reproductions of preexisting artwork made by, for example, lithography, photoengraving, or etching.

Maps: cartographic representations of an area, such as state and county maps, atlases, marine charts, relief maps, and globes.

Photographs: pictorial photographic prints and slides and holograms.

Jewelry designs: 3-dimensional designs applied to rings, pendants, earrings, necklaces, and the like.

Technical drawings: diagrams illustrating scientific or technical information in linear form, such as architectural blueprints or mechanical drawings.

Text: textual material that accompanies pictorial, graphic, or sculptural works, such as comic strips, greeting cards, games rules, commercial prints or labels, and maps.

Architectural works: designs of buildings, including the overall form as well as the arrangement and composition of spaces and elements of the design.

NOTE: Any registration for the underlying architectural plans must be applied for on a separate Form VA, checking the box "Technical drawing."

SPACE 3: Creation and Publication

General Instructions: Do not confuse "creation" with "publication." Every application for copyright registration must state "the year in which creation of the work was completed." Give the date and nation of first publication only if the work has been published.

Creation: Under the statute, a work is "created" when it is fixed in a copy or phonorecord for the first time. Where a work has been prepared over a period of time, the part of the work existing in fixed form on a particular date constitutes the created work on that date. The date you give here should be the year in which the author completed the particular version for which registration is now being sought, even if other versions exist or if further changes or additions are planned.

Publication: The statute defines "publication" as "the distribution of copies or phonorecords of a work to the public by sale or other transfer of ownership, or by rental, lease, or lending"; a work is also "published" if there has been an "offering to distribute copies or phonorecords to a group of persons for purposes of further distribution, public performance, or public display." Give the full date (month, day, year) when, and the country where, publication first occurred. If first publication took place simultaneously in the United States and other countries, it is sufficient to state "U.S.A."

SPACE 4: Claimant(s)

Name(s) and Address(es) of Copyright Claimant(s): Give the name(s) and address(es) of the copyright claimant(s) in this work even if the claimant is the same as the author. Copyright in a work belongs initially to the author of the work (including, in the case of a work made for hire, the employer or other person for whom the work was prepared). The copyright claimant is either the author of the work or a person or organization to whom copyright initially belonging to the author has been transferred.

Transfer: The statute provides that, if the copyright claimant is not the author, the application for registration must contain "a brief statement of how the claimant obtained ownership of the copyright." If any copyright claimant named in space 4 is not an author named in space 2, give a brief statement explaining how the claimant(s) obtained ownership of the copyright. Examples: "By written contract"; "Transfer of all rights by author"; "Assignment"; "By will." Do not attach transfer documents or other attachments or riders.

SPACE 5: Previous Registration

General Instructions: The questions in space 5 are intended to find out whether an earlier registration has been made for this work and, if so, whether there is any basis for a new registration. As a rule, only one basic

copyright registration can be made for the same version of a particular work.

Same Version: If this version is substantially the same as the work covered by a previous registration, a second registration is not generally possible unless: (1) the work has been registered in unpublished form and a second registration is now being sought to cover this first published edition; or (2) someone other than the author is identified as a copyright claimant in the earlier registration, and the author is now seeking registration in his or her own name. If either of these two exceptions applies, check the appropriate box and give the earlier registration number and date. Otherwise, do not submit Form VA; instead, write the Copyright Office for information about supplementary registration or recordation of transfers of copyright ownership.

Changed Version: If the work has been changed and you are now seeking registration to cover the additions or revisions, check the last box in space 5, give the earlier registration number and date, and complete both parts of space 6 in accordance with the instruction below.

Previous Registration Number and Date: If more than one previous registration has been made for the work, give the number and date of the latest registration.

SPACE 6: Derivative Work or Compilation

General Instructions: Complete space 6 if this work is a "changed version," "compilation," or "derivative work," and if it incorporates one or more earlier works that have already been published or registered for copyright, or that have fallen into the public domain. A "compilation" is defined as "a work formed by the collection and assembling of preexisting materials or of data that are selected, coordinated, or arranged in such a way that the resulting work as a whole constitutes an original work of authorship." A "derivative work" is "a work based on one or more preexisting works." Examples of derivative works include reproductions of works of art, sculptures based on drawings, lithographs based on paintings, maps based on previously published sources, or "any other form in which a work may be recast, transformed, or adapted." Derivative works also include works "consisting of editorial revisions, annotations, or other modifications" if these changes, as a whole, represent an original work of authorship.

Preexisting Material (space 6a): Complete this space *and* space 6b for derivative works. In this space identify the preexisting work that has been recast, transformed, or adapted. Examples of preexisting material might be "Grunewald Altarpiece" or "19th century quilt design." Do not complete this space for compilations.

Material Added to This Work (space 6b): Give a brief, general statement of the *additional* new material covered by the copyright claim for which registration is sought. In the case of a derivative work, identify this new material. Examples: "Adaptation of design and additional artistic work"; "Reproduction of painting by photolithography"; "Additional cartographic material"; "Compilation of photographs." If the work is a compilation, give a brief, general statement describing both the material that has been compiled *and* the compilation itself. Example: "Compilation of 19th century political cartoons."

SPACE 7, 8, 9: Fee, Correspondence, Certification, Return Address

Deposit Account: If you maintain a Deposit Account in the Copyright Office, identify it in space 7a. Otherwise, leave the space blank and send the fee with your application and deposit.

Correspondence (space 7b): Give the name, address, area code, telephone number, email address, and fax number (if available) of the person to be consulted if correspondence about this application becomes necessary.

Certification (space 8): The application cannot be accepted unless it bears the date and the *handwritten signature* of the author or other copyright claimant, or of the owner of exclusive right(s), or of the duly authorized agent of the author, claimant, or owner of exclusive right(s).

Address for Return of Certificate (space 9): The address box must be completed legibly since the certificate will be returned in a window envelope.

PRIVACY ACT ADVISORY STATEMENT Required by the Privacy Act of 1974 (P.L. 93 - 579)
The authority for requesting this information is title 17, U.S.C., secs. 409 and 410. Furnishing the requested information is voluntary. But if the information is not furnished, it may be necessary to delay or refuse registration and you may not be entitled to certain relief, remedies, and benefits provided in chapters 4 and 5 of title 17, U.S.C.
The principal uses of the requested information are the establishment and maintenance of a public record and the examination of the application for compliance with the registration requirements of the copyright code.
Other routine uses include public inspection and copying, preparation of public indexes, preparation of public catalogs of copyright registrations, and preparation of search reports upon request.
NOTE: No other advisory statement will be given in connection with this application. Please keep this statement and refer to it if we communicate with you regarding this application.

Form VA, Page 3

Copyright Office fees are subject to change. For current fees, check the Copyright Office website at *www.copyright.gov*, write the Copyright Office, or call (202) 707-3000.

Ⓒ Form VA
For a Work of the Visual Arts
UNITED STATES COPYRIGHT OFFICE

REGISTRATION NUMBER

VA   VAU

EFFECTIVE DATE OF REGISTRATION

Month   Day   Year

DO NOT WRITE ABOVE THIS LINE. IF YOU NEED MORE SPACE, USE A SEPARATE CONTINUATION SHEET.

1

Title of This Work ▼   NATURE OF THIS WORK ▼ See instructions

Previous or Alternative Titles ▼

Publication as a Contribution If this work was published as a contribution to a periodical, serial, or collection, give information about the collective work in which the contribution appeared. **Title of Collective Work ▼**

If published in a periodical or serial give: Volume ▼   Number ▼   Issue Date ▼   On Pages ▼

2

a

NAME OF AUTHOR ▼   DATES OF BIRTH AND DEATH
                                    Year Born ▼   Year Died ▼

NOTE
Under the law, the "author" of a "work made for hire" is generally the employer, not the employee (see instructions). For any part of this work that was "made for hire" check "Yes" in the space provided, give the employer (or other person for whom the work was prepared) as "Author" of that part, and leave the space for dates of birth and death blank.

Was this contribution to the work a "work made for hire"?
☐ Yes
☐ No

Author's Nationality or Domicile
Name of Country
OR { Citizen of _____
     Domiciled in _____

Was This Author's Contribution to the Work
Anonymous?   ☐ Yes ☐ No
Pseudonymous?   ☐ Yes ☐ No
If the answer to either of these questions is "Yes," see detailed instructions.

Nature of Authorship Check appropriate box(es). **See Instructions**
☐ 3-Dimensional sculpture   ☐ Map   ☐ Technical drawing
☐ 2-Dimensional artwork   ☐ Photograph ☐ Text
☐ Reproduction of work of art ☐ Jewelry design ☐ Architectural work

b

Name of Author ▼   Dates of Birth and Death
                                    Year Born ▼   Year Died ▼

Was this contribution to the work a "work made for hire"?
☐ Yes
☐ No

Author's Nationality or Domicile
Name of Country
OR { Citizen of _____
     Domiciled in _____

Was This Author's Contribution to the Work
Anonymous?   ☐ Yes ☐ No
Pseudonymous?   ☐ Yes ☐ No
If the answer to either of these questions is "Yes," see detailed instructions.

Nature of Authorship Check appropriate box(es). **See instructions**
☐ 3-Dimensional sculpture   ☐ Map   ☐ Technical drawing
☐ 2-Dimensional artwork   ☐ Photograph ☐ Text
☐ Reproduction of work of art ☐ Jewelry design ☐ Architectural work

3
a Year in Which Creation of This Work Was Completed
        This information must be given in all cases.   Year
b Date and Nation of First Publication of This Particular Work
Complete this information ONLY if this work has been published.
Month _____ Day _____ Year _____
                                                        Nation

4

See instructions before completing this space.

COPYRIGHT CLAIMANT(S) Name and address must be given even if the claimant is the same as the author given in space 2. ▼

APPLICATION RECEIVED

ONE DEPOSIT RECEIVED

TWO DEPOSITS RECEIVED

FUNDS RECEIVED

DO NOT WRITE HERE
OFFICE USE ONLY.

Transfer If the claimant(s) named here in space 4 is (are) different from the author(s) named in space 2, give a brief statement of how the claimant(s) obtained ownership of the copyright. ▼

MORE ON BACK ▶ · Complete all applicable spaces (numbers 5-9) on the reverse side of this page.
                    · See detailed instructions.   · Sign the form at line 8.

DO NOT WRITE HERE
Page 1 of _____ pages

Form VA, Page 4

DO NOT WRITE ABOVE THIS LINE. IF YOU NEED MORE SPACE, USE A SEPARATE CONTINUATION SHEET.

PREVIOUS REGISTRATION Has registration for this work, or for an earlier version of this work, already been made in the Copyright Office?

☐ Yes ☐ No If your answer is "Yes," why is another registration being sought? (Check appropriate box.) ▼

a. ☐ This is the first published edition of a work previously registered in unpublished form.

b. ☐ This is the first application submitted by this author as copyright claimant.

c. ☐ This is a changed version of the work, as shown by space 6 on this application.

If your answer is "Yes," give: **Previous Registration Number** ▼   **Year of Registration** ▼

5

DERIVATIVE WORK OR COMPILATION Complete both space 6a and 6b for a derivative work; complete only 6b for a compilation.

a. Preexisting Material Identify any preexisting work or works that this work is based on or incorporates. ▼

b. Material Added to This Work Give a brief, general statement of the material that has been added to this work and in which copyright is claimed. ▼

6

a

See instructions
before completing
this space.

b

DEPOSIT ACCOUNT If the registration fee is to be charged to a Deposit Account established in the Copyright Office, give name and number of Account.
Name ▼   **Account Number** ▼

7

a

CORRESPONDENCE Give name and address to which correspondence about this application should be sent. Name/Address/Apt/City/State/Zip ▼

b

Area code and daytime telephone number   (   )   Fax number   (   )

Email

CERTIFICATION* I, the undersigned, hereby certify that I am the

check only one ▶ {
☐ author
☐ other copyright claimant
☐ owner of exclusive right(s)
☐ authorized agent of _____
}
Name of author or other copyright claimant, or owner of exclusive right(s) ▲

of the work identified in this application and that the statements made by me in this application are correct to the best of my knowledge.

8

Typed or printed name and date ▼ If this application gives a date of publication in space 3, do not sign and submit it before that date.

_____ Date _____

Handwritten signature (X) ▼

X _____

**Certificate
will be
mailed in
window
envelope
to this
address:**

Name ▼

Number/Street/Apt ▼

City/State/ZIP ▼

9

*17 USC §506(e): Any person who knowingly makes a false representation of a material fact in the application for copyright registration provided for by section 409, or in any written statement filed in connection with the application, shall be fined not more than $2,500.

Form VA – Full   Rev. 07/2006   Print: 07/2006—30,000   Printed on recycled paper   U.S. Government Printing Office: 2004-320-958/60,125

Form SR, Page 1

 Form SR

Detach and read these instructions before completing this form.
Make sure all applicable spaces have been filled in before you return this form.

BASIC INFORMATION

When to Use This Form: Use Form SR for registration of published or unpublished sound recordings. It should be used when the copyright claim is limited to the sound recording itself, and it may also be used where the same copyright claimant is seeking simultaneous registration of the underlying musical, dramatic, or literary work embodied in the phonorecord.

With one exception, "sound recordings" are works that result from the fixation of a series of musical, spoken, or other sounds. The exception is for the audio portions of audiovisual works, such as a motion picture soundtrack or an audio cassette accompanying a filmstrip. These are considered a part of the audiovisual work as a whole.

Deposit to Accompany Application: An application for copyright registration must be accompanied by a deposit consisting of phonorecords representing the entire work for which registration is to be made.

Unpublished Work: Deposit one complete phonorecord.

Published Work: Deposit two complete phonorecords of the best edition, together with "any printed or other visually perceptible material" published with the phonorecords.

Work First Published Outside the United States: Deposit one complete phonorecord of the first foreign edition.

Contribution to a Collective Work: Deposit one complete phonorecord of the best edition of the collective work.

The Copyright Notice: Before March 1, 1989, the use of copyright notice was mandatory on all published works, and any work first published before that date should have carried a notice. For works first published on and after March 1, 1989, use of the copyright notice is optional. For more information about copyright notice, see Circular 3, *Copyright Notices*.

For Further Information: To speak to a Copyright Office staff member, call (202) 707-3000 (TTY: (202) 707-6737). Recorded information is available 24 hours a day. Order forms and other publications from Library of Congress, Copyright Office, 101 Independence Avenue SE, Washington, DC 20559-6000 or call the Forms and Publications Hotline at (202) 707-9100. Access and download circulars, forms, and other information from the Copyright Office website at *www.copyright.gov*.

> **PRIVACY ACT ADVISORY STATEMENT Required by the Privacy Act of 1974 (P.L. 93-579)**
> The authority for requesting this information is title 17 *USC*, secs. 409 and 410. Furnishing the requested information is voluntary. But if the information is not furnished, it may be necessary to delay or refuse registration and you may not be entitled to certain relief, remedies, and benefits provided in chapters 4 and 5 of title 17 *USC*.
> The principal uses of the requested information are the establishment and maintenance of a public record and the examination of the application for compliance with the registration requirements of the copyright code.
> Other routine uses include public inspection and copying, preparation of public indexes, preparation of public catalogs of copyright registrations, and preparation of search reports upon request.
> NOTE: No other advisory statement will be given in connection with this application. Please keep this statement and refer to it if we communicate with you regarding this application.

LINE-BY-LINE INSTRUCTIONS

Please type or print neatly using black ink. The form is used to produce the certificate.

 SPACE 1: Title

Title of This Work: Every work submitted for copyright registration must be given a title to identify that particular work. If the phonorecords or any accompanying printed material bears a title (or an identifying phrase that could serve as a title), transcribe that wording completely and exactly on the application. Indexing of the registration and future identification of the work may depend on the information you give here.

Previous, Alternative, or Contents Titles: Complete this space if there are any previous or alternative titles for the work under which someone searching for the registration might be likely to look, or under which a document pertaining to the work might be recorded. You may also give the individual contents titles, if any, in this space or you may use a Continuation Sheet. Circle the term that describes the titles given.

SPACE 2: Author(s)

General Instructions: After reading these instructions, decide who are the "authors" of this work for copyright purposes. Then, unless the work is a "collective work," give the requested information about every "author" who contributed any appreciable amount of copyrightable matter to this version of the work. If you need further space, request additional Continuation Sheets. In the case of a collective work such as a collection of previously published or registered sound recordings, give information about the author of the collective work as a whole. If you are submitting this Form SR to cover the recorded musical, dramatic, or literary work as well as the sound recording itself, it is important for space 2 to include full information about the various authors of all of the material covered by the copyright claim, making clear the nature of each author's contribution.

Name of Author: The fullest form of the author's name should be given. Unless the work was "made for hire," the individual who actually created the work is its "author." In the case of a work made for hire, the statute provides that "the employer or other person for whom the work was prepared is considered the author."

What Is a "Work Made for Hire"? A "work made for hire" is defined as: (1) "a work prepared by an employee within the scope of his or her employment"; or (2) "a work specially ordered or commissioned for use as a contribution to a collective work, as a part of a motion picture or other audiovisual work, as a translation, as a supplementary work, as a compilation, as an instructional text, as a test, as answer material for a test, or as an atlas, if the parties expressly agree in a written instrument signed by them that the work shall be considered a work made for hire." If you have checked "Yes" to indicate that the work was "made for hire," you must give the full legal name of the employer (or other person for whom the work was prepared). You may also include the name of the employee along with the name of the employer (for example: "Elster Record Co., employer for hire of John Ferguson").

"Anonymous" or "Pseudonymous" Work: An author's contribution to a work is "anonymous" if that author is not identified on the copies or phonorecords of the work. An author's contribution to a work is "pseudonymous" if that author is identified on the copies or phonorecords under a fictitious name. If the work is "anonymous" you may: (1) leave the line blank; or (2) state "anonymous" on the line; or (3) reveal the author's identity. If the work is "pseudonymous" you may: (1) leave the line blank; or (2) give the pseudonym and identify it as such (for example: "Huntley Haverstock, pseudonym"); or (3) reveal the author's name, making clear which is the real name and which is the pseudonym (for example: "Judith Barton, whose pseudonym is Madeline Elster"). However, the citizenship or domicile of the author *must* be given in all cases.

Dates of Birth and Death: If the author is dead, the statute requires that the year of death be included in the application unless the work is anonymous or pseudonymous. The author's birth date is optional, but is useful as a form of identification. Leave this space blank if the author's contribution was a "work made for hire."

Author's Nationality or Domicile: Give the country in which the author is a citizen, or the country in which the author is domiciled. Nationality or domicile *must* be given in all cases.

Nature of Authorship: Sound recording authorship is the performance, sound production, or both, that is fixed in the recording deposited for registration. Describe this authorship in space 2 as "sound recording." If the claim also covers the underlying work(s), include the appropriate authorship terms for each author, for example, "words," "music," "arrangement of music," or "text."

Generally, for the claim to cover both the sound recording and the underlying work(s), every author should have contributed to both the sound recording *and* the underlying work(s). If the claim includes artwork or photographs, include the appropriate term in the statement of authorship.

Form SR, Page 2

SPACE 3: Creation and Publication

General Instructions: Do not confuse "creation" with "publication." Every application for copyright registration must state "the year in which creation of the work was completed." Give the date and nation of first publication only if the work has been published.

Creation: Under the statute, a work is "created" when it is fixed in a copy or phonorecord for the first time. Where a work has been prepared over a period of time, the part of the work existing in fixed form on a particular date constitutes the created work on that date. The date you give here should be the year in which the author completed the particular version for which registration is now being sought, even if other versions exist or if further changes or additions are planned.

Publication: The statute defines "publication" as "the distribution of copies or phonorecords of a work to the public by sale or other transfer of ownership, or by rental, lease, or lending"; a work is also "published" if there has been an "offering to distribute copies or phonorecords to a group of persons for purposes of further distribution, public performance, or public display." Give the full date (month, date, year) when, and the country where, publication first occurred. If first publication took place simultaneously in the United States and other countries, it is sufficient to state "U.S.A."

SPACE 4: Claimant(s)

Name(s) and Address(es) of Copyright Claimant(s): Give the name(s) and address(es) of the copyright claimant(s) in the work even if the claimant is the same as the author. Copyright in a work belongs initially to the author of the work (including, in the case of a work made for hire, the employer or other person for whom the work was prepared). The copyright claimant is either the author of the work or a person or organization to whom the copyright initially belonging to the author has been transferred.

Transfer: The statute provides that, if the copyright claimant is not the author, the application for registration must contain "a brief statement of how the claimant obtained ownership of the copyright." If any copyright claimant named in space 4a is not an author named in space 2, give a brief statement explaining how the claimant(s) obtained ownership of the copyright. Examples: "By written contract"; "Transfer of all rights by author"; "Assignment"; "By will." Do not attach transfer documents or other attachments or riders.

SPACE 5: Previous Registration

General Instructions: The questions in space 5 are intended to show whether an earlier registration has been made for this work and, if so, whether there is any basis for a new registration. As a rule, only one basic copyright registration can be made for the same version of a particular work.

Same Version: If this version is substantially the same as the work covered by a previous registration, a second registration is not generally possible unless: (1) the work has been registered in unpublished form and a second registration is now being sought to cover this first published edition; or (2) someone other than the author is identified as copyright claimant in the earlier registration and the author is now seeking registration in his or her own name. If either of these two exceptions applies, check the appropriate box and give the earlier registration number and date. Otherwise, do not submit Form SR. Instead, write the Copyright Office for information about supplementary registration or recordation of transfers of copyright ownership.

Changed Version: If the work has been changed and you are now seeking reg-

istration to cover the additions or revisions, check the last box in space 5, give the earlier registration number and date, and complete both parts of space 6 in accordance with the instructions below.

Previous Registration Number and Date: If more than one previous registration has been made for the work, give the number and date of the latest registration.

SPACE 6: Derivative Work or Compilation

General Instructions: Complete space 6 if this work is a "changed version," "compilation," or "derivative work," and if it incorporates one or more earlier works that have already been published or registered for copyright, or that have fallen into the public domain, or sound recordings that were fixed before February 15, 1972. A "compilation" is defined as "a work formed by the collection and assembling of preexisting materials or of data that are selected, coordinated, or arranged in such a way that the resulting work as a whole constitutes an original work of authorship." A "derivative work" is "a work based on one or more preexisting works." Examples of derivative works include recordings reissued with substantial editorial revisions or abridgments of the recorded sounds, and recordings republished with new recorded material, or "any other form in which a work may be recast, transformed, or adapted." Derivative works also include works "consisting of editorial revisions, annotations, or other modifications" if these changes, as a whole, represent an original work of authorship.

Preexisting Material (space 6a): Complete this space and space 6b for derivative works. In this space identify the preexisting work that has been recast, transformed, or adapted. The preexisting work may be material that has been previously published, previously registered, or that is in the public domain. For example, the preexisting material might be: "1970 recording by Sperryville Symphony of Bach Double Concerto."

Material Added to This Work (space 6b): Give a brief, general statement of the additional new material covered by the copyright claim for which registration is sought. In the case of a derivative work, identify this new material. Examples: "Recorded performances on bands 1 and 3"; "Remixed sounds from original multitrack sound sources"; "New words, arrangement, and additional sounds." If the work is a compilation, give a brief, general statement describing both the material that has been compiled and the compilation itself. Example: "Compilation of 1938 Recordings by various swing bands."

SPACE 7,8,9: Fee, Correspondence, Certification, Return Address

Deposit Account: If you maintain a Deposit Account in the Copyright Office, identify it in space 7a. Otherwise, leave the space blank and send the filing fee with your application and deposit. (See space 8 on form.) (Note: Copyright Office fees are subject to change. For current fees, check the Copyright Office website at *www.copyright.gov*, write the Copyright Office, or call (202) 707-3000.)

Correspondence (space 7b): Give the name, address, area code, telephone number, fax number, and email address (if available) of the person to be consulted if correspondence about this application becomes necessary.

Certification (space 8): This application cannot be accepted unless it bears the date and the *handwritten signature* of the author or other copyright claimant, or of the owner of exclusive right(s), or of the duly authorized agent of the author, claimant, or owner of exclusive right(s).

Address for Return of Certificate (space 9): The address box must be completed legibly since the certificate will be returned in a window envelope.

MORE INFORMATION

"Works": "Works" are the basic subject matter of copyright; they are what authors create and copyright protects. The statute draws a sharp distinction between the "work" and "any material object in which the work is embodied."

"Copies" and "Phonorecords": These are the two types of material objects in which "works" are embodied. In general, "copies" are objects from which a work can be read or visually perceived, directly or with the aid of a machine or device, such as manuscripts, books, sheet music, film, and videotape. "Phonorecords" are objects embodying fixations of sounds, such as audio tapes and phonograph disks. For example, a song (the "work") can be reproduced in sheet music ("copies") or phonograph disks ("phonorecords"), or both.

"Sound Recordings": These are "works," not "copies" or "phonorecords." "Sound recordings" are "works that result from the fixation of a series of musical, spoken, or other sounds, but not including the sounds accompanying a motion picture or other audiovisual work." Example: When a record company issues a new release, the release will typically involve two distinct "works": the "musical work" that has been recorded, and the "sound recording" as a separate work in itself. The material objects that the record company sends out are "phonorecords": physical reproductions of both the "musical work" and the "sound recording."

Should You File More Than One Application? If your work consists of a recorded musical, dramatic, or literary work and if both that "work" and the sound recording as a separate "work" are eligible for registration, the application form you should file depends on the following:

File Only Form SR if: The copyright claimant is the same for both the musical, dramatic, or literary work and for the sound recording, and you are seeking a single registration to cover both of these "works."

File Only Form PA (or Form TX) if: You are seeking to register only the musical, dramatic, or literary work, not the sound recording. Form PA is appropriate for works of the performing arts; Form TX is for nondramatic literary works.

Separate Applications Should Be Filed on Form PA (or Form TX) and on Form SR if: (1) The copyright claimant for the musical, dramatic, or literary work is different from the copyright claimant for the sound recording; or (2) You prefer to have separate registrations for the musical, dramatic, or literary work and for the sound recording.

Form SR, Page 3

Copyright Office fees are subject to change. For current fees, check the Copyright Office website at *www.copyright.gov*, write the Copyright Office, or call (202) 707-3000.

Form SR
For a Sound Recording
UNITED STATES COPYRIGHT OFFICE

REGISTRATION NUMBER

_____

	SR	SRU

EFFECTIVE DATE OF REGISTRATION

Month	Day	Year

DO NOT WRITE ABOVE THIS LINE. IF YOU NEED MORE SPACE, USE A SEPARATE CONTINUATION SHEET.

1

TITLE OF THIS WORK ▼

PREVIOUS, ALTERNATIVE, OR CONTENTS TITLES (CIRCLE ONE) ▼

2 a

NAME OF AUTHOR ▼

DATES OF BIRTH AND DEATH
Year Born ▼   Year Died ▼

Was this contribution to the work a "work made for hire"?
❑ Yes
❑ No

AUTHOR'S NATIONALITY OR DOMICILE
Name of Country
OR { Citizen of ▶_____
Domiciled in ▶_____

WAS THIS AUTHOR'S CONTRIBUTION TO THE WORK
Anonymous?   ❑ Yes ❑ No
Pseudonymous? ❑ Yes ❑ No
If the answer to either of these questions is "Yes," see detailed instructions.

NATURE OF AUTHORSHIP Briefly describe nature of material created by this author in which copyright is claimed. ▼

NOTE

Under the law, the "author" of a "work made for hire" is generally the employer, not the employee (see instructions). For any part of this work that was "made for hire," check "Yes" in the space provided, give the employer (or other person for whom the work was prepared) as "Author" of that part, and leave the space for dates of birth and death blank.

b

NAME OF AUTHOR ▼

DATES OF BIRTH AND DEATH
Year Born ▼   Year Died ▼

Was this contribution to the work a "work made for hire"?
❑ Yes
❑ No

AUTHOR'S NATIONALITY OR DOMICILE
Name of Country
OR { Citizen of ▶_____
Domiciled in ▶_____

WAS THIS AUTHOR'S CONTRIBUTION TO THE WORK
Anonymous?   ❑ Yes ❑ No
Pseudonymous? ❑ Yes ❑ No
If the answer to either of these questions is "Yes," see detailed instructions.

NATURE OF AUTHORSHIP Briefly describe nature of material created by this author in which copyright is claimed. ▼

c

NAME OF AUTHOR ▼

DATES OF BIRTH AND DEATH
Year Born ▼   Year Died ▼

Was this contribution to the work a "work made for hire"?
❑ Yes
❑ No

AUTHOR'S NATIONALITY OR DOMICILE
Name of Country
OR { Citizen of ▶_____
Domiciled in ▶_____

WAS THIS AUTHOR'S CONTRIBUTION TO THE WORK
Anonymous?   ❑ Yes ❑ No
Pseudonymous? ❑ Yes ❑ No
If the answer to either of these questions is "Yes," see detailed instructions.

NATURE OF AUTHORSHIP Briefly describe nature of material created by this author in which copyright is claimed. ▼

3 a

YEAR IN WHICH CREATION OF THIS WORK WAS COMPLETED
_____ ◀ Year   This Information must be given in all cases.

b DATE AND NATION OF FIRST PUBLICATION OF THIS PARTICULAR WORK
Complete this information ONLY if this work has been published.
Month ▶_____ Day ▶_____ Year ▶_____ ◀ Nation

4 a

COPYRIGHT CLAIMANT(S) Name and address must be given even if the claimant is the same as the author given in space 2. ▼

See instructions before completing this space.

b

TRANSFER If the claimant(s) named here in space 4 is (are) different from the author(s) named in space 2, give a brief statement of how the claimant(s) obtained ownership of the copyright. ▼

APPLICATION RECEIVED

ONE DEPOSIT RECEIVED

TWO DEPOSITS RECEIVED

FUNDS RECEIVED

DO NOT WRITE HERE OFFICE USE ONLY

MORE ON BACK ▶   • Complete all applicable spaces (numbers 5-9) on the reverse side of this page.
• See detailed instructions.   • Sign the form at line 8.

DO NOT WRITE HERE
Page 1 of _____ pages

Form SR, Page 4

DO NOT WRITE ABOVE THIS LINE. IF YOU NEED MORE SPACE, USE A SEPARATE CONTINUATION SHEET.

PREVIOUS REGISTRATION Has registration for this work, or for an earlier version of this work, already been made in the Copyright Office?

❑ Yes ❑ No If your answer is "Yes," why is another registration being sought? (Check appropriate box) ▼

a. ❑ This work was previously registered in unpublished form and now has been published for the first time.

b. ❑ This is the first application submitted by this author as copyright claimant.

c. ❑ This is a changed version of the work, as shown by space 6 on this application.

If your answer is "Yes," give: **Previous Registration Number** ▼   **Year of Registration** ▼

5

DERIVATIVE WORK OR COMPILATION

Preexisting Material Identify any preexisting work or works that this work is based on or incorporates. ▼

a

6

See instructions
before completing
this space.

Material Added to This Work Give a brief, general statement of the material that has been added to this work and in which copyright is claimed. ▼

b

DEPOSIT ACCOUNT If the registration fee is to be charged to a deposit account established in the Copyright Office, give name and number of Account.

Name ▼   **Account Number** ▼

a

7

CORRESPONDENCE Give name and address to which correspondence about this application should be sent. Name/Address/Apt/City/State/Zip ▼

b

Area code and daytime telephone number   Fax number

Email

CERTIFICATION* I, the undersigned, hereby certify that I am the

Check only one ▼

❑ author

❑ other copyright claimant

❑ owner of exclusive right(s)

❑ authorized agent of _____

Name of author or other copyright claimant, or owner of exclusive right(s) ▲

8

of the work identified in this application and that the statements made by me in this application are correct to the best of my knowledge.

Typed or printed name and date ▼ If this application gives a date of publication in space 3, do not sign and submit it before that date.

_____   Date _____

Handwritten signature ▼

9

Certificate
will be
mailed in
window
envelope
to this
address

Name ▼

Number/Street/Apt ▼

City/State/Zip ▼

*17 *USC* §506(e): Any person who knowingly makes a false representation of a material fact in the application for copyright registration provided for by section 409, or in any written statement filed in connection with the application, shall be fined not more than $2,500.

Form SR-Full   Rev: 11/2006   Print: 11/2006—60,000   Printed on recycled paper   U.S. Government Printing Office: 2007-330-945/60,138

Form PA, Page 1

 Form PA

Detach and read these instructions before completing this form.
Make sure all applicable spaces have been filled in before you return this form.

BASIC INFORMATION

When to Use This Form: Use Form PA for registration of published or unpublished works of the performing arts. This class includes works prepared for the purpose of being "performed" directly before an audience or indirectly "by means of any device or process." Works of the performing arts include: (1) musical works, including any accompanying words; (2) dramatic works, including any accompanying music; (3) pantomimes and choreographic works; and (4) motion pictures and other audiovisual works.

Deposit to Accompany Application: An application for copyright registration must be accompanied by a deposit consisting of copies or phonorecords representing the entire work for which registration is made. The following are the general deposit requirements as set forth in the statute:

Unpublished Work: Deposit one complete copy (or phonorecord).

Published Work: Deposit two complete copies (or one phonorecord) of the best edition.

Work First Published Outside the United States: Deposit one complete copy (or phonorecord) of the first foreign edition.

Contribution to a Collective Work: Deposit one complete copy (or phonorecord) of the best edition of the collective work.

Motion Pictures: Deposit *both* of the following: (1) a separate written description of the contents of the motion picture; and (2) for a published work, one complete copy of the best edition of the motion picture; or, for an unpublished work, one complete copy of the motion picture or identifying material. Identifying material may be either an audiorecording of the entire soundtrack or one frame enlargement or similar visual print from each 10-minute segment.

The Copyright Notice: Before March 1, 1989, the use of copyright notice was mandatory on all published works, and any work first published before that date should have carried a notice. For works first published on and after March 1, 1989, use of the copyright notice is optional. For more information about copyright notice, see Circular 3, *Copyright Notice.*

For Further Information: To speak to a Copyright Office staff member, call (202) 707-3000 (TTY: (202) 707-6737). Recorded information is available 24 hours a day. Order forms and other publications from the address in space 9 or call the Forms and Publications Hotline at (202) 707-9100. Access and download circulars, forms, and other information from the Copyright Office website at *www.copyright.gov.*

LINE-BY-LINE INSTRUCTIONS

Please type or print using black ink. The form is used to produce the certificate.

 SPACE 1: Title

Title of This Work: Every work submitted for copyright registration must be given a title to identify that particular work. If the copies or phonorecords of the work bear a title (or an identifying phrase that could serve as a title), transcribe that wording *completely* and *exactly* on the application. Indexing of the registration and future identification of the work will depend on the information you give here. If the work you are registering is an entire "collective work" (such as a collection of plays or songs), give the overall title of the collection. If you are registering one or more individual contributions to a collective work, give the title of each contribution, followed by the title of the collection. For an unpublished collection, you may give the titles of the individual works after the collection title.

Previous or Alternative Titles: Complete this space if there are any additional titles for the work under which someone searching for the registration might be likely to look, or under which a document pertaining to the work might be recorded.

Nature of This Work: Briefly describe the general nature or character of the work being registered for copyright. Examples: "Music"; "Song Lyrics"; "Words and Music"; "Drama"; "Musical Play"; "Choreography"; "Pantomime"; "Motion Picture"; "Audiovisual Work."

 SPACE 2: Author(s)

General Instructions: After reading these instructions, decide who are the "authors" of this work for copyright purposes. Then, unless the work is a "collective work," give the requested information about every "author" who contributed any appreciable amount of copyrightable matter to this version of the work. If you need further space, request additional Continuation Sheets. In the case of a collective work such as a songbook or a collection of plays, give information about the author of the collective work as a whole.

Name of Author: The fullest form of the author's name should be given. Unless the work was "made for hire," the individual who actually created the work is its "author." In the case of a work made for hire, the statute provides that "the employer or other person for whom the work was prepared is considered the author."

What Is a "Work Made for Hire"? A "work made for hire" is defined as: (1) "a work prepared by an employee within the scope of his or her employment"; or (2) "a work specially ordered or commissioned for use as a contribution to a collective work, as a part of a motion picture or other audiovisual work, as a translation, as a supplementary work, as a compilation, as an instructional text, as a test, as answer material for a test, or as an atlas, if the parties expressly agree in a written instrument signed by them that the work shall be considered a work made for hire." If you have checked "Yes" to indicate that the work was "made for hire," you must give the full legal name of the employer (or other person for whom the work was prepared). You may also include the name of the employee along with the name of the employer (for example: "Elster Music Co., employer for hire of John Ferguson").

"Anonymous" or "Pseudonymous" Work: An author's contribution to a work is "anonymous" if that author is not identified on the copies or phonorecords of the work. An author's contribution to a work is "pseudonymous" if that author is identified on the copies or phonorecords under a fictitious name. If the work is "anonymous" you may: (1) leave the line blank; or (2) state "anonymous" on the line; or (3) reveal the author's identity. If the work is "pseudonymous" you may: (1) leave the line blank; or (2) give the pseudonym and identify it as such (example: "Huntley Haverstock, pseudonym"); or (3) reveal the author's name, making clear which is the real name and which is the pseudonym (for example: "Judith Barton, whose pseudonym is Madeline Elster"). However, the citizenship or domicile of the author *must* be given in all cases.

Dates of Birth and Death: If the author is dead, the statute requires that the year of death be included in the application unless the work is anonymous or pseudonymous. The author's birth date is optional, but is useful as a form of identification. Leave this space blank if the author's contribution was a "work made for hire."

Author's Nationality or Domicile: Give the country of which the author is a citizen, or the country in which the author is domiciled. Nationality or domicile *must* be given in all cases.

Nature of Authorship: Give a brief general statement of the nature of this particular author's contribution to the work. Examples: "Words"; "Coauthor of Music"; "Words and Music"; "Arrangement"; "Coauthor of Book and Lyrics"; "Dramatization"; "Screen Play"; "Compilation and English Translation"; "Editorial Revisions."

Form PA, Page 2

 ## SPACE 3: Creation and Publication

General Instructions: Do not confuse "creation" with "publication." Every application for copyright registration must state "the year in which creation of the work was completed." Give the date and nation of first publication only if the work has been published.

Creation: Under the statute, a work is "created" when it is fixed in a copy or phonorecord for the first time. Where a work has been prepared over a period of time, the part of the work existing in fixed form on a particular date constitutes the created work on that date. The date you give here should be the year in which the author completed the particular version for which registration is now being sought, even if other versions exist or if further changes or additions are planned.

Publication: The statute defines "publication" as "the distribution of copies or phonorecords of a work to the public by sale or other transfer of ownership, or by rental, lease, or lending"; a work is also "published" if there has been an "offering to distribute copies or phonorecords to a group of persons for purposes of further distribution, public performance, or public display." Give the full date (month, day, year) when, and the country where, publication first occurred. If first publication took place simultaneously in the United States and other countries, it is sufficient to state "U.S.A."

SPACE 4: Claimant(s)

Name(s) and Address(es) of Copyright Claimant(s): Give the name(s) and address(es) of the copyright claimant(s) in this work even if the claimant is the same as the author. Copyright in a work belongs initially to the author of the work (including, in the case of a work made for hire, the employer or other person for whom the work was prepared). The copyright claimant is either the author of the work or a person or organization to whom the copyright initially belonging to the author has been transferred.

Transfer: The statute provides that, if the copyright claimant is not the author, the application for registration must contain "a brief statement of how the claimant obtained ownership of the copyright." If any copyright claimant named in space 4 is not an author named in space 2, give a brief statement explaining how the claimant(s) obtained ownership of the copyright. Examples: "By written contract"; "Transfer of all rights by author"; "Assignment"; "By will." Do not attach transfer documents or other attachments or riders.

SPACE 5: Previous Registration

General Instructions: The questions in space 5 are intended to show whether an earlier registration has been made for this work and, if so, whether there is any basis for a new registration. As a general rule, only one basic copyright registration can be made for the same version of a particular work.

Same Version: If this version is substantially the same as the work covered by a previous registration, a second registration is not generally possible unless: (1) the work has been registered in unpublished form and a second registration is now being sought to cover this first published edition; or (2) someone other than the author is identified as copyright claimant in the earlier registration, and the author is now seeking registration in his or her own name. If either of these two exceptions applies, check the appropriate box and give the earlier registration number and date. Otherwise, do not submit Form PA; instead, write the Copyright Office

for information about supplementary registration or recordation of transfers of copyright ownership.

Changed Version: If the work has been changed and you are now seeking registration to cover the additions or revisions, check the last box in space 5, give the earlier registration number and date, and complete both parts of space 6 in accordance with the instructions below.

Previous Registration Number and Date: If more than one previous registration has been made for the work, give the number and date of the latest registration.

 ## SPACE 6: Derivative Work or Compilation

General Instructions: Complete space 6 if this work is a "changed version," "compilation," or "derivative work," and if it incorporates one or more earlier works that have already been published or registered for copyright or that have fallen into the public domain. A "compilation" is defined as "a work formed by the collection and assembling of preexisting materials or of data that are selected, coordinated, or arranged in such a way that the resulting work as a whole constitutes an original work of authorship." A "derivative work" is "a work based on one or more preexisting works." Examples of derivative works include musical arrangements, dramatizations, translations, abridgments, condensations, motion picture versions, or "any other form in which a work may be recast, transformed, or adapted." Derivative works also include works "consisting of editorial revisions, annotations, or other modifications" if these changes, as a whole, represent an original work of authorship.

Preexisting Material (space 6a): Complete this space *and* space 6b for derivative works. In this space identify the preexisting work that has been recast, transformed, or adapted. For example, the preexisting material might be: "French version of Hugo's 'Le Roi s'amuse'." Do not complete this space for compilations.

Material Added to This Work (space 6b): Give a brief, general statement of the *additional* new material covered by the copyright claim for which registration is sought. In the case of a derivative work, identify this new material. Examples: "Arrangement for piano and orchestra"; "Dramatization for television"; "New film version"; "Revisions throughout; Act III completely new." If the work is a compilation, give a brief, general statement describing both the material that has been compiled *and* the compilation itself. Example: "Compilation of 19th Century Military Songs."

SPACE 7, 8, 9: Fee, Correspondence, Certification, Return Address

Deposit Account: If you maintain a Deposit Account in the Copyright Office, identify it in space 7a. Otherwise, leave the space blank and send the fee with your application and deposit.

Correspondence (space 7b): Give the name, address, area code, telephone number, fax number, and email address (if available) of the person to be consulted if correspondence about this application becomes necessary.

Certification (space 8): The application cannot be accepted unless it bears the date and the **handwritten signature** of the author or other copyright claimant, or of the owner of exclusive right(s), or of the duly authorized agent of the author, claimant, or owner of exclusive right(s).

Address for Return of Certificate (space 9): The address box must be completed legibly since the certificate will be returned in a window envelope.

MORE INFORMATION

How to Register a Recorded Work: If the musical or dramatic work that you are registering has been recorded (as a tape, disk, or cassette), you may choose either copyright application Form PA (Performing Arts) or Form SR (Sound Recordings), depending on the purpose of the registration.

Use Form PA to register the underlying musical composition or dramatic work. Form SR has been developed specifically to register a "sound recording" as defined by the Copyright Act—a work resulting from the "fixation of a series of sounds," separate and distinct from the underlying musical or dramatic work. Form SR should be used when the copyright claim is limited to the sound recording. (In one instance, Form SR may also be used to file for a copyright registration for both kinds of works—see (4) below.) Therefore:

(1) File Form PA if you are seeking to register the musical or dramatic work, not the "sound recording," even though what you deposit for copyright purposes may be in the form of a phonorecord.

(2) File Form PA if you are seeking to register the audio portion of an audiovisual work, such as a motion picture soundtrack; these are considered integral parts of the audiovisual work.

(3) File Form SR if you are seeking to register the "sound recording" itself, that is, the work that results from the fixation of a series of musical, spoken, or other sounds, but not the underlying musical or dramatic work.

(4) File Form SR if you are the copyright claimant for both the underlying musical or dramatic work and the sound recording, *and* you prefer to register both on the same form.

(5) File both forms PA and SR if the copyright claimant for the underlying work and sound recording differ, or you prefer to have separate registration for them.

"Copies" and "Phonorecords": To register for copyright, you are required to deposit "copies" or "phonorecords." These are defined as follows:

Musical compositions may be embodied (fixed) in "copies," objects from which a work can be read or visually perceived, directly or with the aid of a machine or device, such as manuscripts, books, sheet music, film, and videotape. They may also be fixed in "phonorecords," objects embodying fixations of sounds, such as tapes and phonograph disks, commonly known as phonograph records. For example, a song (the work to be registered) can be reproduced in sheet music ("copies") or phonograph records ("phonorecords"), or both.

Form PA, Page 3

Copyright Office fees are subject to change. For current fees, check the Copyright Office website at *www.copyright.gov*, write the Copyright Office, or call (202) 707-3000.

Form PA
For a Work of Performing Arts
UNITED STATES COPYRIGHT OFFICE

REGISTRATION NUMBER

_____

PA   PAU

EFFECTIVE DATE OF REGISTRATION

Month   Day   Year

DO NOT WRITE ABOVE THIS LINE. IF YOU NEED MORE SPACE, USE A SEPARATE CONTINUATION SHEET.

1

TITLE OF THIS WORK ▼

PREVIOUS OR ALTERNATIVE TITLES ▼

NATURE OF THIS WORK ▼ See instructions

2

a   NAME OF AUTHOR ▼

DATES OF BIRTH AND DEATH
Year Born ▼   Year Died ▼

Was this contribution to the work a "work made for hire"?
☐ Yes
☐ No

AUTHOR'S NATIONALITY OR DOMICILE
Name of Country
OR { Citizen of _____
Domiciled in _____

WAS THIS AUTHOR'S CONTRIBUTION TO THE WORK
Anonymous? ☐ Yes ☐ No
Pseudonymous? ☐ Yes ☐ No

If the answer to either of these questions is "Yes," see detailed instructions.

NATURE OF AUTHORSHIP   Briefly describe nature of material created by this author in which copyright is claimed. ▼

NOTE

Under the law, the "author" of a "work made for hire" is generally the employer, not the employee (see instructions). For any part of this work that was "made for hire" check "Yes" in the space provided, give the employer (or other person for whom the work was prepared) as "Author" of that part, and leave the space for dates of birth and death blank.

b   NAME OF AUTHOR ▼

DATES OF BIRTH AND DEATH
Year Born ▼   Year Died ▼

Was this contribution to the work a "work made for hire"?
☐ Yes
☐ No

AUTHOR'S NATIONALITY OR DOMICILE
Name of Country
OR { Citizen of _____
Domiciled in _____

WAS THIS AUTHOR'S CONTRIBUTION TO THE WORK
Anonymous? ☐ Yes ☐ No
Pseudonymous? ☐ Yes ☐ No

If the answer to either of these questions is "Yes," see detailed instructions.

NATURE OF AUTHORSHIP   Briefly describe nature of material created by this author in which copyright is claimed. ▼

c   NAME OF AUTHOR ▼

DATES OF BIRTH AND DEATH
Year Born ▼   Year Died ▼

Was this contribution to the work a "work made for hire"?
☐ Yes
☐ No

AUTHOR'S NATIONALITY OR DOMICILE
Name of Country
OR { Citizen of _____
Domiciled in _____

WAS THIS AUTHOR'S CONTRIBUTION TO THE WORK
Anonymous? ☐ Yes ☐ No
Pseudonymous? ☐ Yes ☐ No

If the answer to either of these questions is "Yes," see detailed instructions.

NATURE OF AUTHORSHIP   Briefly describe nature of material created by this author in which copyright is claimed. ▼

3

a   YEAR IN WHICH CREATION OF THIS WORK WAS COMPLETED   This information must be given in all cases.
_____ Year

b   DATE AND NATION OF FIRST PUBLICATION OF THIS PARTICULAR WORK   Complete this information ONLY if this work has been published.
Month _____ Day _____ Year _____
_____ Nation

4

See instructions before completing this space.

COPYRIGHT CLAIMANT(S) Name and address must be given even if the claimant is the same as the author given in space 2. ▼

TRANSFER If the claimant(s) named here in space 4 is (are) different from the author(s) named in space 2, give a brief statement of how the claimant(s) obtained ownership of the copyright. ▼

APPLICATION RECEIVED

ONE DEPOSIT RECEIVED

TWO DEPOSITS RECEIVED

FUNDS RECEIVED

DO NOT WRITE HERE OFFICE USE ONLY

MORE ON BACK ▶ • Complete all applicable spaces (numbers 5-9) on the reverse side of this page.
• See detailed instructions.   • Sign the form at line 8.

DO NOT WRITE HERE
Page 1 of _____ pages

Form PA, Page 4

EXAMINED BY

CHECKED BY

☐ CORRESPONDENCE
Yes

FORM PA

FOR
COPYRIGHT
OFFICE
USE
ONLY

DO NOT WRITE ABOVE THIS LINE. IF YOU NEED MORE SPACE, USE A SEPARATE CONTINUATION SHEET.

PREVIOUS REGISTRATION Has registration for this work, or for an earlier version of this work, already been made in the Copyright Office?
☐ Yes ☐ No If your answer is "Yes," why is another registration being sought? (Check appropriate box.) ▼ If your answer is No, do **not** check box A, B, or C.
a. ☐ This is the first published edition of a work previously registered in unpublished form.
b. ☐ This is the first application submitted by this author as copyright claimant.
c. ☐ This is a changed version of the work, as shown by space 6 on this application.
If your answer is "Yes," give: **Previous Registration Number** ▼   **Year of Registration** ▼

5

DERIVATIVE WORK OR COMPILATION Complete both space 6a and 6b for a derivative work; complete only 6b for a compilation.
Preexisting Material Identify any preexisting work or works that this work is based on or incorporates. ▼

Material Added to This Work Give a brief, general statement of the material that has been added to this work and in which copyright is claimed. ▼

a
6
See instructions
before completing
this space.
b

DEPOSIT ACCOUNT If the registration fee is to be charged to a Deposit Account established in the Copyright Office, give name and number of Account.
Name ▼   **Account Number** ▼

a
7

CORRESPONDENCE Give name and address to which correspondence about this application should be sent. Name/Address/Apt/City/State/Zip▼

b

Area code and daytime telephone number   (   )   Fax number   (   )
Email

CERTIFICATION* I, the undersigned, hereby certify that I am the
Check only one ▶ {
☐ author
☐ other copyright claimant
☐ owner of exclusive right(s)
☐ authorized agent of
Name of author or other copyright claimant, or owner of exclusive right(s) ▲
of the work identified in this application and that the statements made by me in this application are correct to the best of my knowledge.

8

Typed or printed name and date ▼ If this application gives a date of publication in space 3, do not sign and submit it before that date.

Date

Handwritten signature (X) ▼
x

Certificate
will be
mailed in
window
envelope
to this
address:

Name ▼

Number/Street/Apt ▼

City/State/Zip ▼

YOU MUST:
• Complete all necessary spaces
• Sign your application in space 8
SEND ALL 3 ELEMENTS
IN THE SAME PACKAGE:
1. Application form
2. Nonrefundable filing fee in check or money
order payable to *Register of Copyrights*
3. Deposit material
MAIL TO:
Library of Congress
Copyright Office
101 Independence Avenue SE
Washington, DC 20559-6000

9

*17 USC §506(e): Any person who knowingly makes a false representation of a material fact in the application for copyright registration provided for by section 409, or in any written statement filed in connection with the application, shall be fined not more than $2,500.

Form PA – Full Rev: 07/2006 Print: 07/2006 — xx,000 Printed on recycled paper   U.S. Government Printing Office: 2006-xxx-xxx/60,xxx

Form SE, Page 1

 Form SE

Detach and read these instructions before completing this form.
Make sure all applicable spaces have been filled in before you return this form.

BASIC INFORMATION

When to Use This Form: Use a separate Form SE for registration of each individual issue of a serial. A serial is defined as a work issued or intended to be issued in successive parts bearing numerical or chronological designations and intended to be continued indefinitely. This class includes a variety of works: periodicals; newspapers; annuals; the journals, proceedings, transactions, etc., of societies. Do not use Form SE to register an individual contribution to a serial. Request Form TX for such contributions.

Deposit to Accompany Application: An application for copyright registration must be accompanied by a deposit consisting of copies or phonorecords representing the entire work for which registration is to be made. The following are the general deposit requirements as set forth in the statute:

Unpublished Work: Deposit one complete copy (or phonorecord).

Published Work: Deposit two complete copies (or one phonorecord) of the best edition.

Work First Published Outside the United States: Deposit one complete copy (or phonorecord) of the first foreign edition.

Mailing Requirements: It is important that you send the application, the deposit copy or copies, and the registration fee together in the same envelope or package. The Copyright Office cannot process them unless they are received together. Send to: *Library of Congress, Copyright Office, 101 Independence Avenue SE, Washington DC 20559-6000.*

The Copyright Notice: Before March 1, 1989, the use of copyright notice was mandatory on all published works, and any work first published before that date should have carried a notice. For works first published on and after March 1, 1989, use of the copyright notice is optional. For more information about copyright notice, see Circular 3, *Copyright Notices.*

For Further Information: To speak to a Copyright Office staff member, call (202) 707-3000 (TTY: (202) 707-6737). Recorded information is available 24 hours a day. Order forms and other publications from the address in space 9 or call the Forms and Publications Hotline at (202) 707-9100. Access and download circulars, forms, and other information from the Copyright Office website at *www.copyright.gov.*

PRIVACY ACT ADVISORY STATEMENT Required by the Privacy Act of 1974 (P.L. 93-579)
The authority for requesting this information is title 17, *USC* secs. 409 and 410. Furnishing the requested information is voluntary. But if the information is not furnished, it may be necessary to delay or refuse registration and you may not be entitled to certain relief, remedies, and benefits provided in chapters 4 and 5 of title 17, *USC.* The principal uses of the requested information are the establishment and maintenance of a public record and the examination of the application for compliance with the registration requirements of the copyright code. Other routine uses include public inspection and copying, preparation of public indexes, preparation of public catalogs of copyright registrations, and preparation of search reports upon request.
NOTE: No other advisory statement will be given in connection with this application. Please keep this statement and refer to it if we communicate with you regarding this application.

LINE-BY-LINE INSTRUCTIONS
Please type or print using black ink. The form is used to produce the certificate.

 ### SPACE 1: Title

Title of This Serial: Every work submitted for copyright registration must be given a title to identify that particular work. If the copies or phonorecords of the work bear a title (or an identifying phrase that could serve as a title), copy that wording *completely* and *exactly* on the application. Give the volume and number of the periodical issue for which you are seeking registration. The "Date on Copies" in space 1 should be the date appearing on the actual copies (for example: "June 1981," "Winter 1981"). Indexing of the registration and future identification of the work will depend on the information you give here.

Previous or Alternative Titles: Complete this space only if there are any additional titles for the serial under which someone searching for the registration might be likely to look or under which a document pertaining to the work might be recorded.

 ### SPACE 2: Author(s)

General Instructions: After reading these instructions, decide who are the "authors" of this work for copyright purposes. In the case of a serial issue, the organization that directs the creation of the serial issue as a whole is generally considered the author of the "collective work" (see "Nature of Authorship") whether it employs a staff or uses the efforts of volunteers. Where, however, an individual is independently responsible for the serial issue, name that person as author of the "collective work."

Name of Author: The fullest form of the author's name should be given. In the case of a "work made for hire," the statute provides that "the employer or other person for whom the work was prepared is considered the author." If this issue is a "work made for hire," the author's name will be the full legal name of the hiring organization, corporation, or individual. The title of the periodical should not ordinarily be listed as "author" because the title itself does not usually correspond to a legal entity capable of authorship. When an individual creates an issue of a serial independently and not as an "employee" of an organization or corporation, that individual should be listed as the "author."

Author's Nationality or Domicile: Give the country of which the author is a citizen, or the country in which the author is domiciled. Nationality or domicile *must* be given in all cases. The citizenship of an organization formed under U.S. federal or state law should be stated as "U.S.A."

What Is a "Work Made for Hire"? A "work made for hire" is defined as (1) "a work prepared by an employee within the scope of his or her employment"; or (2) "a work specially ordered or commissioned for use as a contribution to a collective work, as a part of a motion picture or other audiovisual work, as a translation, as a supplementary work, as a compilation, as an instructional text, as a test, as answer material for a test, or as an atlas, if the parties expressly agree in a written instrument signed by them that the work shall be considered a work made for hire." An organization that uses the efforts of volunteers in the creation of a "collective work" (see "Nature of Authorship") may also be considered the author of a "work made for hire" even though those volunteers were not specifically paid by the organization. In the case of a "work made for hire," give the full legal name of the employer and check "Yes" to indicate that the work was made for hire. You may also include the name of the employee along with the name of the employer (for example: "Elster Publishing Co., employer for hire of John Ferguson").

"Anonymous" or "Pseudonymous" Work: Leave this space *blank* if the serial is a "work made for hire." An author's contribution to a work is "anonymous" if that author is not identified on the copies or phonorecords of the work. An author's contribution to a work is "pseudonymous" if that author is identified on the copies or phonorecords under a fictitious name. If the work is "anonymous" you may: (1) leave the line blank; or (2) state "anonymous" on the line; or (3) reveal the author's identify. If the work is "pseudonymous" you may: (1) leave the line blank; or (2) give the pseudonym and identify it as such (for example: "Huntley Haverstock, pseudonym"); or (3) reveal the author's name, making clear which is the real name and which is the pseudonym (for example: "Judith Barton, whose pseudonym is Madeline Elster"). However, the citizenship or domicile of the author *must* be given in all cases.

Dates of Birth and Death: Leave this space blank if the author's contribution was a "work made for hire." If the author is dead, the statute requires that the year of death be included in the application unless the work is anonymous

Form SE, Page 2

or pseudonymous. The author's birth date is optional but is useful as a form of identification.

Nature of Authorship: Give a brief statement of the nature of the particular author's contribution to the work. If an organization directed, controlled, and supervised the creation of the serial issue as a whole, check the box "collective work." The term "collective work" means that the author is responsible for compilation and editorial revision and may also be responsible for certain individual contributions to the serial issue. Further examples of "Authorship" which may apply both to organizational and to individual authors are "Entire text"; "Text and illustrations"; "Editorial revision, compilation, and additional new material."

 SPACE 3: Creation and Publication

General Instructions: Do not confuse "creation" with "publication." Every application for copyright registration must state "the year in which creation of the work was completed." Give the date and nation of first publication only if the work has been published.

Creation: Under the statute, a work is "created" when it is fixed in a copy or phonorecord for the first time. Where a work has been prepared over a period of time, the part of the work existing in fixed form on a particular date constitutes the created work on that date. The date you give here should be the year in which this particular issue was completed.

Publication: The statute defines "publication" as "the distribution of copies or phonorecords of a work to the public by sale or other transfer of ownership or by rental, lease, or lending"; a work is also "published" if there has been an "offering to distribute copies or phonorecords to a group of persons for purposes of further distribution, public performance, or public display." Give the full date (month, day, year) when, and the country where, publication of this particular issue first occurred. If first publication took place simultaneously in the United States and other countries, it is sufficient to state "U.S.A."

 SPACE 4: Claimant(s)

Name(s) and Address(es) of Copyright Claimant(s): This space must be completed. Give the name(s) and address(es) of the copyright claimant(s) of this work even if the claimant is the same as the author named in space 2. Copyright in a work belongs initially to the author of the work (including, in the case of a work made for hire, the employer or other person for whom the work was prepared). The copyright claimant is either the author of the work or a person or organization to whom the copyright initially belonging to the author has been transferred.

Transfer: The statute provides that, if the copyright claimant is not the author, the application for registration must contain "a brief statement of how the claimant obtained ownership of the copyright." If any copyright claimant named in space 4 is not an author named in space 2, give a brief statement explaining how the claimant(s) obtained ownership of the copyright. Examples: "By written contract"; "Transfer of all rights by author"; "Assignment"; "By will." Do not attach transfer documents or other attachments or riders.

 SPACE 5: Previous Registration

General Instructions: This space rarely applies to serials. Complete space 5 if this particular issue has been registered earlier or if it contains a substantial amount of material that has been previously registered. Do not complete this space if the previous registrations are simply those made for earlier issues.

Previous Registration:
a. Check this box if this issue has been registered in unpublished form and a second registration is now sought to cover the first published edition.

b. Check this box if someone other than the author is identified as copyright claimant in the earlier registration and the author is now seeking registration in his or her own name. If the work in question is a contribution to a collective work as opposed to the issue as a whole, file Form TX, not Form SE.

c. Check this box (and complete space 6) if this particular issue or a substantial portion of the material in it has been previously registered and you are now seeking registration for the additions and revisions that appear in this issue for the first time.

Previous Registration Number and Date: Complete this line if you checked one of the boxes above. If more than one previous registration has been made for the issue or for material in it, give only the number and year date for the latest registration.

 SPACE 6: Derivative Work or Compilation

General Instructions: Complete space 6 if this issue is a "changed version," "compilation," or "derivative work" that incorporates one or more earlier works that have already been published or registered for copyright or that have fallen into the public domain. Do not complete space 6 for an issue consisting of entirely new material appearing for the first time such as a new issue of a continuing serial. A "compilation" is defined as "a work formed by the collection and assembling of preexisting materials or of data that are selected, coordinated, or arranged in such a way that the resulting work as a whole constitutes an original work of authorship." A "derivative work" is "a work based on one or more preexisting works." Examples of derivative works include translations, fictionalizations, abridgments, condensations, or "any other form in which a work may be recast, transformed, or adapted." Derivative works also include works "consisting of editorial revisions, annotations, or other modifications" if these changes, as a whole, represent an original work of authorship.

Preexisting Material (space 6a): For derivative works, complete this space *and* space 6b. In space 6a identify the preexisting work that has been recast, transformed, adapted, or updated. Example: "1978 Morgan Co. Sales Catalog." Do not complete space 6a for compilations.

Material Added to This Work (space 6b): Give a brief, general statement of the new material covered by the copyright claim for which registration is sought. *Derivative work* examples include: "Editorial revisions and additions to the Catalog"; "Translation"; "Additional material." If a periodical issue is a *compilation*, describe both the compilation itself and the material that has been compiled. Examples: "Compilation of previously published journal articles"; "Compilation of previously published data." An issue may be both a derivative work and a compilation, in which case a sample statement might be: "Compilation of [describe] and additional new material."

 SPACE 7,8,9: Fee, Correspondence, Certification, Return Address

Deposit Account (Space 7a): If you maintain a deposit account in the Copyright Office, identify it in space 7a. Otherwise leave the space blank and send the fee with your application and deposit.

Correspondence (space 7b): This space should contain the name, address, area code, and telephone and fax numbers and email address of the person to be consulted if correspondence about this application becomes necessary.

Certification (space 8): The application cannot be accepted unless it bears the date and the *handwritten signature* of the author or other copyright claimant, or of the owner of exclusive right(s), or of the duly authorized agent of the author, claimant, or owner of exclusive right(s).

Address for Return of Certificate (space 9): The address box must be completed legibly since the certificate will be returned in a window envelope.

Form SE, Page 3

Copyright Office fees are subject to change. For current fees, check the Copyright Office website at *www.copyright.gov*, write the Copyright Office, or call (202) 707-3000.

Form SE
For a Serial
UNITED STATES COPYRIGHT OFFICE

REGISTRATION NUMBER

U

EFFECTIVE DATE OF REGISTRATION

Month   Day   Year

DO NOT WRITE ABOVE THIS LINE. IF YOU NEED MORE SPACE, USE A SEPARATE CONTINUATION SHEET.

1

TITLE OF THIS SERIAL ▼

Volume ▼   Number ▼   Date of Copies ▼   Frequency of Publication ▼

PREVIOUS OR ALTERNATIVE TITLES ▼

2

a

NAME OF AUTHOR ▼

DATES OF BIRTH AND DEATH
Year Born ▼   Year Died ▼

Was this contribution to the work a "work made for hire"?
☐ Yes
☐ No

AUTHOR'S NATIONALITY OR DOMICILE
Name of Country
OR { Citizen of ▶_____
{ Domiciled in ▶_____

WAS THIS AUTHOR'S CONTRIBUTION TO THE WORK
Anonymous?   ☐ Yes ☐ No
Pseudonymous?   ☐ Yes ☐ No

If the answer to either of these questions is "Yes," see detailed instructions.

NATURE OF AUTHORSHIP Briefly describe nature of material created by this author in which copyright is claimed. ▼
☐ Collective Work   Other:

NOTE

Under the law, the "author" of a "work made for hire" is generally the employer, not the employee (see instructions). For any part of this work that was "made for hire" check "Yes" in the space provided, give the employer (or other person for whom the work was prepared) as "Author" of that part, and leave the space for dates of birth and death blank.

b

NAME OF AUTHOR ▼

DATES OF BIRTH AND DEATH
Year Born ▼   Year Died ▼

Was this contribution to the work a "work made for hire"?
☐ Yes
☐ No

AUTHOR'S NATIONALITY OR DOMICILE
Name of Country
OR { Citizen of ▶_____
{ Domiciled in ▶_____

WAS THIS AUTHOR'S CONTRIBUTION TO THE WORK
Anonymous?   ☐ Yes ☐ No
Pseudonymous?   ☐ Yes ☐ No

If the answer to either of these questions is "Yes," see detailed instructions.

NATURE OF AUTHORSHIP Briefly describe nature of material created by this author in which copyright is claimed. ▼
☐ Collective Work   Other:

c

NAME OF AUTHOR ▼

DATES OF BIRTH AND DEATH
Year Born ▼   Year Died ▼

Was this contribution to the work a "work made for hire"?
☐ Yes
☐ No

AUTHOR'S NATIONALITY OR DOMICILE
Name of Country
OR { Citizen of ▶_____
{ Domiciled in ▶_____

WAS THIS AUTHOR'S CONTRIBUTION TO THE WORK
Anonymous?   ☐ Yes ☐ No
Pseudonymous?   ☐ Yes ☐ No

If the answer to either of these questions is "Yes," see detailed instructions.

NATURE OF AUTHORSHIP Briefly describe nature of material created by this author in which copyright is claimed. ▼
☐ Collective Work   Other:

3

a YEAR IN WHICH CREATION OF THIS WORK WAS COMPLETED This information must be given ◀Year in all cases.

b DATE AND NATION OF FIRST PUBLICATION OF THIS PARTICULAR WORK
Complete this information ONLY if this work has been published.
Month ▶_____ Day▶_____ Year▶_____ ◀ Nation

4

See instructions before completing this space.

COPYRIGHT CLAIMANT(S) Name and address must be given even if the claimant is the same as the author given in space 2. ▼

APPLICATION RECEIVED

ONE DEPOSIT RECEIVED

TWO DEPOSITS RECEIVED

FUNDS RECEIVED

TRANSFER If the claimant(s) named here in space 4 is (are) different from the author(s) named in space 2, give a brief statement of how the claimant(s) obtained ownership of the copyright. ▼

DO NOT WRITE HERE
OFFICE USE ONLY

MORE ON BACK ▶ • Complete all applicable spaces (numbers 5–9) on the reverse side of this page.
• See detailed instructions.   • Sign the form at line 8.

DO NOT WRITE HERE
Page 1 of _____ pages

Form SE, Page 4

EXAMINED BY

CHECKED BY

☐ CORRESPONDENCE
  Yes

FORM SE

FOR
COPYRIGHT
OFFICE
USE
ONLY

DO NOT WRITE ABOVE THIS LINE. IF YOU NEED MORE SPACE, USE A SEPARATE CONTINUATION SHEET.

PREVIOUS REGISTRATION Has registration for this work, or for an earlier version of this work, already been made in the Copyright Office?

☐ Yes ☐ No If your answer is "Yes," why is another registration being sought? (Check appropriate box.) ▼

a. ☐ This is the first published edition of a work previously registered in unpublished form.

b. ☐ This is the first application submitted by this author as copyright claimant.

c. ☐ This is a changed version of the work, as shown by space 6 on this application.

If your answer is "Yes," give: **Previous Registration Number** ▶   **Year of Registration** ▶

5

DERIVATIVE WORK OR COMPILATION Complete both space 6a and 6b for a derivative work; complete only 6b for a compilation.

Preexisting Material Identify any preexisting work or works that this work is based on or incorporates. ▼

a

6

Material Added to This Work Give a brief, general statement of the material that has been added to this work and in which copyright is claimed. ▼

b

See instructions
before completing
this space.

DEPOSIT ACCOUNT If the registration fee is to be charged to a Deposit Account established in the Copyright Office, give name and number of Account.

Name ▼   **Account Number** ▼

a

7

CORRESPONDENCE Give name and address to which correspondence about this application should be sent.   Name/Address/Apt/City/State/Zip ▼

b

Area code and daytime telephone number ▶   Fax number ▶

Email ▶

CERTIFICATION* I, the undersigned, hereby certify that I am the

Check only one ▶

☐ author
☐ other copyright claimant
☐ owner of exclusive right(s)
☐ authorized agent of _____

of the work identified in this application and that the statements made
by me in this application are correct to the best of my knowledge.

Name of author or other copyright claimant, or owner of exclusive right(s) ▲

8

Typed or printed name and date ▼ If this application gives a date of publication in space 3, do not sign and submit it before that date.

_____   Date ▶ _____

Handwritten signature ▼

Certificate
will be
mailed in
window
envelope
to this
address:

Name ▼

Number/Street/Apt ▼

City/State/Zip ▼

YOU MUST:
• Complete all necessary spaces
• Sign your application in space 8

**SEND ALL 3 ELEMENTS
IN THE SAME PACKAGE:**
1. Application form
2. Nonrefundable filing fee in check or money
   order payable to *Register of Copyrights*
3. Deposit material

MAIL TO:
Library of Congress
Copyright Office
101 Independence Avenue SE
Washington, DC 20559-6222

9

*17 *USC* §506(e): Any person who knowingly makes a false representation of a material fact in the application for copyright registration provided for by section 409, or in any written statement filed in connection with the application, shall be fined not more than $2,500.

Form SE–Full Rev: 11/2006 Print: 11/2006 Printed on recycled paper   U.S. Government Printing Office: 2006-xxx-xxx/xx,xxx

Copyright Fees, Page 1

Copyright Office Fees

For detailed information on fees charged by the Copyright Office for services it provides, see Circular 4, *Copyright Office Fees*.

Copyright Office fees are subject to change. For current fees, check the Copyright Office website at *www.copyright.gov*, write the Copyright Office, or call (202) 707-3000.

For Further Information

BY INTERNET · Circulars, announcements, regulations, other related materials, and all copyright application forms are available on the Copyright Office website at *www.copyright.gov*.

BY TELEPHONE · For general information about copyright, call the Copyright Public Information Office at (202) 707-3000. The TTY number is (202) 707-6737. Copyright Office staff members are on duty from 8:30 AM to 5:00 PM, eastern time, Monday through Friday, except federal holidays. Recorded information is available 24 hours a day. Or, if you know which application forms and circulars you want, you may request them from the Forms and Publications Hotline at (202) 707-9100 24 hours a day. You may leave a recorded message.

BY REGULAR MAIL · Write to—
Library of Congress
Copyright Office
Publications Section
101 Independence Avenue SE
Washington, DC 20559-6000

Copyright Fees, Page 2

ⓒ Copyright Office Fees

Effective as of July 1, 2006

Basic Registrations

Fee to accompany an application and deposit for registration of a claim to copyright

$45 Form TX, Short Form TX, Form VA, Short Form VA, Form PA, Short Form PA, Form SE, Short Form SE, Form SR, & Form GATT
— Form GR/CP (*This form is an adjunct to Forms VA, PA, and TX. There is no additional charge.*)

Renewal Registrations

For works published or registered before January 1, 1978

$75 Form RE
$220 Addendum to Form RE

Group Registrations

Fee to register a group of related claims, where appropriate

$25 Form SE/Group (serials) (*per issue, with minimum 2 issues*)
$70 Form G/DN (daily newspapers and newsletters)
$45 Published phographs (*Form VA. Up to 750 published photographs may be identified on form GR/PPh/CON with a single filing fee.*)

Supplementary Registrations

Fee to make a correction or amplification to a completed registration

$115 Form CA
$115 Form DC
$100 Preregistration

Miscellaneous Registrations

$200 Form D-VH (vessel hulls)
$95 Form MW (mask works)

Special Services Related to Registration (Optional Services)

Special Handling for Registration of Qualified Copyright Claims

Fee to expedite processing of qualified claims

$685 Special handling fee (*per claim*)
$50 Additional fee for each (nonspecial handling) claim using the same deposit

Other Fees Associated with Registration

$425 Full-term retention of published copyright deposit
$150 Secure test processing (*$/hr*)
$45 Handling extra copy for certification

Requests for Reconsideration
(*For claims previously refused registration*)

$250 First request
$25 Additional claim in related group (*each*)
$500 Second request
$25 Additional claim in related group (*each*)

Other Copyright Service Fees

Recordation of Documents Relating to Copyrighted Works

Fee to make a public record of an assignment of rights or other document

$95 Recordation of a document, including a Notice of Intention to Enforce, containing no more than one title
$25 Additional titles (*per group of 10 or fewer titles*)
$435 Special handling of recordation of documents

Reference & Bibliography Reports on Copyrighted Works

Fee for searching copyright records and preparing an official report

$100 Estimate of search fee
$150 Preparation of a report from official records (*$/hr*)
$400 Expedited Reference and Bibliography reports (*$/hr*)

Certification & Documents Services: Preparing Copies of Copyright Office Records

Fees for locating, retrieving, and reproducing records

$150 Locating and/or retrieving Copyright Office records (*$/hr*)
$40 Additional certificate of registration
$150 Certification of Copyright Office records (*$/hr*)
— Copying fee: variable depending on format and size
$150 Locating and/or retrieving in-process materials (*$/hr*)
$240 Surcharge for expedited Certification & Documents services listed above or for certification of a Reference & Bibliography search report (*$/hr*)

Miscellaneous Fees

$20 Receipt for deposit without registration (*Section 407 deposit*)
$80 Online Service Provider Designation (Recordation of an Interim Designation of Agent to Receive Notification of Claimed Infringement under §512(c)(2))
$50 Notice to Libraries and Archives (*each additional title: $20*)

Deposit Account Service Charges

$150 Overdraft
$75 Dishonored replenishment check

For Licensing Division fees, request SL-4L.

Copyright Office fees are subject to change. For current fees, check the Copyright Office website at www.copyright.gov, write the Copyright Office, or call (202) 707-3000.

Term of Copyright

Appendix C1 – Term of Copyright

WHEN WORKS PASS INTO THE PUBLIC DOMAIN

DATE OF WORK	CONDITIONS	TERM
Created On or After January 1, 1978	Published with copyright notice	Life + 70 years Work For Hire: The shorter of 95 years from publication or 120 years from creation
Between 1978 and March 1, 1989	Published without any copyright notice and without subsequent registration	In Public Domain
Between 1978 and March 1, 1989	Published without any copyright notice, but with subsequent registration	Life + 70 years Work For Hire: The shorter of 95 years from publication or 120 years from creation
Published before 1923		In Public Domain
Published Between 1923 and 1963	When published with copyright notice	28 years + Could be reviewed for up to 67 years. If not renewed, in public domain
Published Between 1964 and 1977	When published with copyright notice	28 years for first term Automatic extension of 67 years for second term
Published between 1923 and 1978	Published without any copyright notice	In Public Domain
Created before 1978 but not published	Protected from January 1, 1978	Longer of: Life + 70 years or December 31,2002
Created before 1978 but not published between 1978 and the end of 2002	Protected from January 1, 1978	Longer of: Life + 70 years or December 31, 2047

Glossary

102 Reference. A prior art reference that is used to teach each and every limitation of a claim of a patent application. A 102 reference is also said to "anticipate" the claim.

102(b) Bar. Where your patent application was filed more than a year after you first sold your invention or offered your invention for sale, or your invention was published. The sale, offer for sale, or publication bars you from obtaining a patent.

103 Reference. A prior art reference that is used to make obvious a claim of a patent application. The 103 reference may be used by itself or with another prior art reference.

112, First Paragraph Requirements. The requirements for written description, enablement and best mode when preparing a patent application, found in Section 112 of Title 35 of the patent law.

Abstract (or Abstract of Disclosure). A brief narrative of the disclosure of a patent application in 150 words or less.

Accused Device (or Product). A competitive device (or product) accused of infringing intellectual property rights.

Acquired Distinctiveness (Interchangeable with "Secondary Meaning"). Occurs when a descriptive word or design has been used and advertised extensively by a company, so that consumers recognize that it is a trademark or service mark referring to the company as the particular source of the goods or services.

Actual Reduction to Practice. The making of a prototype of an invention.

Allowance (of a Patent). When the USPTO sends a Notice of Allowance, indicating that all claims are allowed, with the Issue Fee remaining to be paid.

Amend Claims. A revision to the wording of the claims of a patent application, typically to overcome a rejection made by a patent examiner.

Amendment After Final. An option for a patent applicant after receiving a final rejection from the patent examiner. With an Amendment After Final, the applicant amends the application in minor ways that don't require substantive review by the examiner, such as cleaning up typographical errors or canceling rejected claims to leave only allowed claims.

Annuities. Annual fees paid to foreign patent offices to maintain your foreign patents. In the U.S., there are patent maintenance fees that are paid to the USPTO to maintain your patent (and which are due at 3½, 7½ and 11½ years from issuance).

Answer. A document that responds point-by-point to the complaint, either denying or admitting the factual allegations made in the complaint.

Anticipation. A type of rejection made by the USPTO when examining your patent application, indicating that every limitation of your claim is taught by a single prior art reference. In other words, an issued patent, an earlier filed patent application, or a prior invention already covers what you have included in your patent claim.

Appeal (after a Final Office Action). An option for a patent applicant after receiving a final rejection from the patent examiner. The applicant files an Appeal of the Final Office Action with the Board of Patent Appeals and Interferences. The applicant presents his arguments first in writing, and then orally before the Board.

Applicant. The person or persons applying for a patent, copyright, or trademark.

Arbitrary Marks. Trademarks or service marks that are comprised of recognizable words, but the words do not suggest or describe any aspect of the goods or services being sold. Examples of arbitrary marks include APPLE® computers and SATURN® for cars.

Article of Manufacture. A tangible product, which, if it has a new, original and ornamental design, can be protected by a design patent.

Assignee. The owner of a patent, copyright, or trademark, or the recipient of the IP from another entity (the Assignor).

Assignment. A legal document conveying ownership of an IP right. In the context of patents, an assignment may convey ownership of a patent application from the inventors to the company or other owner. Because inventors are the presumed owners of a patent application, an assignment is typically filed to provide proof of a transfer of ownership to the company or other owner.

Assignor. The entity who transfers the IP right to another (the Assignee).

Background of the Invention. In a patent application, the Background contains a description of the technology related to the invention. Sometimes the Background will identify and describe prior patents or publications addressing the same or similar problem that the patent application itself is intending to address. The Background can also be more general, simply describing in brief some of the prior ways others have attempted to solve similar problems.

Best Mode. A requirement that your patent specification describe the best, or preferred, way of carrying out the invention.

Body (of a Claim). The language following the Preamble that sets forth the limitations of the claim.

Board of Patent Appeals and Interferences (aka Board of Appeals). The federal administrative body that will receive, hear, and decide Appeals of Final Office Actions and patent interferences.

Brief Description of the Drawings. In a patent application, the portion of the specification briefly describing each of the drawings.

Broadening Reissue. An application filed based upon an already issued patent where the applicant seeks to broaden the scope claims of the issued claims based upon an inadvertent failure to do so originally. Such an application can only be filed within two years of original issuance.

Cancellation Action. An action filed in the TTAB to cancel a federal trademark registration.

Case Management Conference. The conference set by the court once the pleadings (complaint, answer, reply) are filed. It is a first opportunity for the parties to educate the judge on the big picture issues in the case and tell the court a little bit about the parties and where they expect the case to go. It's also an opportunity for the court to set dates for the case; for example, discovery dates, trial date, etc.

Certificate of Correction. A document that a patentee may file with the USPTO to correct minor typographical errors.

Claim Construction. The process in which a court is asked to define the meaning and scope of disputed terms and phrases in a patent claim. Like the interpretation of a contract, the courts are given the authority to decide how patent claim terms should be defined so that the parties can litigate whether such claims, as construed by the court, are infringed or are invalid.

Claim Limitation. A requirement specified in the language of a claim that must be found in an accused device in order for it to be infringing.

Claiming Priority (of a Patent). Making a reference to an earlier filed patent application so that one or more claims of the patent may be treated as filed on the date of the earlier filed patent application.

Claims. The numbered paragraphs at the end of a patent specification defining the legal scope or coverage of the invention.

Close-Ended Claim. A claim, typically using the transition phrase "consisting of," indicating that the claim requires only the limitations that follow, such that an accused device must only have the limitations specified in the claim.

Coined Marks. Interchangeable with "Fanciful Marks." Trademarks or service marks that are made-up words. They do not exist in any language. Examples include KODAK® and EXXON®.

Complaint. A document filed with a court that sets forth a legal claim against one or more entities or property. A lawsuit officially starts with the filing of a complaint. However, the proceedings do not effectively begin until the complaint is served upon at least one of the defendants. In most courts, if a complaint filed with a court is not served upon the defendant(s) within a certain period of time, the court will dismiss the case.

Constructive Reduction to Practice. The filing of a patent application.

Continuation. A type of patent application claiming priority to an earlier filed patent application that does not add any new subject matter versus the earlier filed patent application.

Continuation-in-Part. A type of patent application claiming priority to an earlier filed patent application that repeats some or all of the subject matter of the earlier filed patent application, and adds new subject matter.

Copyright. A form of protection provided by United States law to authors of "original works of authorship."

Copyright Office. An office of public record for copyright registration and deposit of copyright material.

Counterclaims. Claims by the defendant against the plaintiff.

Cross-license. A license given to a third party in exchange for a license to their intellectual property.

Declaration (in a Patent). A signed statement made by the inventor or inventors of a patent application required to be filed in a patent application.

Dependent Claim. A claim that includes the limitations not only of the claim itself, but also of another claim. The other claim could be either an independent claim or another dependent claim.

Deposit (in connection with a copyright application). Along with the completed application and the filing fee, you are required to submit a copy of the "best edition" of the work being registered. The requirements for what you send as the deposit copy are different depending on the type of work being registered.

Deposition. A proceeding in which oral testimony is taken of a witness outside of a courtroom setting. Depositions are most often conducted by an attorney for one of the parties in a lawsuit for purposes of gathering information from the witness. The witness is placed under oath and the testimony is recorded by an official court reporter. Depositions may be videotaped upon the request of the examining party.

Derivative Work. A work of authorship that is *based upon* one or more pre-existing works of authorship.

Design Around. A redesign of your product to avoid problematic patents.

Design Patent. A type of patent used to protect any new, original, and ornamental design for an article of manufacture.

Descriptive Marks. Words or designs that describe some characteristic, quality, or aspect of the goods or services with which they are used. No one can claim exclusive trademark rights in descriptive terms until they have acquired distinctiveness or secondary meaning. Technically there is no such thing as a descriptive mark; it should be called a "descriptive potential mark."

Detailed Description of Preferred Embodiments. In a patent application, the Detailed Description forms the majority of the text of the specification, generally providing a full and thorough description of the invention. This description is usually written with extensive reference to the drawings or figures, with each component of each figure labeled with a reference number that is described in detail in the specification.

Disclosure. A synonym for Specification. Also used to refer to the invention's disclosure of an invention to a patent attorney.

Discovery. The process by which a party to a lawsuit gathers information from other parties to the lawsuit or from non-parties that may have information relevant to the lawsuit. Discovery is permitted in the U.S. as a litigation tool to provide the exchange of evidence so that parties can prove their case or disprove the other party's case. While discovery is not unique to the United States, it is certainly permitted to a greater degree by U.S. courts than other countries. Discovery can include written requests for certain documents, written questions (known as interrogatories), requests for admission (as to facts or positions), and depositions (oral testimony of witnesses).

Divisional. A type of patent application claiming priority to an earlier-filed patent application, but directed to a patentably distinct invention than the earlier-filed patent application. Divisional patent applications often result from a patent examiner issuing a Restriction Requirement.

Doctrine of Equivalents. A legal principle in which a product or process could still be found to infringe a patent claim even though the product or process does not literally infringe the claim. The principle finds its origins in the recognition by courts that the invention could still be exploited without the accused product or process literally meeting every word of a patent claim if the differences are insubstantial or insignificant.

Domain Name. An address on the internet. It can be trademarked if goods or services are sold on the web site.

Double Patenting. A rejection made by a patent examiner when two patents or patent applications are filed by an applicant for the same invention. There are two types of double patenting: (i) same invention, when the claims of both patents or applications are the same, and (ii) obviousness-type, where the claims are not identical but are considered obvious in view of one another.

Drawings (of a Patent). Illustrations included in the patent specification that are referred to in the Detailed Description.

Due Diligence. The investigation by a potential investor or acquirer into a target company or its IP to determine whether an investment or acquisition is justified.

Effective Filing Date. When a patent application claims priority to one or more earlier-filed patent applications, the earliest date to which a claim in the patent application is entitled.

Enablement. A requirement that your patent specification describe the invention in such terms that one skilled in the art can make and use the claimed invention.

Embodiment. An example of how an invention may be implemented.

Exit Strategy. The ultimate goal of many companies. Particularly for a start-up company, the exit strategy may be an acquisition or an initial public offering (IPO).

Fanciful Marks (Interchangible with "Coined Marks"). Trademarks or service marks that are made-up words. They do not exist in any language. Examples include KODAK® and EXXON®.

Federal Circuit. Shorthand for one of the federal appellate courts that hears all appeals from patent cases. The Court of Appeals for the Federal Circuit consists of eleven judges who sit in Washington, D.C., to hear issues that have been appealed from all patent cases, and from other select categories of lawsuits. A patent case appealed to the Federal Circuit will typically be heard before a panel of three judges who will rule on the issues presented and either affirm the lower court's decision, reverse the lower court's decision, or a combination of both.

Federal Court. Distinct from the state courts, the federal courts are courts of the United States that are provided under the auspices of the U.S. Constitution. Federal Courts are courts of limited jurisdiction, which means they can only preside over certain types of cases; usually those involving federal claims, those involving parties from different states, and those seeking damages above a set amount.

Federal Trademark Registration. A certificate of registration issued by the USPTO which confers a number of important rights to the trademark owner.

Field of the Invention. In a patent application, a single sentence or two at the beginning of the patent application, describing the general field of technology. This information is helpful to the examiner in performing her search for relevant patents, publications, or other information predating your invention.

Figures (of a Patent). Illustrations included in the patent specification that are referred to in the Detailed Description.

File History (aka File Wrapper). The written record of the communication between the patent or trademark applicant and the USPTO. Synonymous with "Prosecution History."

Filing Date (of a Patent). The date a patent application is submitted (usually by mail or electronically) to the USPTO.

Final Office Action (aka Final Rejection). A type of Office Action sent by a patent examiner that closes substantive prosecution of your patent application. This means that the examiner is maintaining her position and doesn't agree with the arguments you made in your response to her Office Action.

Formal Documents (in a Patent Application). The Assignment, Power of Attorney, and Declaration that an applicant files with the USPTO.

Freedom to Operate Analysis. An analysis to determine whether making or selling your product would infringe the intellectual property rights of others. Synonymous with "Right to Practice Analysis" and "Market Clearance Analysis."

Generic Words. Words that name a good or service. Generic words can never become exclusive trademarks, no matter how much a company advertises them. Examples of generic words include APPLE for apples, and HEALTH CENTER for health centers.

Grace Period. A time period after the sale, offer for sale, or publication of an invention within which a patent application can still be filed. In the U.S., the grace period is one year.

Incorporation by Reference. A statement made in a patent application indicating that the document incorporated by reference, which may be another patent or application, forms a part of the patent application itself.

Independent Claim. A claim that stands on its own, meaning that it does not refer to any other claim.

Inequitable Conduct. A defense against a claim of infringement that is based upon improper conduct by a patent applicant during prosecution. Inequitable conduct typically refers to a failure of an applicant to supply important information to the patent office under the duty of candor or where an applicant misrepresents information to the patent office.

Information Disclosure Statement (aka IDS). A list of references provided by the patent applicant for consideration by the patent examiner in examining your patent application.

Infringement. The violation of your patent, trademark, copyright, trade secret, or other intellectual property right.

Infringer. Someone who violates your patent, trademark, copyright, trade secret, or other intellectual property right.

Inherently Distinctive Marks. Trademarks that are protectable without the owner having to prove that they function as trademarks. Inherently distinctive marks include coined, fanciful, arbitrary, and suggestive marks.

Intellectual Property (aka IP). A right typically granted by the government to protect intangible property. The four major types of IP are patents, trademarks, copyrights, and trade secrets.

Intent to Use. Before filing an application to register a trademark in the USPTO, the applicant must have a bona fide, or honest, intention to use the mark on the goods or services listed in the application. This is to prevent companies from filing lots of applications just to "stockpile" marks so that others cannot use them.

Interference. A proceeding before the USPTO to determine who should be awarded a patent when two or more inventors are seeking separate patents for the same invention.

Invalidity (of a Patent). When a patent is found not patentable after the patent has issued, and therefore cannot be enforced.

Inventor. A person who made an inventive contribution, either individually or jointly, to the subject matter of at least one claim in a patent application.

Inventor's Declaration. A signed statement made by the inventor or inventors of a patent application required to be filed in a patent application.

IP Audit. An evaluation, typically conducted by a patent attorney, evaluating a company's offensive strategy, defensive strategy and ownership with respect to its IP.

Issue Date (of a Patent). The date that a patent is granted by the Patent Office. A patent cannot be enforced until the patent issues.

Issue Fee (of a Patent). The fee due to receive a patent after receipt of a Notice of Allowance.

Large Entity. An entity that does not qualify as a Small Entity, meaning that it will have to pay the normal fees before the USPTO.

Likelihood of Confusion. The test used by the courts and the USPTO to decide if there is trademark infringement. The marks and the goods or services do not need to be identical to find infringement. They need be only sufficiently similar that consumers would associate them with one another.

Limitation. A requirement specified in the language of a claim that must be found in an accused device in order for it to be infringing.

Literal Infringement. Where a product or process includes literally every feature and/or limitation expressed in a patent claim. It is distinct from Infringement under the Doctrine of Equivalents.

"Look for" Advertising. Advertising that specifically points out a company's trademarks, e.g., "Look for the socks with the gold toe," or "Look for the pink insulation." Such advertising is very helpful in proving that consumers recognize specific features or descriptions as trademarks.

Madrid Protocol. An international trademark treaty that provides a single International Registration covering multiple countries.

Maintenance Fees. Fees payable to the USPTO at 3½, 7½ and 11½ years from issuance of a U.S. patent to maintain the patent in force.

Market Clearance Analysis. An analysis to determine whether making or selling your product would infringe the intellectual property rights of others. Synonymous with "Freedom to Operate Analysis" and "Right to Practice Analysis."

Marking. The placement of a patent number or "Patent Pending" on a patented article to provide notice to the public of the patent or patent application. Marking of an issued patent number on a patented article may be required to collect damages against an infringer.

Markman Hearing. A separate proceeding in a patent infringement lawsuit held by the judge to determine how the claims in a patent should be interpreted (or words in the claim should be defined).

National Phase. The stage of a PCT application after it is filed in individual foreign countries. This typically occurs 30 months after the earliest priority date.

Non-disclosure Agreement (aka NDA). An agreement obligating a party to maintain the confidentiality of the information disclosed.

Non-functional. The aspects of a product that are not necessary for its function. Examples could be an elaborate design on a spoon handle, or the unusual shape of a container. These non-functional aspects may be protectable as trademarks, copyrights, or by design patents.

Non-provisional patent application. A utility patent application that is not a provisional application. Synonymous with regular patent application.

Notice of Allowance. The official notice issued by the patent examiner that a patent application is in condition for allowance. The Notice of Allowance also specifies a deadline (which is three months from the date of the Notice of Allowance) by which the applicant needs to pay the Issue Fee in order to obtain the patent.

Notice of Appeal. The document that an applicant files with the Board of Patent Appeals and Interferences to appeal a Final Office Action.

Notice to File Missing Parts (of a Patent Application). A notice received from the USPTO specifying that a patent application is missing certain requirements. A typical Missing Parts response may require the filing of a Declaration or a filing fee.

Nonobviousness. A requirement for a patent application that the invention not be obvious.

Novelty. A requirement for a patent application that the invention be new.

Obviousness. A type of rejection made by the USPTO when examining your patent application, indicating that the limitations of your claim are made obvious by one or more prior art references.

Offer for Sale. The offering of an invention for sale that triggers the start of the one-year grace period, or the offering of a product for sale to infringe a patent.

Office Action. A written communication from the USPTO detailing the results of examination of your patent or trademark application.

One-year Grace Period. The one-year time period after the sale, offer for sale, or publication of an invention within which a U.S. patent application can still be filed.

On-sale Bar. Where your patent application was filed more than a year after you first sold your invention or offered your invention for sale. The sale or offer for sale bars you from obtaining a patent.

Open-Ended Claim. A claim, typically using the transition phrase "comprising," indicating that the claim requires all of the limitations that follow, but can still be infringed if an infringing device includes more than just those limitations.

Opposition. An action filed in the TTAB to oppose the registration of a trademark. There is a 30-day period in which anyone who believes they may be damaged by the registration of a mark may oppose the application.

Ordinary Skill in the Art. A term used to describe a person of a typical skill level in a particular technology field.

Ornamental. A requirement of a design patent that a feature be non-functional or aesthetic. Also, a merely ornamental design that does not function as an identifier of source is not a trademark.

Patent. A right granted to inventors by the government to exclude others from making, selling, offering for sale, using, or importing an invention.

Patent Agent. A scientist who is registered to practice before the U.S. Patent Office, but who is not a lawyer.

Patent Attorney. A lawyer who is registered to practice before the U.S. Patent Office.

Patent Examiner. An employee of the U.S. Patent Office trained to examine patent applications in a particular technology area.

Patent Number. The number used to identify a patent.

Patentability Search. A search of the prior art to determine whether an invention may be patentable.

Patent Term. The length of time that a patent is in force.

Patentee. The applicant for a patent, or the party to whom the patent is granted. Sometimes this will refer to the inventor(s) of a patent application, and other times it will refer to the owner of the patent.

PCT Application. An international patent application filed through the Patent Cooperation Treaty to preserve the ability to file patent applications in most countries of the world.

Plant Patent. A type of patent used to protect any asexually reproduced distinct and new variety of plant.

Pleadings. The complaint, answer, and reply in litigation. The pleadings identify the claims and high-level issues that the parties will litigate in the case.

Power of Attorney. A document signed on behalf of the owner of the patent application (which may be the inventors themselves, if their rights have not been assigned), appointing an attorney as the agent to represent the owner before the USPTO on the particular patent application.

Practice (as with an Invention). The manufacture, use, or sale of an invention. Typically referred to in the context of your ability to manufacture, use, or sell your invention without liability to others.

Preamble. The first portion of a claim that serves to introduce the claim and provide an indication of the nature of the subject matter to follow.

Preferred Embodiments. In a patent application, the examples in the specification describing the best way of making and using your invention.

Presumption of Validity. All patents issued by the U.S Patent and Trademark Office are presumed to be valid. That simply means that anyone challenging the validity of a patent in court must overcome the presumption by showing that the claimed invention is unpatentable using clear and convincing evidence.

Prior Art. The universe of references, such as prior patents, publications, or other information, that can be used by the examiner to reject a patent application.

Priority (of a Patent). A reference to an earlier-filed patent application so that one or more claims of the patent may to be treated as filed on the date of the earlier filed patent application.

Priority Date. When a patent application claims priority to an earlier-filed patent application, the date of the earlier-filed patent application.

Product Configuration Marks. When the shape of a product is distinctive, and is not necessary for the function of the product, it may be registrable as a trademark. Examples of product configuration marks include the shape of a WEBER® barbecue, and the shape of a LIFESAVER® candy.

Production of Documents. During proceedings before a court or the TTAB, a party can demand that the other party provide copies of documents that pertain to the issues in dispute.

Prosecution. The process of navigating a patent or trademark application through the USPTO.

Prosecution History. The written record of the communication between the patent or trademark applicant and the USPTO. Synonymous with "File History."

Prosecution History Estoppel. A legal principle in which a patent holder is prevented from arguing that an accused product or process infringes the patent under the doctrine of equivalents. The principle applies where the patent applicant made statements and/or changes to the application during prosecution that relates to the issue of whether such accused product or process is covered by the patent.

Provisional Patent Application. An informal patent application filed for the purpose of securing an early filing date with the USPTO. For the claims of a regular utility application to obtain the benefit of the provisional application, the regular application must be filed within one year of the provisional filing, and the provisional must satisfy the requirements of written description, enablement, and best mode.

Provisional Rights (Against Potential Infringers). Upon publication of a patent application, rights obtained by sending a letter to potential infringers notifying them of the publication. If the patent ultimately issues with claims substantially the same as in the publication, the patentee may be entitled to a reasonable royalty from the potential infringers.

PTO. The Patent and Trademark Office. Synonymous with "USPTO."

Public Domain. When the rights grant by intellectual property expire or are abandoned, allowing the public to make, use, or sell the intellectual property for itself without the need to license it from another.

Publication of a Work. The distribution of copies of a copyrighted work to the public by sale or other transfer of ownership, or by rental, lease, or lending.

Publication of a Patent Application. The publication by the USPTO of a patent application 18 months after its earliest priority date.

Published Work. A copyrighted work that has been distributed to the public by sale or other transfer of ownership, or by rental, lease, or lending.

Reduction to Practice. The prototyping of an invention (actual reduction to practice) or the filing of a patent application (constructive reduction to practice).

Reexamination. An examination conducted by the USPTO after a patent has issued based on prior patents or printed publications raising a substantial new question of patentability. Reexamination may be *ex parte*, meaning that only the patent holder and the USPTO communicate with one another, or *inter partes*, meaning that both the requestor of the reexamination and the patent holder have the opportunity to correspond with the USPTO.

Reference. A document that may be used by a patent or trademark examiner in a rejection against a patent or trademark application.

Registered Patent Attorney. Synonymous with Patent Attorney.

Regular patent application. Another term used to refer to a utility patent application.

Reissue. A type of patent application filed to correct an error in the original patent. A reissue application reopens prosecution of the patent application.

Request for Continued Examination (aka RCE). A request filed after receipt of a Final Office Action. A Request for Continued Examination gives the applicant another opportunity to convince the patent examiner of the patentability of the invention.

Request for Accelerated Examination. A request filed with the USPTO where the applicant seeks quicker examination of the patent application.

Restriction Requirement. When your patent application is found to have more than one patentable invention, a requirement by a patent examiner to choose one invention.

Right to Practice. A term referring to the ability to make, use and sell your invention without violating the intellectual property rights of others.

Right to Practice Analysis. An analysis to determine whether making or selling your product would infringe the intellectual property rights of others. Synonymous with "Freedom to Operate Analysis" and "Market Clearance Analysis."

Secondary Considerations of Nonobviousness. Factors such as unexpected results, commercial success, long-felt need, failure of others, copying by others, and skepticism of expert, that may be used to try to convince a patent examiner that an invention is not obvious.

Secondary Meaning. Interchangeable with "Acquired Distinctiveness." Occurs when a descriptive word or design has been used and advertised extensively by a company, so that consumers recognize that it is a trademark or service mark referring to the company as the particular source of the goods or services.

Secret Prior Art. Prior art that may be used to reject a patent application but may not have been known at the time of filing the patent application. One example is where a patent application was filed before your patent application was filed, but did not publish until after your filing date.

Service Mark. A word, phrase, logo, design, color, sound, smell, or virtually anything that is used to identify the source of a service and distinguish it from competitors' services. The terms "trademark" or "mark" are often used interchangeably to refer to either a trademark or service mark.

Small Entity. An independent inventor, small business, or non-profit organization qualified to pay reduced fees before the USPTO.

Specification. The written disclosure of a patent application describing the invention.

State Registration. Certificate of registration issued by any of the 50 states which gives the owner exclusive trademark rights throughout the state.

Suggestive Marks. Marks that suggest a quality of a product or service, but stop short of describing them. Suggestive marks are inherently distinctive.

Summary Judgment Motion. A set of papers filed with the court by one party for the purpose of asking the court to rule in favor of that party without need for trial.

Swearing Behind. The process of swearing behind a prior art reference by proving an earlier date of invention.

Terminal Disclaimer. A document filed by a patent applicant tying the term of a patent to another patent.

Testimony Period. The time period during an opposition or cancellation action in which a witness is deposed by his own attorney, and his comments are recorded by a court reporter. The transcript is then read by the judges of the TTAB, rather than having the witness appear live at a hearing.

Title of the Invention. A brief title of a patent application.

Trade Dress. The combination of elements that creates a unique overall impression of a product and its packaging. Distinctive and non-functional aspects of trade dress can be registerable as trademarks.

Trade Secret. Information that (1) provides economic benefit to the holder of the information; (2) is generally not known by others; and (3) is subject to reasonable measures to preserve its secrecy. A customer list could be a trade secret. A manufacturing recipe could be a trade secret. Information that is generally known cannot serve as a trade secret.

Trade Secret Misappropriation. Trade secret information that has been used and/or disclosed without authority by someone with access to the information. A person cannot be liable for misappropriation for independently creating the information.

Trademark. A word, phrase, logo, design, color, sound, smell, or virtually anything that is used to identify the source of a product and distinguish it from competitors' products. The terms "trademark" or "mark" are often used interchangeably to refer to either a trademark or service mark.

Trademark Examiner. An attorney at the USPTO who examines trademark applications.

Trademark Notice. ® may be used only after a mark is registered in the USPTO. TM may be used for trademarks, and SM may be used for service marks, at any time, even before a trademark application has been filed.

Trademark Search. The search that a company does before adopting a trademark, to see if it will infringe the rights of others.

Trade Name. A name used to distinguish businesses, as opposed to a mark used to distinguish goods or services.

Transition. The second portion of a claim that bridges the preamble with the body of the claim, and determines whether the claim is open-ended or close-ended. An open-ended claim is infringed even if the infringing product includes more than just what is recited by the claim. A close-ended claim is infringed only if the infringing includes the limitations recited by the claim, and nothing more. The most common transition phrases are "comprising," "consisting of," and "consisting essentially of."

Treble Damages. Enhanced damages that may be awarded when infringement is found to be willful.

USPTO. Interchangeable with "PTO." The United States Patent and Trademark Office.

Utility. A requirement for patentability that an invention have usefulness.

Utility Patent. A type of patent used to protect any new and useful process, machine, manufacture, or composition of matter, or any new and useful improvement thereof.

Watching Services. Independent companies offer a service by which they will notify a trademark owner if another company files applications for similar marks. These services are both national and international.

Work or Work of Authorship. A creative or artistic work that is entitled to copyright protection because it is original to the creator or author and is fixed in a tangible form of expression, including, literary and textual works, musical works and accompanying lyrics, dramatic works, pictorial, graphic and sculptural works, audiovisual works, and architectural works.

Work Made for Hire. An exception to the general rule of copyright ownership which provides that an *employer* owns the copyrights in works created by full-time employees within the scope of their employment.

Written Description. A requirement that your patent specification describe your invention in writing in order to demonstrate that the inventor is in possession of the claimed invention.

About the Authors

The authors are attorneys with Knobbe, Martens, Olson & Bear, LLP, one of the largest law firms in the United States specializing in intellectual property law. Knobbe, Martens serves clients around the globe in all areas of intellectual property law. Its clients include public and private companies at various stages of growth, from start-up businesses to Fortune 500 companies. The firm's impressive client list includes Oakley, Quiksilver, Razor USA, Yamaha Motor Corporation, Specialized Bicycle, Carl Karcher Enterprises (Carl's Jr.), Toshiba, Hansen Beverage Company, Monster Energy®, BJ's Restaurants, Samsung, Ticketmaster, Nobu Matsuhisa,

Stanford University, Medtronic Inc. (medical technology), Össur (prosthetic solutions), and numerous biotech and pharmaceutical companies.

Patents, trademarks, copyrights, unfair competition, trade secrets, and rights of publicity are all components of the firm's practice. That practice includes consulting with clients, licensing, preparation, and procurement of patents and trademarks, copyright applications, appeals, oppositions, and cancellations, and intellectual property litigation before federal and state courts.

Lawyers at Knobbe, Martens are registered to practice before the U.S. Patent and Trademark Office. Most of the firm's lawyers have degrees in engineering or science, and many also have graduate or medical degrees, or work experience as engineers or scientists in high-tech industries. The firm's international practice is supported by several lawyers and patent attorneys who were educated and trained in Europe and Asia.

The firm's litigation lawyers have accumulated vast experience within the field of intellectual property law and by specializing in this area, have unsurpassed skills and knowledge in intellectual property litigation. The firm's litigation practice is also supported by numerous scientists and paralegals, which enables the firm to handle intellectual property cases of all sizes, regardless of the technology at issue.

Knobbe, Martens' expertise is recognized in international surveys. The firm repeatedly has been voted number one in both litigation and non-litigation aspects of IP law. In addition, several members of the firm have been voted among the world's leading IP lawyers.

Catherine J. Holland is a partner with Knobbe, Martens, Olson & Bear. She specializes in all aspects of domestic and international trademark selection, protection, licensing, and enforcement. Ms. Holland represents clients in a wide range of industries, including the software, hardware, motor vehicle, medical device, apparel, publishing, financial, restaurant, and food and beverage industries. In surveys conducted by *Los Angeles* magazine and *Super Lawyer* magazine, Ms. Holland was named a California Super Lawyer in 2003 and 2007. In a 2006 survey conducted by *Managing Intellectual Property* of 4,000 practitioners in 60 countries, Ms. Holland was named one of the World's Leading Trademark Practitioners. She has earned the highest ranking (AV) by Martindale Hubbell.

Vito A. Canuso III is a partner with Knobbe, Martens, Olson & Bear. His practice includes both IP litigation and patent and trademark prosecution matters. Mr. Canuso manages numerous IP litigation matters dealing primarily with the enforcement and defense of patent infringement and trademark infringement, rights of publicity, and unfair competition issues. The technology involved in many of those litigation matters has included computer electronics, medical devices, semiconductor processing equipment, pharmaceuticals, telephony, automotive and mechanical devices, and accounting business methods. Mr. Canuso has litigated cases before district courts throughout the United States and before the International Trade Commission, as well as appeals to the Federal Circuit. His patent prosecution docket is focused primarily on medical devices for numerous life sciences companies in the cardiovascular and pulmonary fields.

Diane M. Reed is a partner with Knobbe, Martens, Olson & Bear. Ms. Reed's practice focuses primarily on licensing, distribution, manufacturing, and development agreements, on domestic and international trademark and copyright counseling, prosecution, maintenance, and enforcement, and on trademark portfolio development and management. Ms. Reed works with clients in numerous industries, including the clothing, consumer product, software, medical device, and entertainment industries.

Sabing H. Lee is a partner with Knobbe, Martens, Olson & Bear. He specializes in patent protection and other forms of intellectual property protection. Mr. Lee's practice includes strategic patent procurement, patent portfolio management, general counseling on infringement and licensing issues, and other related issues. Mr. Lee currently represents clients in a wide range of technologies, including medical devices, nanotechnology, and semiconductor fabrication.

Andrew I. Kimmel is an associate attorney with Knobbe, Martens, Olson & Bear. His practice involves protecting intellectual property rights through patent and trademark portfolio development, management, and strategic planning. He has worked with a diverse range of technologies, including medical devices, computer hardware and software systems, and wireless and wired network communications and control. Prior to joining the firm, Mr. Kimmel was the vice president of engineering and regulatory affairs with a medical device manufacturer of solid state laser systems for dentistry and medicine, where he was responsible for product design, development, and regulatory approvals by organizations such as the Food and Drug Administration, UL, and CE.

Wendy K. Peterson is the General Counsel of Knobbe, Martens, Olson & Bear. As General Counsel, Ms. Peterson advises the firm on all internal legal matters, including ethics, employment, contracts, and real estate issues. Prior to joining the firm, Ms. Peterson was General Counsel of Wynn Oil Company, a subsidiary of Parker-Hannifin Corporation and client of Knobbe, Martens, and prior to that was Assistant General Counsel and Secretary to Wynn's International, Inc., an NYSE-listed company. Ms. Peterson began her legal career in 1985 as a corporate and securities lawyer at O'Melveny & Myers. She has 22 years of experience in counseling businesses, from start-ups to publicly traded companies. She has supervised patent and trademark portfolios and IP litigation for the businesses she served.

For information about Knobbe, Martens, Olson & Bear, LLP, please visit www.kmob.com.

Index

A

Appendix A, Smart
   Umbrella, 325–338
Appendix B, USPTO
   Fees and Information,
   339–350
Appendix C, Forms,
   351–374

C

Cease-and-desist
   letter and infringe-
   ment suits, 287–295
   assessing the seri-
     ousness of the
     threat, 288
   options in
     responding,
     288–290
   stopping competi-
     tors from
     sending cease
     and desist let
     ters, 290–291

what to do if you
   are sued for
   infringing
   patents, trade-
   marks, or
   copyrights,
   291–295
Company name as trade-
   mark, 22
Copyright, 213–253
   author's rights,
     223–224
   challenges to your
     registration, 260
   co-authors of, 227
   concept of "publi-
     cation" of a
     work, 238
   contract workers,
     224–225
   copyrighting a
     web site,
     221–222
   derivative works,
     234, 239

   doctrine of fair use,
     241–243
   explained, 11
   expression that is not
     copyrightable, 218
   getting ownership of
     copyrights you do not
     own, 230–231
   in your *Raingod* umbrella,
     219, 220, 221
   length of, 236
   marking catalogs and mar-
     keting materials with
     copyright notice,
     251–253
   minimal amount of origi-
     nality requirement,
     218–219
   obtaining permission or
     "license," 241
   only protects the expres-
     sion of an idea,
     219–220
   other factors affecting
     the term of, 237–238

overview of, 214–215
ownership in your *Raingod*
  umbrella, 227–230
protection and how long it lasts,
  233–238
protection in foreign countries,
  253
protection limited to artistic
  expression, 220–221
public domain and, 238
registering your, 245–250, 259–260
test and remedies for
  infringement, 234–236
using copies of works, 240
using copyrighted work owned by
  others in your business, 239–243
using only a small portion of a
  work, 240–241
what can be protected by, 217–218
who can claim, 223–231
work made for hire, 225–227
works created before, on, or after
  January 1, 1978, 236–237, 238

D

Design patent cover page, Figure 9.2,
  70
Design patents, 9, 73–75

E

Employee incentives to file invention
  disclosure documents, 8
Enforcing your IP rights, 299–305

F

Figure 4.1, Trademark spectrum of
  strength, 27
Figure 8.1, Trademark foreign filing
  priority, 58
Figure 9.1, Cover page of a utility
  patent, 69
Figure 9.2, Cover page of a design
  patent, 70
Figure 9.3, Cover page of a plant
  patent, 71
Figure 10.1, Timeline to preserve
  United States patent rights, 81
Figure 10.2, Timeline to preserve for-
  eign patent rights, 83
Figure 10.3, Drawing found in patent
  application for umbrella inven-
  tion, 86
Figure 10.4, An umbrella as defined
  by claim 1, 95
Figure 11.1, Lab notebook page of
  umbrella invention, 114
Figure 12.1, Typical patent applica-
  tion prosecution timeline, 120
Figure 13.1, Cover page of a United
  States patent publication, 144
Figure 13.2, Cover page of a utility
  patent, 145
Figure 14.1, Cover page of PCT
  application, 152

Figure 15.1, Cover page of a reissue
  patent, 158
Figure 15.2, Claims of reissue patent,
  showing claims deleted and claims
  added, 159
Figure 15.3, Sample pages of a reexamination certificate, 162–163
Figure 15.4, Example of utility patent
  expiring 20 years from filing, 165
Figure 15.5, Example of utility patent
  claiming multiple priorities
  (including to a provisional), 167
Figure 15.6, Example of utility patent
  filed before June 8, 1995, expiring
  17 years from issuance, 168
Figure 15.7, Example of utility patent
  filed before June 8, 1995, expiring
  20 years from filing, 169
Figure 15.8, Example of patent having
  term adjustment, 171
Figure 15.9, Example of a utility
  patent with a terminal disclaimer
  note, 173
Figure 30.1, Litigation flowchart, 308
Foreign patent protection, 149–154
Forms, Appendix C, 351–374

G

Glossary, 375–394

H

How different types of IP protect different aspects of your business, 4

I

Improvements to existing devices as
  patentable, 8
Innovation, purpose of patent system
  is to stimulate, 7–8
Intellectual property (IP) protection,
  benefits of, 257–260
Intellectual property (IP) rights,
  enforcing your, 299–305
Intellectual property (IP) types
  brief summary of, 1–11
  table 1.1, Comparison of different
    types of (IP) intellectual
    property, 12
Invention can occur in any department of company, 8
Invention disclosure documents, 8

L

License and cross-license strategies, 6, 72
Litigation flowchart, Figure 301.1, 308
Litigation, intellectual property (IP),
  302–323
Litigation, the nature and cost of
  going to trial for intellectual
  property (IP), 307–323
  "Markman Hearings," 317–318
  allegations in the complaint, 311
  alternative defenses, 311
  answer of the defendant
    infringer, 311

appealing your case, 323
case management conference,
  313–314
claim construction, 317–318
complaint, the, 309
counterclaims, 312
discovery process, 314–316
expert witnesses, 318–319
litigation costs, 323
location of lawsuit, 309
plaintiff's reply to counterclaims, 312
pleadings, 312–313
post-trial proceedings, 322–323
trial, the, 319–321
whom should you sue?, 309–310

M

Madrid Protocol, 59–61

O

Once your patent issues, 155–174

P

Patent applications, 119–127
  18-month publication, 142–143
  after a patent application
    publication, 142
  amendment after final rejection,
    filing a, 126
  anticipation rejection, 121–123
  appeal, filing an, 127
  continuation applications,
    126–127, 130
  continuations, 130–131
  continuations-in-part, 133–136
  continuing application limits, 138
  continuing applications and
    patent term, 139
  disclosure, 136–137
  divisionals, 131–132
  establishing priority, 136
  Figure 12.1, Typical patent appli-
    cation prosecution timeline, 120
  Figure 13.1, Cover page of a
    United States patent
    publication, 144
  Figure 13.2, Cover page of a
    utility patent, 145
  final rejection, 125–126
  how does a patent get allowed?,
    127–128
  inventorship, 136
  non-publication requests, 143, 146
  obviousness rejection, 123–125
  office action, 120–125
  pendency, 136
  priority claim, 137–138
  provisional patent application,
    139–142
  provisional rights, 146–147
  request for continued examina-
    tion (RCE), filing a, 126
  restriction requirements, 132
Patent Cooperation Treaty (PCT),
  150–154

Figure 14.1, Cover page of PCT application, 152
Patent fees, selected USPTO, Appendix B, 339–352
Patent infringement not guaranteed by holder of intellectual property right, 7, 68
Patent protection, worldwide, 149–154
Patent publication, continuing application, provisional applications and, 129–147
Patent review meetings to help identify inventions generated within your company, 8
Patent strategy, 175–193
    considering the useful, marketable life of your technology, 179
    cost considerations, 186–188
    defensive analysis: how to avoid infringing someone else's patents, 188–190
    establishing ownership, 190–192
    filing provisional patent applications to defer costs, 182–183
    filing under the patent cooperation treaty to defer costs, 183–185
    generating licensing revenue from your patent protection, 193
    intellectual property (IP) audits, 176–177
    maintaining inventions as trade secrets, 178, 198
    offensive plan: developing a patent portfolio, 177–188
    purchasing patent protection, 192
    requesting nonpublication of your patent application, 180
    searching to assess patentability, 178–179
    Table 16.1, Filing strategies, 185
    what to patent, 180 181
    when to file your patent applications, 181–182
    where to apply for patent protection, 185–186
    whether to patent, 177–178
Patent term, 164–174
    Figure 15.4, Example of utility patent expiring 20 years from filing, 165
    Figure 15.5, Example of utility patent claiming multiple priorities (including to a provisional), 167
    Figure 15.6, Example of utility patent filed before June 8, 1995, expiring 17 years from issuance, 168
    Figure 15.7, Example of utility patent filed before June 8, 1995, expiring 20 years from filing, 169

Figure 15.8, Example of patent having term adjustment, 171
Figure 15.9, Example of a utility patent with a terminal disclaimer note, 173
    measuring terms, 166
    ways it can be cut short, 170–174
    ways to extend the patent term, 166, 170
Patent, once its issued, 155–174
    a reexamination, 160–164
    errors, 156–160
    Figure 15.1, Cover page of a reissue patent, 158
    Figure 15.2, Claims of reissue patent, showing claims deleted and claims added, 159
    Figure 15.3, Sample pages of a reexamination certificate, 162–163
    marking a product with the patent number, 156
Patentability, requirements for, 103–117
    anticipation, 104–105
    Figure 11.1, Lab notebook page of umbrella invention, 114
    obviousness, 105–106
Patent searching, 117
    prior art, different types of, 106–112
    Table 11.1, Different types of prior art references, 108
    the examiner and prior art, 115–117
    utility, novelty, and nonobviousness, 104
    what is an interference?, 112–115
Patents
    claims, 93–98
    design, 73–75
    explained, 5–9, 65–66, 68
    fees, filing, 99
    Figure 10.1, Timeline to preserve United States patent rights, 81
    Figure 10.2, Timeline to preserve foreign patent rights, 83
    Figure 10.4, an umbrella as defined by claim 1, 95
    filing your application, 77–102
    inventorship, 99–102
    items to file with a patent application, 98–102
    myths about, 258
    other documents to file with patent application, 102
    preserving foreign rights by filing before any public disclosure, 82–83
    preserving U.S. rights by filing within one year, 80–82
    provide only a right to exclude, 68, 72

requirements to file a patent application, 83–84
specification (also referred to as the "disclosure"), the, 85–88
Table 10.1, differences between written description and enablement, 92
three types of United States, utility, design and plant, 66–68
unenforceable protection, 6–7
what can you patent?, 72–73
when to file your application, 80–82
written description, enablement, and best mode, 88–93
Patents, protecting yourself from an infringement claim, 263–286
    "market clearance," 276
    being sued and the chances of winning, 276–278
    buying the patent vs. obtaining a license under the patent, 280–281
    compensation, 284
    conducting a technology/patent search: figuring out what is unprotected and what is protected, 264–265
    cost of an opinion of counsel, 275–276
    cross-licensing, 284
    design-arounds, 271–272
    focus on the new features as first step, 263–264
    hiring a professional patent searcher, 265–267
    invalidating the problematic patent, 284–286
    need for an opinion of counsel, 272–275
    obtaining a license under someone else's patent, 283
    obtaining the rights to the problematic patent, 280
    patent licenses vs. product licenses, 281–282
    patent search, after the, 270–271
    patent search, analyzing results of, 268–270
    patents are complicated, 272–273
    protect yourself from an accusation of willful infringement, 273–275
    reliability of patent searches, 267–268
    risk-aversion and the problematic patent, 279
    terms of a patent lease, 283–284
    trolls, 278–279
    what you pay for a patent license, 284
Plant patent cover page, Figure 9.3, 71
Processes as patentable, 8
Product's shape and packaging "trade dress," protecting your, 30–31

Protecting your business's driving forces through an intellectual property (IP) strategy, 4
Protecting your company name—incorporating and fictitious name statement is not enough, 21–22
Protecting yourself from a patent infringement claim, 263–286

R

Rain Alert Inc., (Smart Umbrella product) hypothetical company to illustrate IP strategy, and how each type of intellectual property can arise, 17–18

S

Smart Umbrella, Appendix A, 325–338
Solutions to problems may be patentable inventions, 8
Sound marks, 31

T

Table 1.1, Comparison of different types of intellectual property, 12
Table 11.1, Different types of prior art references, 108
Table 16.1, Filing strategies, 185
Testing your IP knowledge, 13–18
Trade dress protection and registration, 9, 30–31
Trade name, definition of, 28
Trade secrets, 197–210
confidentiality agreements, employee, 204
enforcing, 206–207
entrance interviews, employee, 203
exit interviews, employee, 204
explained, 10
informing employees about your confidential information, 202
legal requirements for, 199–200
losing protection, 205–206
non-disclosure agreement (NDA) and, 10
nondisclosure agreements with third parties, 207–210
protecting and enforcing your, 201–210
reminders, employee, 203–204
using technology to safeguard your, 205
what information should be secret, 202
Trademark foreign filing priority, Figure 8.1, 58
Trademarks
"genericide," 47
and domain names, 49–50
care and maintenance of your, 45–50

coined and arbitrary, 24–25
company name as, 22
cost to obtain foreign registrations, 61–62
definition of, 24
descriptive, 25–26
determining whether to claim multiple, 29
European Community Trademark Application or CTM, 57
evaluating for your umbrella, 27–29
explained, 9
Figure 4.1, spectrum of strength, 27
Figure 8.1, Trademark foreign filing priority, 58
finding good, 23–31
foreign filing strategies for, 57
foreign national applications, 57–59
foreign pirates, 56
generic words can never function as, 27
goodwill and assignments, 48
licensing, 49
Madrid Protocol, 59–61
marking your products and marketing materials with a trademark notice, 45–46
notice in foreign countries, 61
oppositions and cancellation actions, 51–54
policing your, 47–48
product configuration marks, 29–31
protection in foreign countries, 55–62
rights provided by a registration, 258–259
search, definition of, 35
searching and registering your, 33–44
selecting a strong, 24
sound marks, 31
suggestive, 26
trade dress protection, 9, 30–31
sing a mark properly to maintain its value, 46–47
watching services, 48
Trademarks, registering your, 36–44
describing and classifying the goods, 38–39
federal registration cost, 41–42
federal registration length, 42–43
filing a trademark before using a mark application, 37–38
fraud, 41
publication for opposition, 39–40
state registration, 43–44
statement of use, 40–41
the application, 37
the office action, 39

Trademarks, searching your, 33–36
definition of search, 35
filing an application to register it in the USPTO, 36–44
Internet searching, 35
obtaining a legal opinion post-search results, 35–36
professional search companies, 34–35
USPTO database searching, 34

U

Utility patent cover page, Figure 9.1, 69
Utility patents, 9

W

Worldwide patent protection, 149–154